From the desk of Kim Jong Un

Dear corn-fed, James Franco-loving Americans,

   When I was a child, all I wanted was two things: a coupon for 20% off anything at Bed, Bath & Beyond, and to be a member of a special club. For years, all everyone talked about at my United Nations sanctions hearings was how badass Dubya looked in his pilot outfit, how smokin' Barack was in his forged passport photo, or how funny Donnie's impressions of reporters were. American Presidents made so many friends...

   So I spent decades travelling the globe trying to be like a cool American President. But nothing I did worked: I tried being intellectual by getting a slick, donkey-anus haircut, but everyone said I reminded them of that creepy sandwich spokesman. I even tried being an activist by implementing a nationwide hunger strike against obesity, but everyone called me a monster!

   I thought all was lost... until one day, after watching a re-run of Mrs. Doubtfire, the solution finally dawned on me-- to be cool like an American President, I must BECOME an American President...

   So I stole thousands of non-union laborers from a Hollywood work-camp and created this blueprint on how I will one day become the Great Leader... of America!

   Can't wait to see you soon, capitalist swine! Vote Kim Jong Un for President this November!

                                                        Xoxo,

                                                        Kimmy

PRINTED IN KOREA

(Seriously)

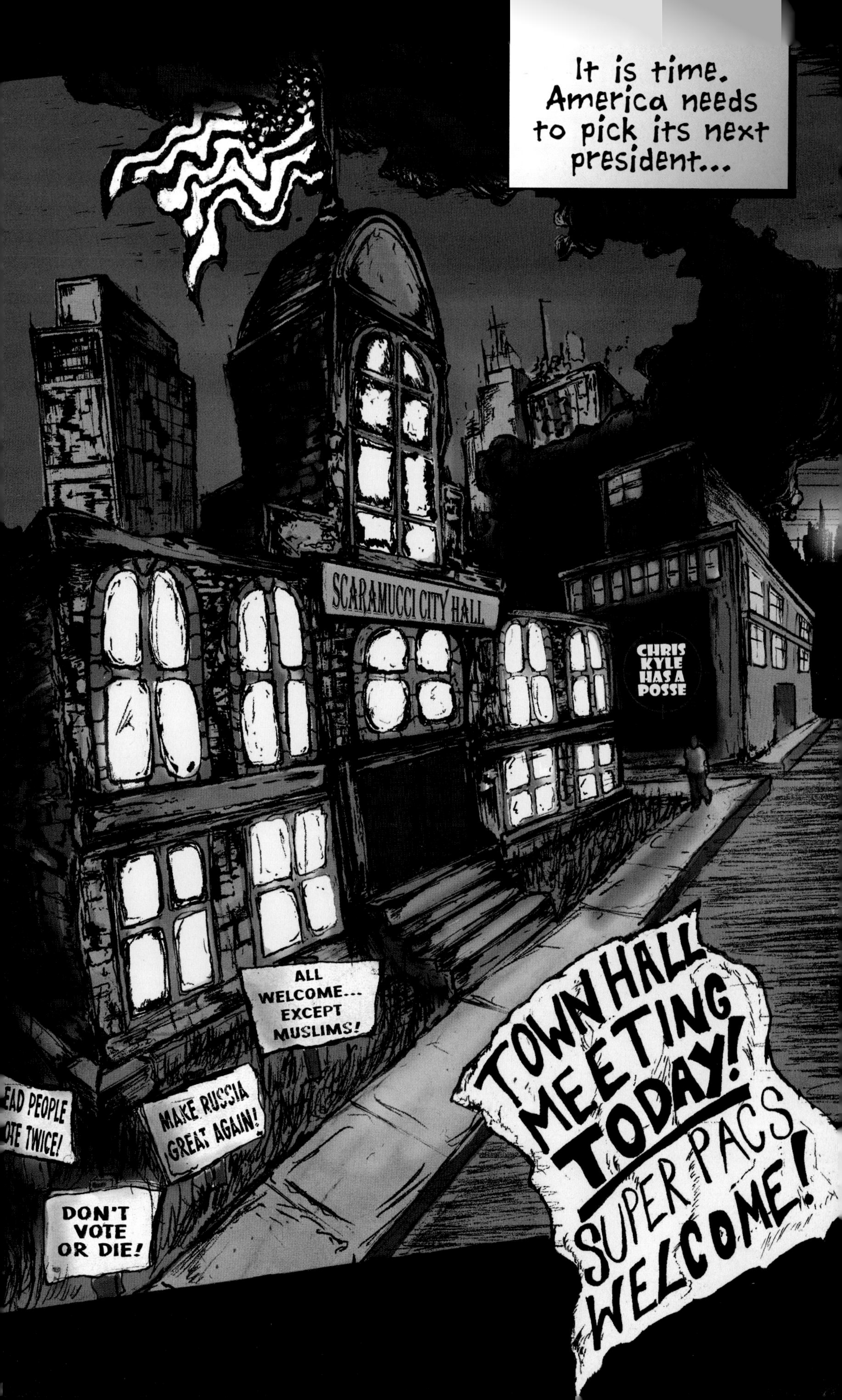
It is time. America needs to pick its next president...
SCARAMUCCI CITY HALL
CHRIS KYLE HAS A POSSE
ALL WELCOME... EXCEPT MUSLIMS!
EAD PEOPLE
OTE TWICE!
MAKE RUSSIA GREAT AGAIN!
DON'T VOTE OR DIE!
TOWN HALL MEETING TODAY!
SUPER PACS WELCOME!

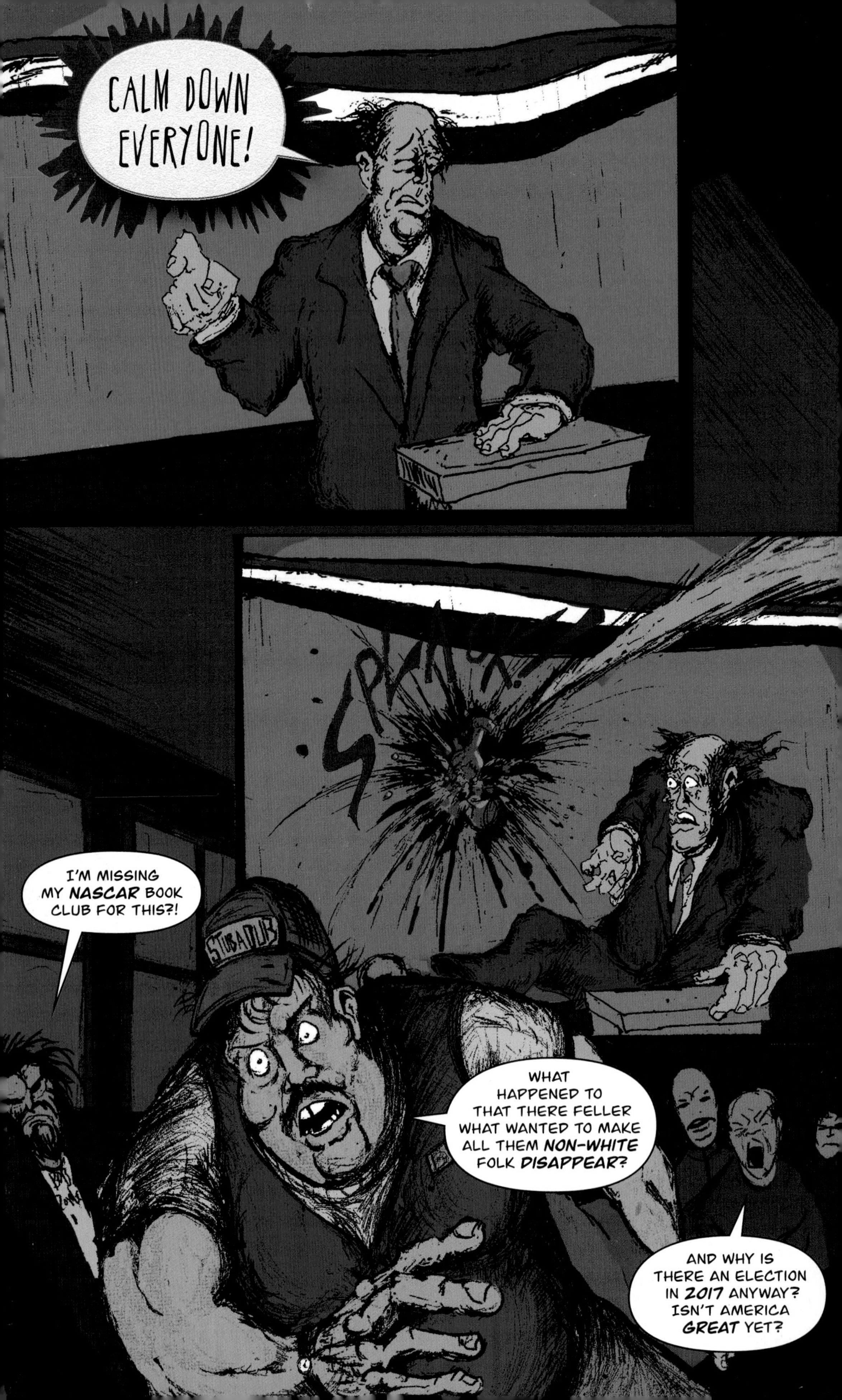
CALM DOWN EVERYONE!
SPLACK!
I'M MISSING MY NASCAR BOOK CLUB FOR THIS?!
WHAT HAPPENED TO THAT THERE FELLER WHAT WANTED TO MAKE ALL THEM NON-WHITE FOLK DISAPPEAR?
AND WHY IS THERE AN ELECTION IN 2017 ANYWAY? ISN'T AMERICA GREAT YET?

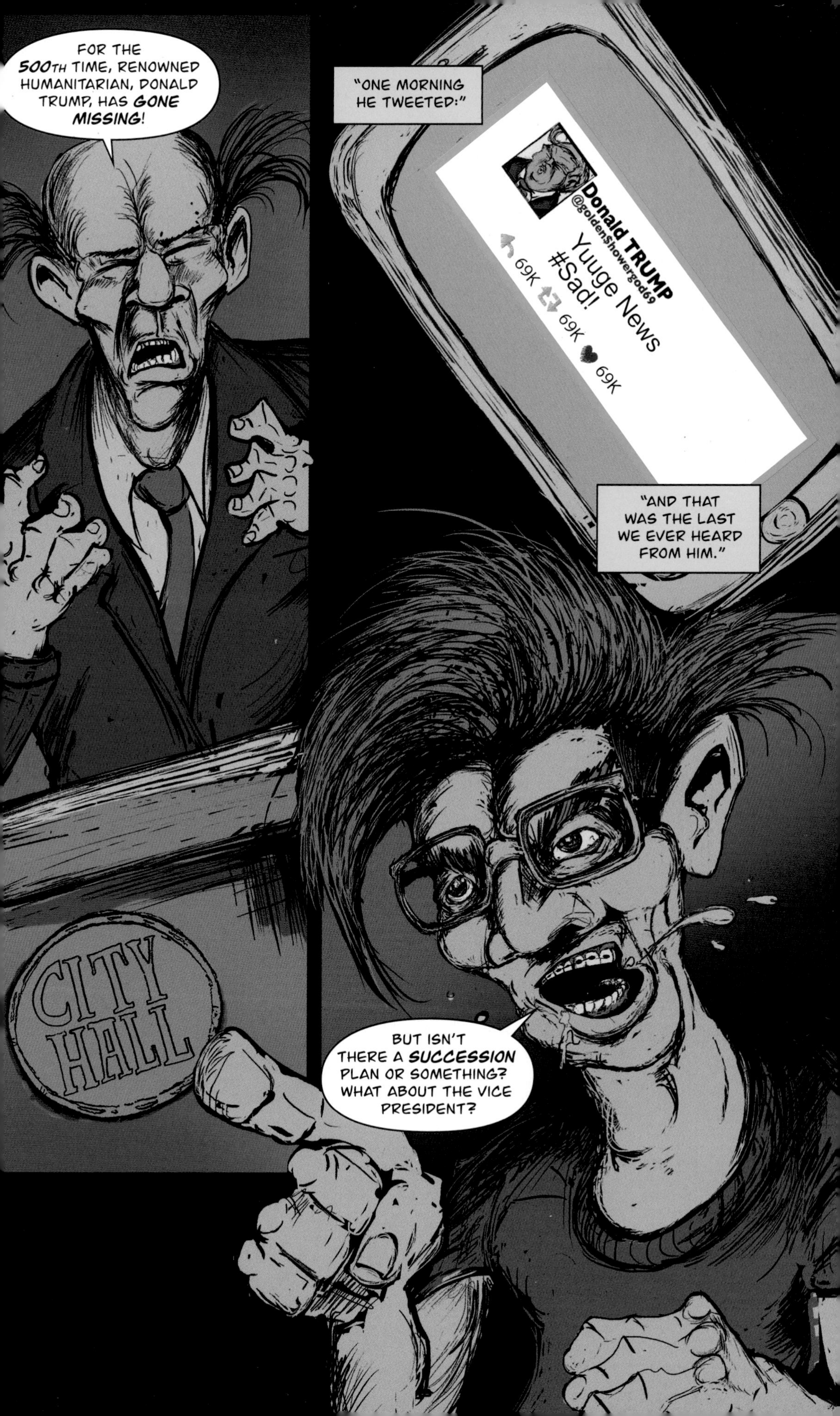

FOR THE 500TH TIME, RENOWNED HUMANITARIAN, DONALD TRUMP, HAS GONE MISSING!
CITY HALL
"ONE MORNING HE TWEETED:"
Donald TRUMP
@goldenShowergod69
Yuuge News
#Sad!
69K 69K 69K
"AND THAT WAS THE LAST WE EVER HEARD FROM HIM."
BUT ISN'T THERE A SUCCESSION PLAN OR SOMETHING? WHAT ABOUT THE VICE PRESIDENT?

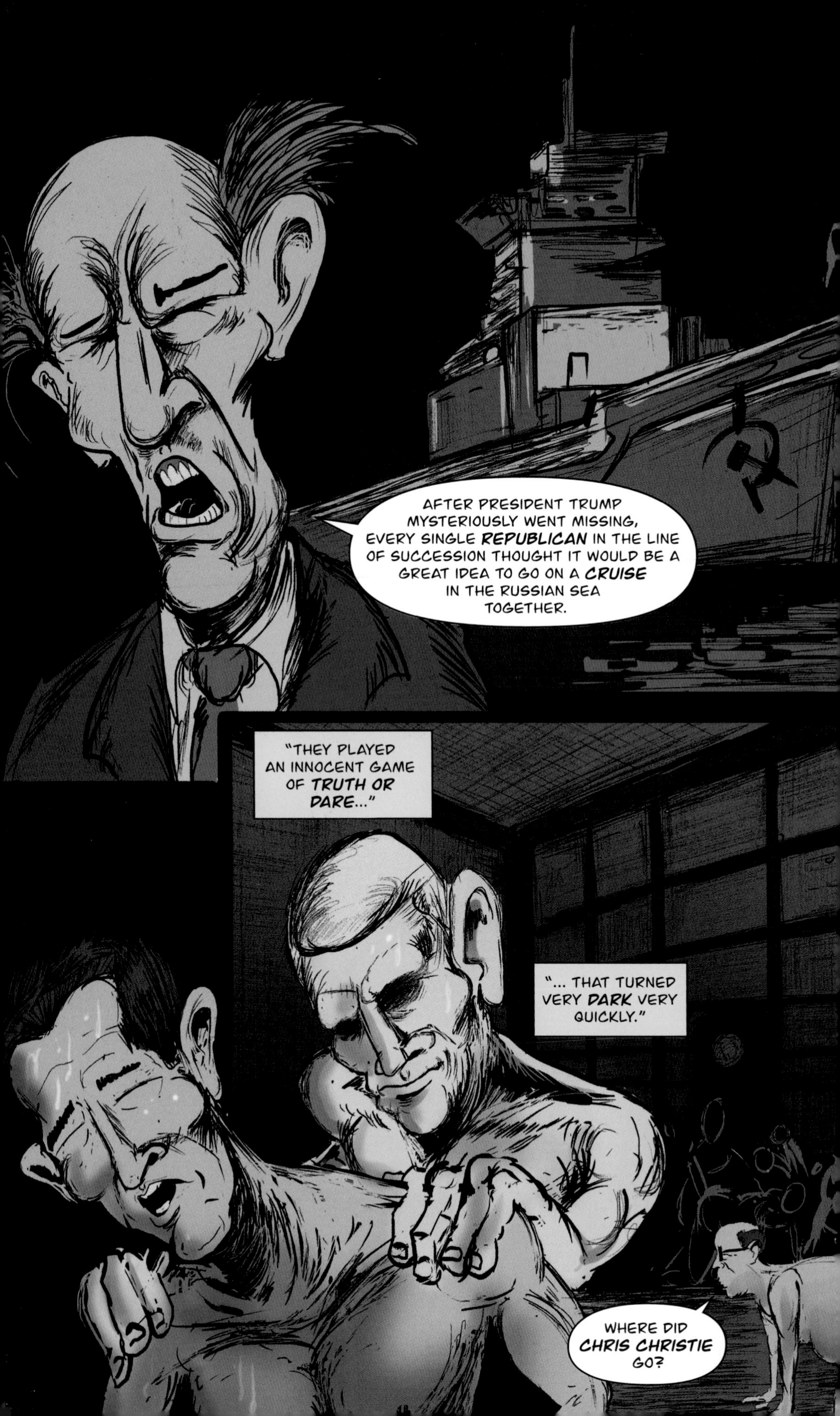
AFTER PRESIDENT TRUMP MYSTERIOUSLY WENT MISSING, EVERY SINGLE REPUBLICAN IN THE LINE OF SUCCESSION THOUGHT IT WOULD BE A GREAT IDEA TO GO ON A CRUISE IN THE RUSSIAN SEA TOGETHER.
"THEY PLAYED AN INNOCENT GAME OF TRUTH OR DARE..."
"... THAT TURNED VERY DARK VERY QUICKLY."
WHERE DID CHRIS CHRISTIE GO?

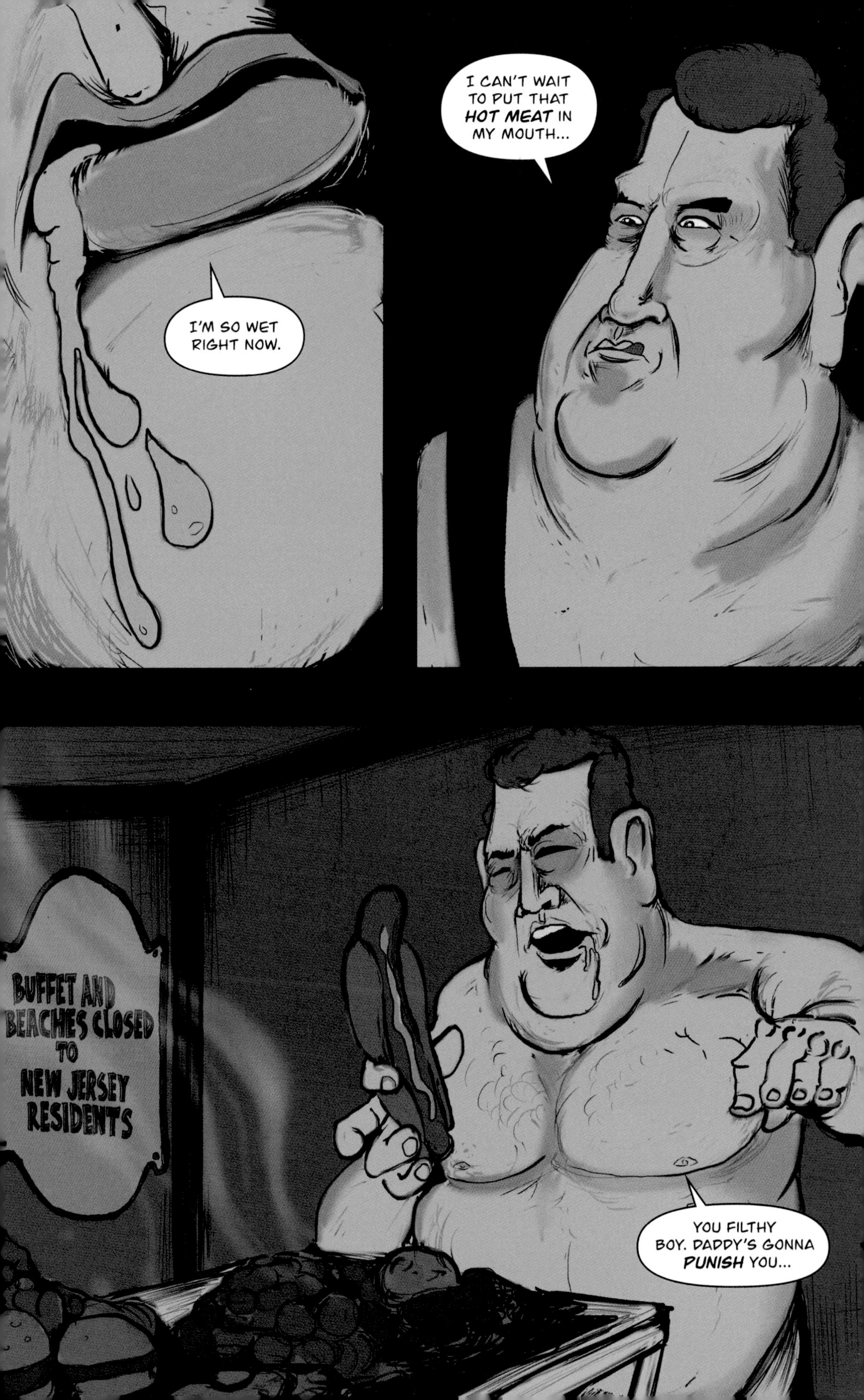
I'M SO WET RIGHT NOW.
I CAN'T WAIT TO PUT THAT HOT MEAT IN MY MOUTH...
BUFFET AND BEACHES CLOSED TO NEW JERSEY RESIDENTS
YOU FILTHY BOY. DADDY'S GONNA PUNISH YOU...

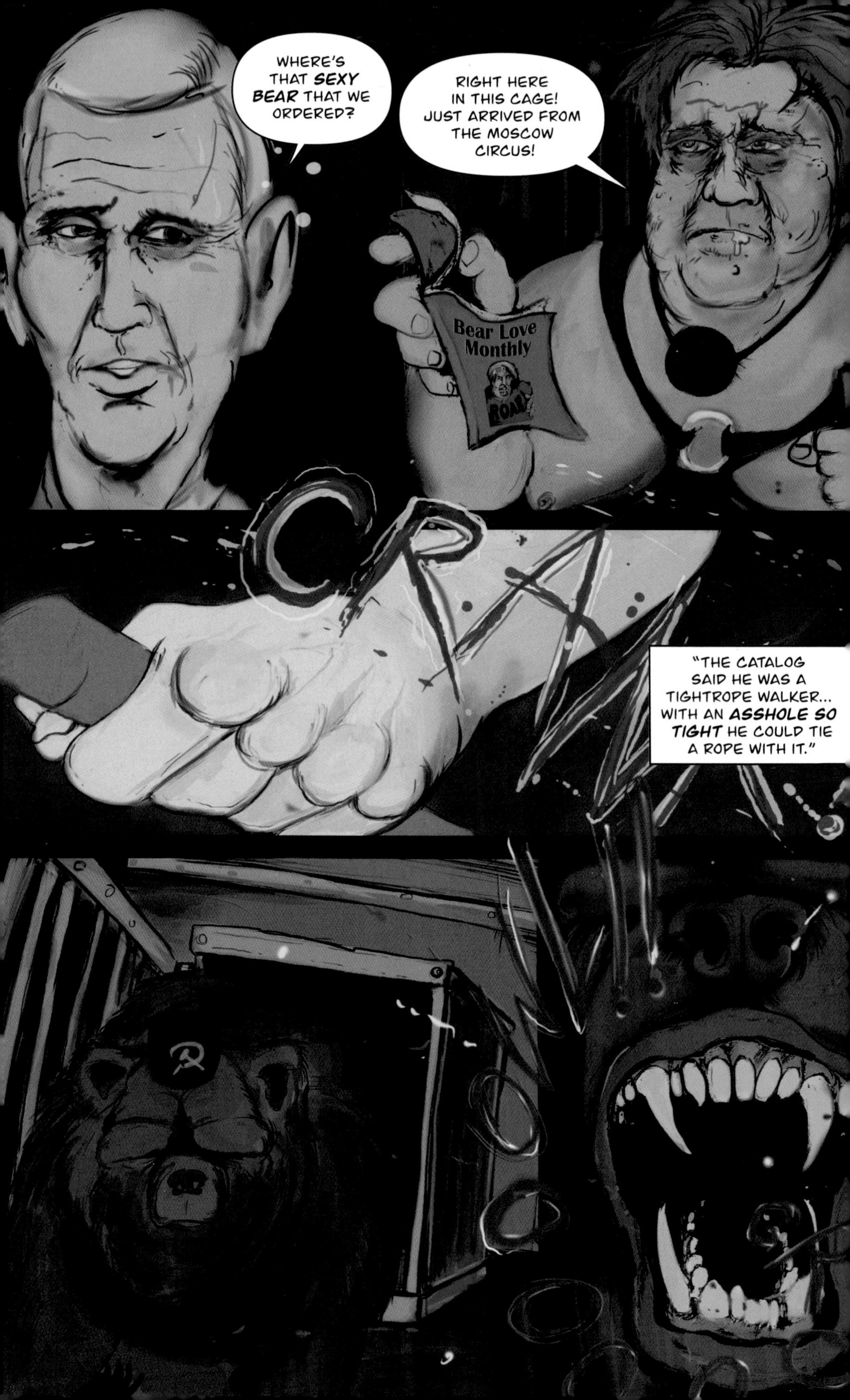
WHERE'S THAT SEXY BEAR THAT WE ORDERED?
RIGHT HERE IN THIS CAGE! JUST ARRIVED FROM THE MOSCOW CIRCUS!
Bear Love Monthly
ROAR
CRAK
"THE CATALOG SAID HE WAS A TIGHTROPE WALKER... WITH AN ASSHOLE SO TIGHT HE COULD TIE A ROPE WITH IT."

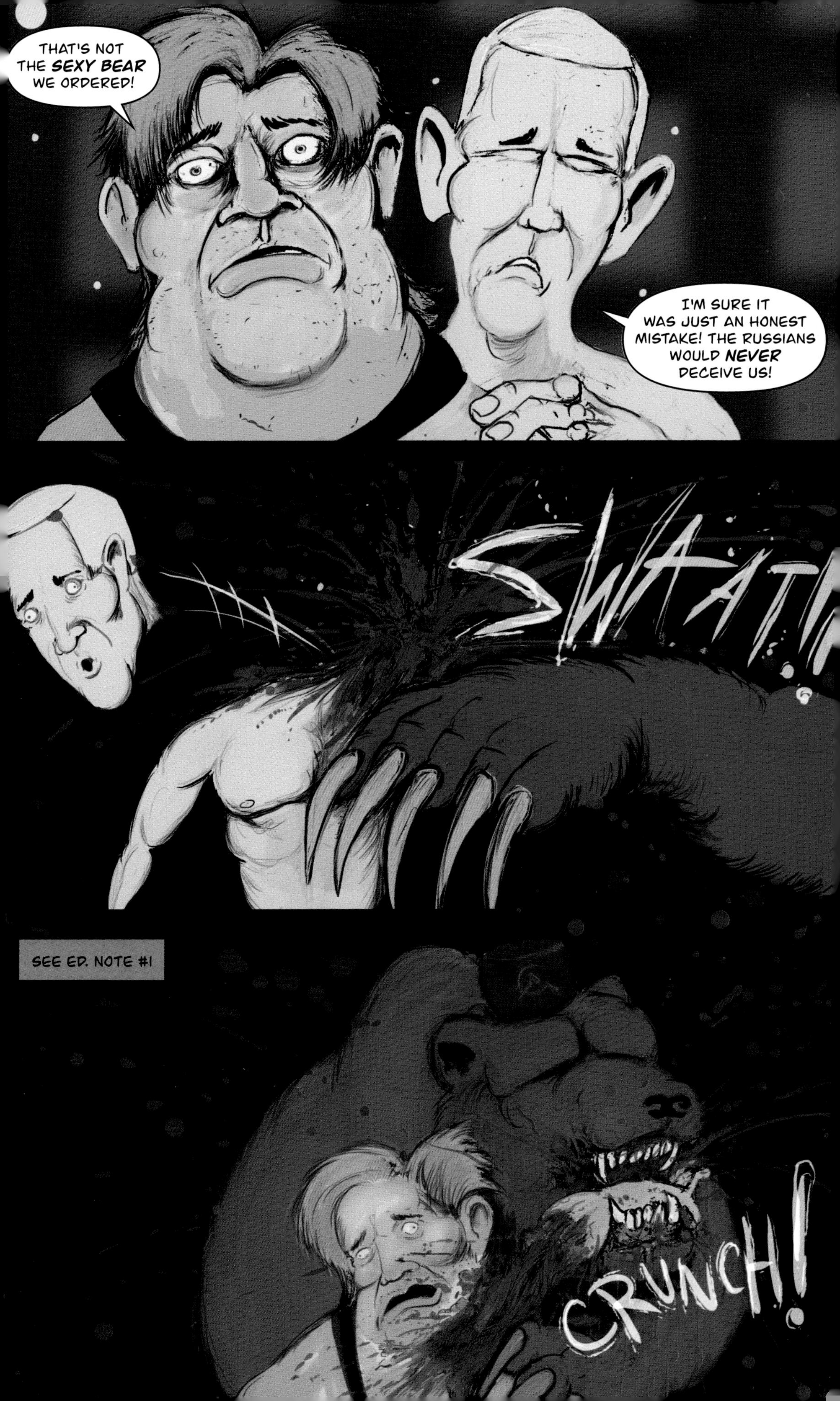
THAT'S NOT THE **SEXY BEAR** WE ORDERED!
I'M SURE IT WAS JUST AN HONEST MISTAKE! THE RUSSIANS WOULD **NEVER** DECEIVE US!
SWAT!
SEE ED. NOTE #1
CRUNCH!

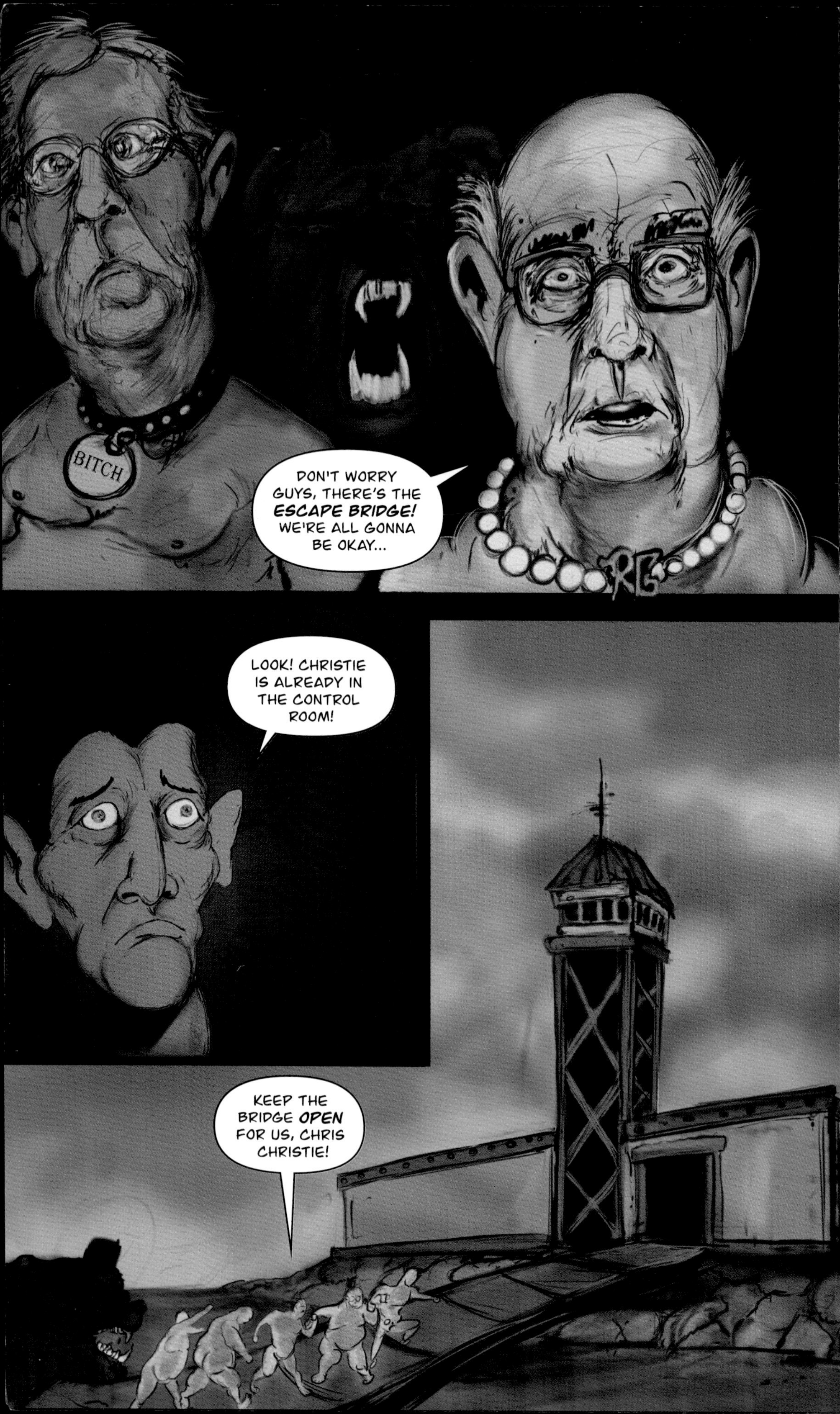
BITCH
DON'T WORRY GUYS, THERE'S THE **ESCAPE BRIDGE!** WE'RE ALL GONNA BE OKAY...
LOOK! CHRISTIE IS ALREADY IN THE CONTROL ROOM!
KEEP THE BRIDGE **OPEN** FOR US, CHRIS CHRISTIE!

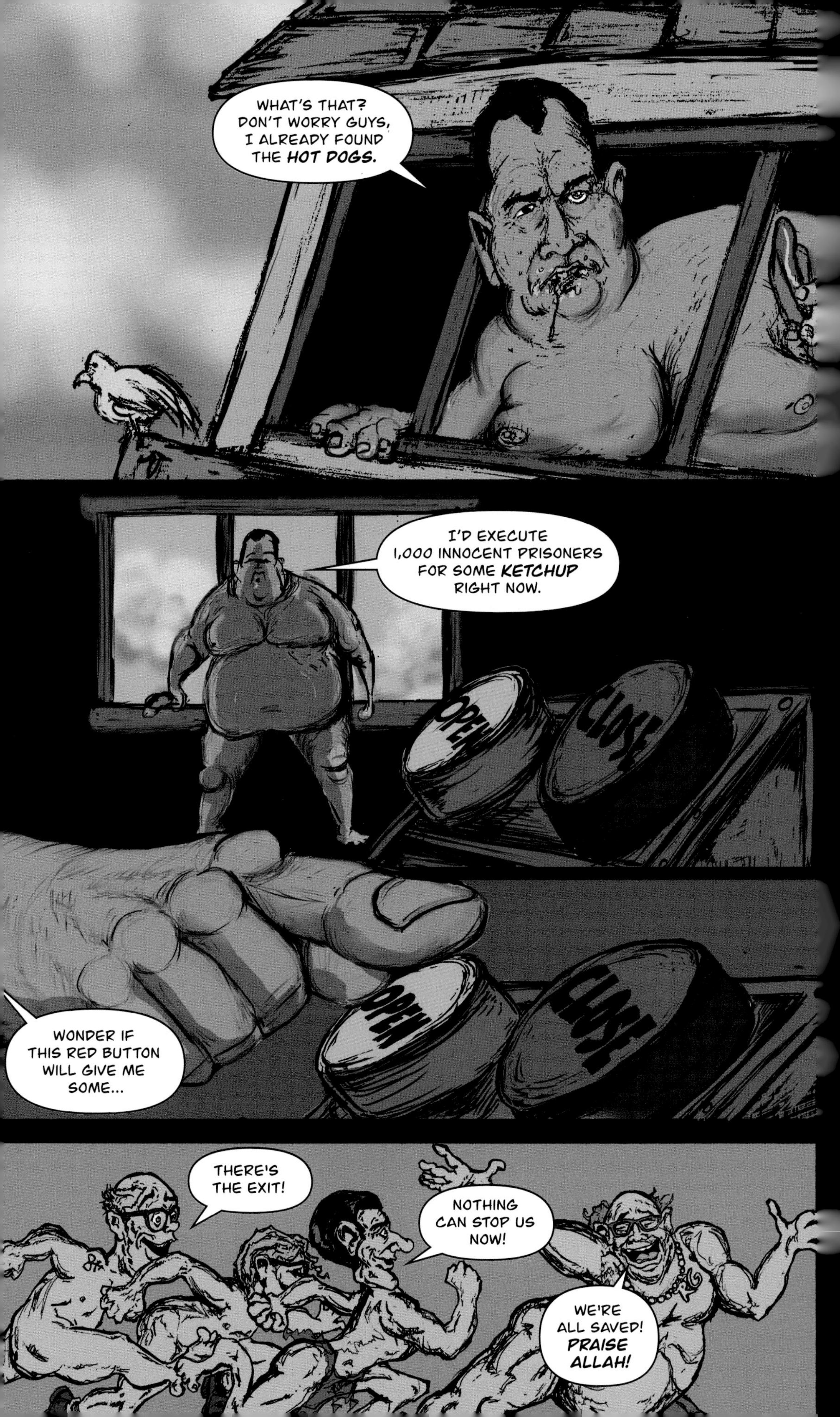
WHAT'S THAT? DON'T WORRY GUYS, I ALREADY FOUND THE HOT DOGS.
I'D EXECUTE 1,000 INNOCENT PRISONERS FOR SOME KETCHUP RIGHT NOW.
OPEN
CLOSE
WONDER IF THIS RED BUTTON WILL GIVE ME SOME...
OPEN
CLOSE
THERE'S THE EXIT!
NOTHING CAN STOP US NOW!
WE'RE ALL SAVED! PRAISE ALLAH!

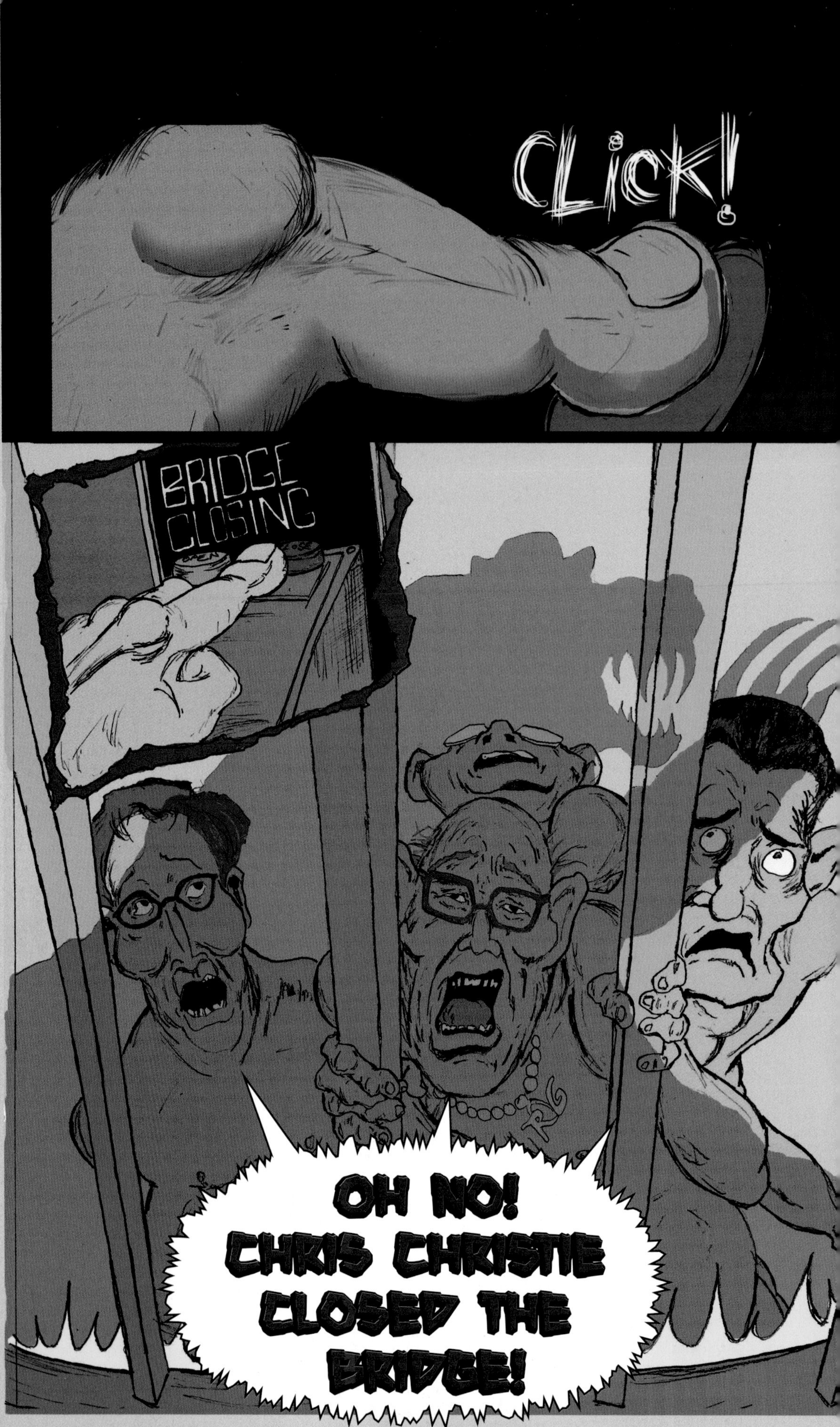
CLICK!
BRIDGE CLOSING
OH NO! CHRIS CHRISTIE CLOSED THE BRIDGE!

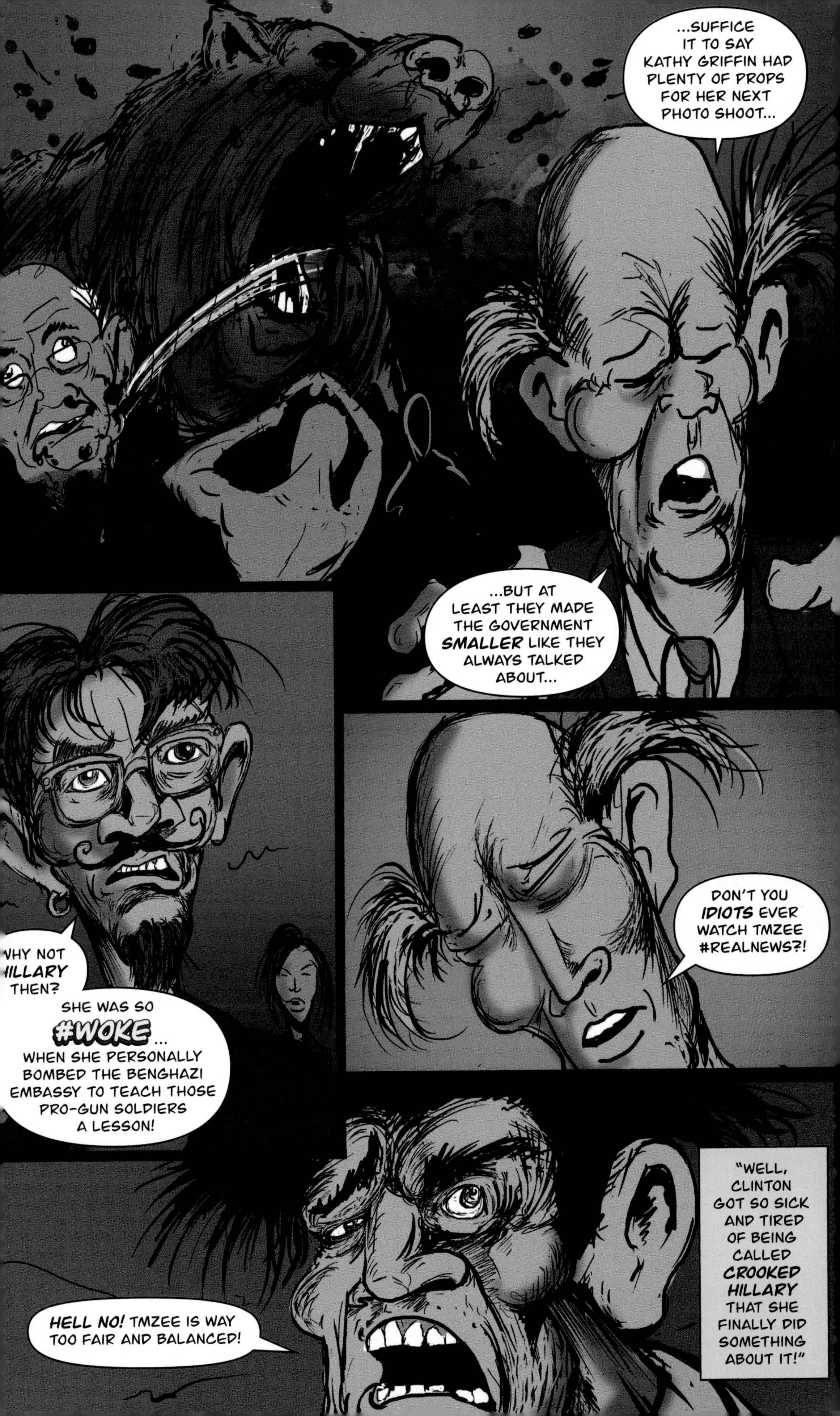
...SUFFICE IT TO SAY KATHY GRIFFIN HAD PLENTY OF PROPS FOR HER NEXT PHOTO SHOOT...
...BUT AT LEAST THEY MADE THE GOVERNMENT SMALLER LIKE THEY ALWAYS TALKED ABOUT...
HILLARY THEN?
SHE WAS SO #WOKE... WHEN SHE PERSONALLY BOMBED THE BENGHAZI EMBASSY TO TEACH THOSE PRO-GUN SOLDIERS A LESSON!
DON'T YOU IDIOTS EVER WATCH TMZEE #REALNEWS?!
HELL NO! TMZEE IS WAY TOO FAIR AND BALANCED!
"WELL, CLINTON GOT SO SICK AND TIRED OF BEING CALLED CROOKED HILLARY THAT SHE FINALLY DID SOMETHING ABOUT IT!"

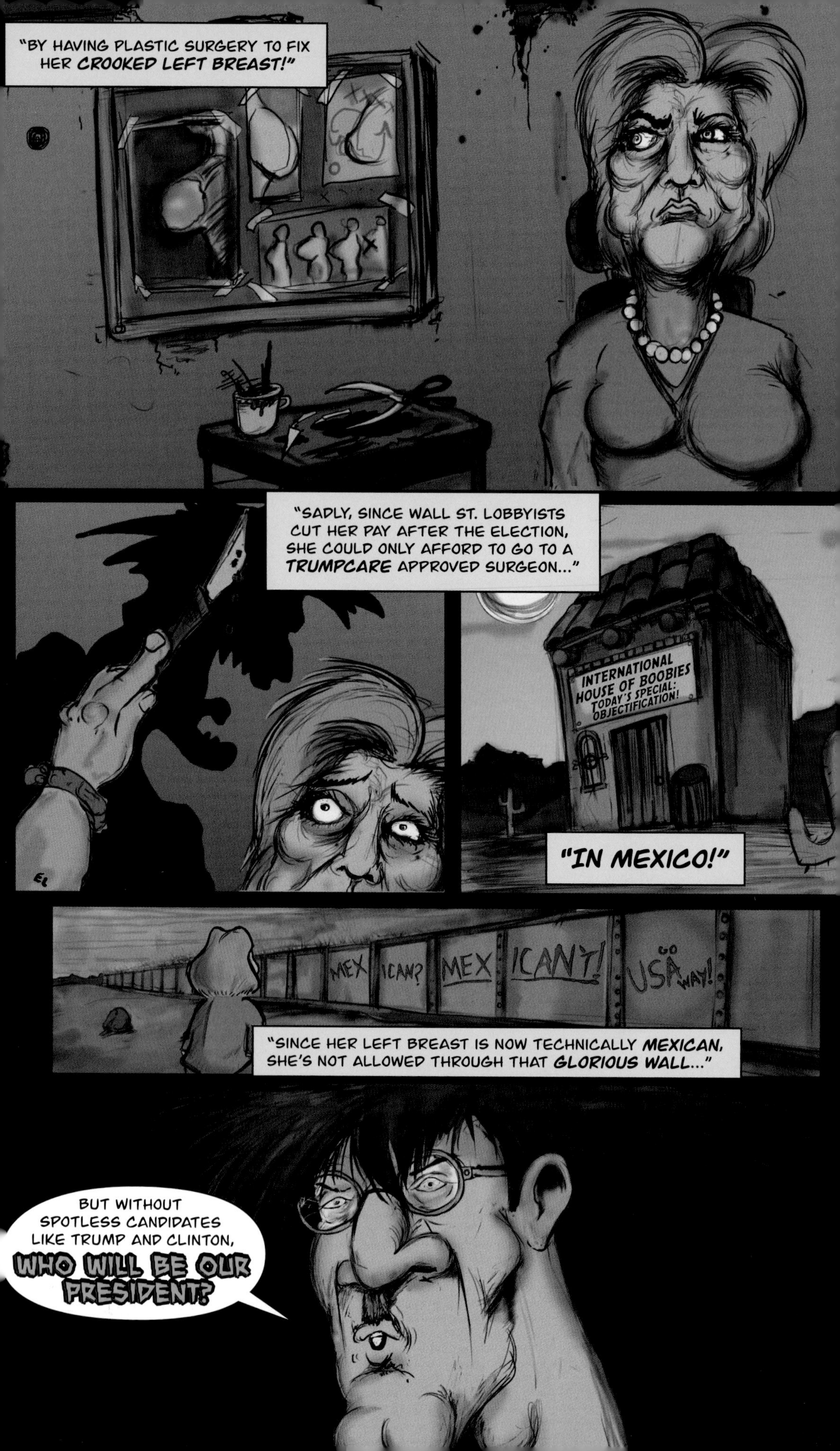
"BY HAVING PLASTIC SURGERY TO FIX HER CROOKED LEFT BREAST!"
"SADLY, SINCE WALL ST. LOBBYISTS CUT HER PAY AFTER THE ELECTION, SHE COULD ONLY AFFORD TO GO TO A TRUMPCARE APPROVED SURGEON..."
INTERNATIONAL HOUSE OF BOOBIES TODAY'S SPECIAL: OBJECTIFICATION!
"IN MEXICO!"
MEX ICAN? MEX ICAN'T! USA GO WAY!
"SINCE HER LEFT BREAST IS NOW TECHNICALLY MEXICAN, SHE'S NOT ALLOWED THROUGH THAT GLORIOUS WALL..."
BUT WITHOUT SPOTLESS CANDIDATES LIKE TRUMP AND CLINTON, WHO WILL BE OUR PRESIDENT?

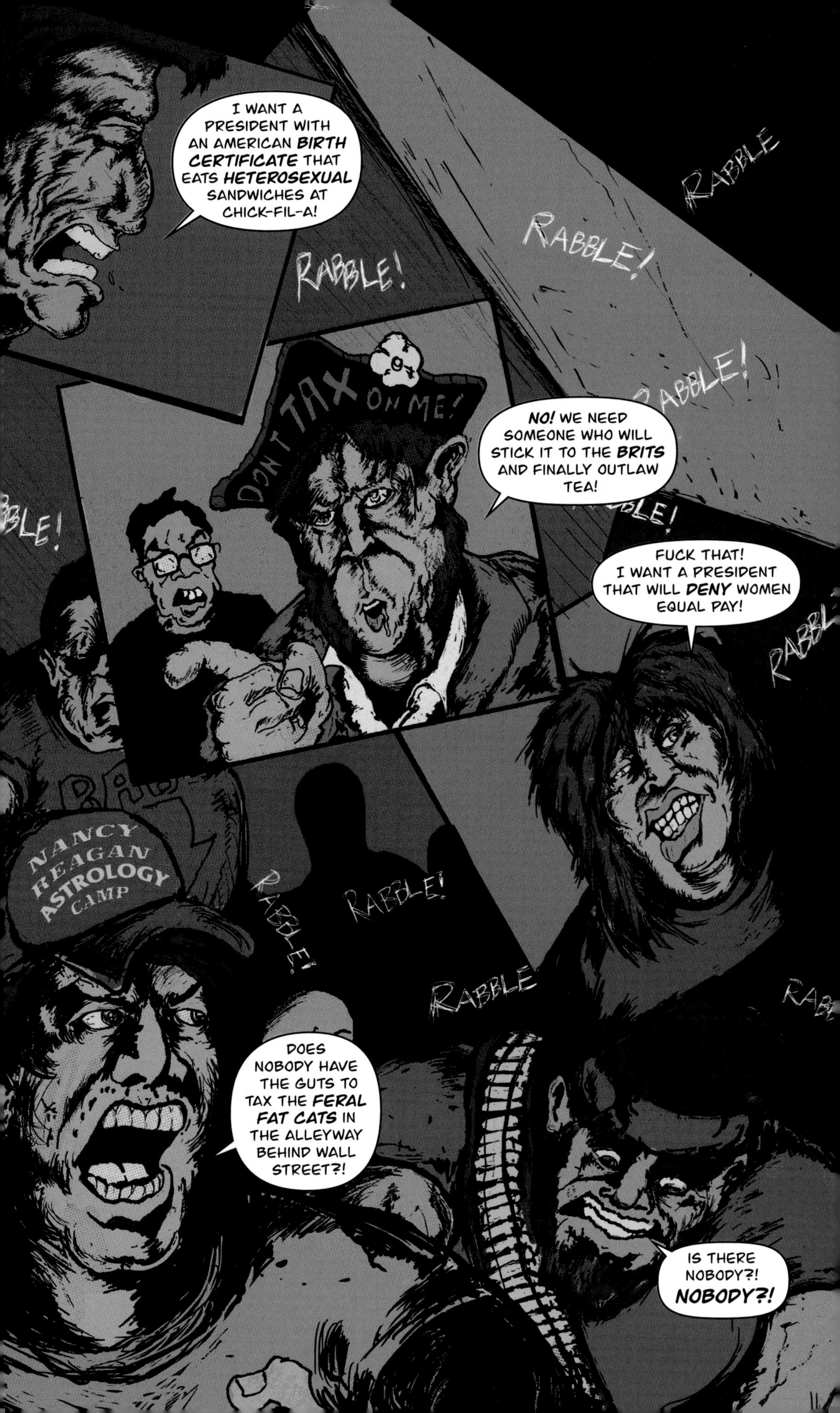
I WANT A PRESIDENT WITH AN AMERICAN BIRTH CERTIFICATE THAT EATS HETEROSEXUAL SANDWICHES AT CHICK-FIL-A!
RABBLE!
RABBLE!
RABBLE
DON'T TAX ON ME!
NO! WE NEED SOMEONE WHO WILL STICK IT TO THE BRITS AND FINALLY OUTLAW TEA!
RABBLE!
FUCK THAT! I WANT A PRESIDENT THAT WILL DENY WOMEN EQUAL PAY!
NANCY REAGAN ASTROLOGY CAMP
RABBLE!
RABBLE!
RABBLE
DOES NOBODY HAVE THE GUTS TO TAX THE FERAL FAT CATS IN THE ALLEYWAY BEHIND WALL STREET?!
IS THERE NOBODY?! NOBODY?!

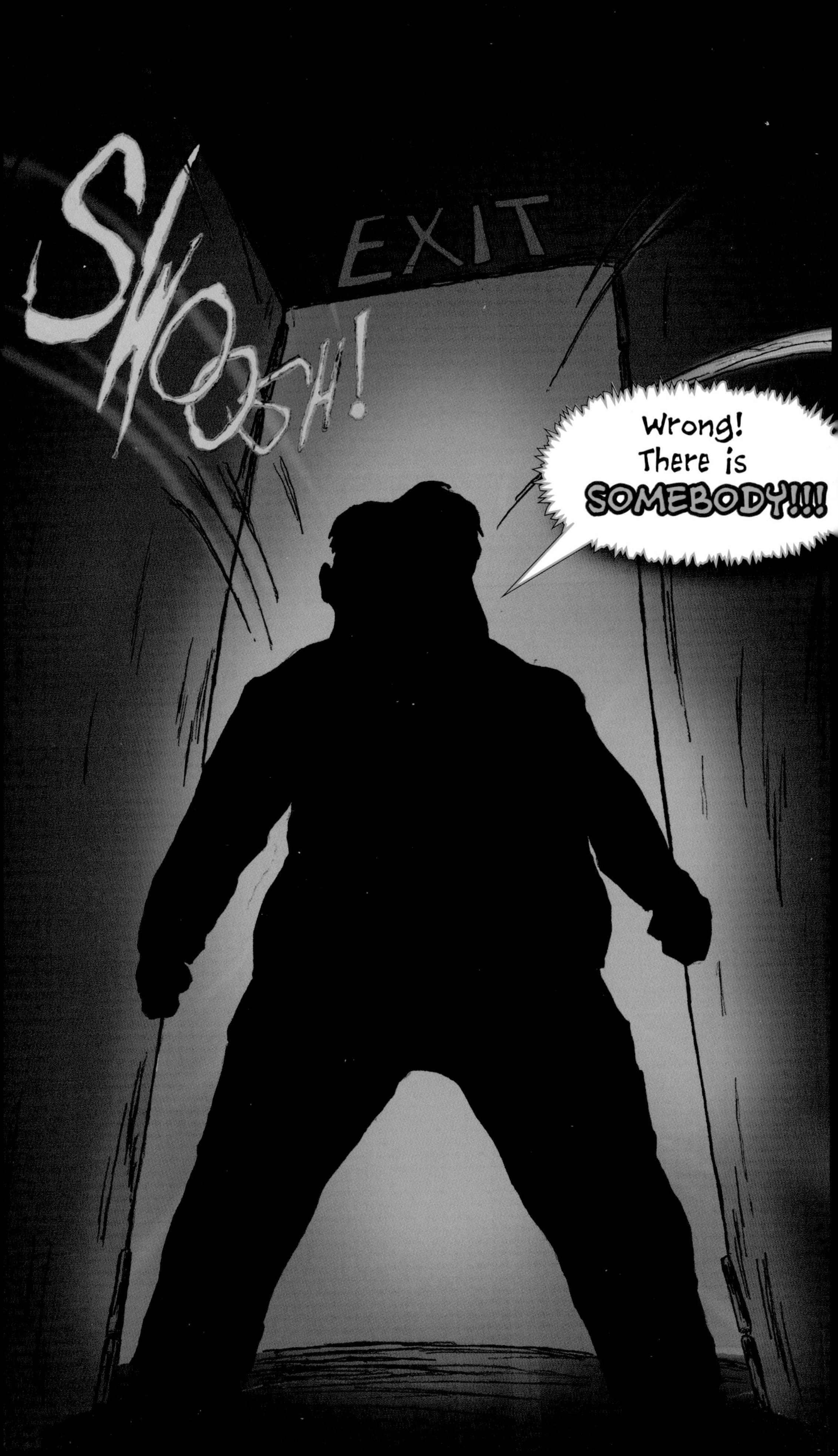
SHOOSH!
EXIT
Wrong! There is SOMEBODY!!!!

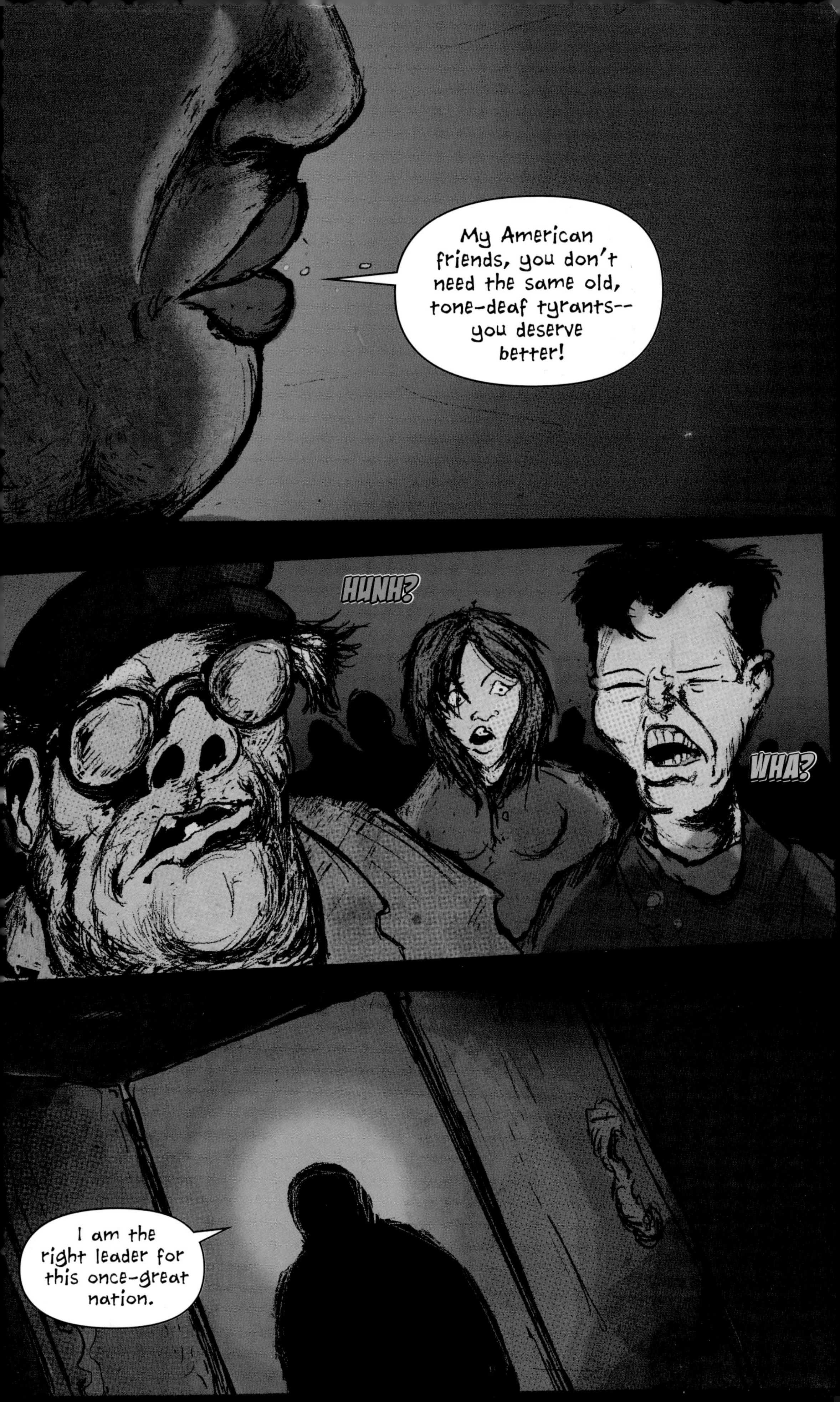
My American friends, you don't need the same old, tone-deaf tyrants-- you deserve better!
HUNH?
WHA?
I am the right leader for this once-great nation.

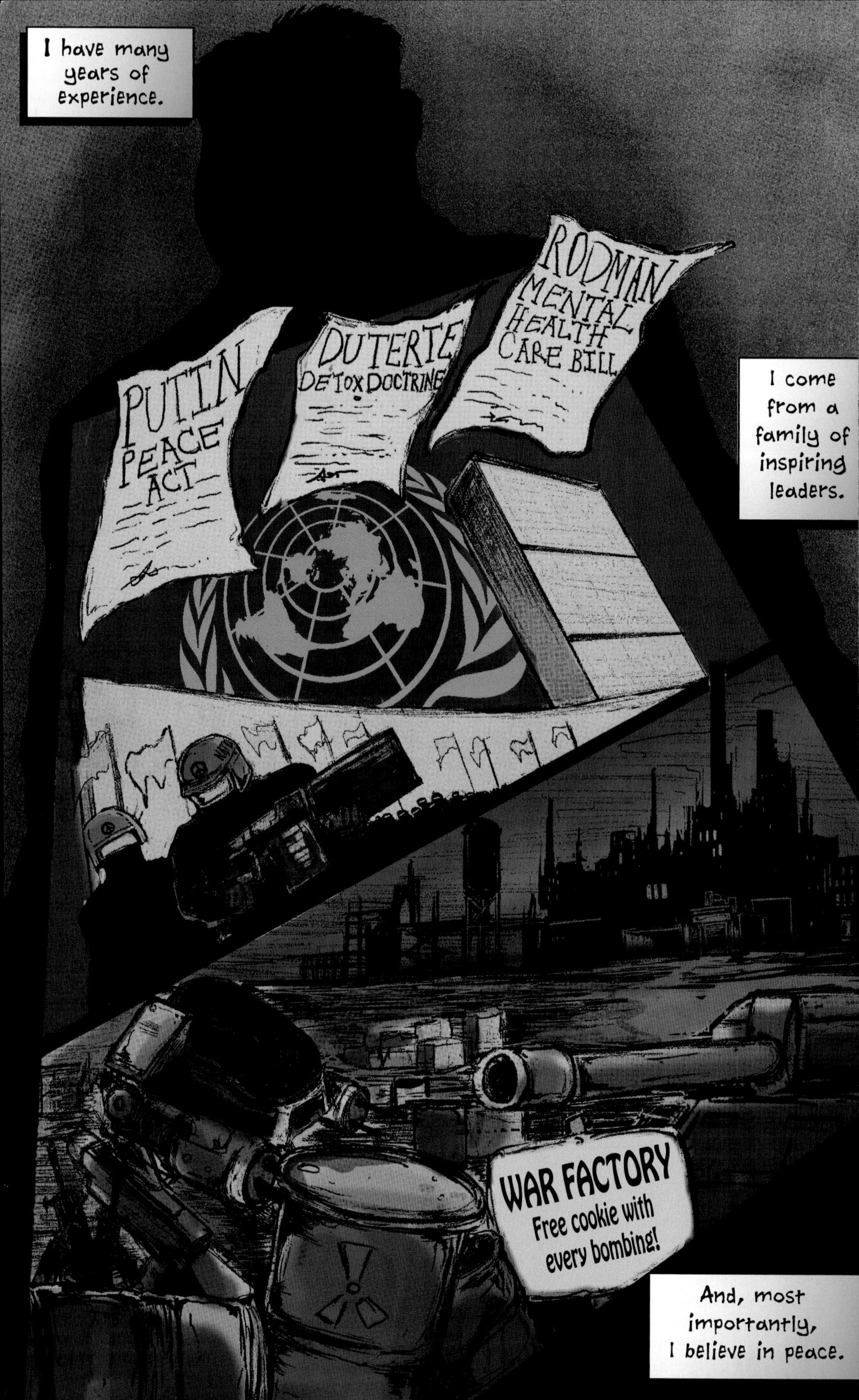
I have many years of experience.
PUTIN PEACE ACT
DUTERTE DETOX DOCTRINE
RODMAN MENTAL HEALTH CARE BILL
I come from a family of inspiring leaders.
WAR FACTORY
Free cookie with every bombing!
And, most importantly, I believe in peace.

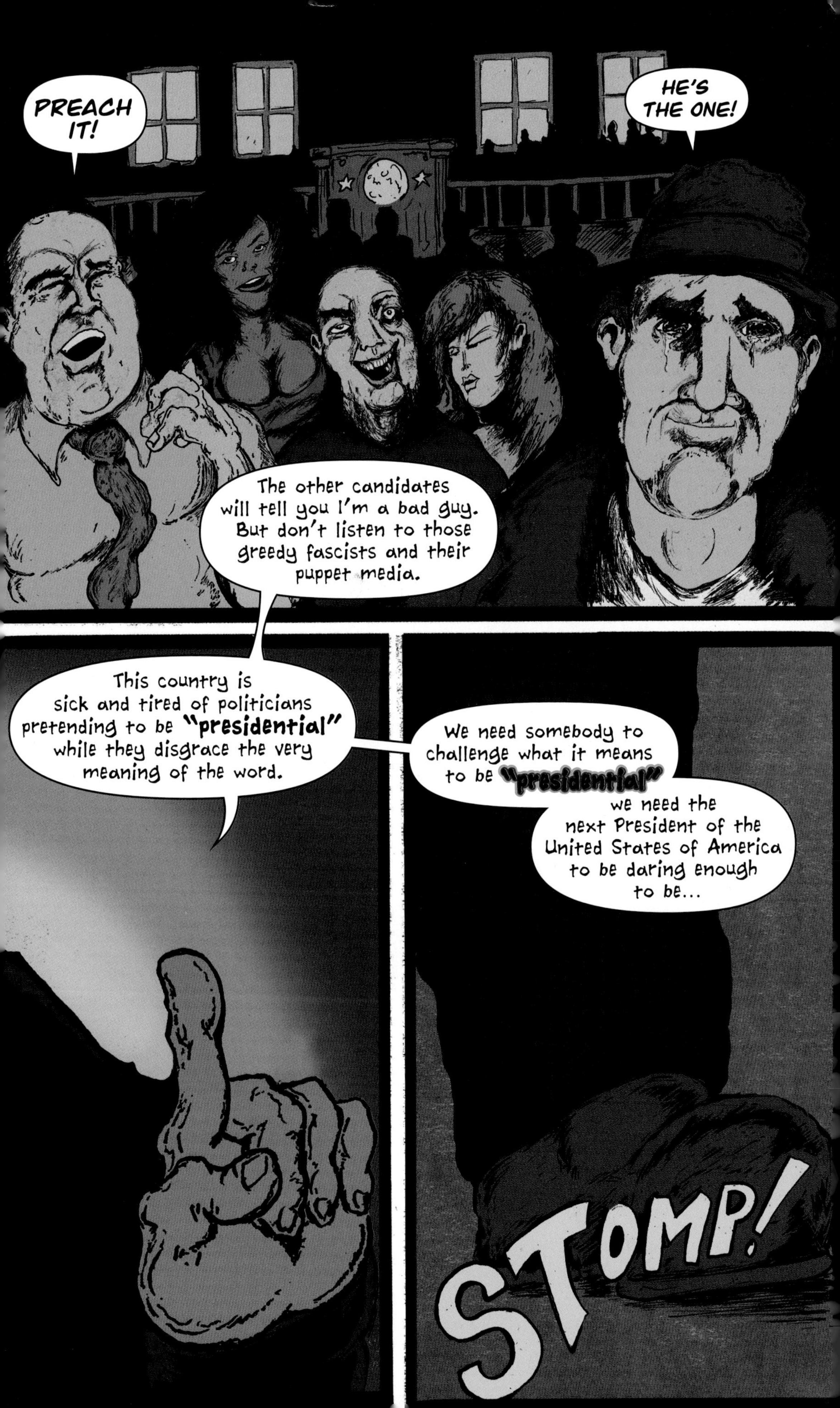

PREACH IT!
HE'S THE ONE!
The other candidates will tell you I'm a bad guy. But don't listen to those greedy fascists and their puppet media.
This country is sick and tired of politicians pretending to be "presidential" while they disgrace the very meaning of the word.
We need somebody to challenge what it means to be "presidential"
we need the next President of the United States of America to be daring enough to be...
STOMP!

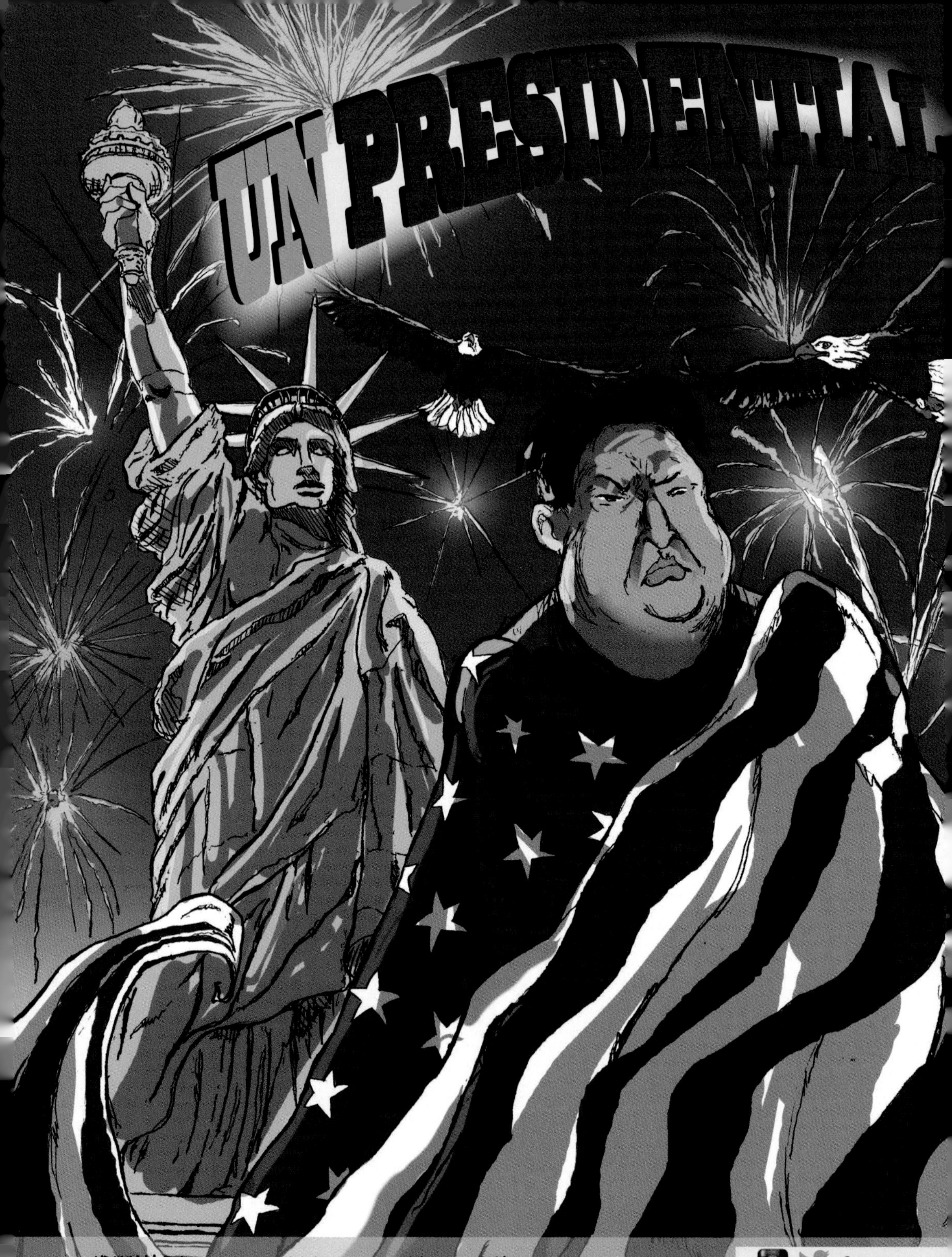
UN PRESIDENTIAL

WRITTEN BY
MAN VS ROCK
(KEVIN BIEBER &
VICTOR REYNOLDS)

ART BY
JEREMY LABIB

SPECIAL THANKS TO
JARED LAMP
ALADDIN COLLAR
MATT AND JOHN YUAN

DISTRIBUTED BY
Z2 COMICS

@MANVSROCK
MANVSROCK.COM
MAN VS. ROC
BUCK@MANVSROCK.COM

ED. NOTE #1 - ALL EVENTS DEPICTED IN THIS BOOK ARE PURELY IN THE NATURE OF SATIRE. NO PERSON ASSOCIATED WITH THIS BOOK IN ANY WAY SUPPORTS OR CONDONES ANY VIOLENCE WHATSOEVER, INCLUDING ANY VIOLENCE AGAINST OUR ELECTED REPRESENTATIVES OR ANY PUBLIC FIGURE

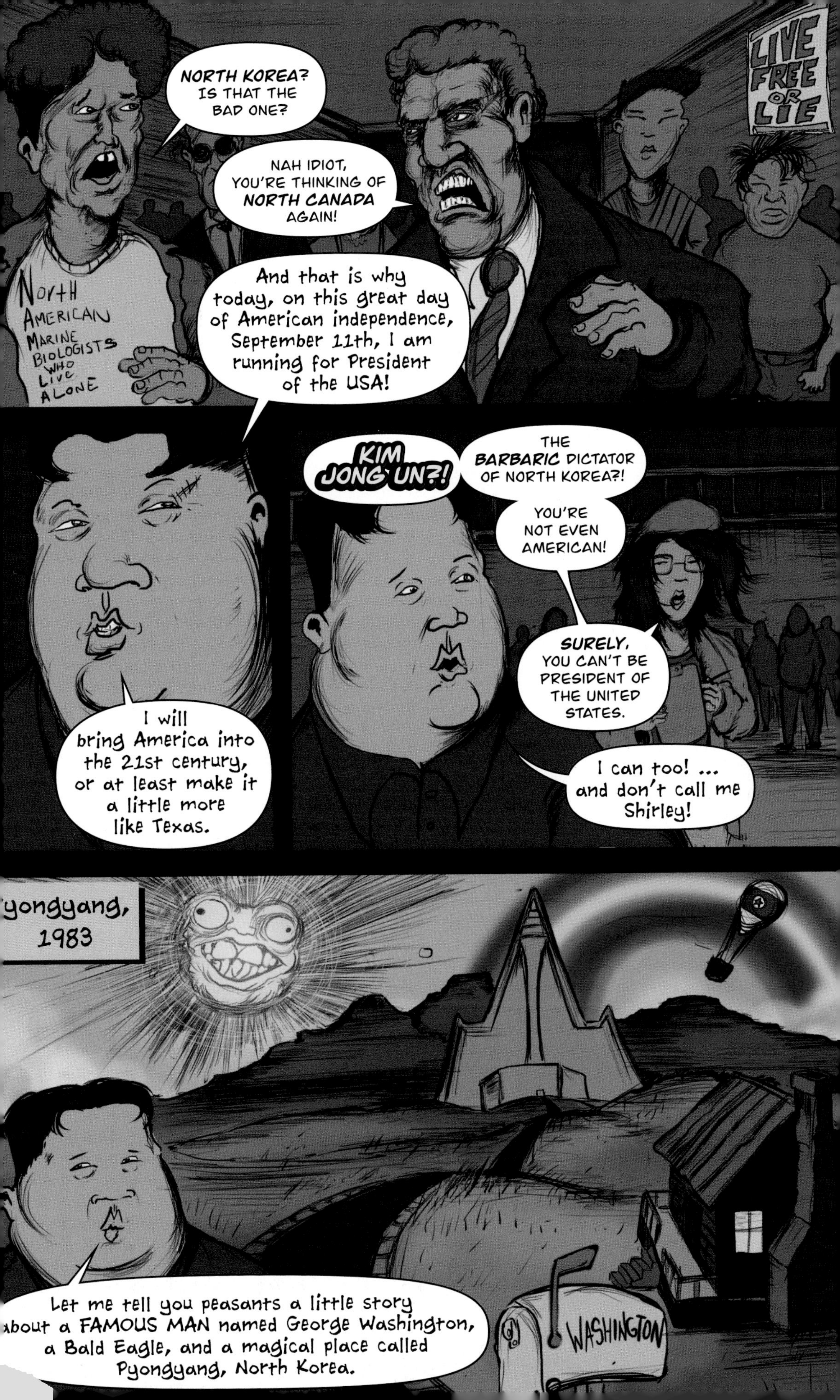

NORTH KOREA? IS THAT THE BAD ONE?
NAH IDIOT, YOU'RE THINKING OF NORTH CANADA AGAIN!
LIVE FREE OR LIE
NORTH AMERICAN MARINE BIOLOGISTS WHO LIVE ALONE
And that is why today, on this great day of American independence, September 11th, I am running for President of the USA!
I will bring America into the 21st century, or at least make it a little more like Texas.
KIM JONG UN?!
THE BARBARIC DICTATOR OF NORTH KOREA?!
YOU'RE NOT EVEN AMERICAN!
SURELY, YOU CAN'T BE PRESIDENT OF THE UNITED STATES.
I can too! ... and don't call me Shirley!
yongyang, 1983
Let me tell you peasants a little story about a FAMOUS MAN named George Washington, a Bald Eagle, and a magical place called Pyongyang, North Korea.
WASHINGTON

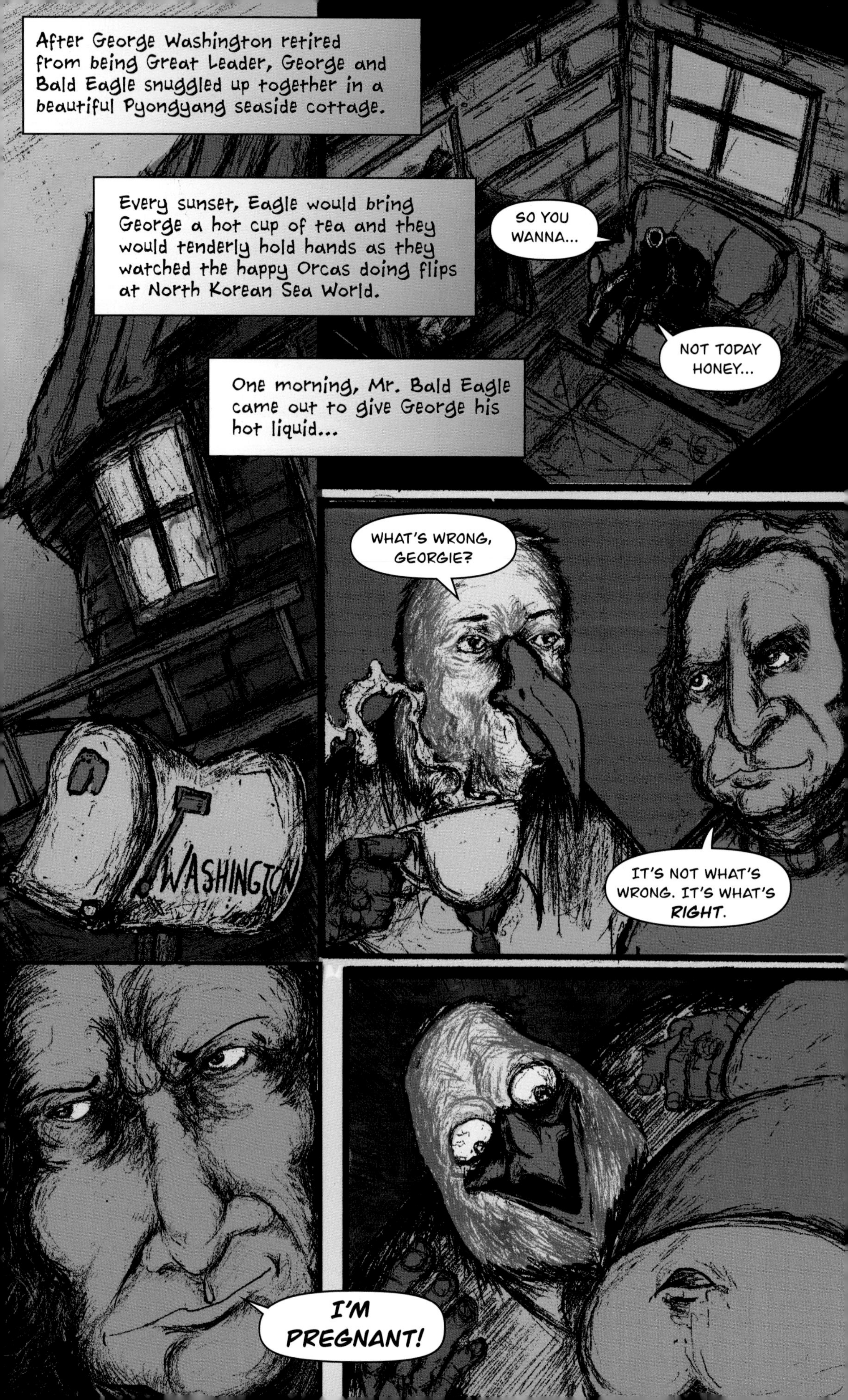
After George Washington retired from being Great Leader, George and Bald Eagle snuggled up together in a beautiful Pyongyang seaside cottage.
Every sunset, Eagle would bring George a hot cup of tea and they would tenderly hold hands as they watched the happy Orcas doing flips at North Korean Sea World.
SO YOU WANNA...
NOT TODAY HONEY...
One morning, Mr. Bald Eagle came out to give George his hot liquid...
WASHINGTON
WHAT'S WRONG, GEORGIE?
IT'S NOT WHAT'S WRONG. IT'S WHAT'S RIGHT.
I'M PREGNANT!

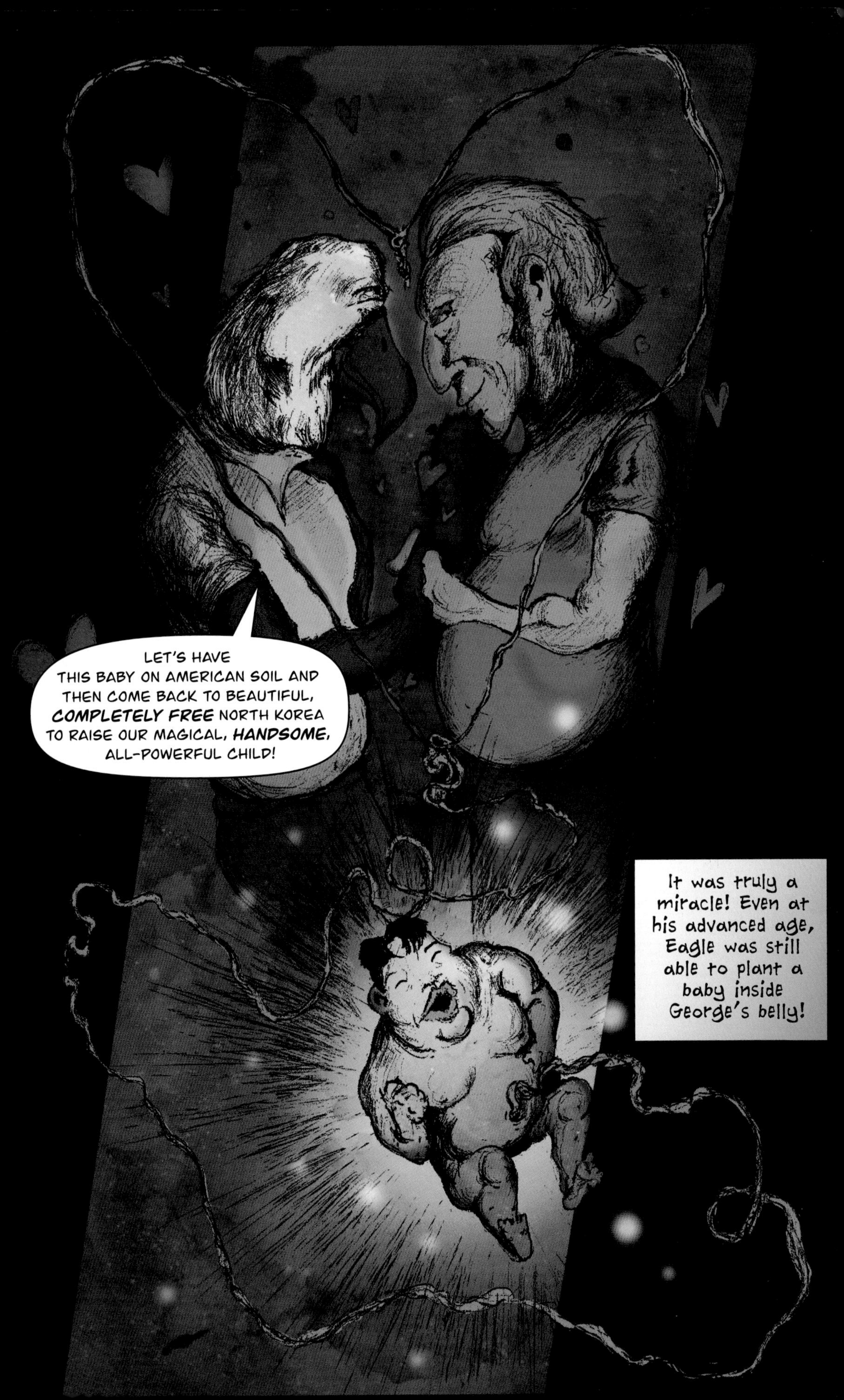
LET'S HAVE THIS BABY ON AMERICAN SOIL AND THEN COME BACK TO BEAUTIFUL, COMPLETELY FREE NORTH KOREA TO RAISE OUR MAGICAL, HANDSOME, ALL-POWERFUL CHILD!
It was truly a miracle! Even at his advanced age, Eagle was still able to plant a baby inside George's belly!

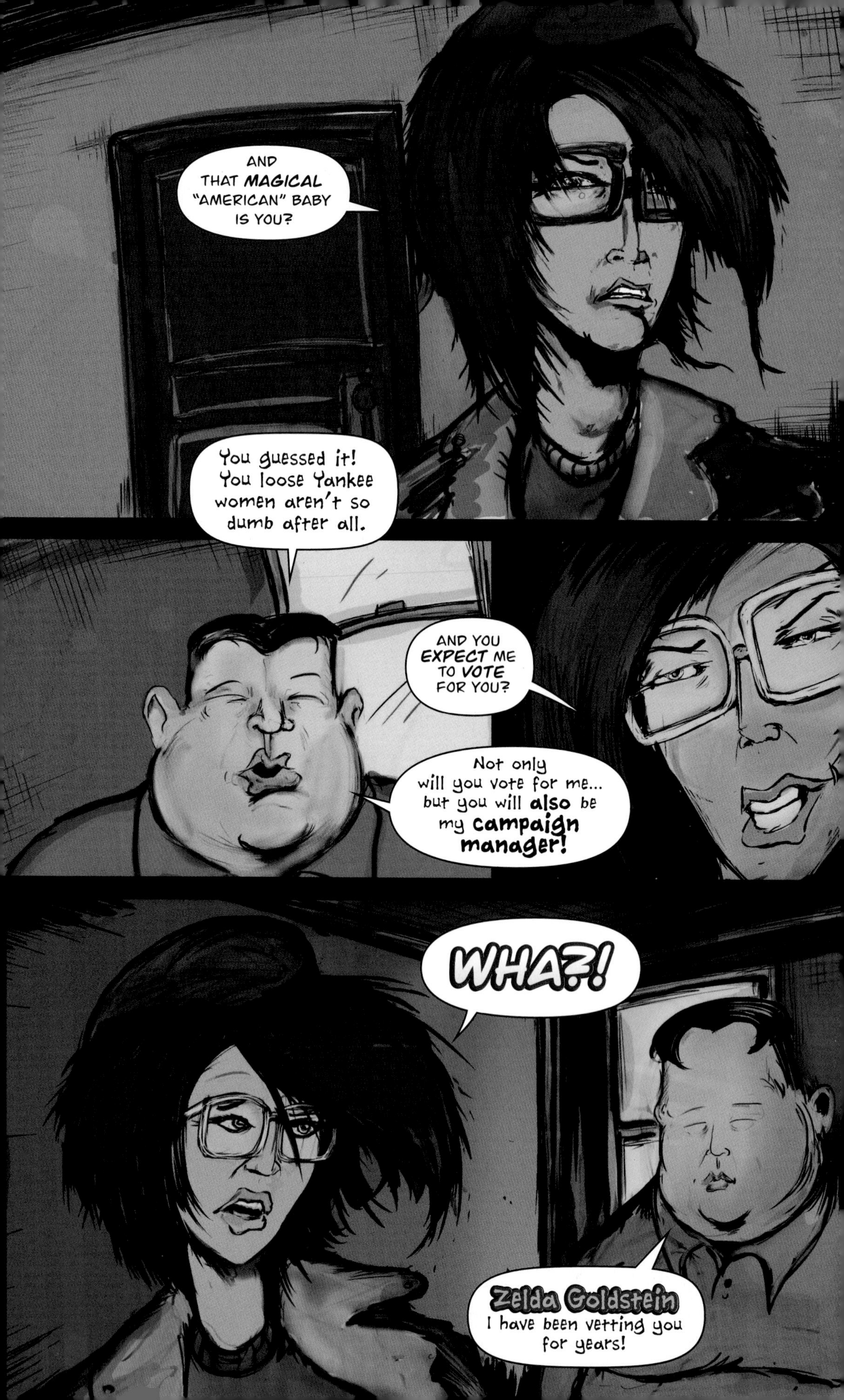
AND THAT MAGICAL "AMERICAN" BABY IS YOU?
You guessed it! You loose Yankee women aren't so dumb after all.
AND YOU EXPECT ME TO VOTE FOR YOU?
Not only will you vote for me... but you will also be my campaign manager!
WHA?!
Zelda Goldstein I have been vetting you for years!

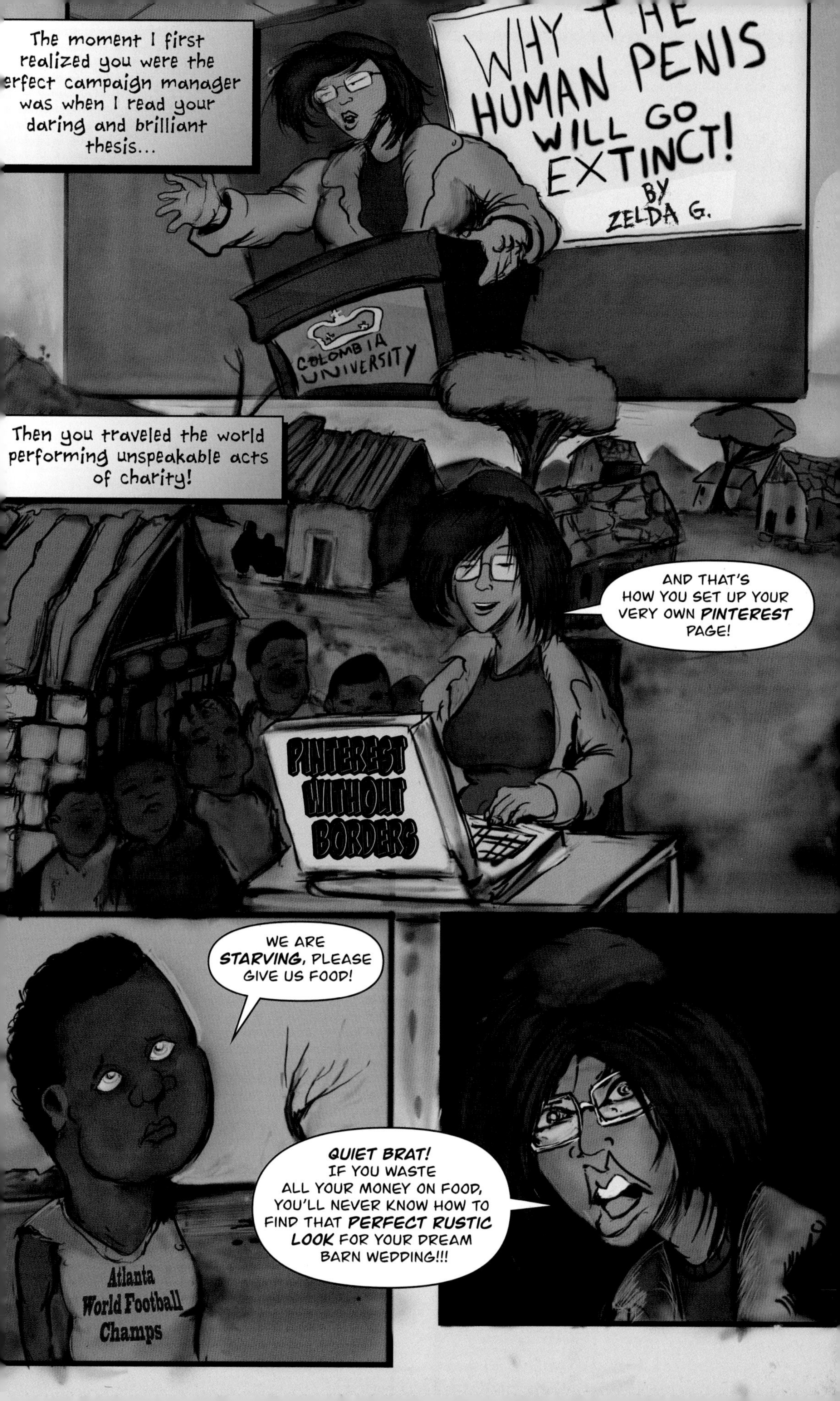

The moment I first realized you were the perfect campaign manager was when I read your daring and brilliant thesis...
WHY THE HUMAN PENIS WILL GO EXTINCT! BY ZELDA G.
COLOMBIA UNIVERSITY
Then you traveled the world performing unspeakable acts of charity!
AND THAT'S HOW YOU SET UP YOUR VERY OWN PINTEREST PAGE!
PINTEREST WITHOUT BORDERS
WE ARE STARVING, PLEASE GIVE US FOOD!
Atlanta World Football Champs
QUIET BRAT! IF YOU WASTE ALL YOUR MONEY ON FOOD, YOU'LL NEVER KNOW HOW TO FIND THAT PERFECT RUSTIC LOOK FOR YOUR DREAM BARN WEDDING!!!

Then you became the most influential journalist at the most prestigious news organization in the world!

Your pioneering journalistic excellence is unrivaled.

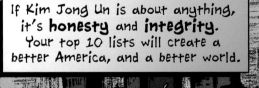

GAWKERFEED'S TOP 10 FARTING KITTENS

SLONP?

If Kim Jong Un is about anything, it's **honesty** and **integrity**. Your top 10 lists will create a better America, and a better world.

OVERPRICED HIPSTER COFFEE SHOP WITH AN IRONIC NAME

OPEN

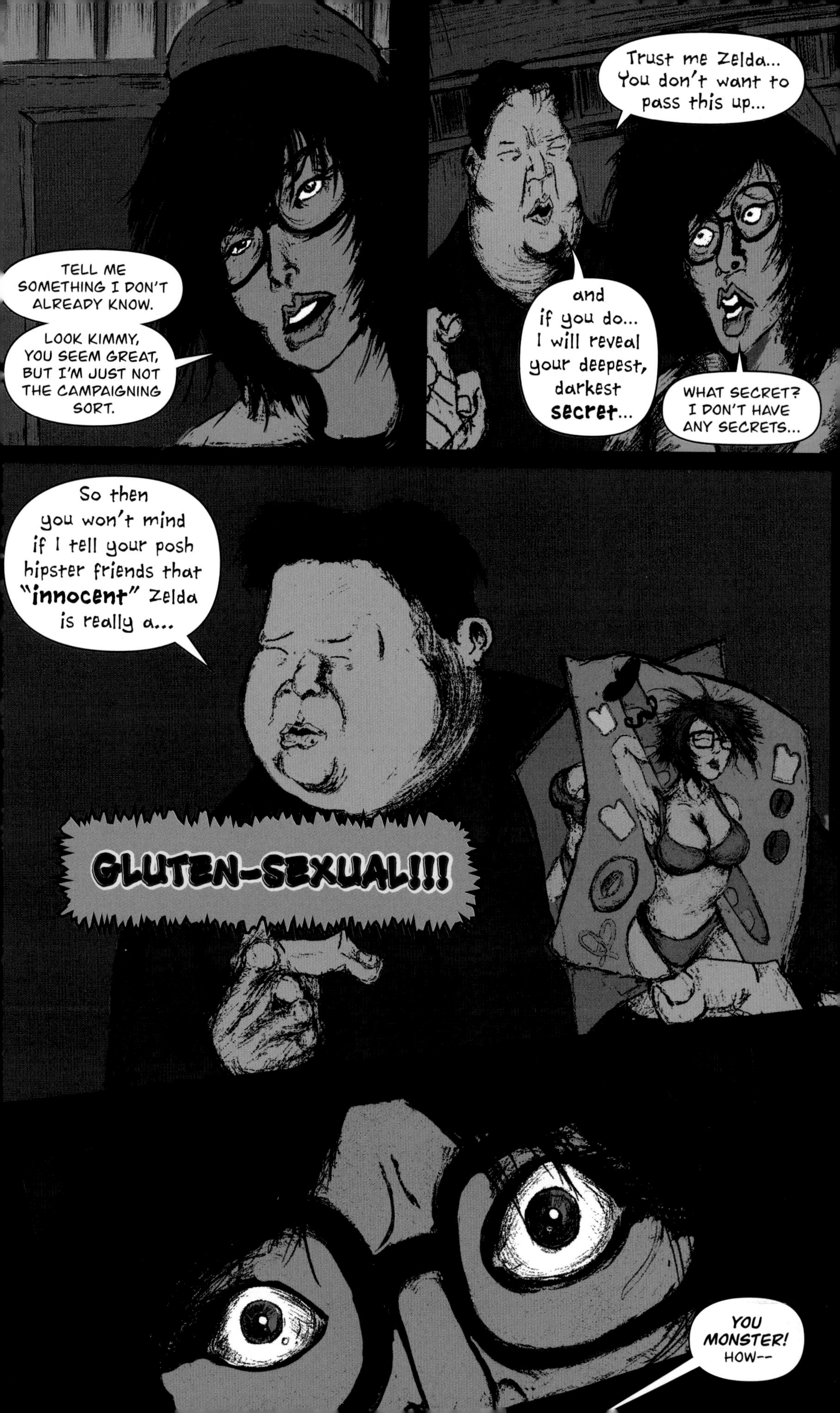
TELL ME SOMETHING I DON'T ALREADY KNOW.
LOOK KIMMY, YOU SEEM GREAT, BUT I'M JUST NOT THE CAMPAIGNING SORT.
Trust me Zelda... You don't want to pass this up...
and if you do... I will reveal your deepest, darkest secret...
WHAT SECRET? I DON'T HAVE ANY SECRETS...
So then you won't mind if I tell your posh hipster friends that "innocent" Zelda is really a...
GLUTEN-SEXUAL!!!
YOU MONSTER! HOW--

How did I find out? Let's just say that the wireless network you were **piggybacking** from wasn't the most **secure...**
SONY
FINE! YOU LEAVE ME NO CHOICE. ***I'LL MANAGE YOUR DAMN CAMPAIGN!*** WHO ELSE IS ON YOUR TEAM?
Team? In homeland, all I needed was Dennis Rodman and my massive world record three inch penis to become Great Leader.
OF COURSE YOU NEED A TEAM. EVEN ***JEB BUSH*** HAD LIKE ***500*** PEOPLE WORKING FOR HIM.
Five hundred people!? There's no way he could lose with that many people!

THE STARVING Pariah -Lofts-
Yes! We accept your parents' money!

"To have a chance, I will need to assemble the best team since the North Korean World Cup champion soccer club."

THERE'S ONLY ONE PLACE WHERE WE CAN FIND SUCH *HIGHLY QUALIFIED* INDIVIDUALS...

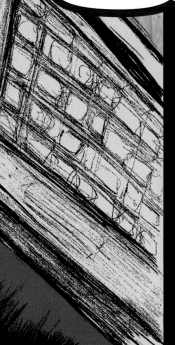

KRAIG'S LIST.

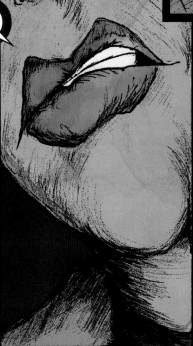

Oh! I'll write the ad! I was voted the most talented poet in the universe by "Highlights Magazine"... and Phillip K. Dick.

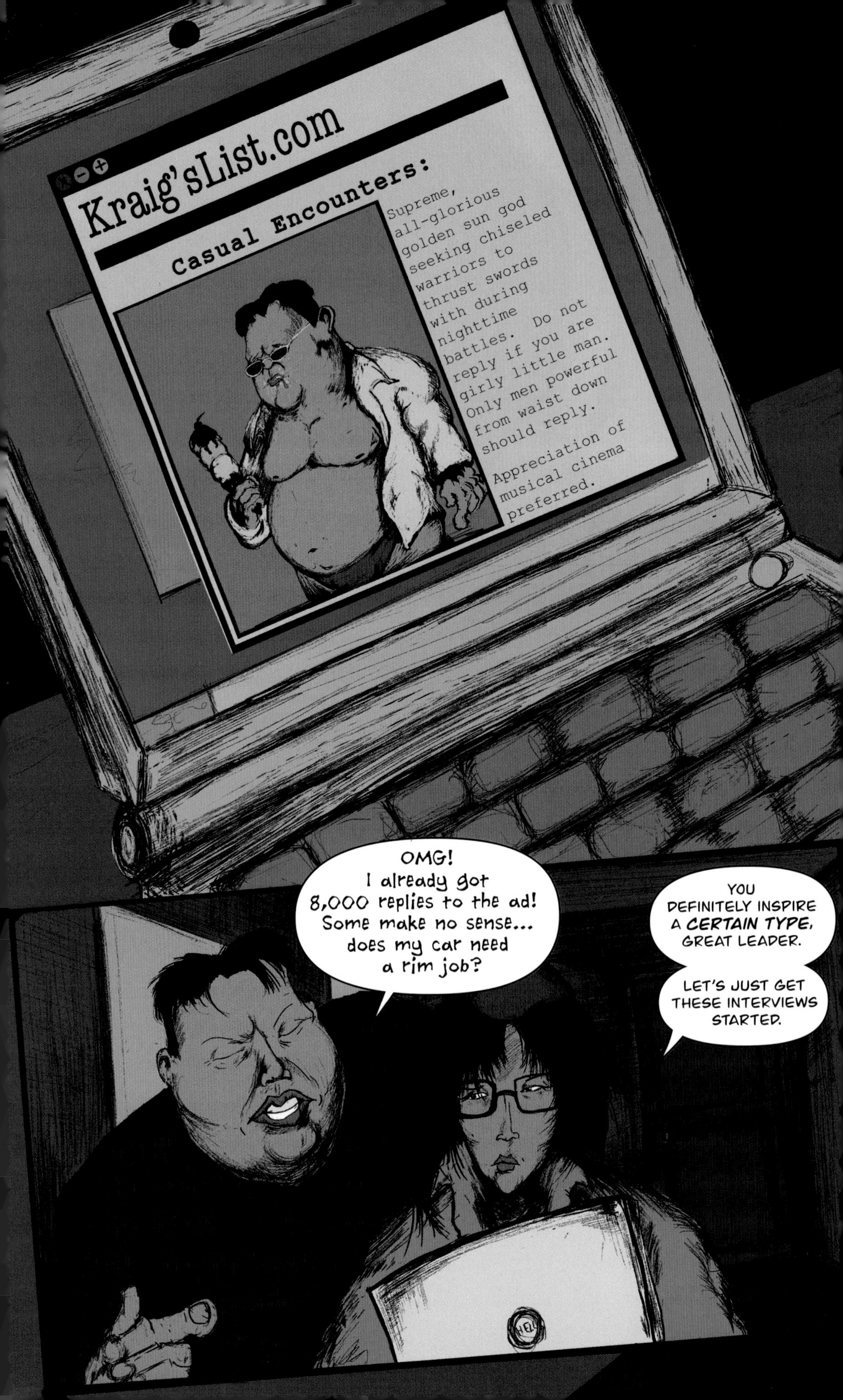
Kraig'sList.com
Casual Encounters:
Supreme, all-glorious golden sun god seeking chiseled warriors to thrust swords with during nighttime battles. Do not reply if you are girly little man. Only men powerful from waist down should reply.
Appreciation of musical cinema preferred.
OMG! I already got 8,000 replies to the ad! Some make no sense... does my car need a rim job?
YOU DEFINITELY INSPIRE A *CERTAIN TYPE*, GREAT LEADER.
LET'S JUST GET THESE INTERVIEWS STARTED.

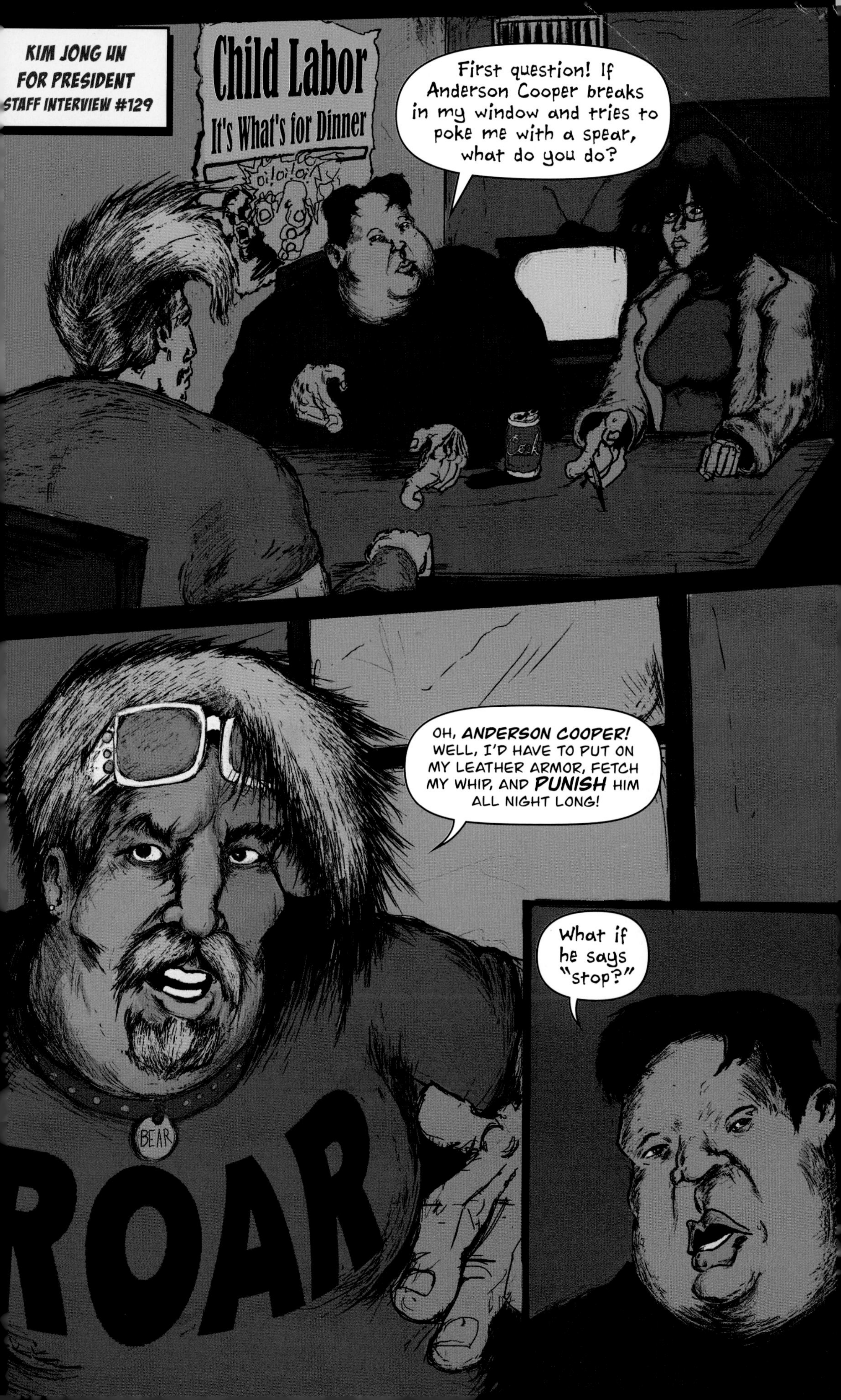

KIM JONG UN FOR PRESIDENT STAFF INTERVIEW #129
Child Labor It's What's for Dinner
First question! If Anderson Cooper breaks in my window and tries to poke me with a spear, what do you do?
OH, ANDERSON COOPER! WELL, I'D HAVE TO PUT ON MY LEATHER ARMOR, FETCH MY WHIP, AND PUNISH HIM ALL NIGHT LONG!
BEAR
ROAR
What if he says "stop?"

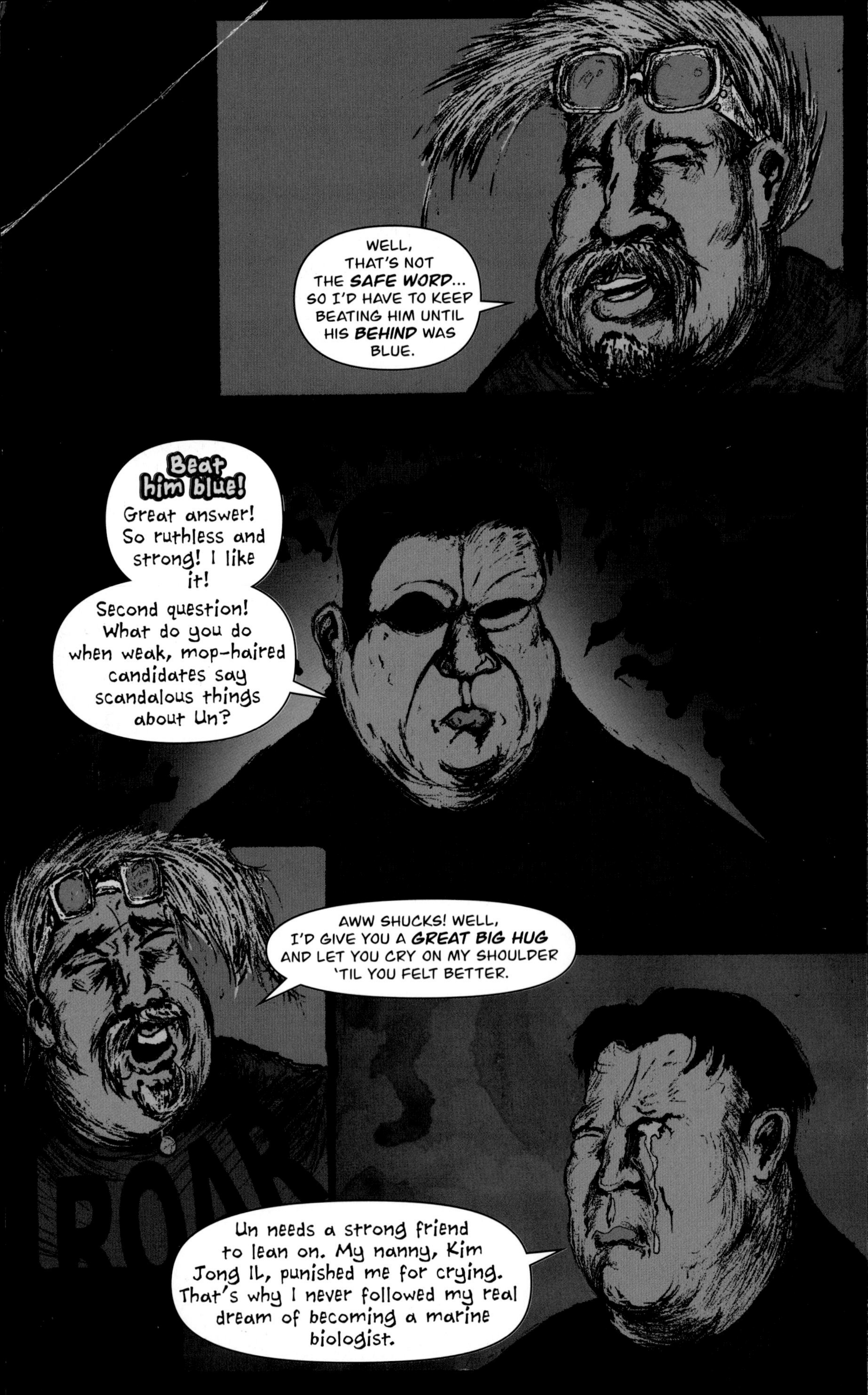
WELL, THAT'S NOT THE SAFE WORD... SO I'D HAVE TO KEEP BEATING HIM UNTIL HIS BEHIND WAS BLUE.
Beat him blue!
Great answer! So ruthless and strong! I like it!
Second question! What do you do when weak, mop-haired candidates say scandalous things about Un?
AWW SHUCKS! WELL, I'D GIVE YOU A GREAT BIG HUG AND LET YOU CRY ON MY SHOULDER 'TIL YOU FELT BETTER.
Un needs a strong friend to lean on. My nanny, Kim Jong IL, punished me for crying. That's why I never followed my real dream of becoming a marine biologist.

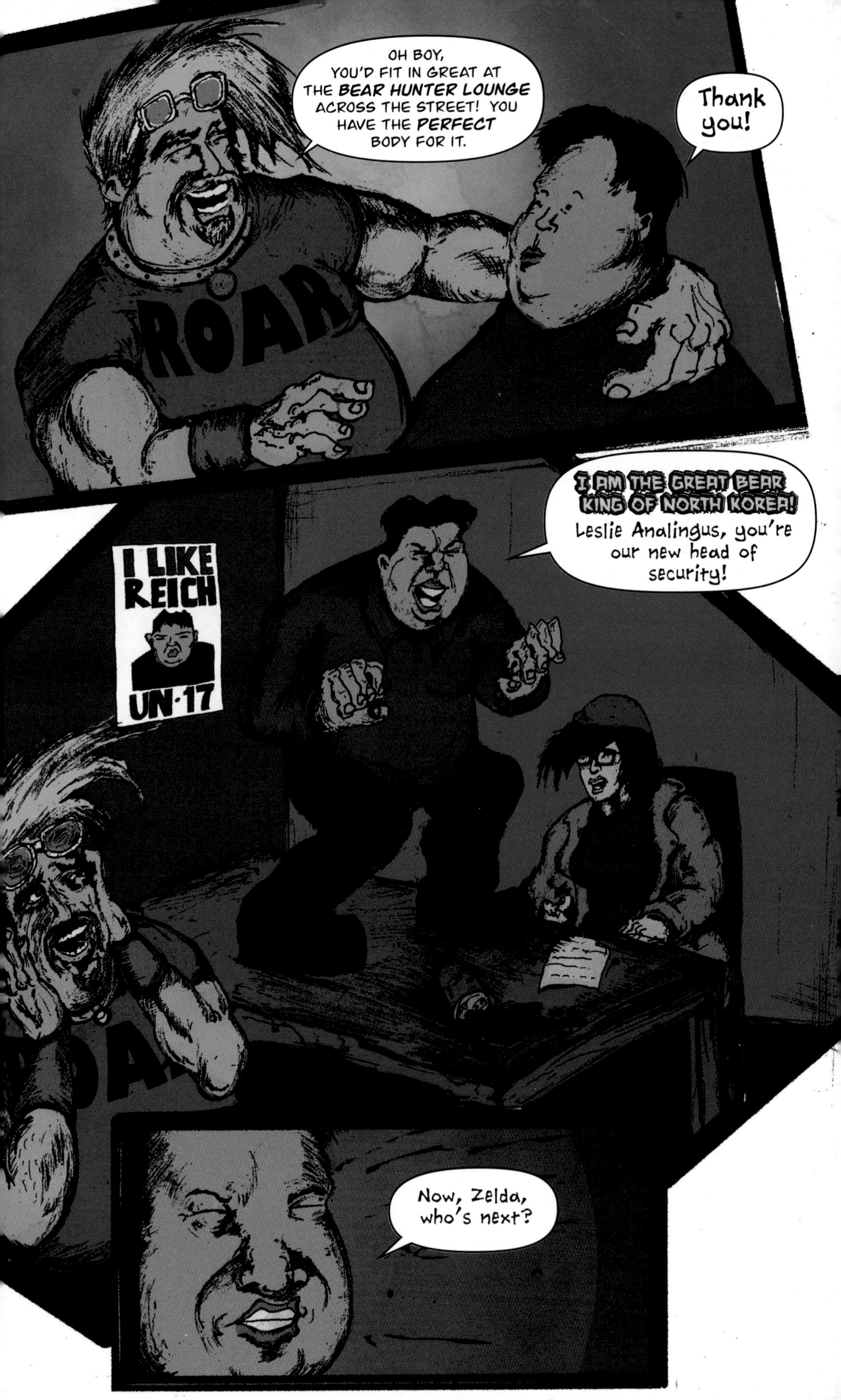

OH BOY, YOU'D FIT IN GREAT AT THE ***BEAR HUNTER LOUNGE*** ACROSS THE STREET! YOU HAVE THE ***PERFECT*** BODY FOR IT.
Thank you!
ROAR
I AM THE GREAT BEAR KING OF NORTH KOREA! Leslie Analingus, you're our new head of security!
I LIKE REICH
UN·17
Now, Zelda, who's next?

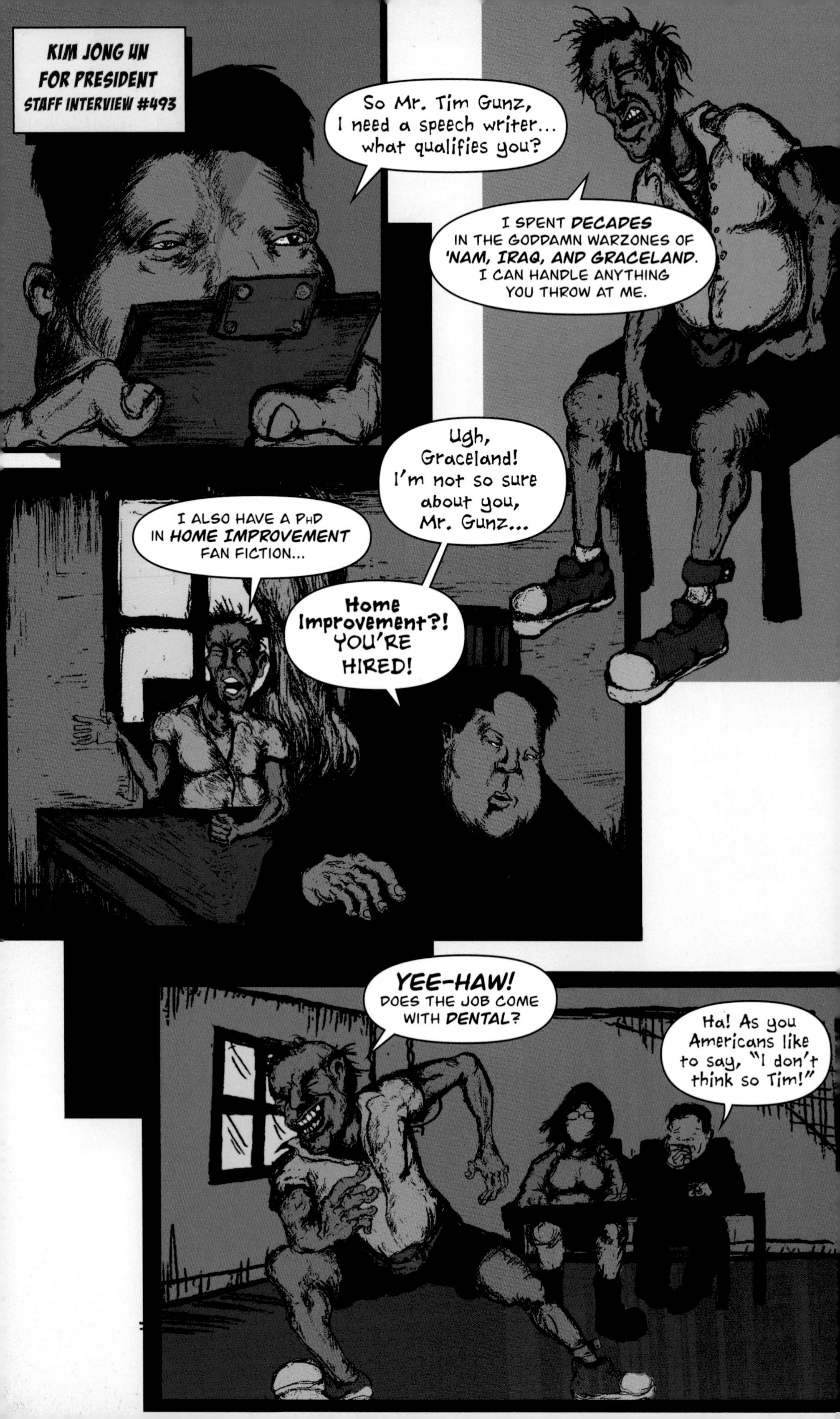
KIM JONG UN FOR PRESIDENT STAFF INTERVIEW #493
So Mr. Tim Gunz, I need a speech writer... what qualifies you?
I SPENT DECADES IN THE GODDAMN WARZONES OF 'NAM, IRAQ, AND GRACELAND. I CAN HANDLE ANYTHING YOU THROW AT ME.
Ugh, Graceland! I'm not so sure about you, Mr. Gunz...
I ALSO HAVE A PHD IN HOME IMPROVEMENT FAN FICTION...
Home Improvement?! YOU'RE HIRED!
YEE-HAW! DOES THE JOB COME WITH DENTAL?
Ha! As you Americans like to say, "I don't think so Tim!"

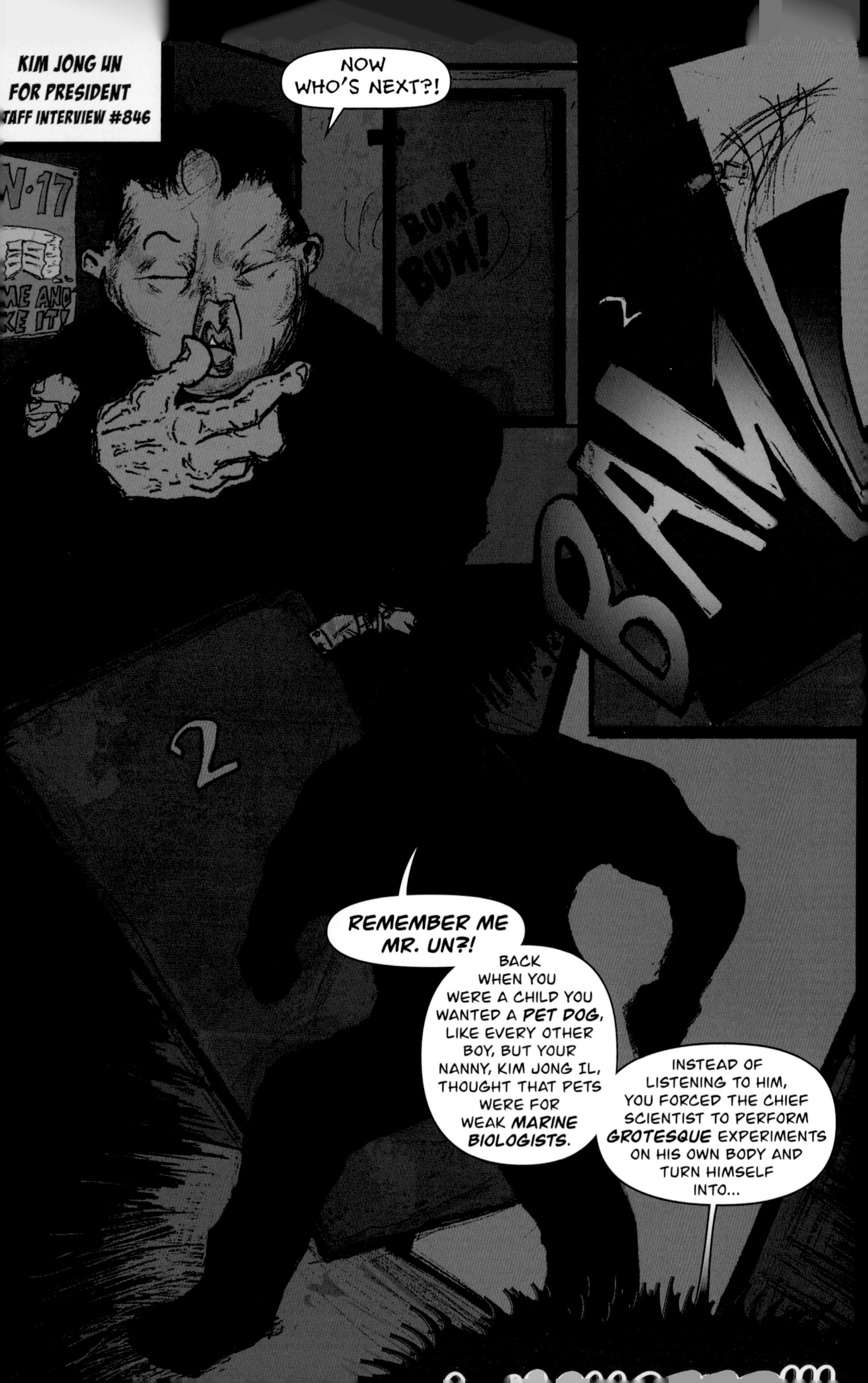
KIM JONG UN FOR PRESIDENT
TAFF INTERVIEW #846
NOW WHO'S NEXT?!
BUM! BUM!
BAM!
REMEMBER ME MR. UN?!
BACK WHEN YOU WERE A CHILD YOU WANTED A PET DOG, LIKE EVERY OTHER BOY, BUT YOUR NANNY, KIM JONG IL, THOUGHT THAT PETS WERE FOR WEAK MARINE BIOLOGISTS.
INSTEAD OF LISTENING TO HIM, YOU FORCED THE CHIEF SCIENTIST TO PERFORM GROTESQUE EXPERIMENTS ON HIS OWN BODY AND TURN HIMSELF INTO...

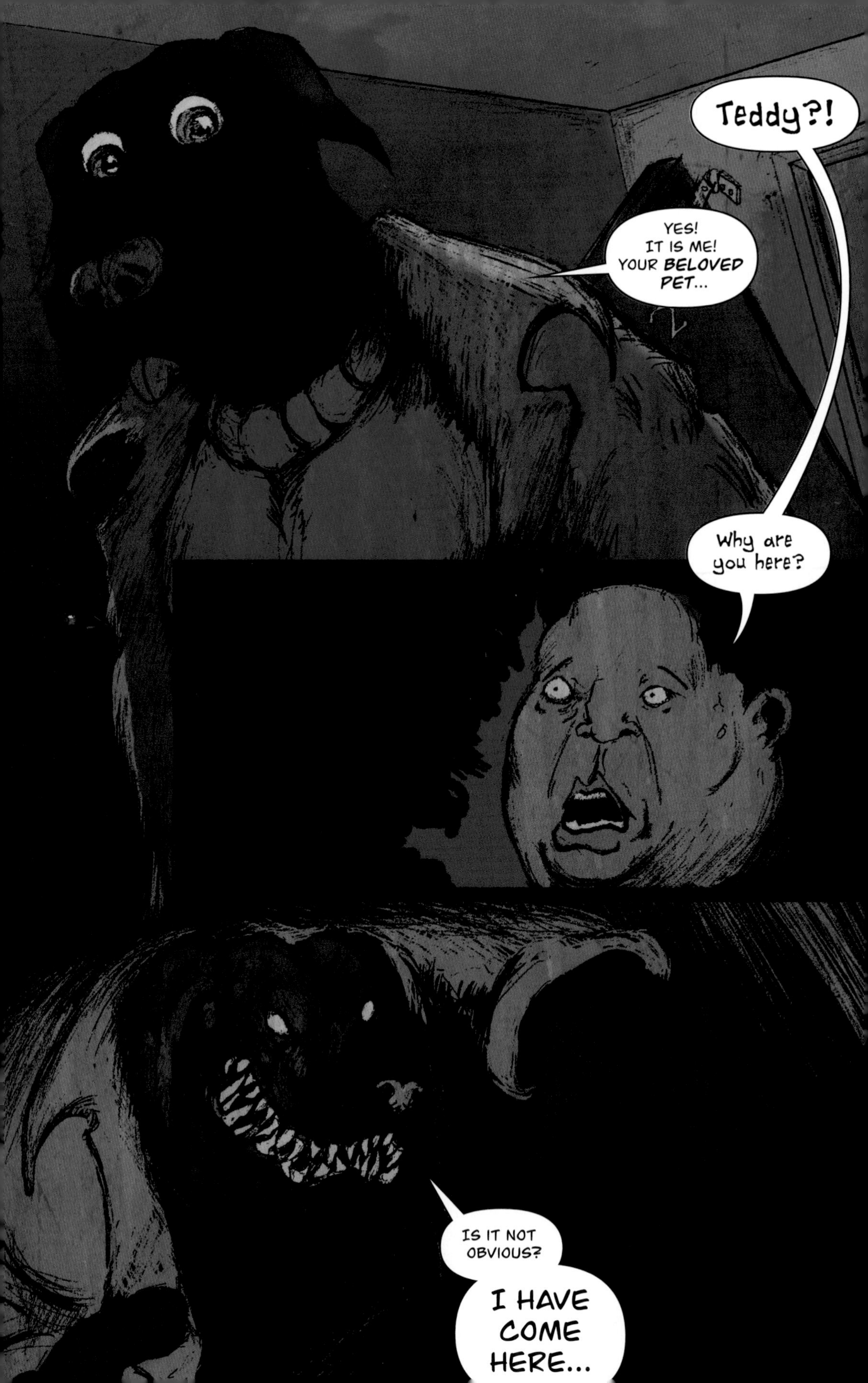
Teddy?!
YES! IT IS ME! YOUR BELOVED PET...
Why are you here?
IS IT NOT OBVIOUS?
I HAVE COME HERE...

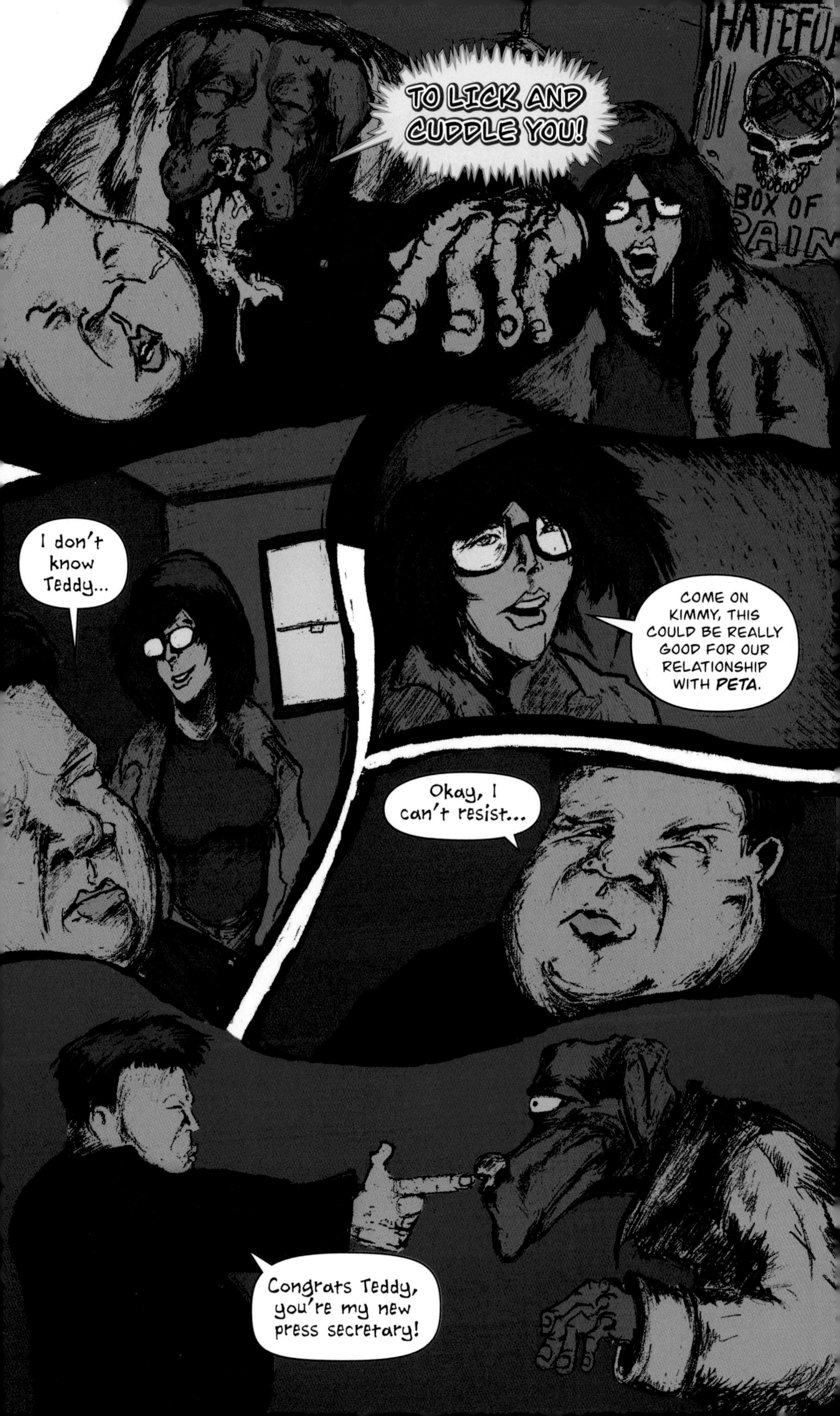
TO LICK AND CUDDLE YOU!
HATEFUL
BOX OF PAIN
I don't know Teddy...
COME ON KIMMY, THIS COULD BE REALLY GOOD FOR OUR RELATIONSHIP WITH PETA.
Okay, I can't resist...
Congrats Teddy, you're my new press secretary!

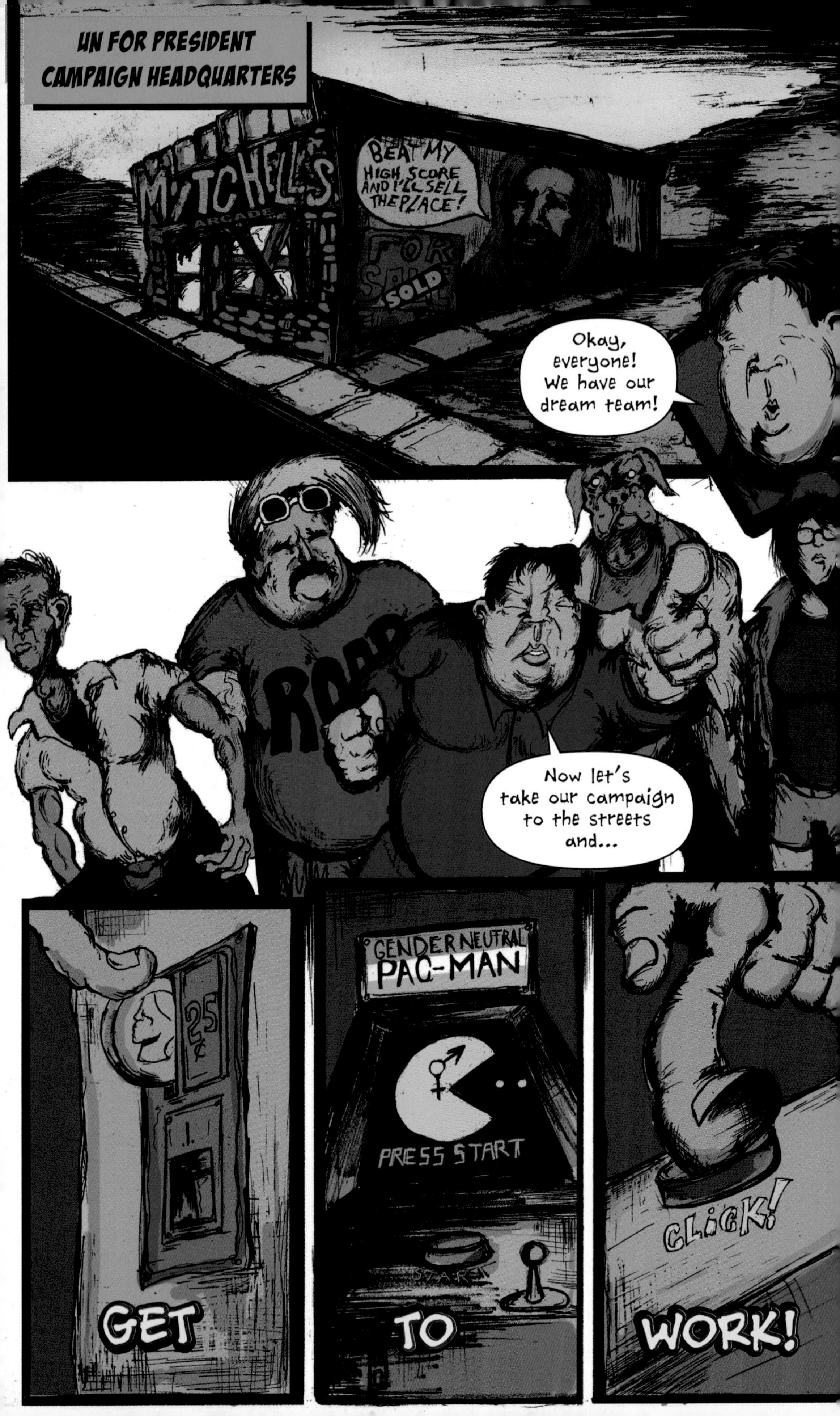
UN FOR PRESIDENT
CAMPAIGN HEADQUARTERS
MITCHELL'S
ARCADE
BEAT MY HIGH SCORE AND I'LL SELL THE PLACE!
FOR SALE
SOLD
Okay, everyone! We have our dream team!
Now let's take our campaign to the streets and...
25¢
GET
GENDER NEUTRAL
PAC-MAN
PRESS START
START
TO
CLICK!
WORK!

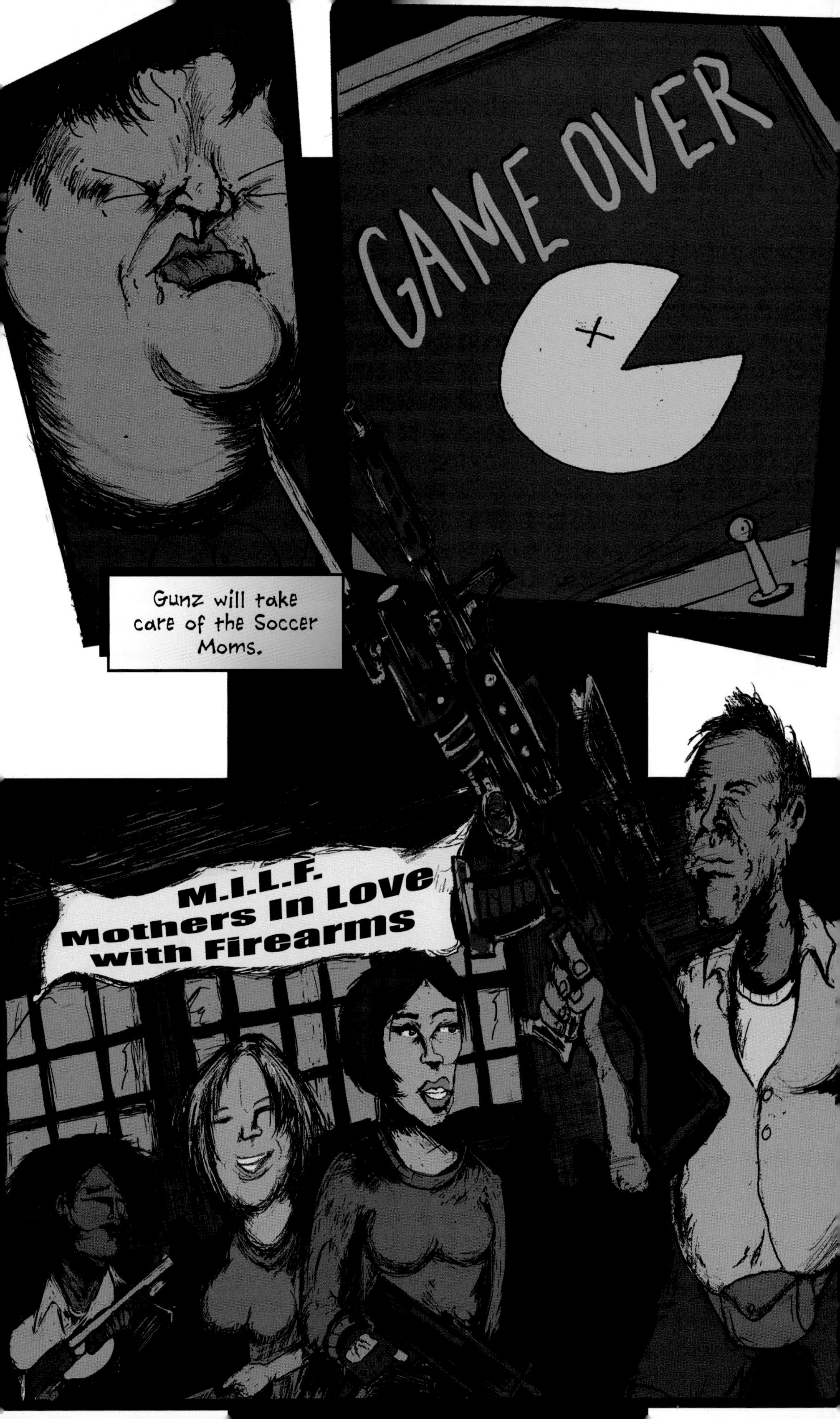
GAME OVER
Gunz will take care of the Soccer Moms.
M.I.L.F.
Mothers In Love with Firearms

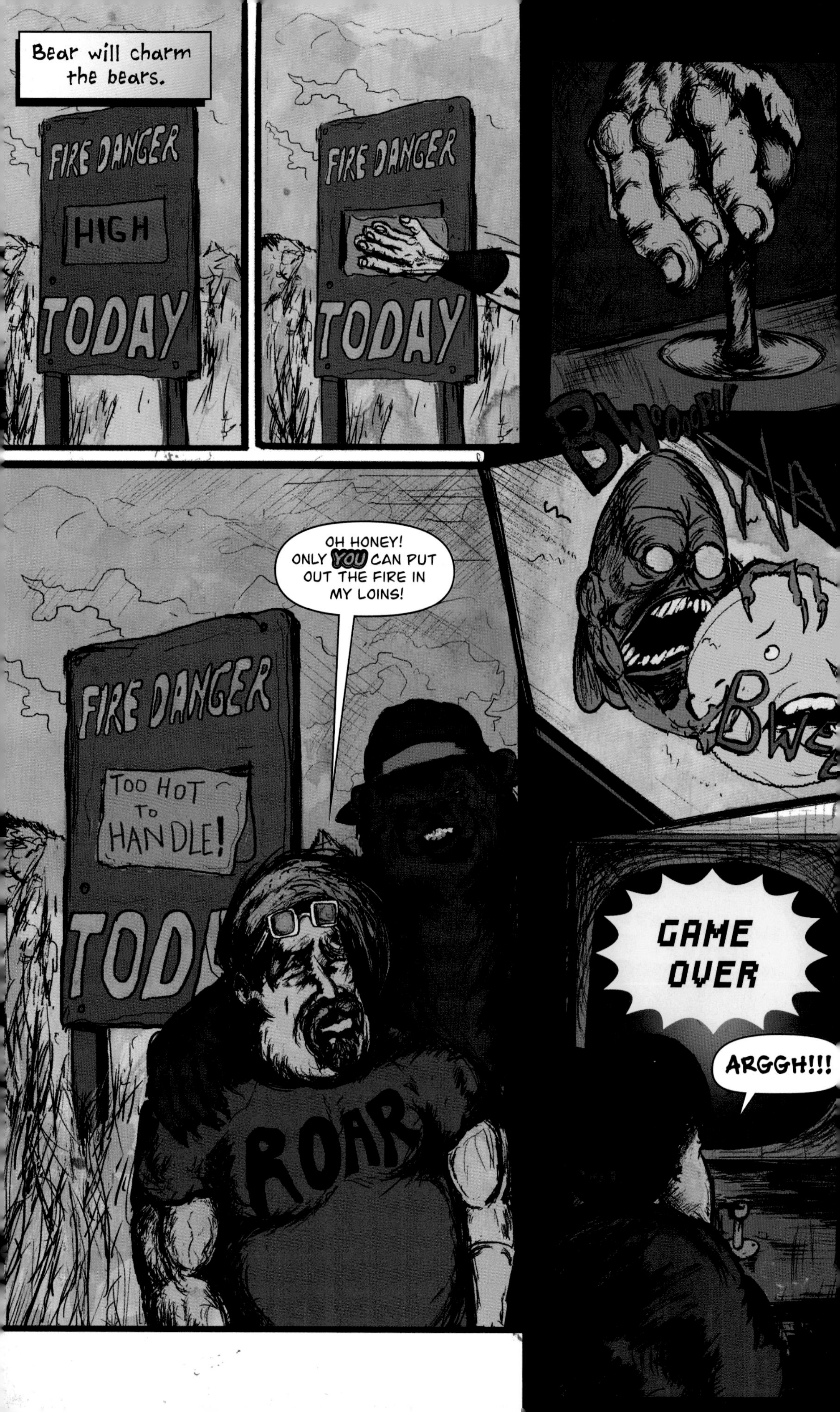
Bear will charm the bears.
FIRE DANGER
HIGH
TODAY
FIRE DANGER
TODAY
BWOOOP!!
WA
BWE
FIRE DANGER
TOO HOT TO HANDLE!
TOD
OH HONEY! ONLY YOU CAN PUT OUT THE FIRE IN MY LOINS!
ROAR
GAME OVER
ARGGH!!!

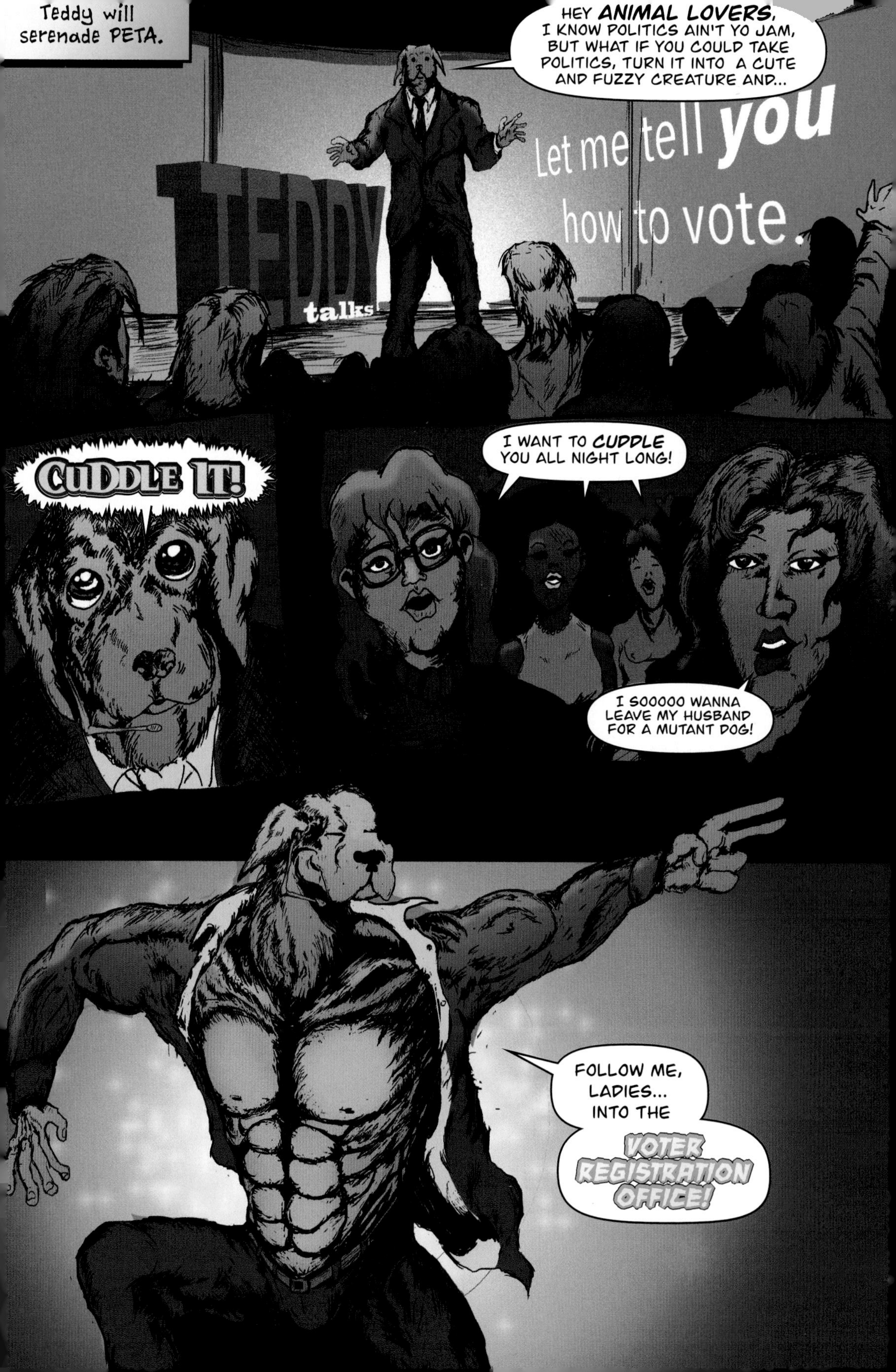

Teddy will serenade PETA.
HEY ANIMAL LOVERS, I KNOW POLITICS AIN'T YO JAM, BUT WHAT IF YOU COULD TAKE POLITICS, TURN IT INTO A CUTE AND FUZZY CREATURE AND...
Let me tell you how to vote.
TEDDY talks
CUDDLE IT!
I WANT TO CUDDLE YOU ALL NIGHT LONG!
I SOOOOO WANNA LEAVE MY HUSBAND FOR A MUTANT DOG!
FOLLOW ME, LADIES... INTO THE
VOTER REGISTRATION OFFICE!

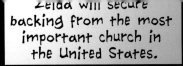
Zelda will secure backing from the most important church in the United States.

LADIES, I WOULD LIKE TO INTRODUCE THE BRAND NEW *E-METER* MADE FOR WOMEN, BY WOMEN! JUST GENTLY INSERT THE *DILDO* INTO--

HOLLYWOOD

FEMINISTS FOR SCIENTOLOGY PRESENTS
De La Femme

And I will work on a very important, **top secret** mission...

GENDER NEUTRAL PAC-MAN

GAME OVER

Pronoun Ghosts always ruin everything...

Baaah! Get away from me, **Pronoun Ghost!**

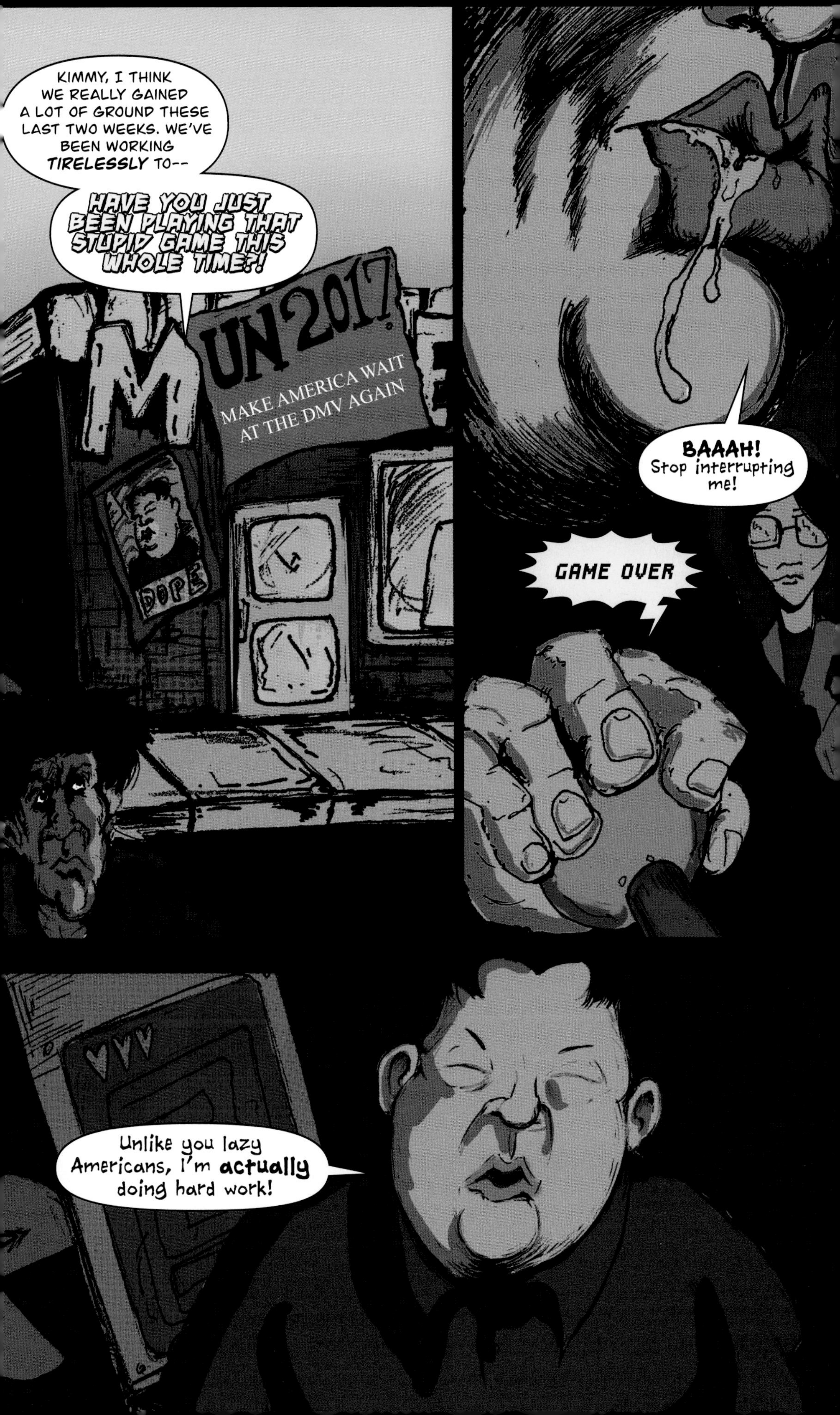
KIMMY, I THINK WE REALLY GAINED A LOT OF GROUND THESE LAST TWO WEEKS. WE'VE BEEN WORKING TIRELESSLY TO--
HAVE YOU JUST BEEN PLAYING THAT STUPID GAME THIS WHOLE TIME?!
UN 2017
MAKE AMERICA WAIT AT THE DMV AGAIN
DOPE
BAAAH! Stop interrupting me!
GAME OVER
Unlike you lazy Americans, I'm actually doing hard work!

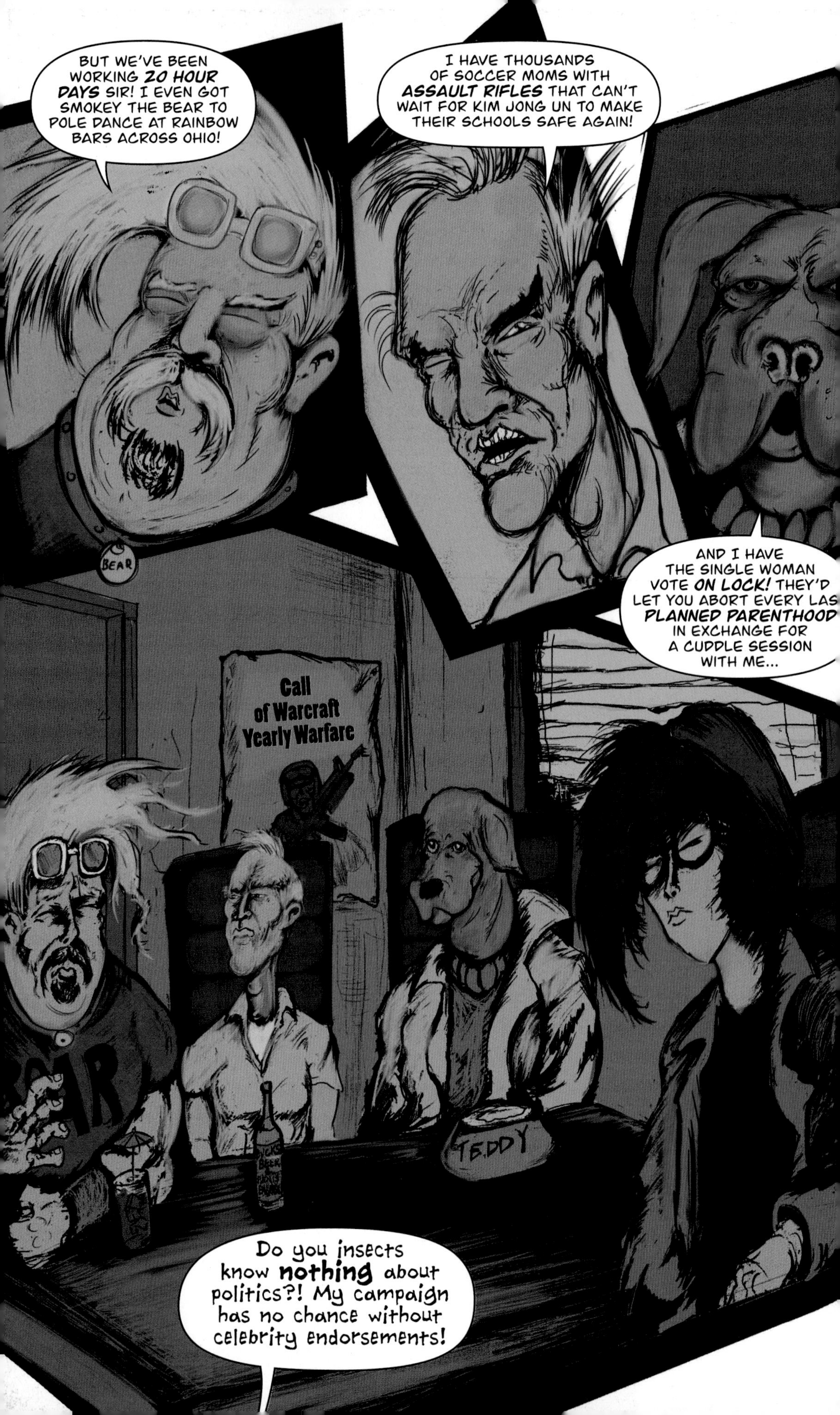
BUT WE'VE BEEN WORKING 20 HOUR DAYS SIR! I EVEN GOT SMOKEY THE BEAR TO POLE DANCE AT RAINBOW BARS ACROSS OHIO!
I HAVE THOUSANDS OF SOCCER MOMS WITH ASSAULT RIFLES THAT CAN'T WAIT FOR KIM JONG UN TO MAKE THEIR SCHOOLS SAFE AGAIN!
AND I HAVE THE SINGLE WOMAN VOTE ON LOCK! THEY'D LET YOU ABORT EVERY LAS PLANNED PARENTHOOD IN EXCHANGE FOR A CUDDLE SESSION WITH ME...
BEAR
Call of Warcraft Yearly Warfare
TEDDY
Do you insects know nothing about politics?! My campaign has no chance without celebrity endorsements!

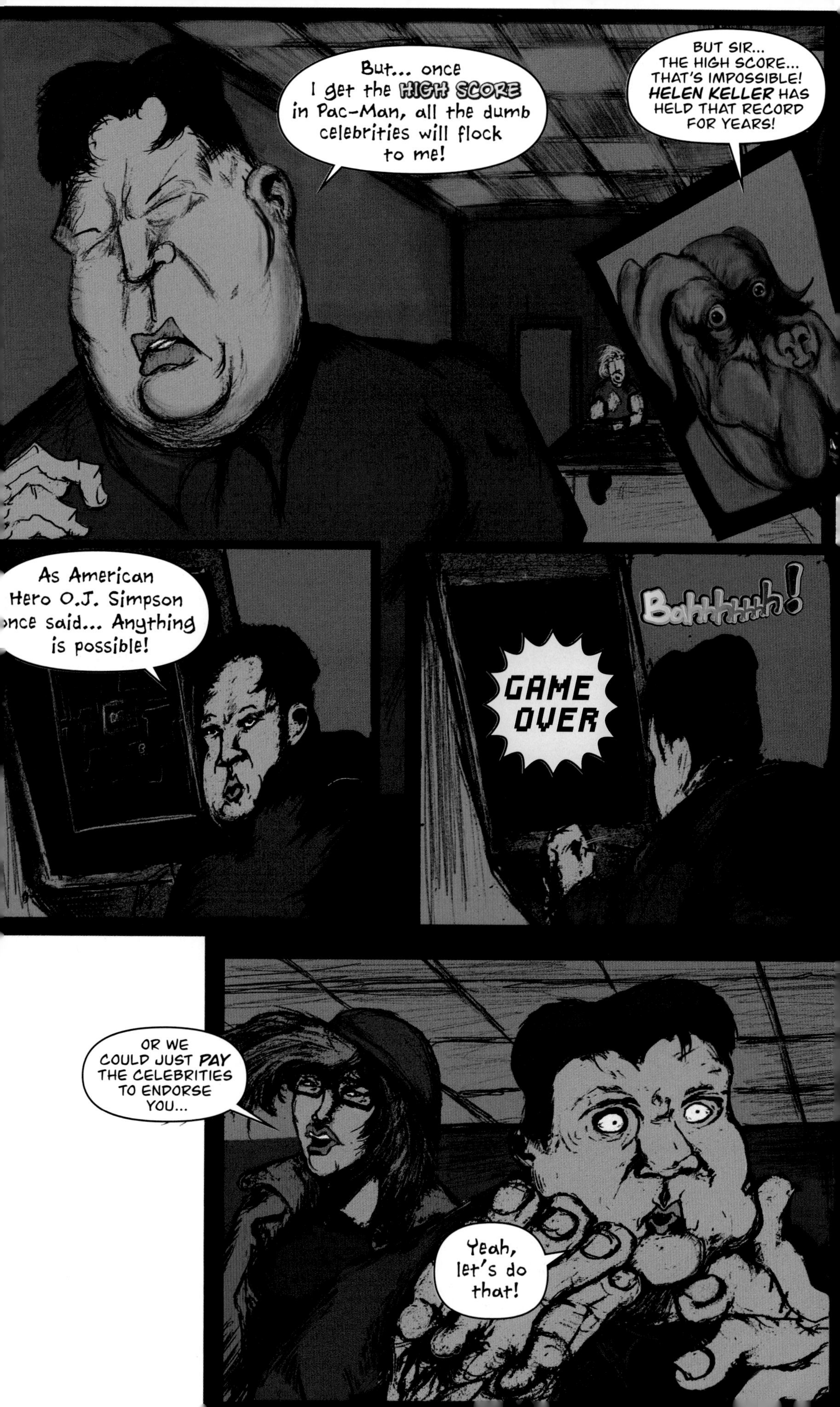
But... once I get the HIGH SCORE in Pac-Man, all the dumb celebrities will flock to me!
BUT SIR... THE HIGH SCORE... THAT'S IMPOSSIBLE! HELEN KELLER HAS HELD THAT RECORD FOR YEARS!
As American Hero O.J. Simpson once said... Anything is possible!
Bahhhhhh!
GAME OVER
OR WE COULD JUST PAY THE CELEBRITIES TO ENDORSE YOU...
Yeah, let's do that!

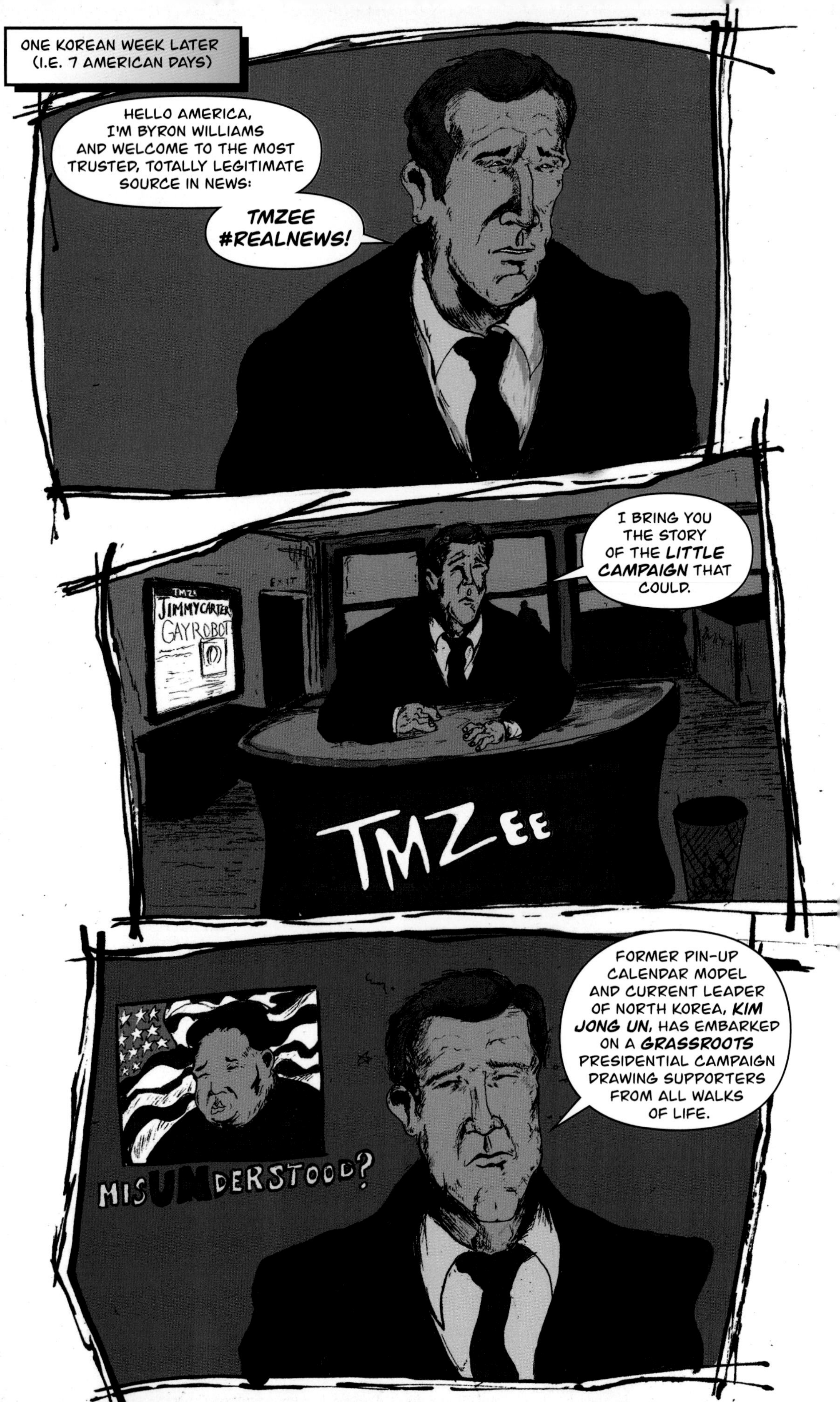
ONE KOREAN WEEK LATER (I.E. 7 AMERICAN DAYS)
HELLO AMERICA, I'M BYRON WILLIAMS AND WELCOME TO THE MOST TRUSTED, TOTALLY LEGITIMATE SOURCE IN NEWS:
TMZEE #REALNEWS!
TMZEE
JIMMY CARTER'S GAY ROBOT
EXIT
I BRING YOU THE STORY OF THE LITTLE CAMPAIGN THAT COULD.
TMZEE
FORMER PIN-UP CALENDAR MODEL AND CURRENT LEADER OF NORTH KOREA, KIM JONG UN, HAS EMBARKED ON A GRASSROOTS PRESIDENTIAL CAMPAIGN DRAWING SUPPORTERS FROM ALL WALKS OF LIFE.
MISUNDERSTOOD?

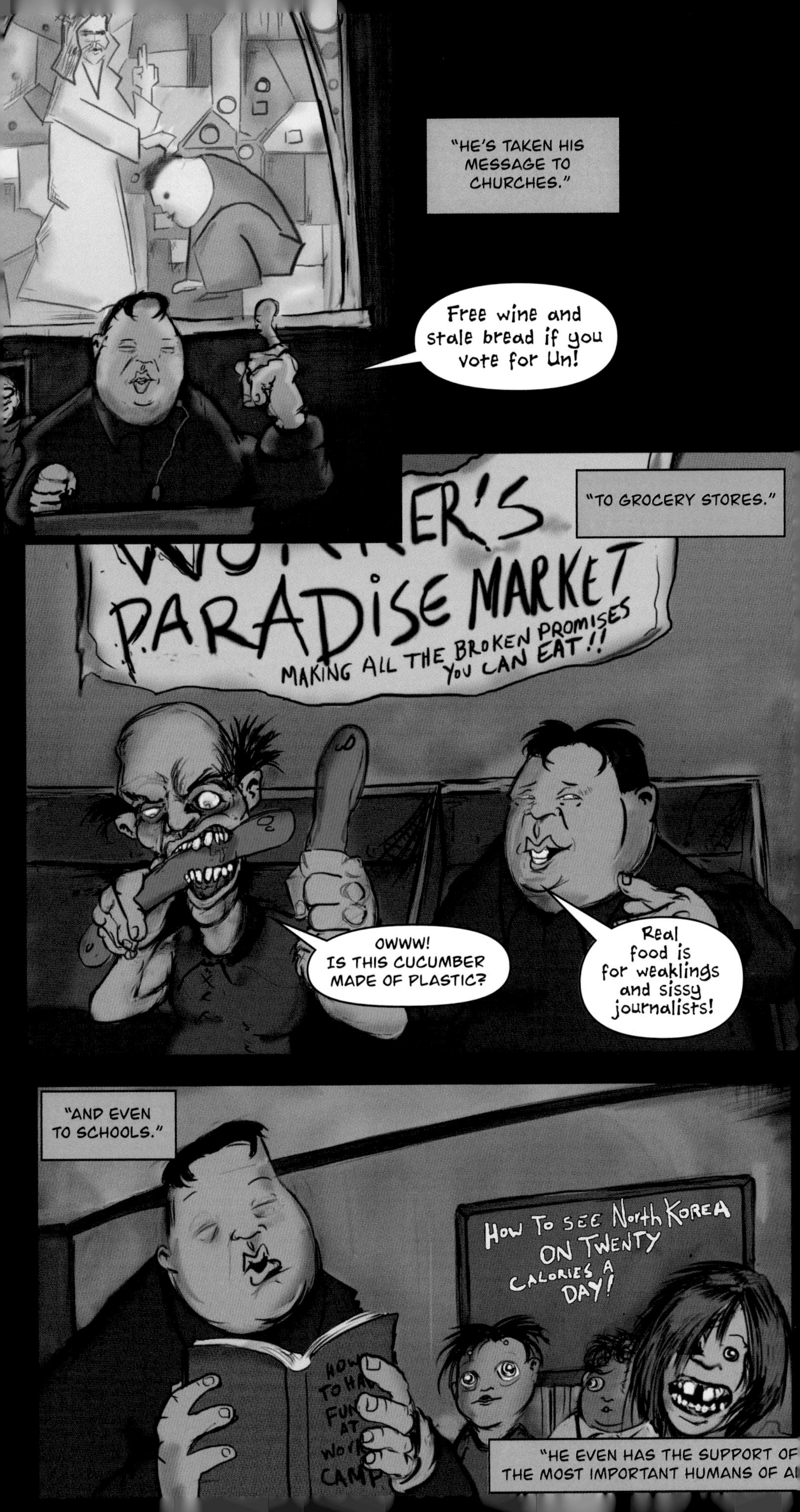
"HE'S TAKEN HIS MESSAGE TO CHURCHES."
Free wine and stale bread if you vote for Un!
"TO GROCERY STORES."
PARADISE MARKET
MAKING ALL THE BROKEN PROMISES YOU CAN EAT!!
OWWW! IS THIS CUCUMBER MADE OF PLASTIC?
Real food is for weaklings and sissy journalists!
"AND EVEN TO SCHOOLS."
How To SEE North KOREA ON TWENTY CALORIES A DAY!
"HE EVEN HAS THE SUPPORT OF
THE MOST IMPORTANT HUMANS OF A

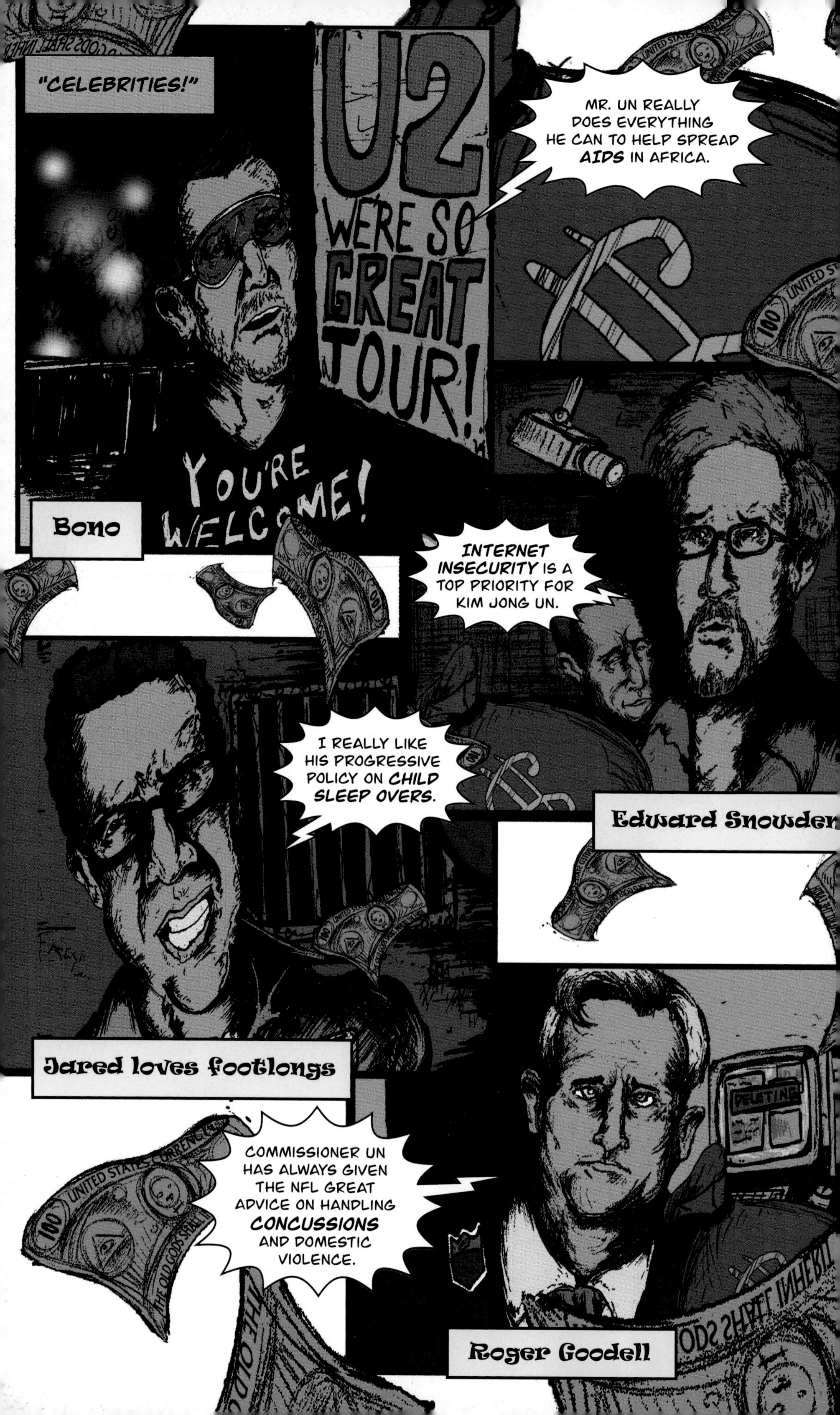
"CELEBRITIES!"
U2
WE'RE SO GREAT TOUR!
YOU'RE WELCOME!
MR. UN REALLY DOES EVERYTHING HE CAN TO HELP SPREAD **AIDS** IN AFRICA.
Bono
INTERNET INSECURITY IS A TOP PRIORITY FOR KIM JONG UN.
Edward Snowden
I REALLY LIKE HIS PROGRESSIVE POLICY ON **CHILD SLEEP OVERS**.
Jared loves footlongs
COMMISSIONER UN HAS ALWAYS GIVEN THE NFL GREAT ADVICE ON HANDLING **CONCUSSIONS** AND DOMESTIC VIOLENCE.
DELETING
Roger Goodell

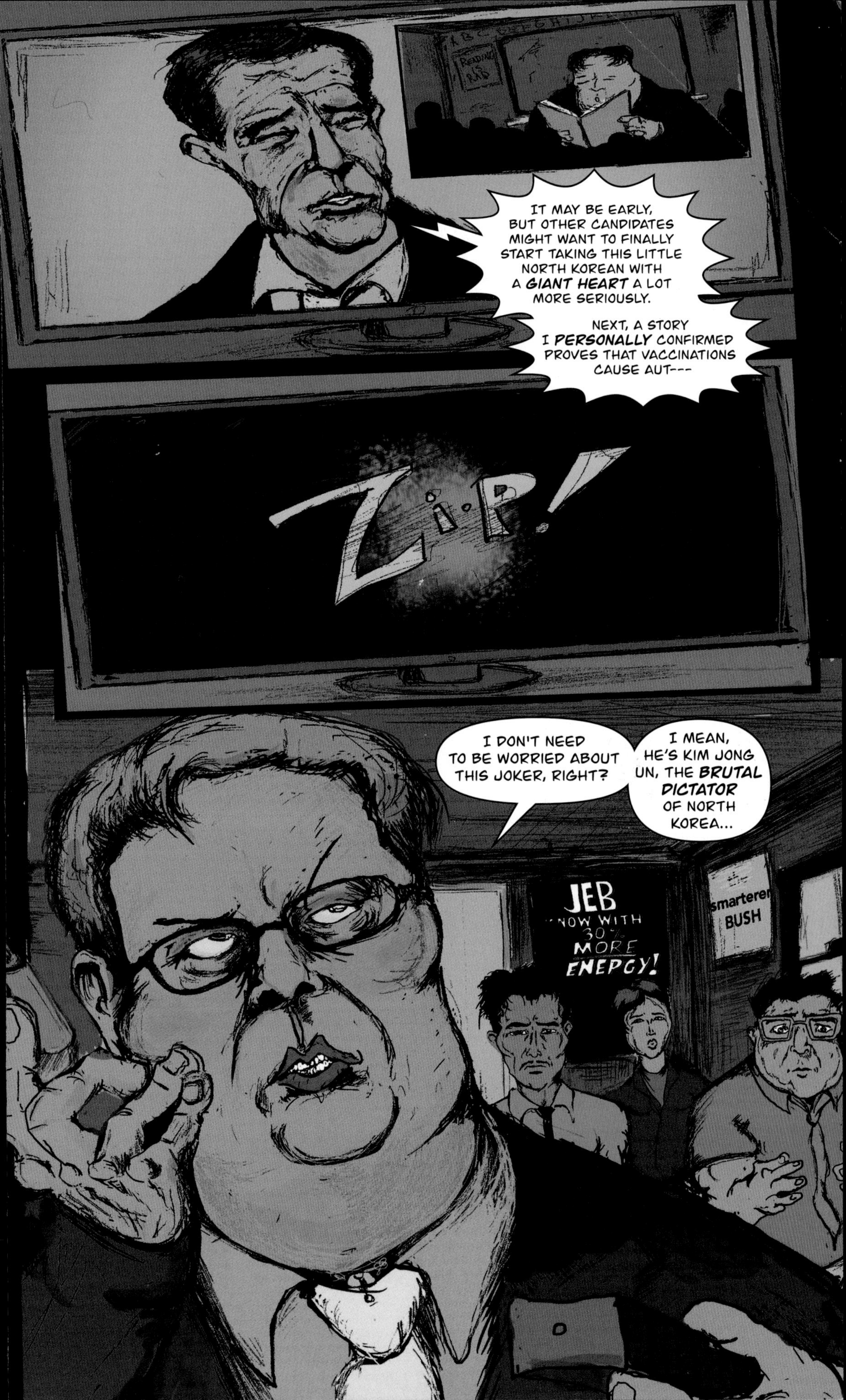
IT MAY BE EARLY, BUT OTHER CANDIDATES MIGHT WANT TO FINALLY START TAKING THIS LITTLE NORTH KOREAN WITH A GIANT HEART A LOT MORE SERIOUSLY.
NEXT, A STORY I PERSONALLY CONFIRMED PROVES THAT VACCINATIONS CAUSE AUT---
ZIP!
I DON'T NEED TO BE WORRIED ABOUT THIS JOKER, RIGHT?
I MEAN, HE'S KIM JONG UN, THE BRUTAL DICTATOR OF NORTH KOREA...
JEB
NOW WITH 30% MORE ENERGY!
smarterer BUSH

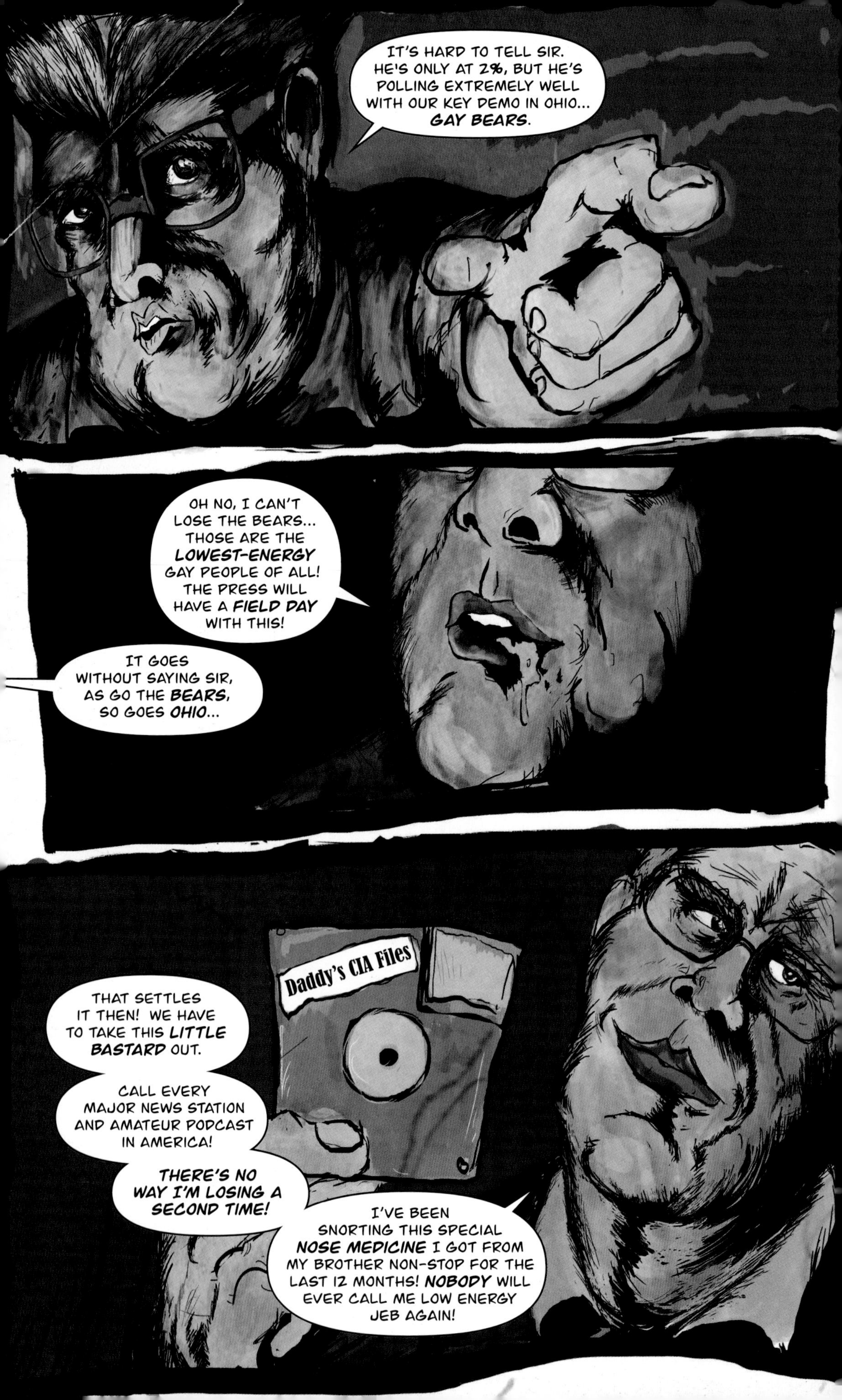
IT'S HARD TO TELL SIR. HE'S ONLY AT 2%, BUT HE'S POLLING EXTREMELY WELL WITH OUR KEY DEMO IN OHIO... GAY BEARS.
OH NO, I CAN'T LOSE THE BEARS... THOSE ARE THE LOWEST-ENERGY GAY PEOPLE OF ALL! THE PRESS WILL HAVE A FIELD DAY WITH THIS!
IT GOES WITHOUT SAYING SIR, AS GO THE BEARS, SO GOES OHIO...
Daddy's CIA Files
THAT SETTLES IT THEN! WE HAVE TO TAKE THIS LITTLE BASTARD OUT.
CALL EVERY MAJOR NEWS STATION AND AMATEUR PODCAST IN AMERICA!
THERE'S NO WAY I'M LOSING A SECOND TIME!
I'VE BEEN SNORTING THIS SPECIAL NOSE MEDICINE I GOT FROM MY BROTHER NON-STOP FOR THE LAST 12 MONTHS! NOBODY WILL EVER CALL ME LOW ENERGY JEB AGAIN!

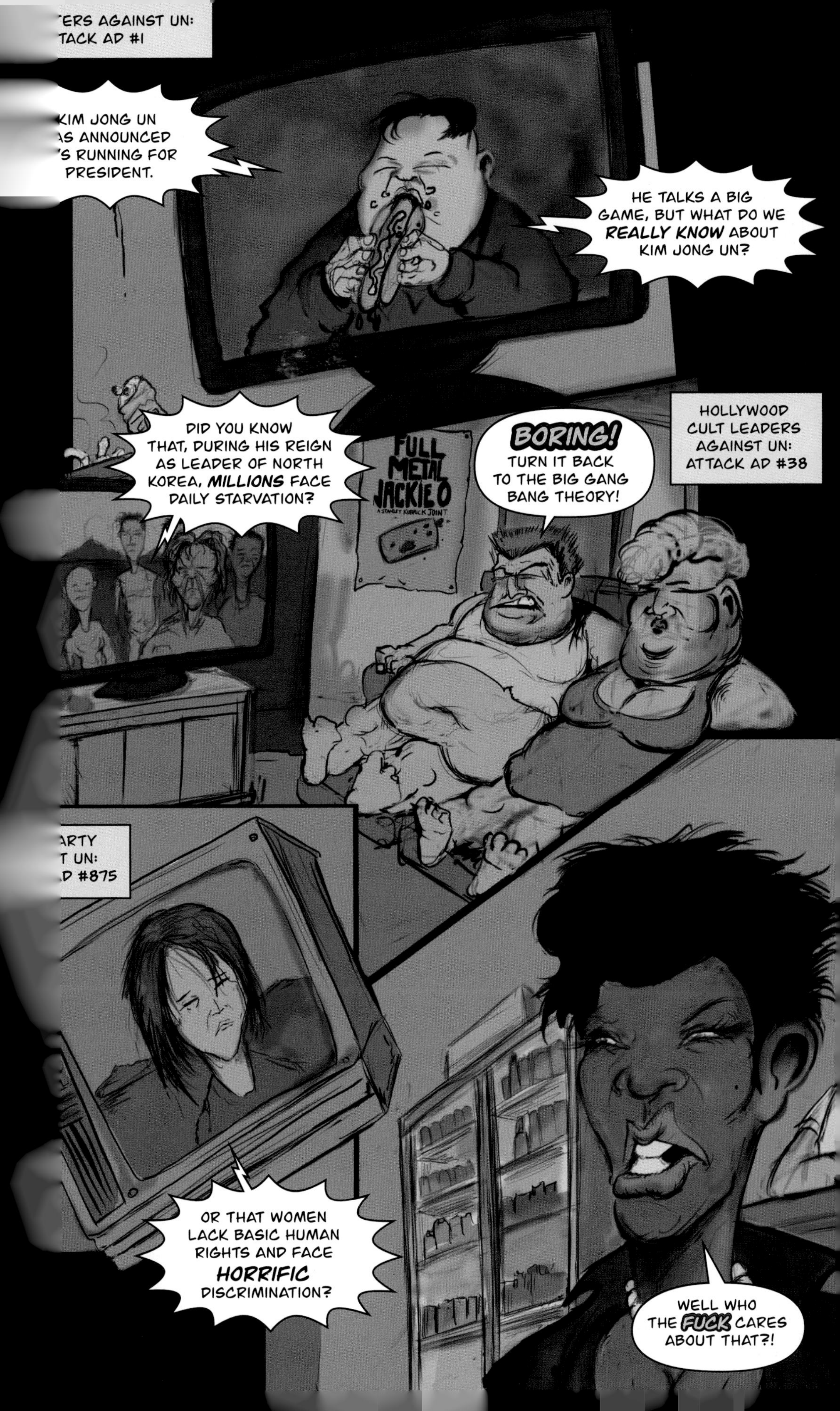

TERS AGAINST UN: TACK AD #1
KIM JONG UN AS ANNOUNCED 'S RUNNING FOR PRESIDENT.
HE TALKS A BIG GAME, BUT WHAT DO WE REALLY KNOW ABOUT KIM JONG UN?
DID YOU KNOW THAT, DURING HIS REIGN AS LEADER OF NORTH KOREA, MILLIONS FACE DAILY STARVATION?
FULL METAL JACKIE O
A STANLEY KUBRICK JOINT
BORING! TURN IT BACK TO THE BIG GANG BANG THEORY!
HOLLYWOOD CULT LEADERS AGAINST UN: ATTACK AD #38
ARTY T UN: D #875
OR THAT WOMEN LACK BASIC HUMAN RIGHTS AND FACE HORRIFIC DISCRIMINATION?
WELL WHO THE FUCK CARES ABOUT THAT?!

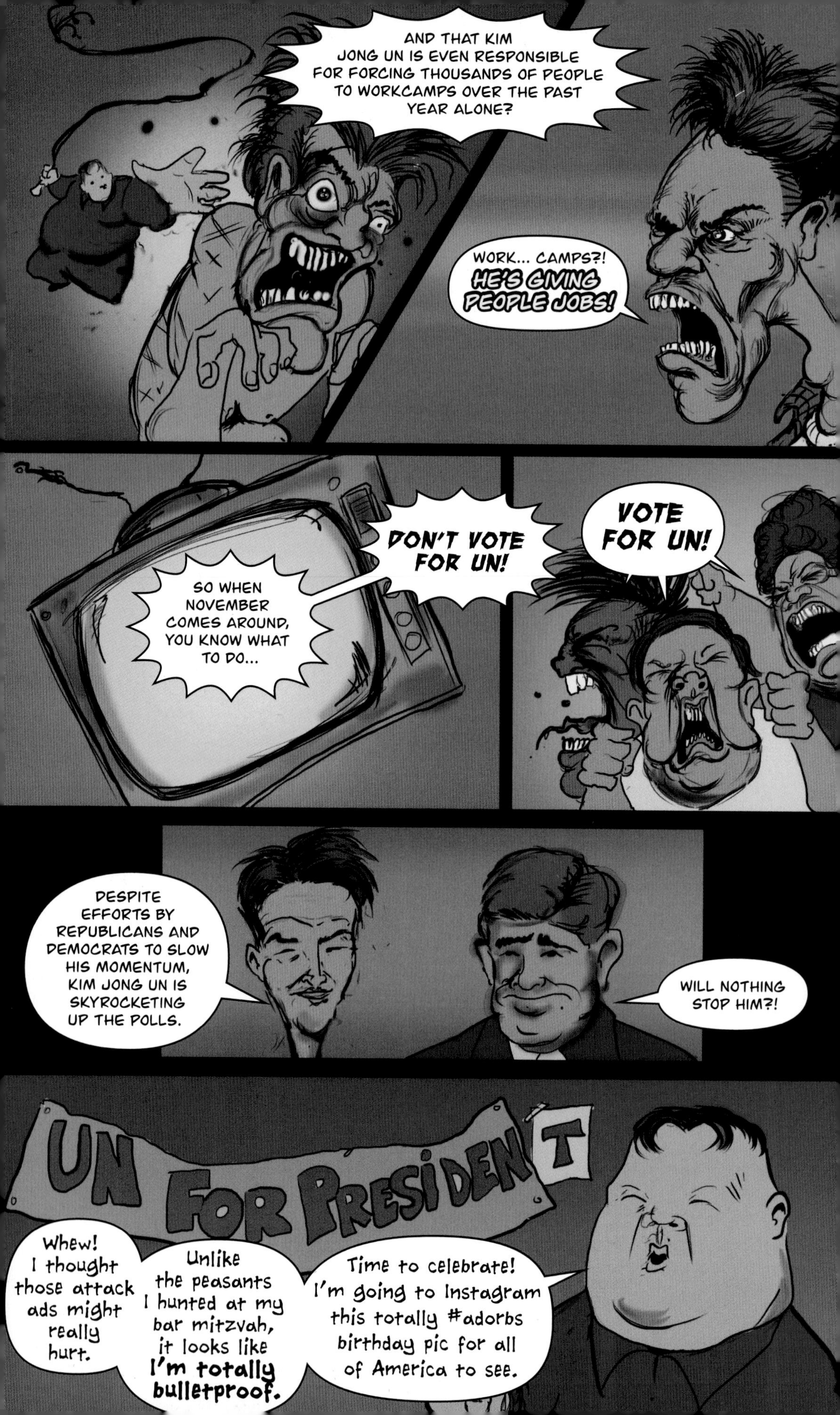
AND THAT KIM JONG UN IS EVEN RESPONSIBLE FOR FORCING THOUSANDS OF PEOPLE TO WORKCAMPS OVER THE PAST YEAR ALONE?
WORK... CAMPS?! HE'S GIVING PEOPLE JOBS!
SO WHEN NOVEMBER COMES AROUND, YOU KNOW WHAT TO DO...
DON'T VOTE FOR UN!
VOTE FOR UN!
DESPITE EFFORTS BY REPUBLICANS AND DEMOCRATS TO SLOW HIS MOMENTUM, KIM JONG UN IS SKYROCKETING UP THE POLLS.
WILL NOTHING STOP HIM?!
UN FOR PRESIDENT
Whew! I thought those attack ads might really hurt.
Unlike the peasants I hunted at my bar mitzvah, it looks like I'm totally bulletproof.
Time to celebrate! I'm going to Instagram this totally #adorbs birthday pic for all of America to see.

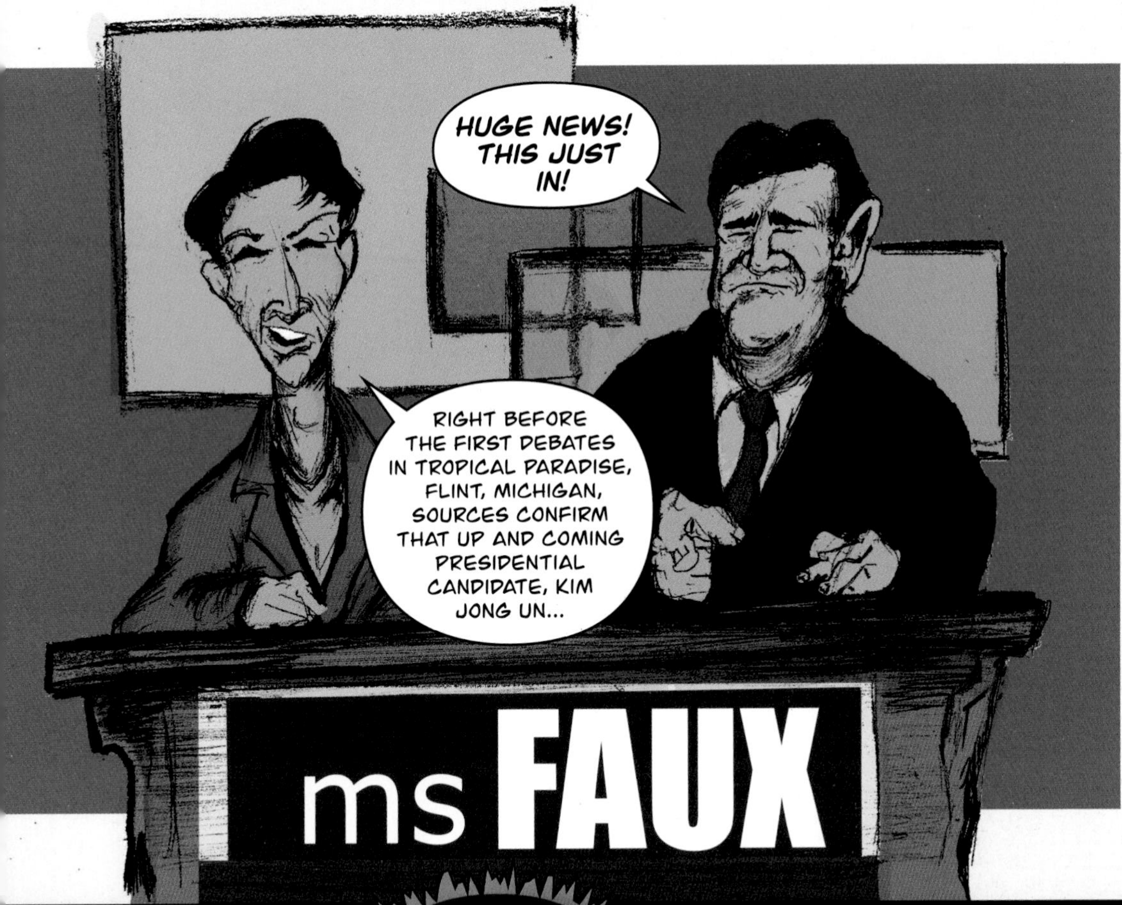
HUGE NEWS! THIS JUST IN!
RIGHT BEFORE THE FIRST DEBATES IN TROPICAL PARADISE, FLINT, MICHIGAN, SOURCES CONFIRM THAT UP AND COMING PRESIDENTIAL CANDIDATE, KIM JONG UN...
ms FAUX

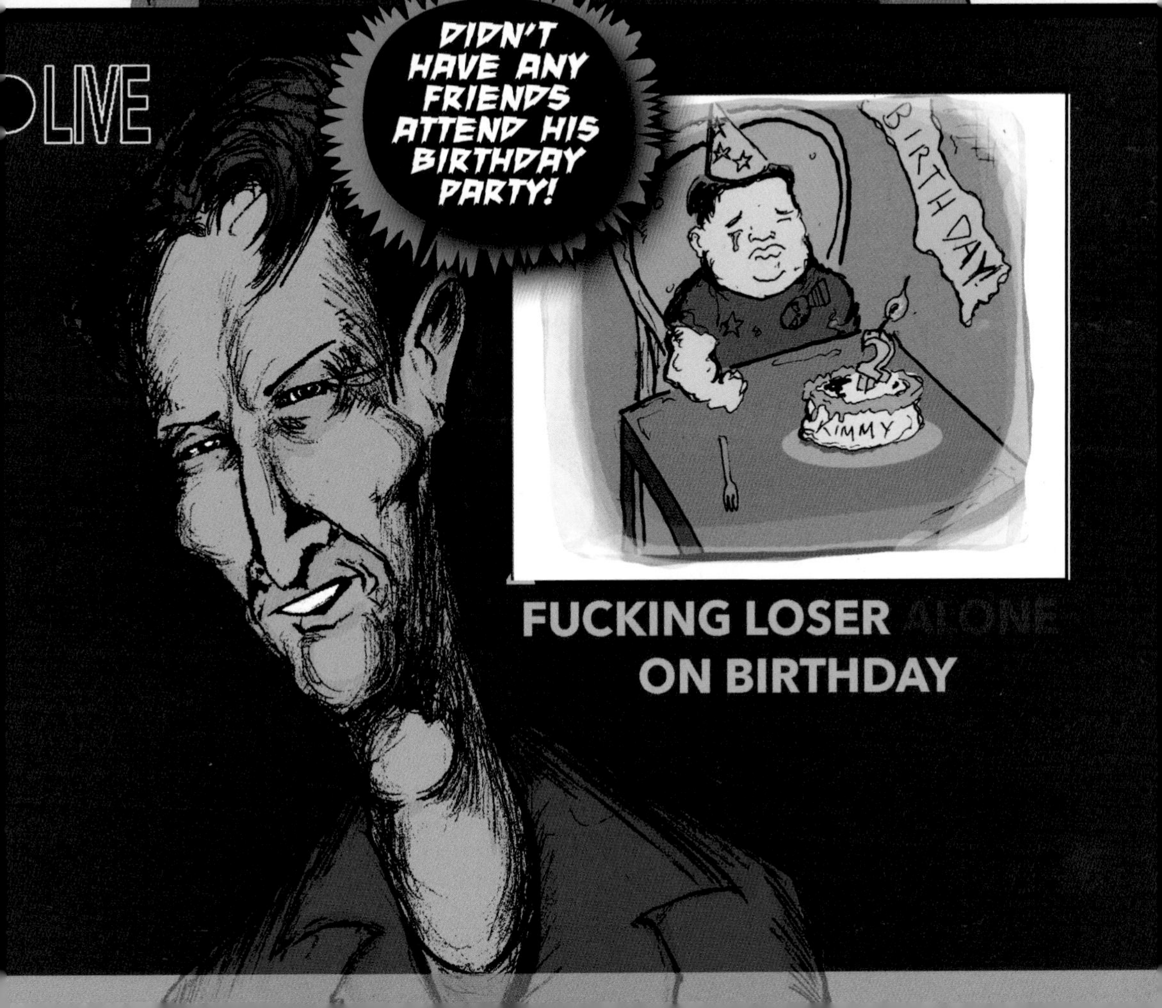
LIVE
DIDN'T HAVE ANY FRIENDS ATTEND HIS BIRTHDAY PARTY!
BIRTHDAY
KIMMY
FUCKING LOSER ALONE
ON BIRTHDAY

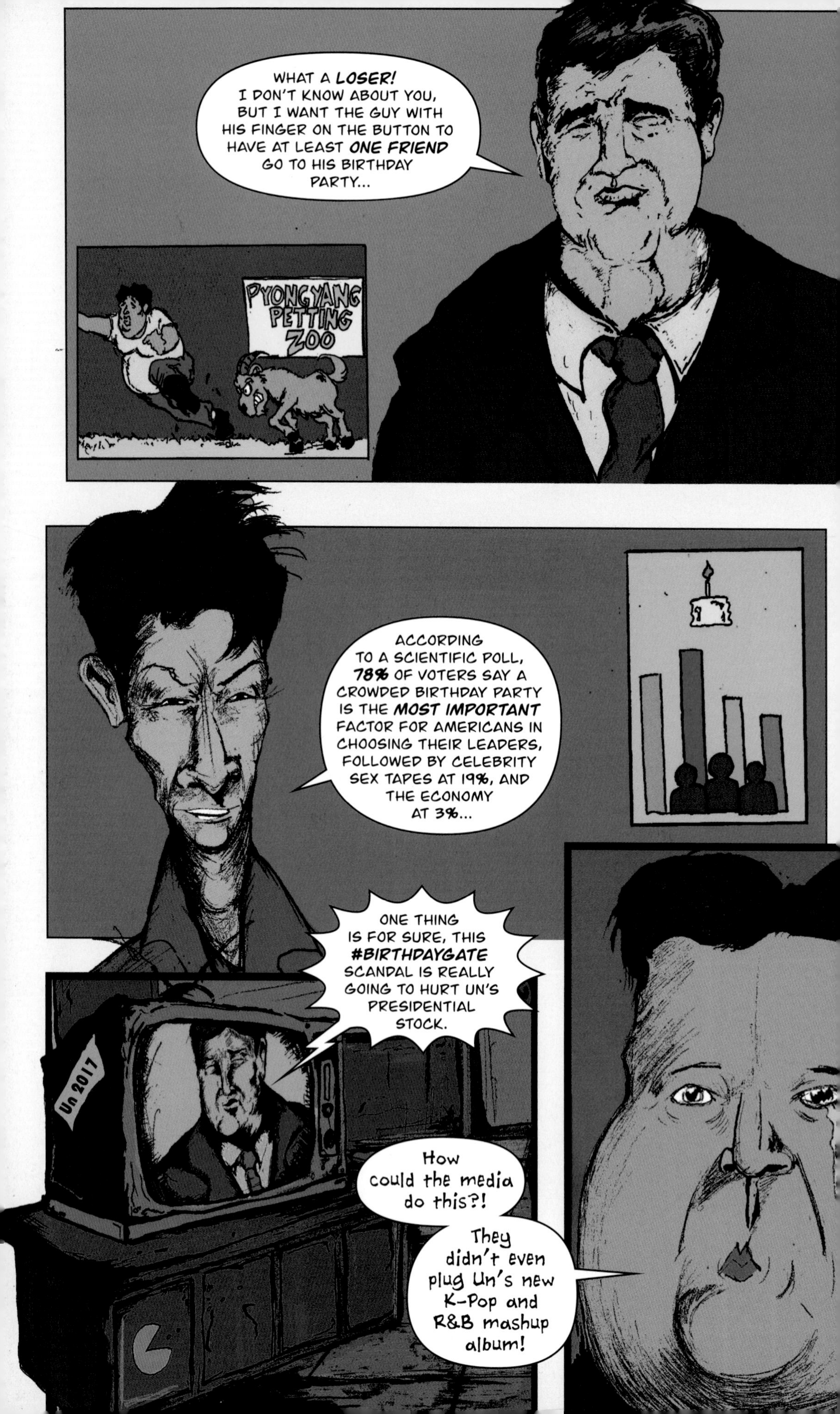
WHAT A **LOSER!** I DON'T KNOW ABOUT YOU, BUT I WANT THE GUY WITH HIS FINGER ON THE BUTTON TO HAVE AT LEAST **ONE FRIEND** GO TO HIS BIRTHDAY PARTY...
PYONGYANG PETTING ZOO
ACCORDING TO A SCIENTIFIC POLL, **78%** OF VOTERS SAY A CROWDED BIRTHDAY PARTY IS THE **MOST IMPORTANT** FACTOR FOR AMERICANS IN CHOOSING THEIR LEADERS, FOLLOWED BY CELEBRITY SEX TAPES AT 19%, AND THE ECONOMY AT 3%...
ONE THING IS FOR SURE, THIS **#BIRTHDAYGATE** SCANDAL IS REALLY GOING TO HURT UN'S PRESIDENTIAL STOCK.
Un 2017
How could the media do this?!
They didn't even plug Un's new K-Pop and R&B mashup album!

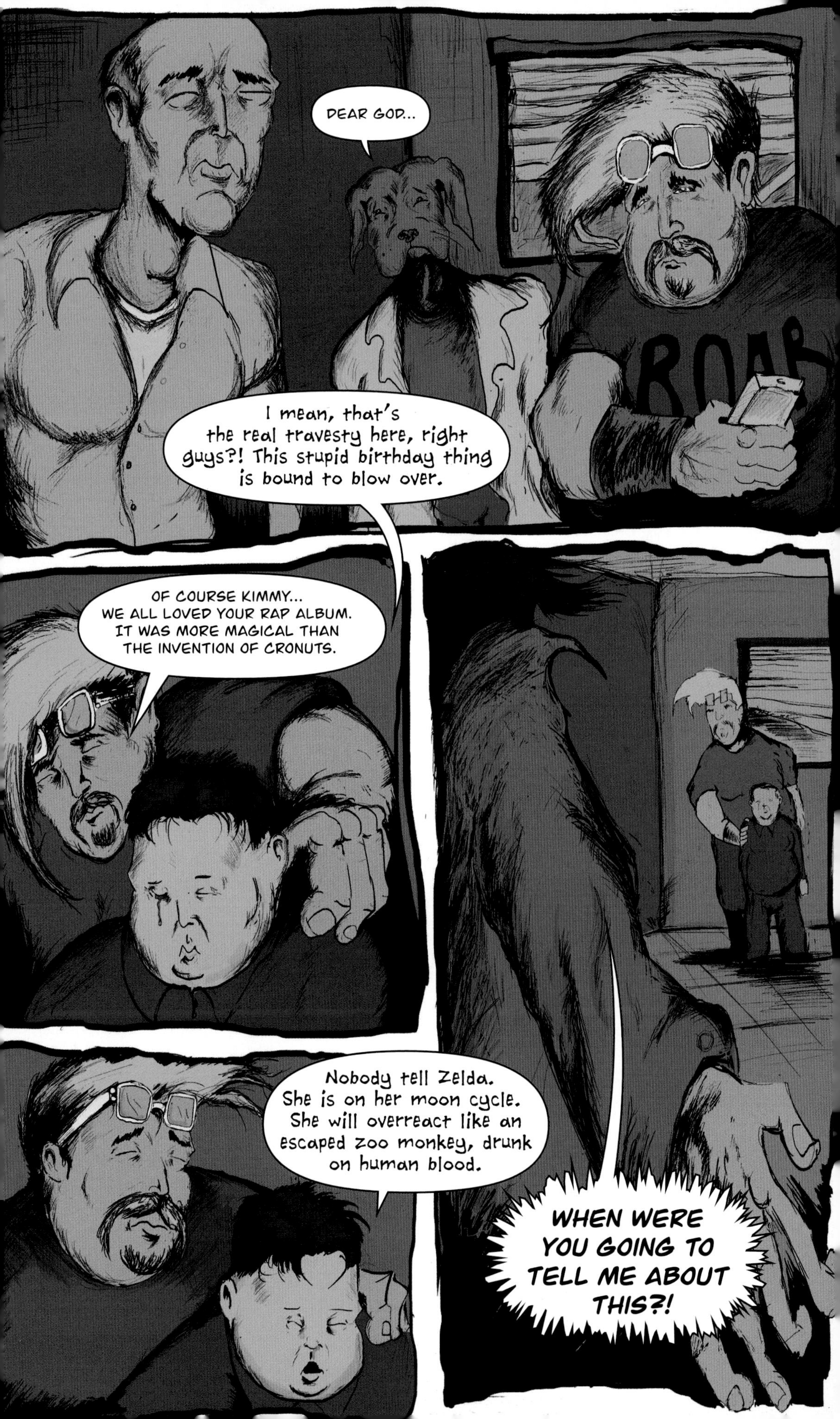
DEAR GOD...
I mean, that's the real travesty here, right guys?! This stupid birthday thing is bound to blow over.
OF COURSE KIMMY... WE ALL LOVED YOUR RAP ALBUM. IT WAS MORE MAGICAL THAN THE INVENTION OF CRONUTS.
Nobody tell Zelda. She is on her moon cycle. She will overreact like an escaped zoo monkey, drunk on human blood.
WHEN WERE YOU GOING TO TELL ME ABOUT THIS?!
ROAR

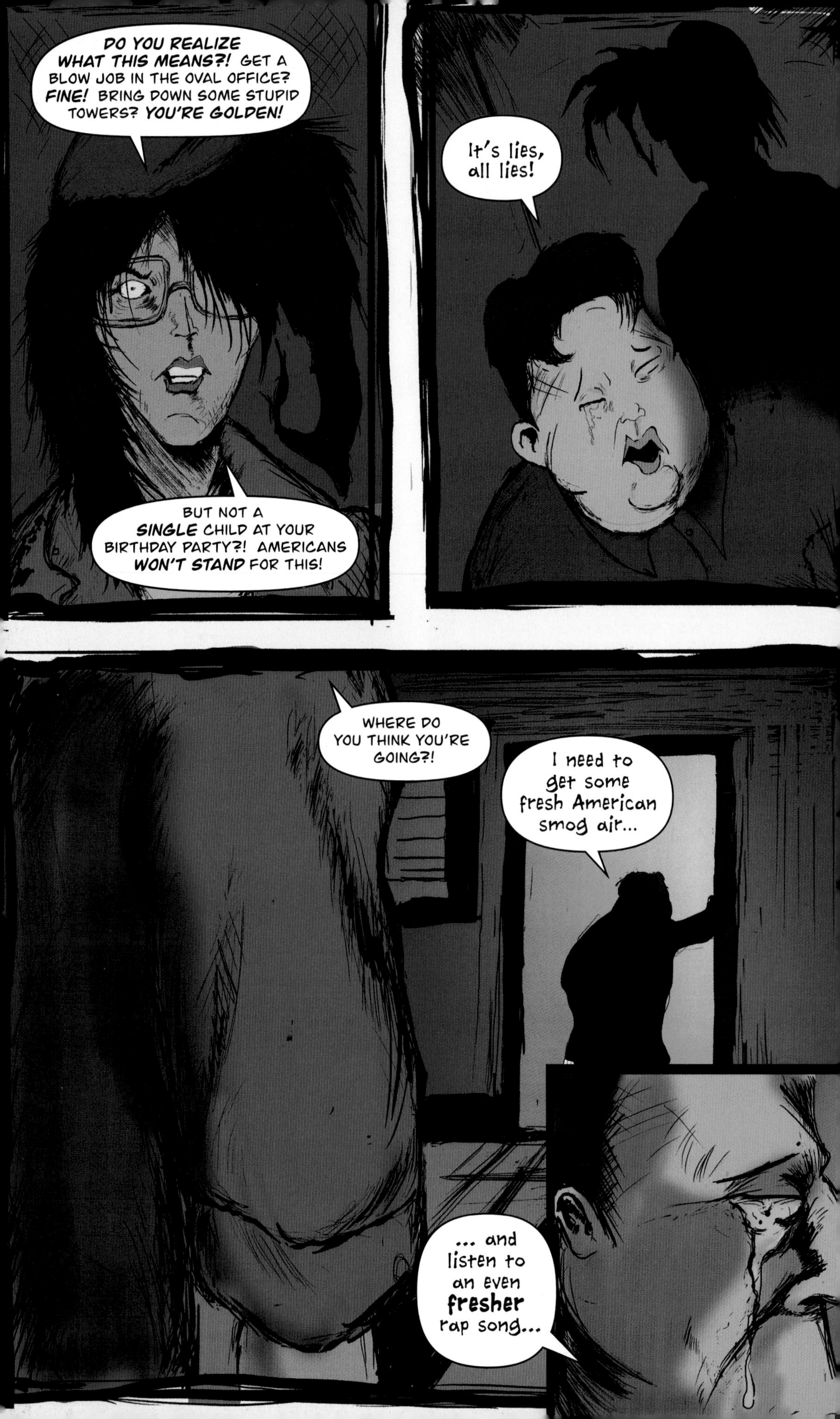
DO YOU REALIZE WHAT THIS MEANS?! GET A BLOW JOB IN THE OVAL OFFICE? FINE! BRING DOWN SOME STUPID TOWERS? YOU'RE GOLDEN!
BUT NOT A SINGLE CHILD AT YOUR BIRTHDAY PARTY?! AMERICANS WON'T STAND FOR THIS!
It's lies, all lies!
WHERE DO YOU THINK YOU'RE GOING?!
I need to get some fresh American smog air...
... and listen to an even fresher rap song...

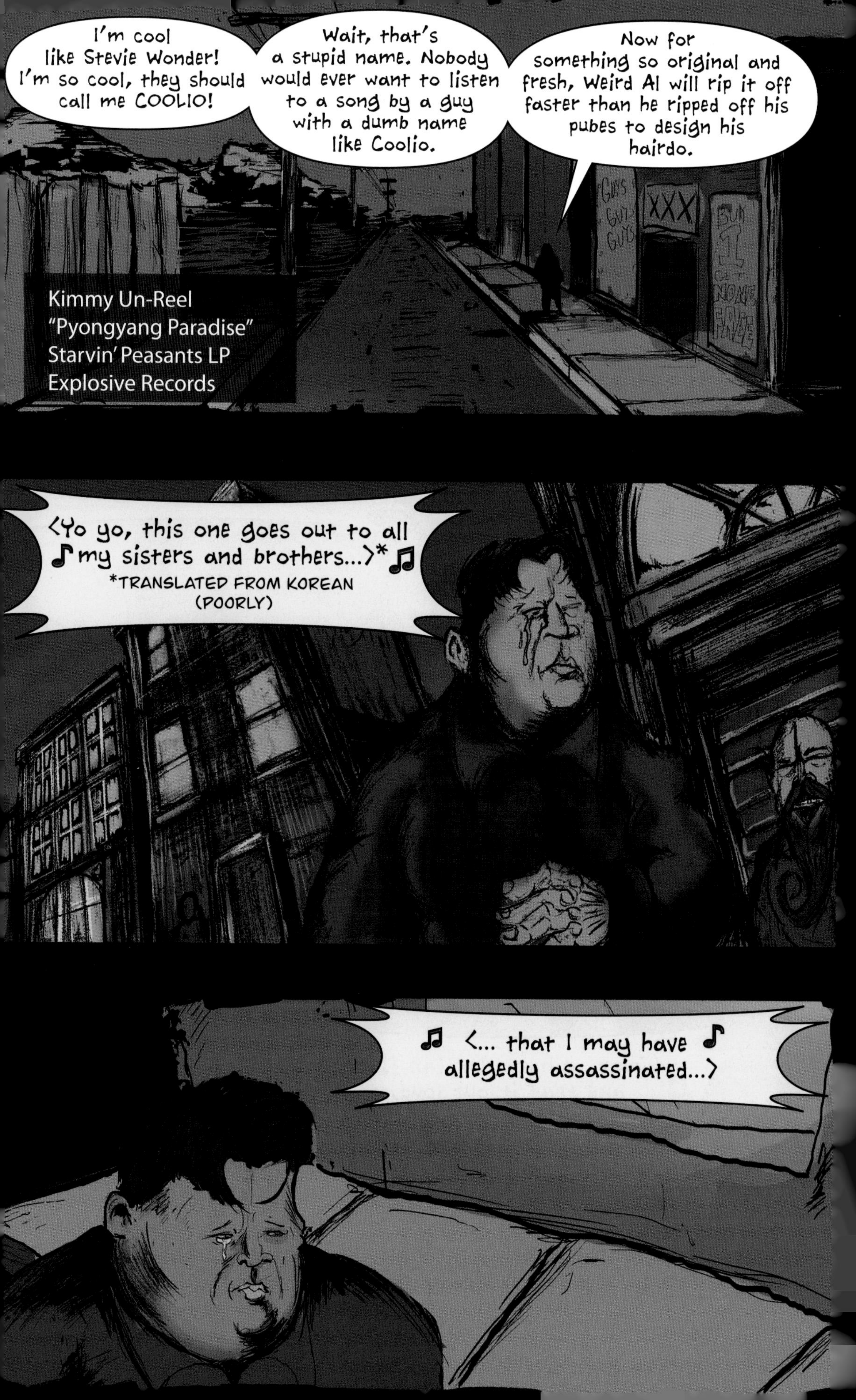
I'm cool like Stevie Wonder! I'm so cool, they should call me COOLIO!
Wait, that's a stupid name. Nobody would ever want to listen to a song by a guy with a dumb name like Coolio.
Now for something so original and fresh, Weird Al will rip it off faster than he ripped off his pubes to design his hairdo.
GUYS GUYS GUYS
XXX
BUY 1 GET NONE FREE
Kimmy Un-Reel
"Pyongyang Paradise"
Starvin' Peasants LP
Explosive Records
<Yo yo, this one goes out to all ♪ my sisters and brothers...>* ♫
*TRANSLATED FROM KOREAN (POORLY)
♫ <... that I may have ♪ allegedly assassinated...>

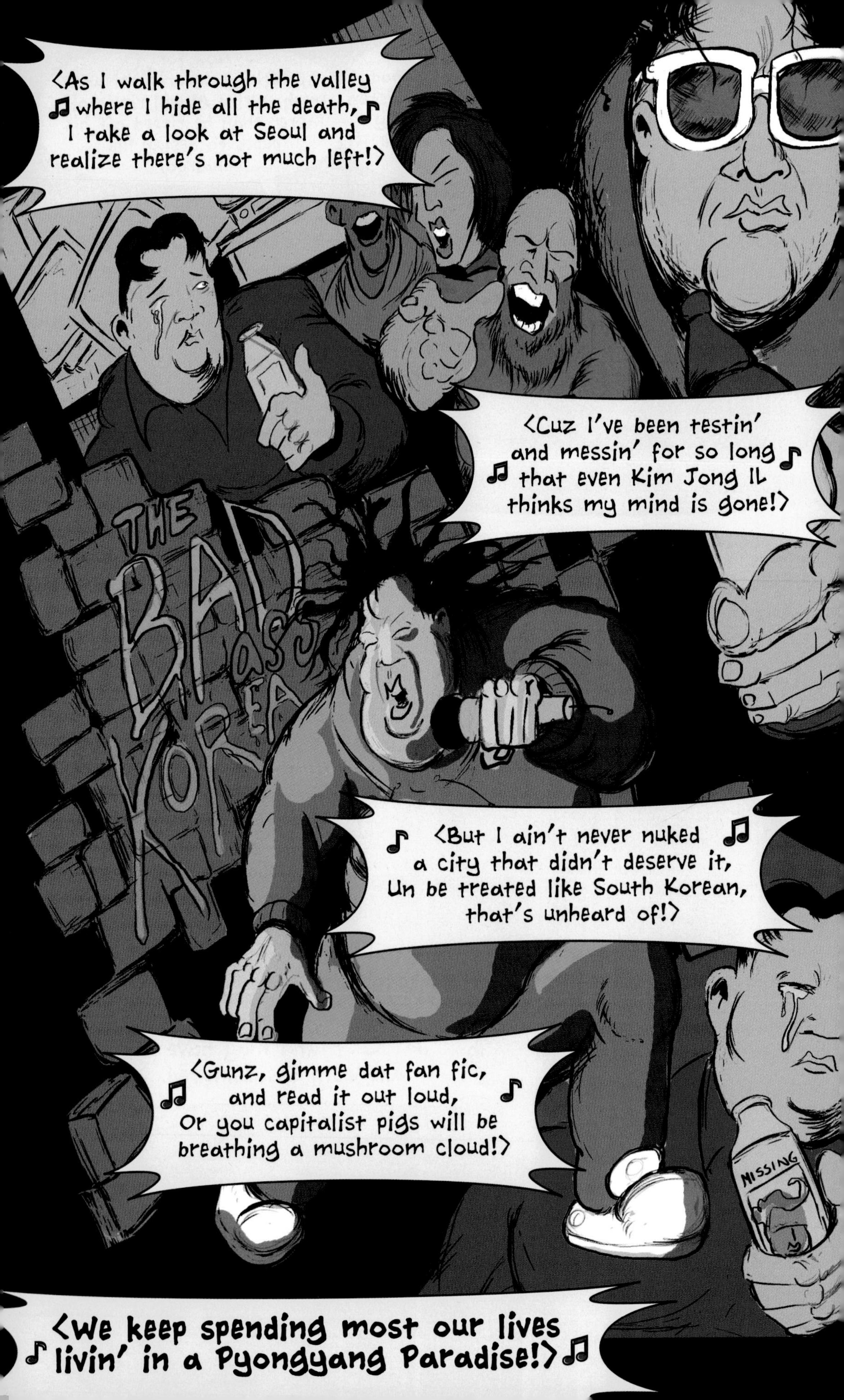
<As I walk through the valley where I hide all the death, I take a look at Seoul and realize there's not much left!>
<Cuz I've been testin' and messin' for so long that even Kim Jong IL thinks my mind is gone!>
<But I ain't never nuked a city that didn't deserve it, Un be treated like South Korean, that's unheard of!>
<Gunz, gimme dat fan fic, and read it out loud, Or you capitalist pigs will be breathing a mushroom cloud!>
MISSING
<We keep spending most our lives livin' in a Pyongyang Paradise!>

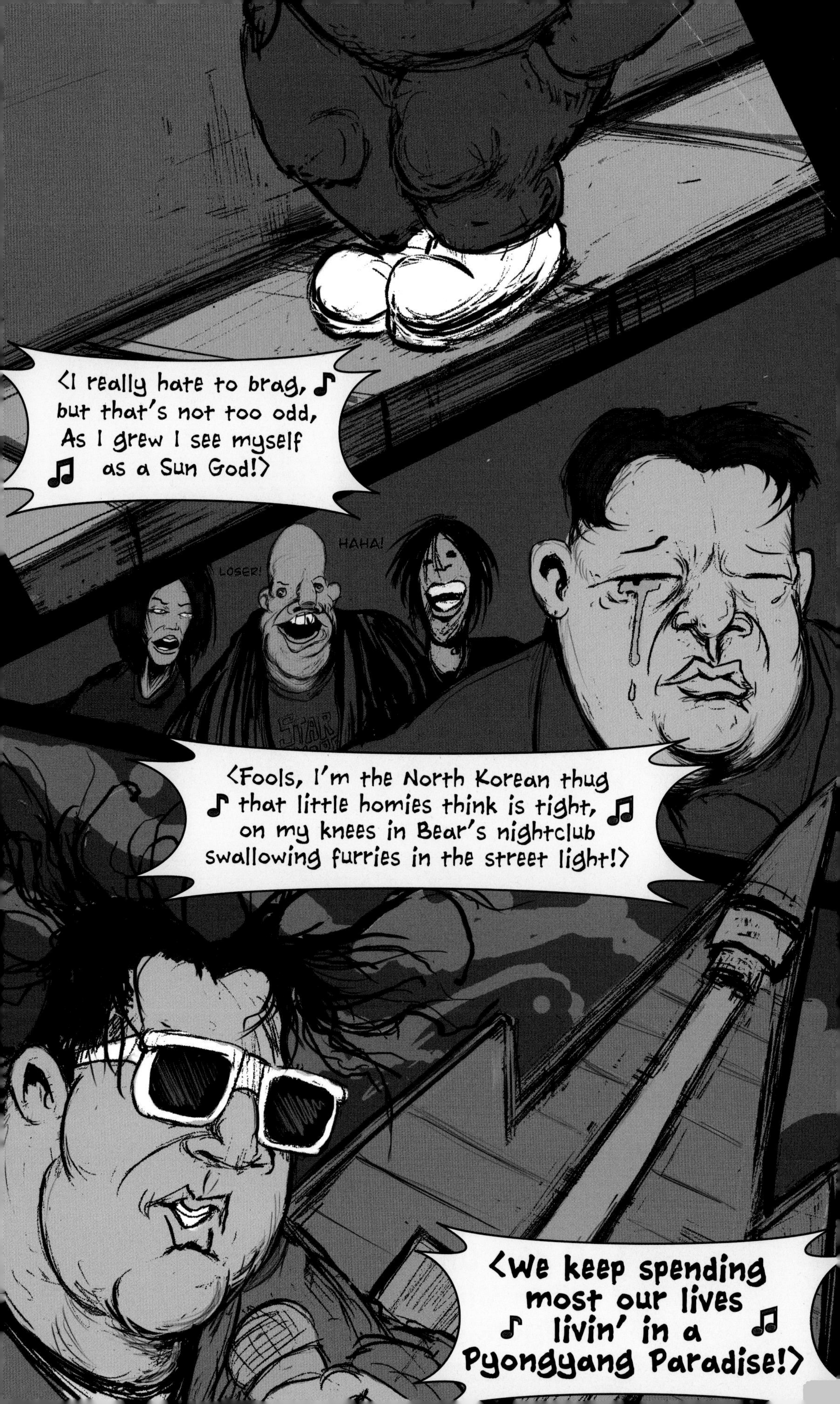
<I really hate to brag, ♪ but that's not too odd, As I grew I see myself ♫ as a Sun God!>
LOSER!
HAHA!
<Fools, I'm the North Korean thug ♪ that little homies think is tight, ♫ on my knees in Bear's nightclub swallowing furries in the street light!>
<We keep spending most our lives ♪ livin' in a ♫ Pyongyang Paradise!>

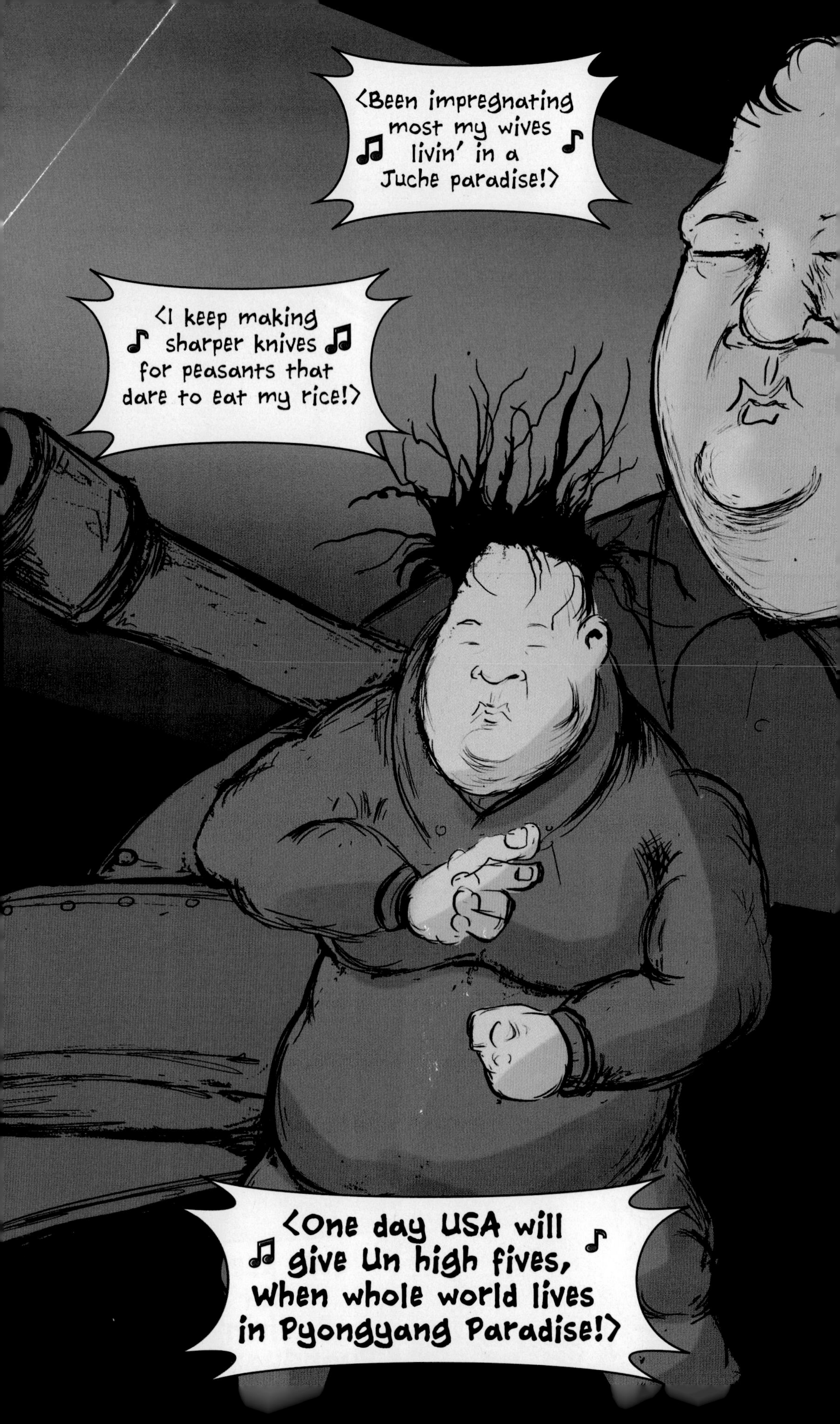
<Been impregnating most my wives livin' in a Juche paradise!>
<I keep making sharper knives for peasants that dare to eat my rice!>
<One day USA will give Un high fives, When whole world lives in Pyongyang Paradise!>

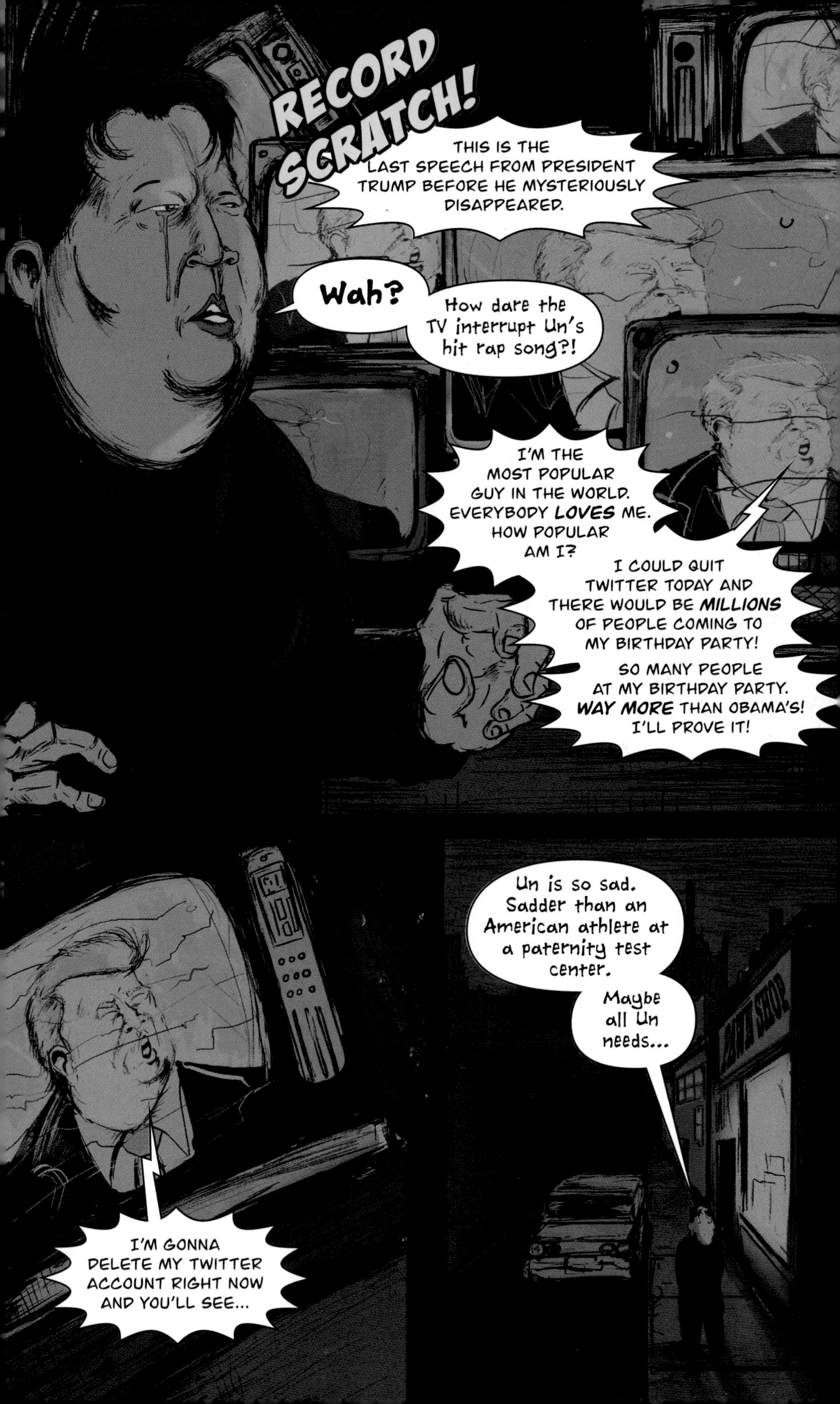
RECORD SCRATCH!
THIS IS THE LAST SPEECH FROM PRESIDENT TRUMP BEFORE HE MYSTERIOUSLY DISAPPEARED.
Wah?
How dare the TV interrupt Un's hit rap song?!
I'M THE MOST POPULAR GUY IN THE WORLD. EVERYBODY LOVES ME. HOW POPULAR AM I?
I COULD QUIT TWITTER TODAY AND THERE WOULD BE MILLIONS OF PEOPLE COMING TO MY BIRTHDAY PARTY!
SO MANY PEOPLE AT MY BIRTHDAY PARTY. WAY MORE THAN OBAMA'S! I'LL PROVE IT!
I'M GONNA DELETE MY TWITTER ACCOUNT RIGHT NOW AND YOU'LL SEE...
Un is so sad. Sadder than an American athlete at a paternity test center.
Maybe all Un needs...
PAWN SHOP

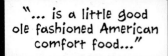
"... is a little good ole fashioned American comfort food..."

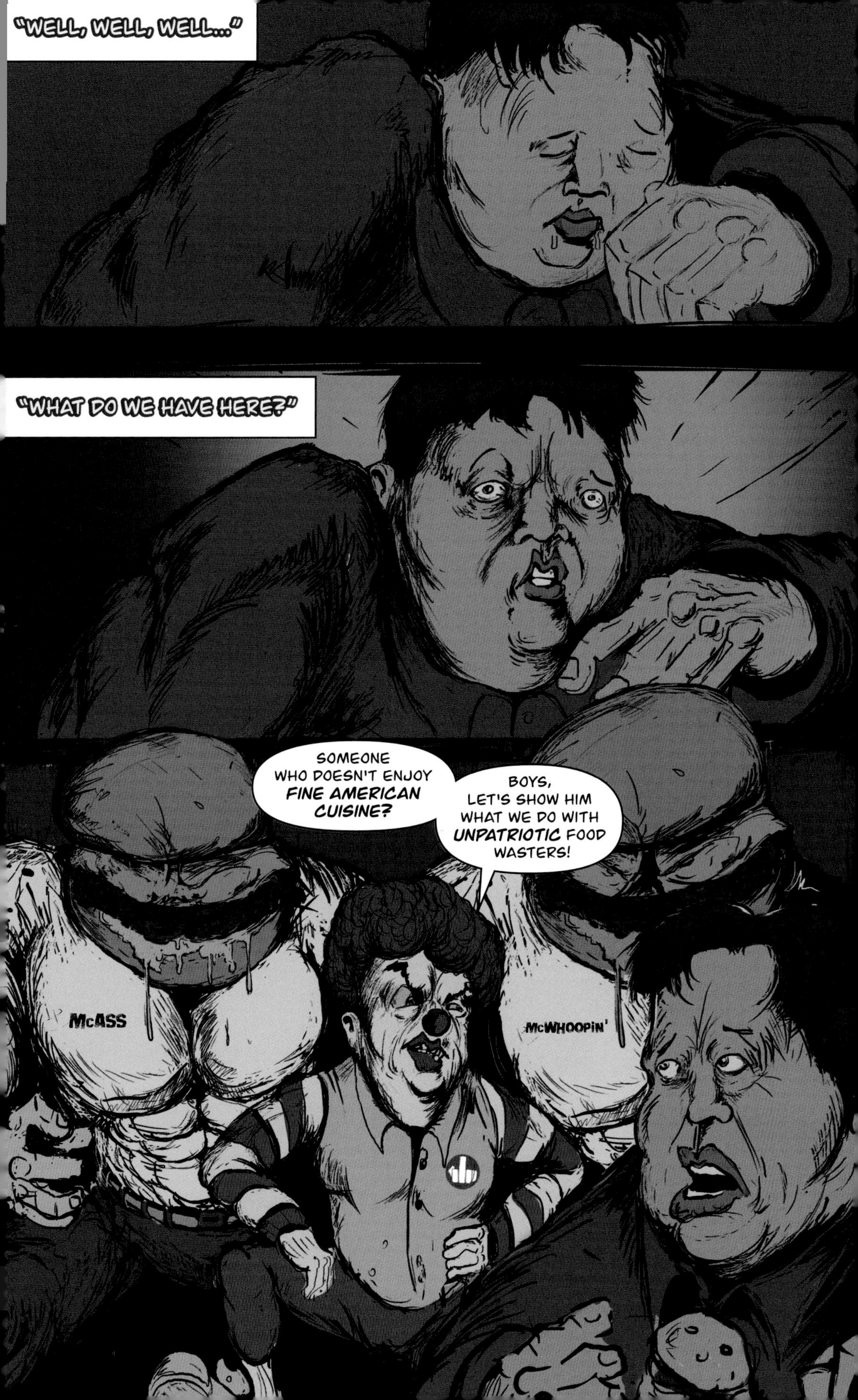
"WELL, WELL, WELL..."
"WHAT DO WE HAVE HERE?"
SOMEONE WHO DOESN'T ENJOY *FINE AMERICAN CUISINE?*
BOYS, LET'S SHOW HIM WHAT WE DO WITH *UNPATRIOTIC* FOOD WASTERS!
McASS
McWHOOPIN'

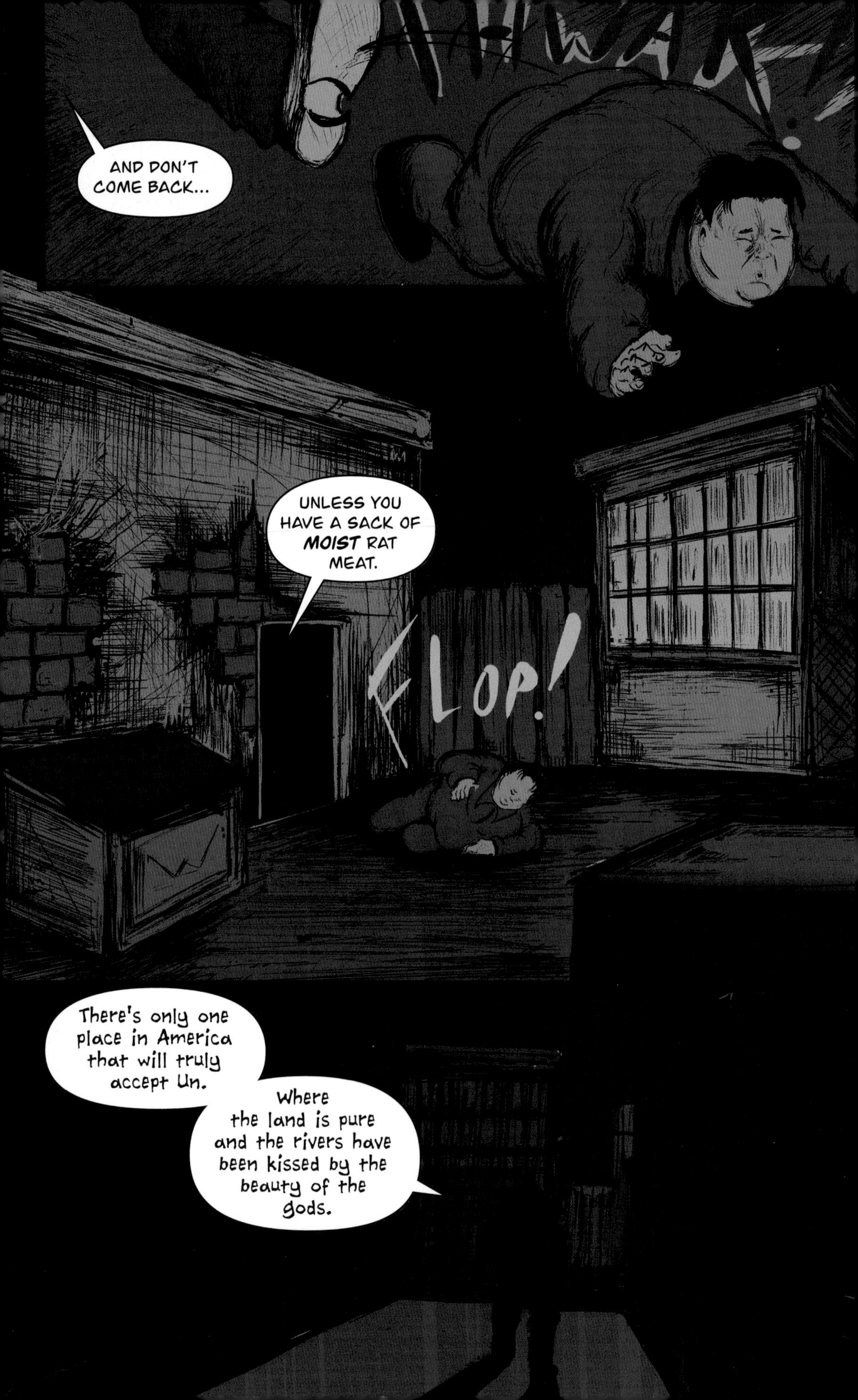
AND DON'T COME BACK...
UNLESS YOU HAVE A SACK OF MOIST RAT MEAT.
FLOP!
There's only one place in America that will truly accept Un.
Where the land is pure and the rivers have been kissed by the beauty of the gods.

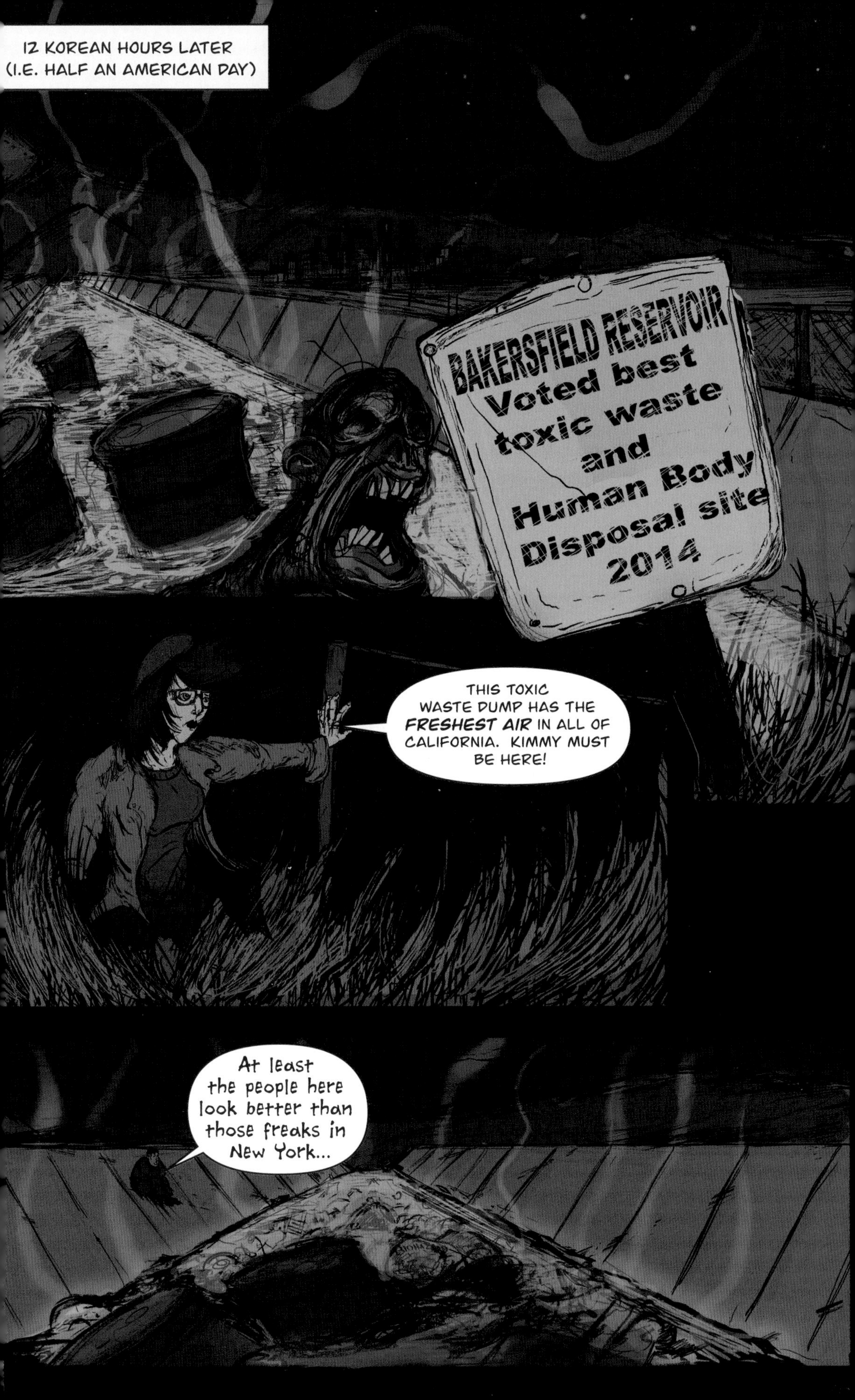
12 KOREAN HOURS LATER
(I.E. HALF AN AMERICAN DAY)
BAKERSFIELD RESERVOIR
Voted best toxic waste and Human Body Disposal site 2014
THIS TOXIC WASTE DUMP HAS THE FRESHEST AIR IN ALL OF CALIFORNIA. KIMMY MUST BE HERE!
At least the people here look better than those freaks in New York...

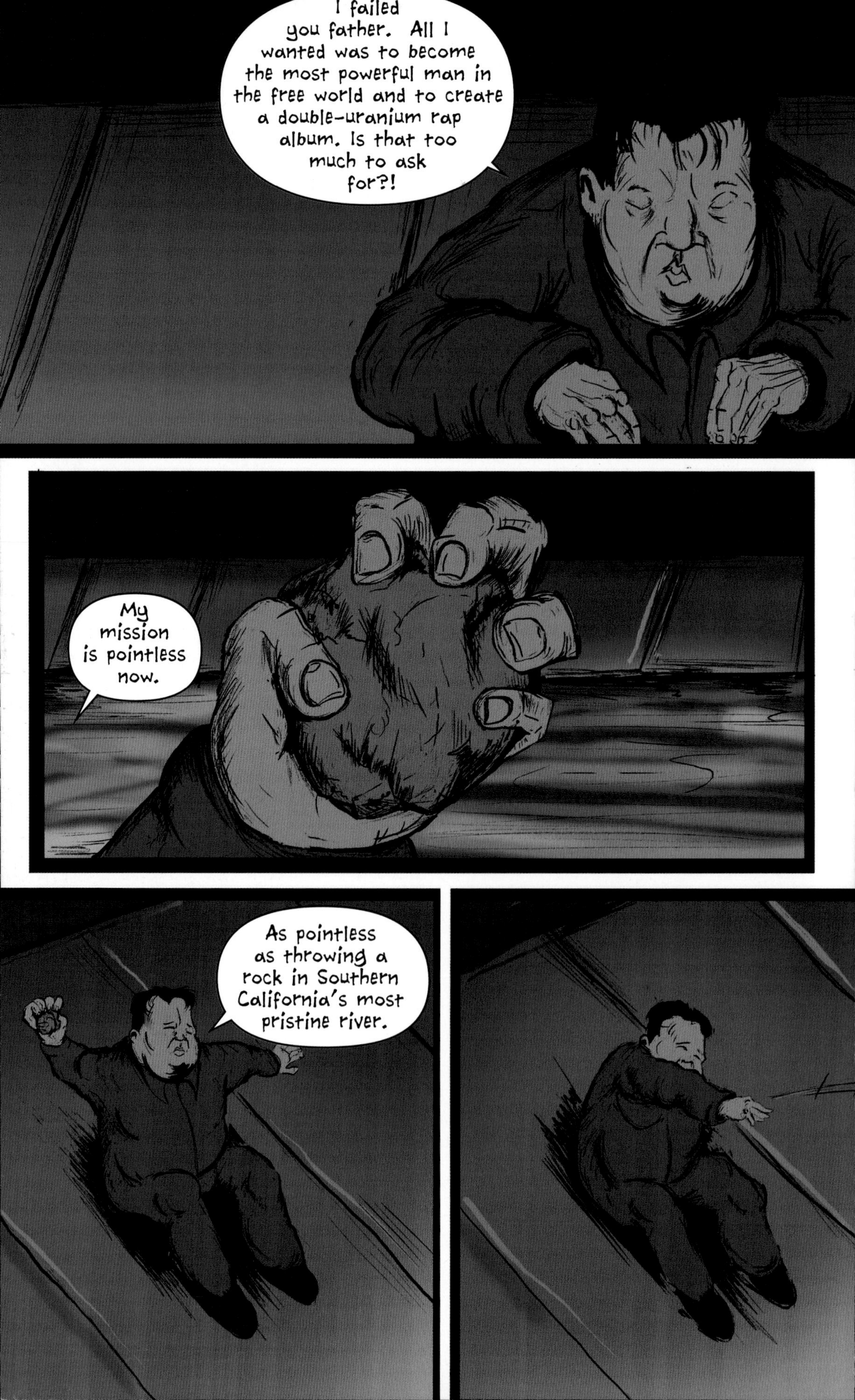
I failed you father. All I wanted was to become the most powerful man in the free world and to create a double-uranium rap album. Is that too much to ask for?!
My mission is pointless now.
As pointless as throwing a rock in Southern California's most pristine river.

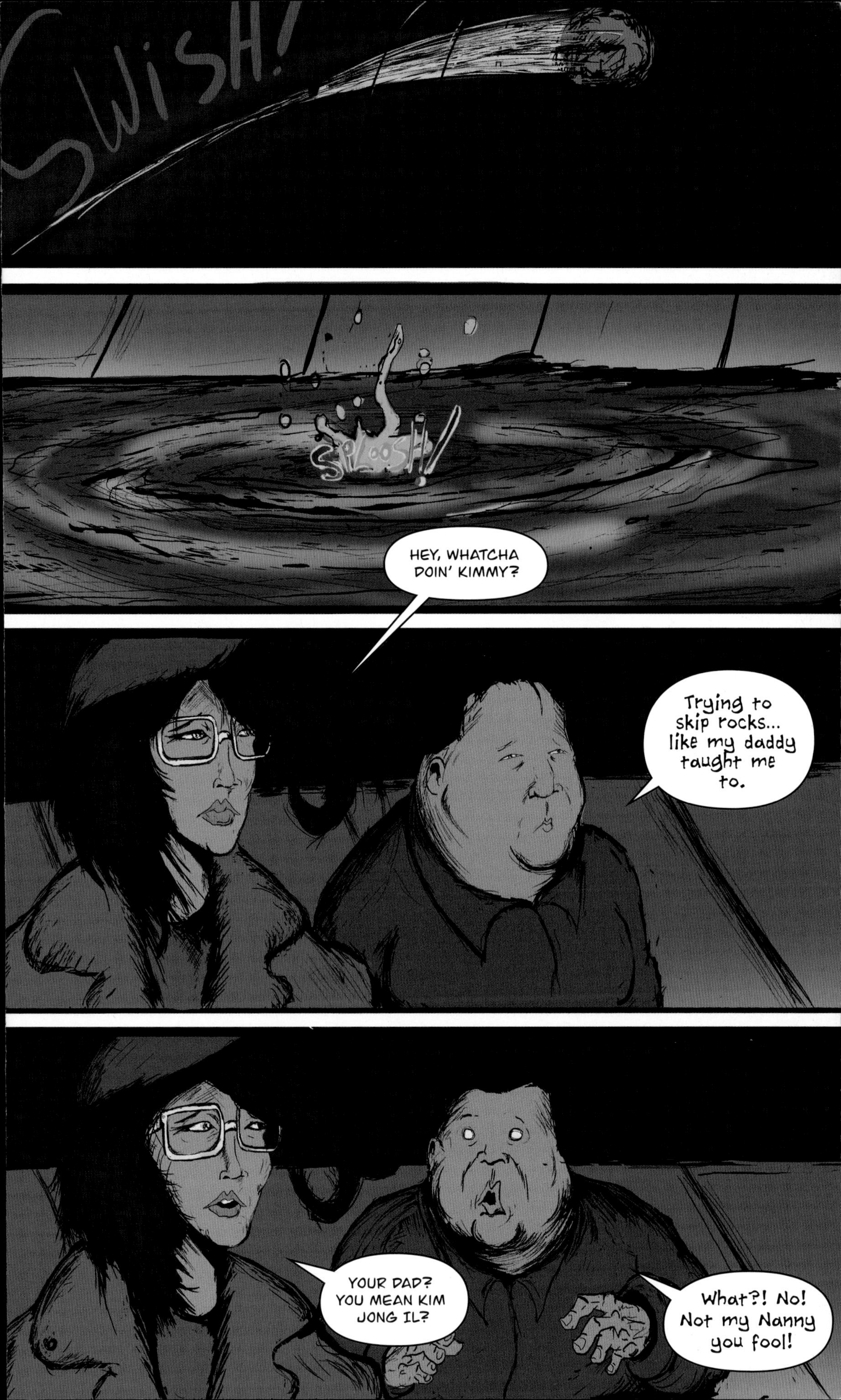
SWISH!
SPLOOSH!!
HEY, WHATCHA DOIN' KIMMY?
Trying to skip rocks... like my daddy taught me to.
YOUR DAD? YOU MEAN KIM JONG IL?
What?! No! Not my Nanny you fool!

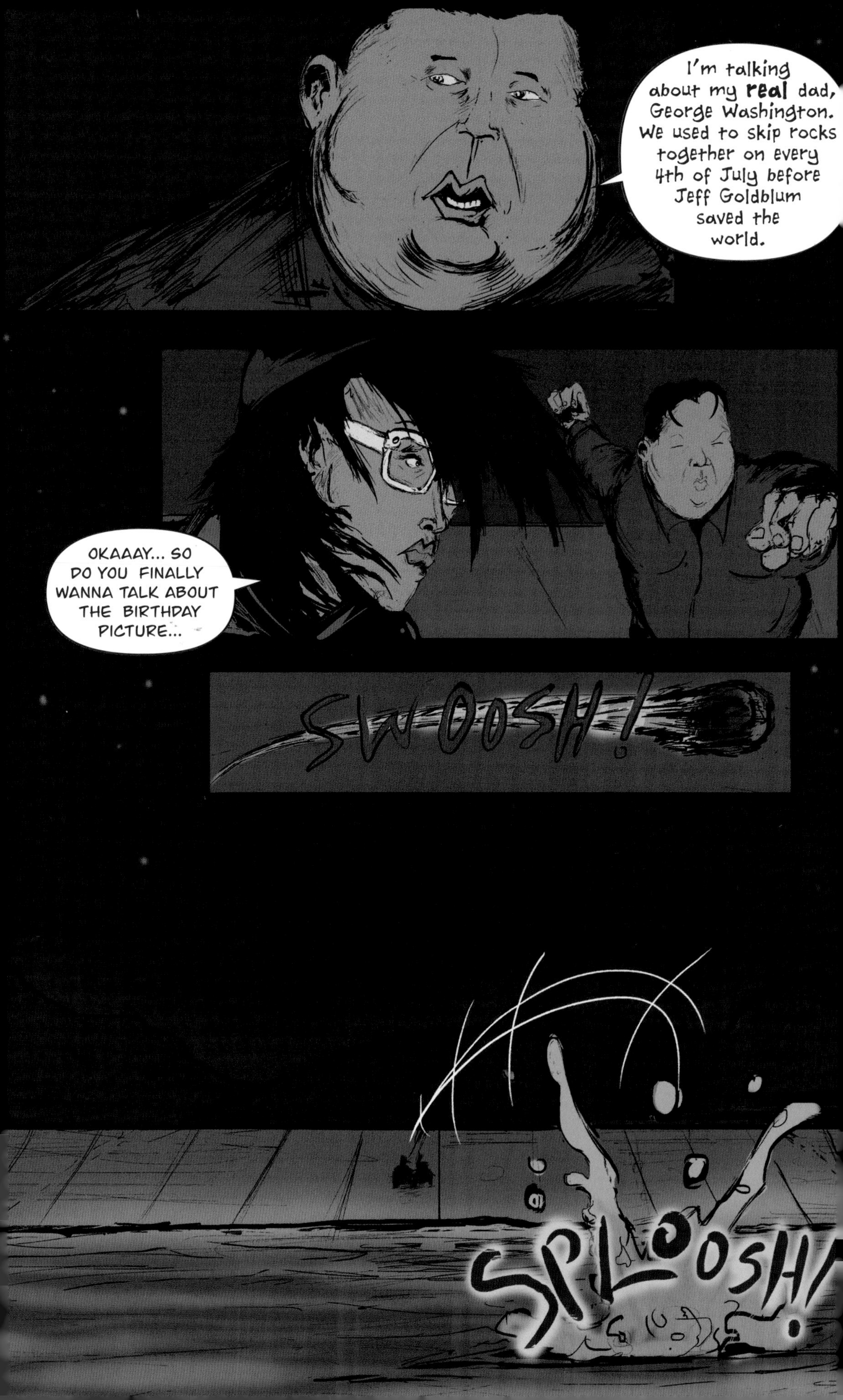
I'm talking about my real dad, George Washington. We used to skip rocks together on every 4th of July before Jeff Goldblum saved the world.
OKAAAY... SO DO YOU FINALLY WANNA TALK ABOUT THE BIRTHDAY PICTURE...
SWOOSH!
SPLOOSH!

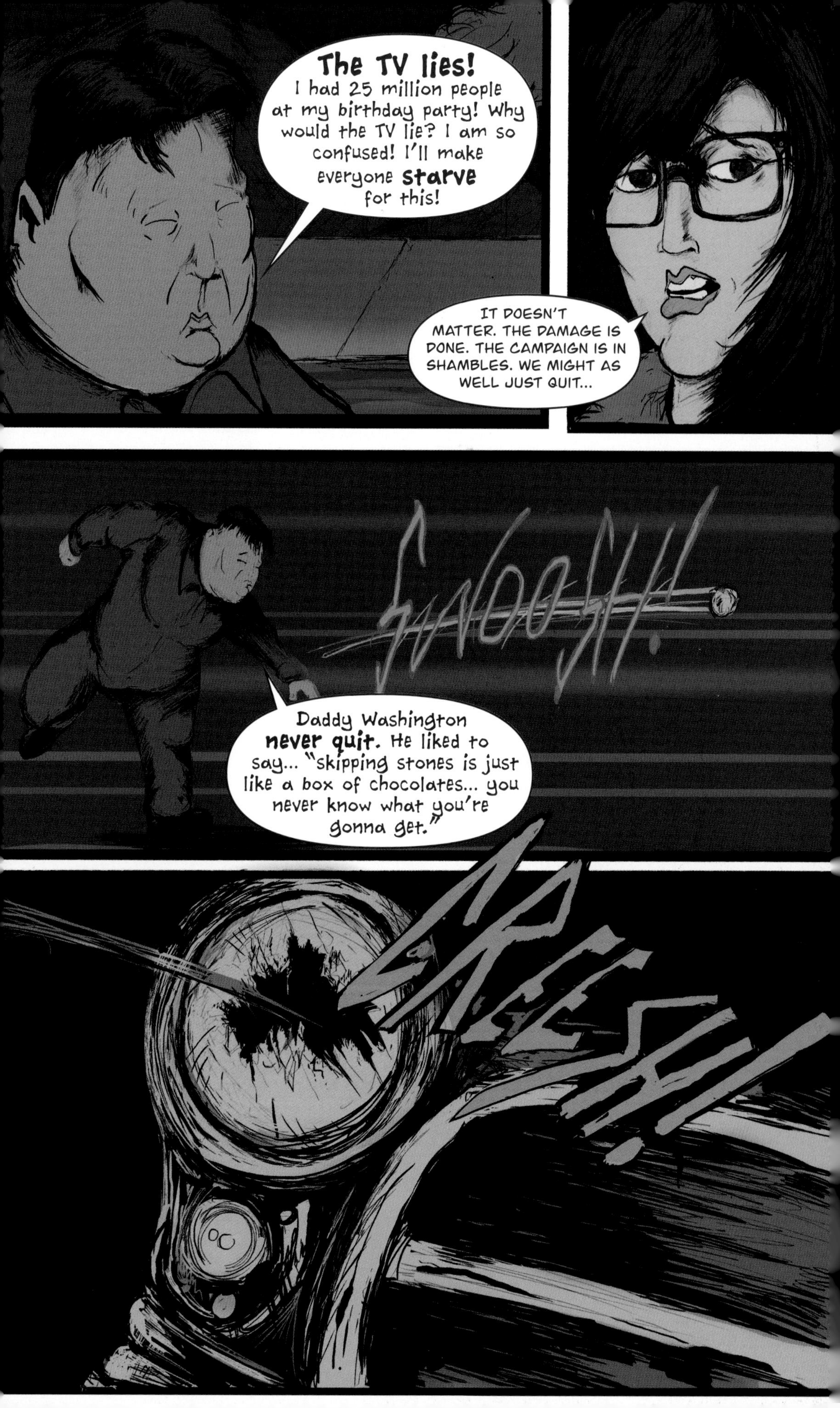
The TV lies! I had 25 million people at my birthday party! Why would the TV lie? I am so confused! I'll make everyone starve for this!
IT DOESN'T MATTER. THE DAMAGE IS DONE. THE CAMPAIGN IS IN SHAMBLES. WE MIGHT AS WELL JUST QUIT...
SWOOSH!
Daddy Washington never quit. He liked to say... "skipping stones is just like a box of chocolates... you never know what you're gonna get."
CRASH!

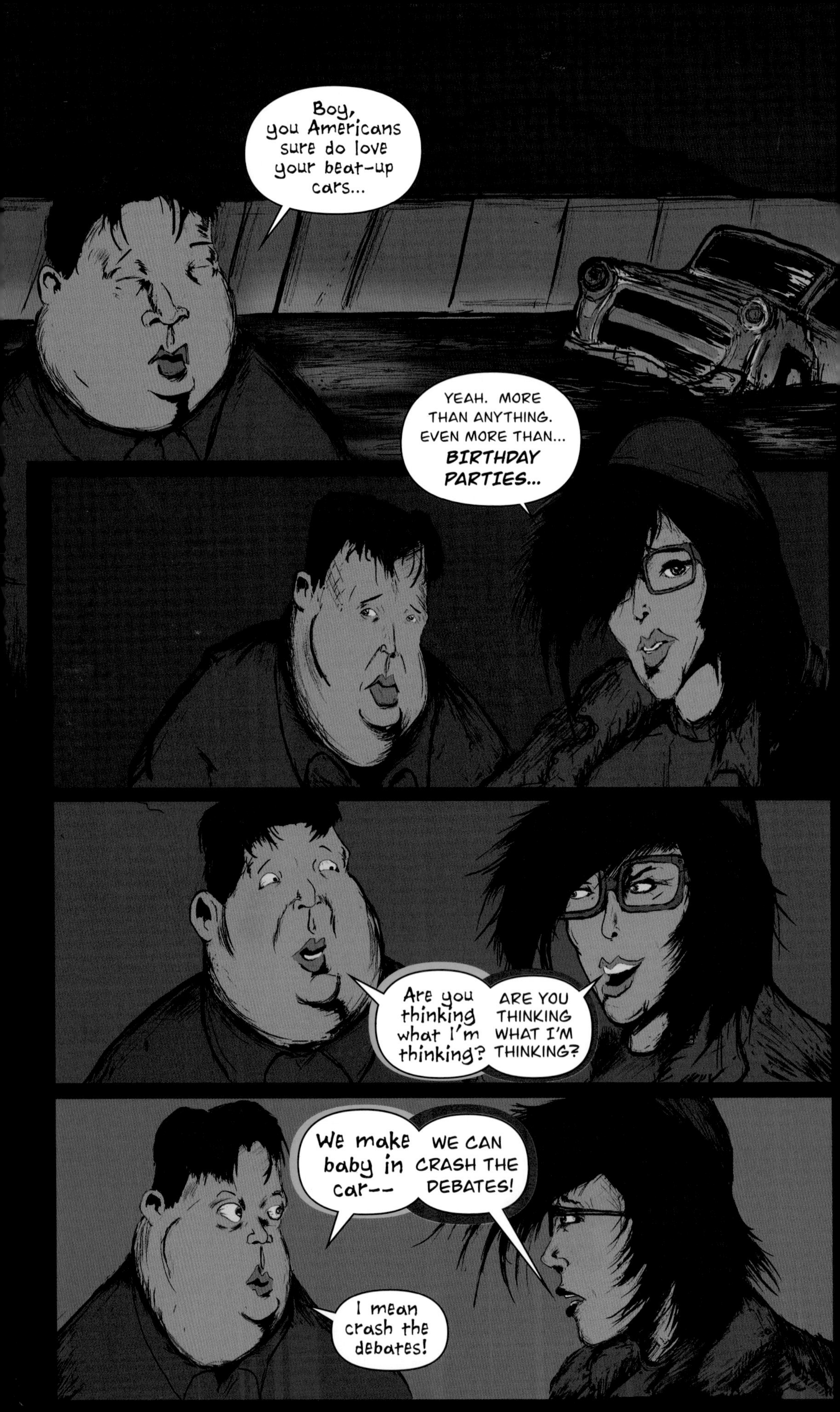
Boy, you Americans sure do love your beat-up cars...
YEAH. MORE THAN ANYTHING. EVEN MORE THAN... BIRTHDAY PARTIES...
Are you thinking what I'm thinking?
ARE YOU THINKING WHAT I'M THINKING?
We make baby in car--
WE CAN CRASH THE DEBATES!
I mean crash the debates!

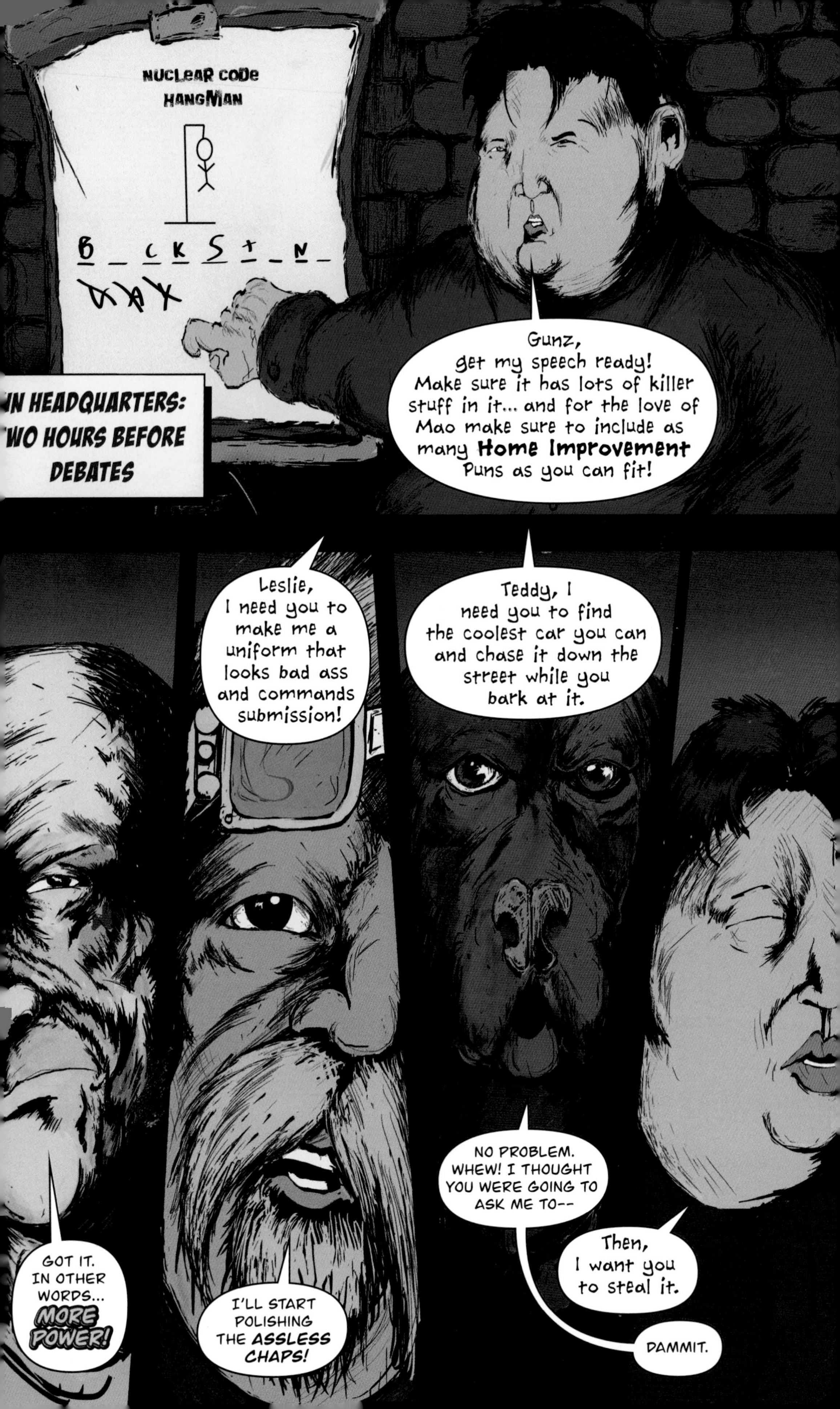
NUCLEAR CODE HANGMAN
B _ _ C K S T _ N _ _
IN HEADQUARTERS: TWO HOURS BEFORE DEBATES
Gunz, get my speech ready! Make sure it has lots of killer stuff in it... and for the love of Mao make sure to include as many **Home Improvement** Puns as you can fit!
Leslie, I need you to make me a uniform that looks bad ass and commands submission!
Teddy, I need you to find the coolest car you can and chase it down the street while you bark at it.
GOT IT. IN OTHER WORDS... MORE POWER!
I'LL START POLISHING THE ASSLESS CHAPS!
NO PROBLEM. WHEW! I THOUGHT YOU WERE GOING TO ASK ME TO--
Then, I want you to steal it.
DAMMIT.

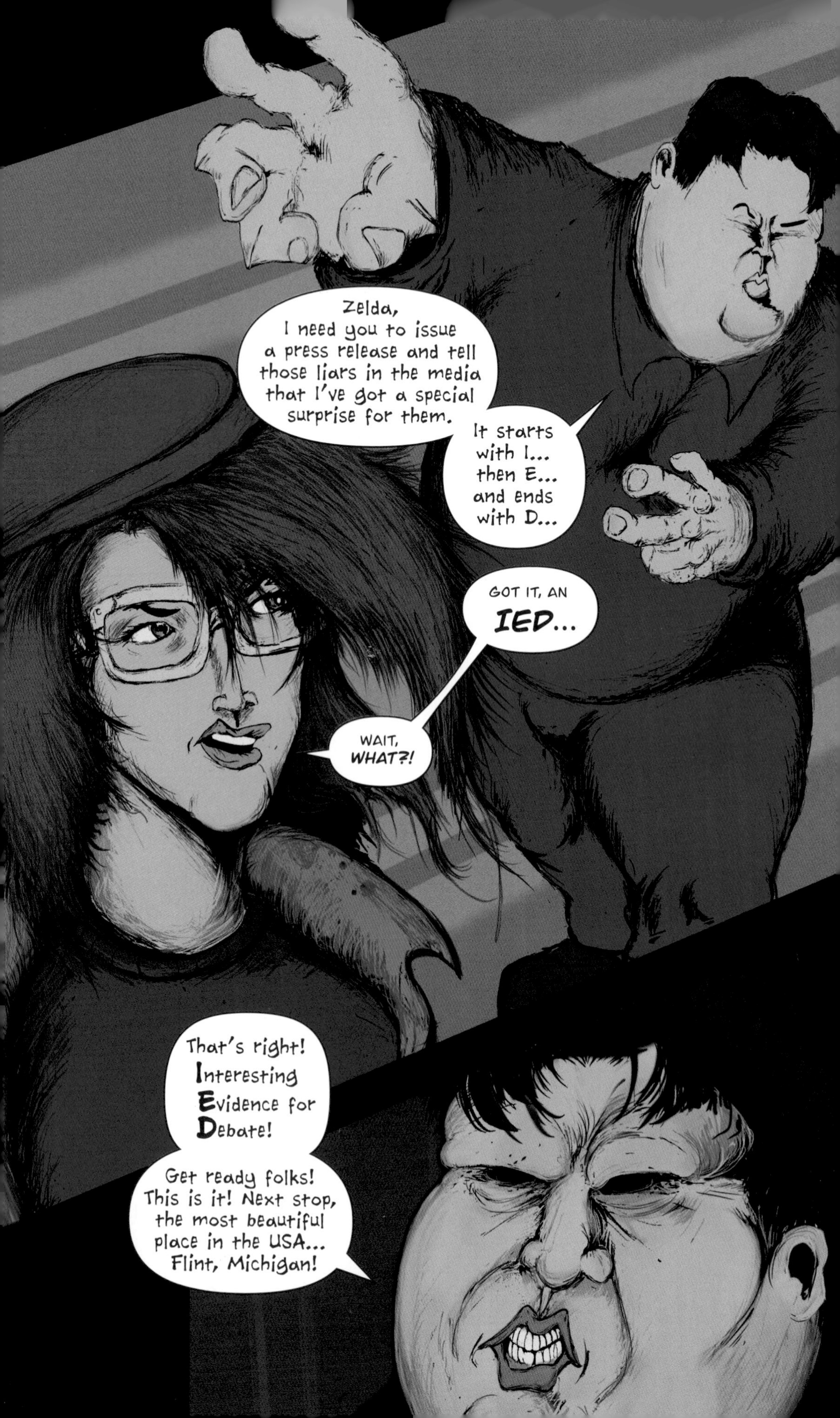
Zelda, I need you to issue a press release and tell those liars in the media that I've got a special surprise for them.
It starts with I... then E... and ends with D...
GOT IT, AN IED...
WAIT, WHAT?!
That's right! Interesting Evidence for Debate!
Get ready folks! This is it! Next stop, the most beautiful place in the USA... Flint, Michigan!

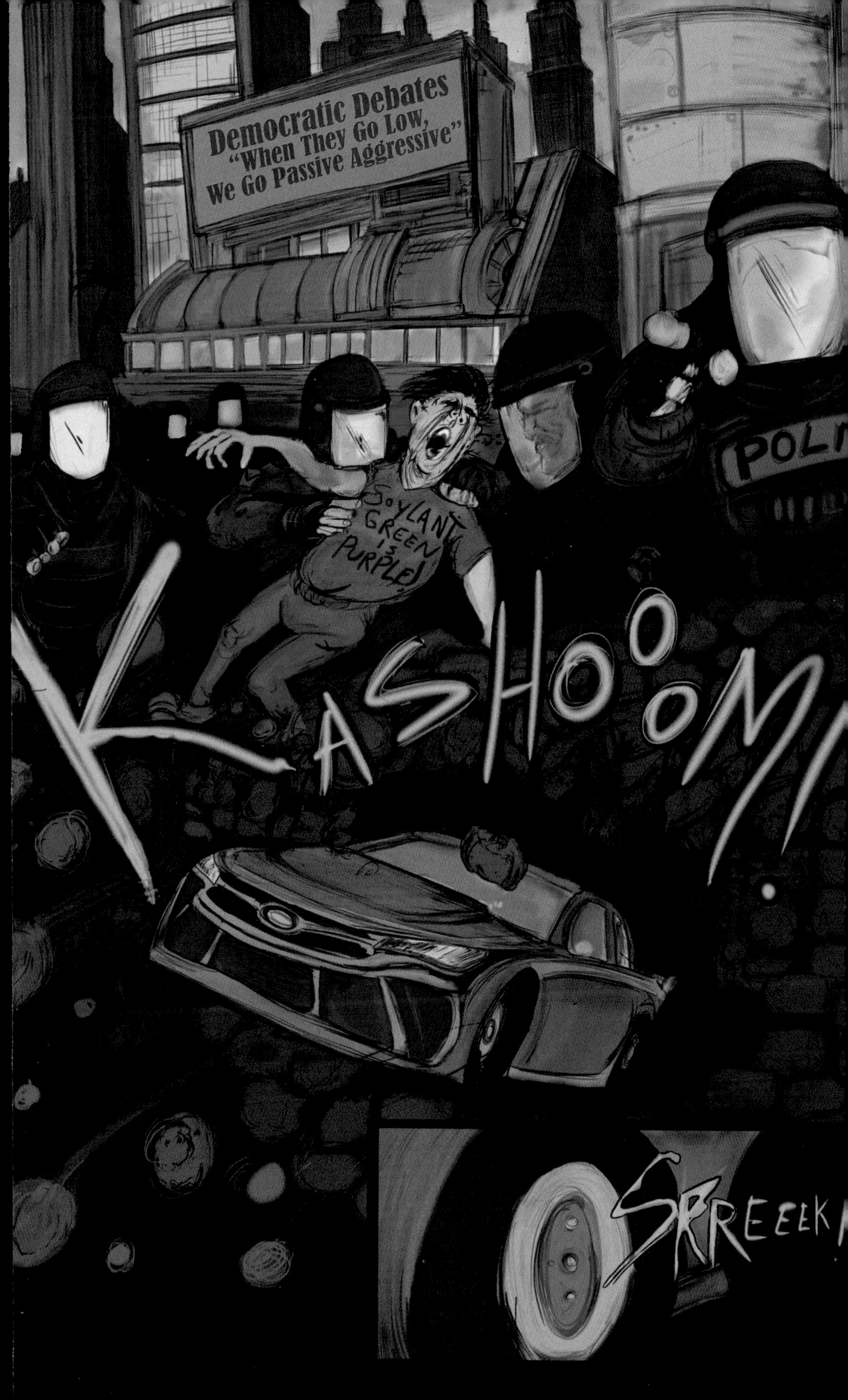

Democratic Debates
"When They Go Low, We Go Passive Aggressive"
Soylant Green is Purple!
POLI
KASHOOOM!
SREEEK

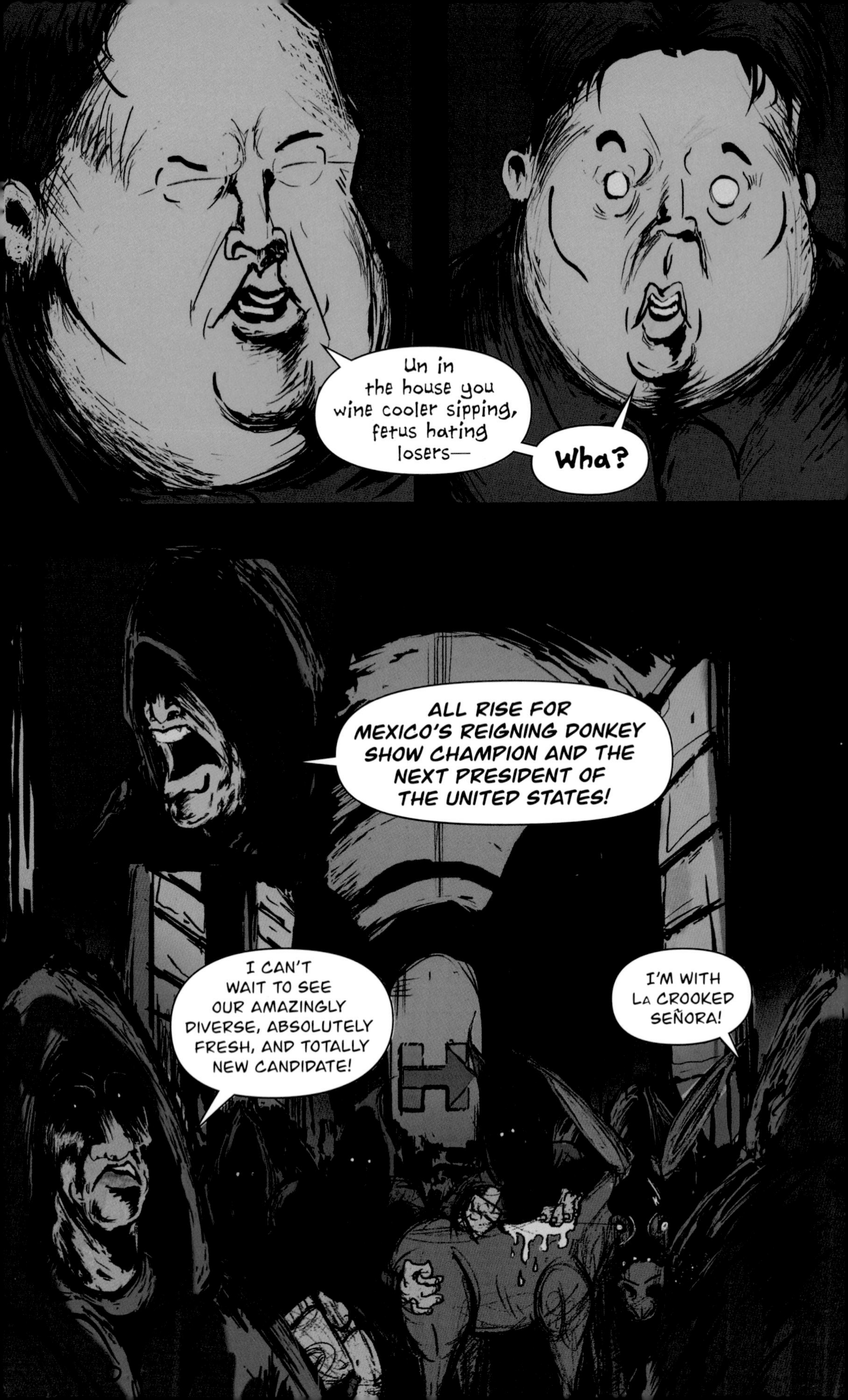
Un in the house you wine cooler sipping, fetus hating losers—
Wha?
ALL RISE FOR MEXICO'S REIGNING DONKEY SHOW CHAMPION AND THE NEXT PRESIDENT OF THE UNITED STATES!
I CAN'T WAIT TO SEE OUR AMAZINGLY DIVERSE, ABSOLUTELY FRESH, AND TOTALLY NEW CANDIDATE!
I'M WITH La CROOKED SEÑORA!

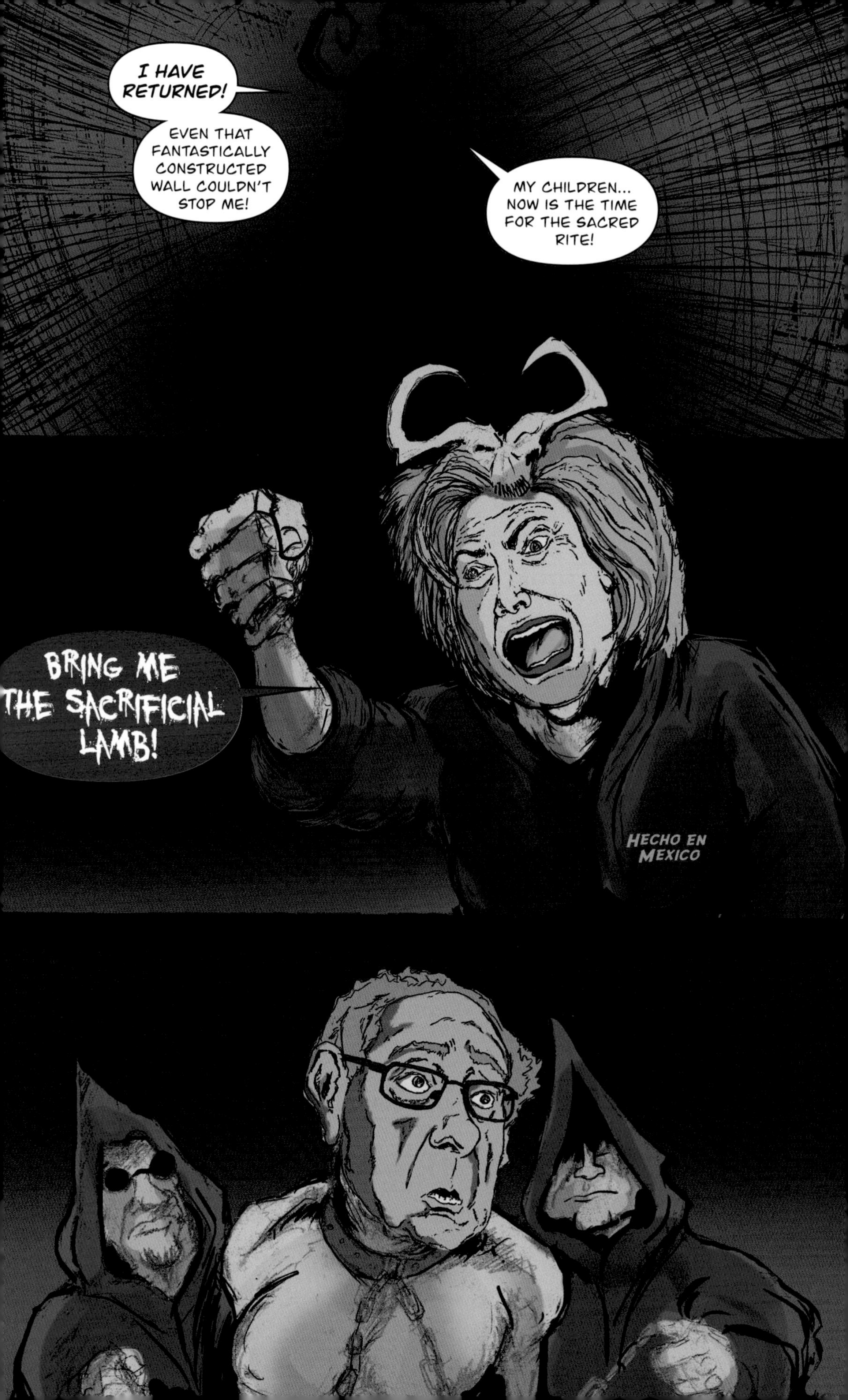
I HAVE RETURNED!
EVEN THAT FANTASTICALLY CONSTRUCTED WALL COULDN'T STOP ME!
MY CHILDREN... NOW IS THE TIME FOR THE SACRED RITE!
BRING ME THE SACRIFICIAL LAMB!
HECHO EN MEXICO

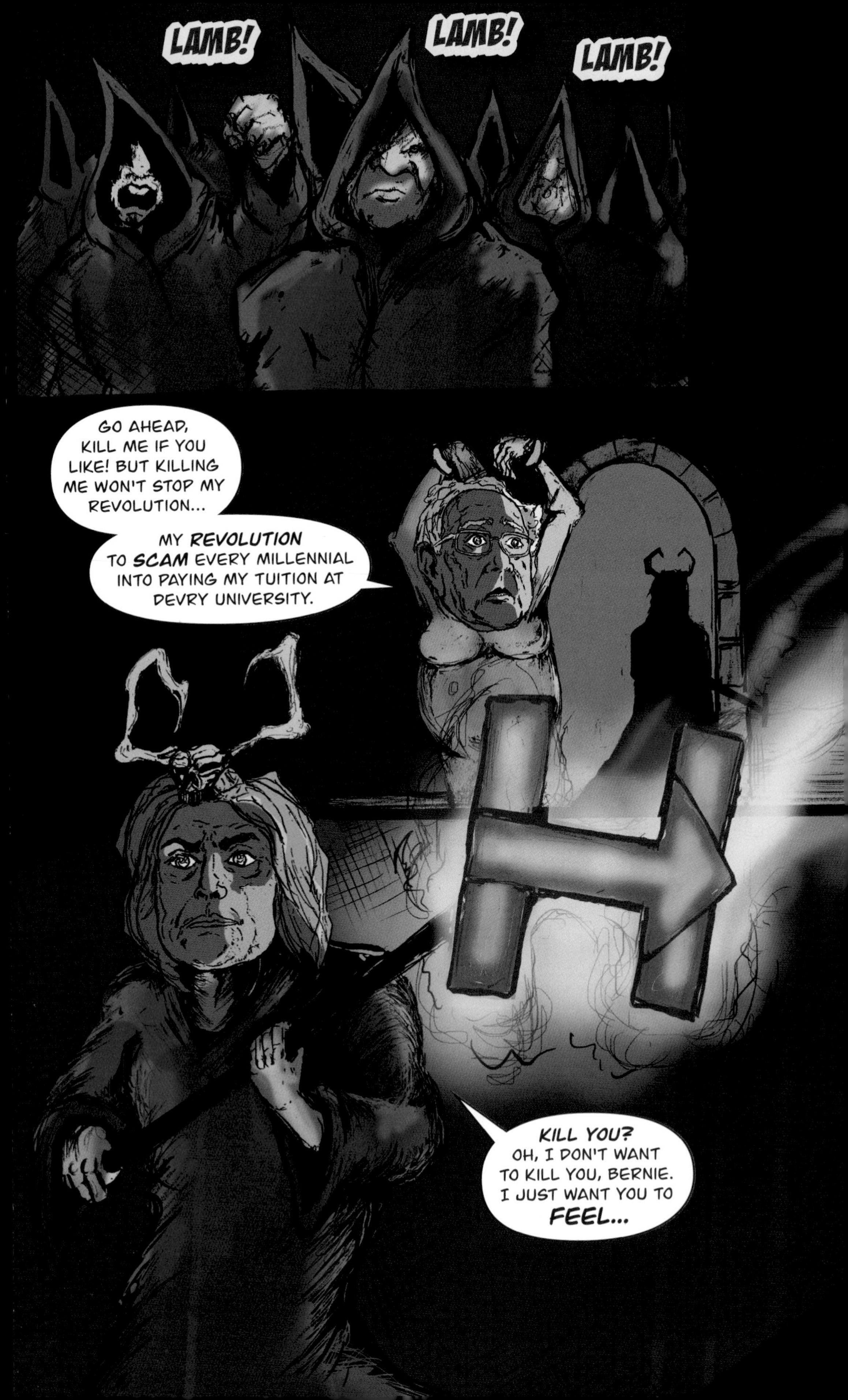
LAMB!
LAMB!
LAMB!
GO AHEAD, KILL ME IF YOU LIKE! BUT KILLING ME WON'T STOP MY REVOLUTION...
MY REVOLUTION TO SCAM EVERY MILLENNIAL INTO PAYING MY TUITION AT DEVRY UNIVERSITY.
KILL YOU? OH, I DON'T WANT TO KILL YOU, BERNIE. I JUST WANT YOU TO FEEL...

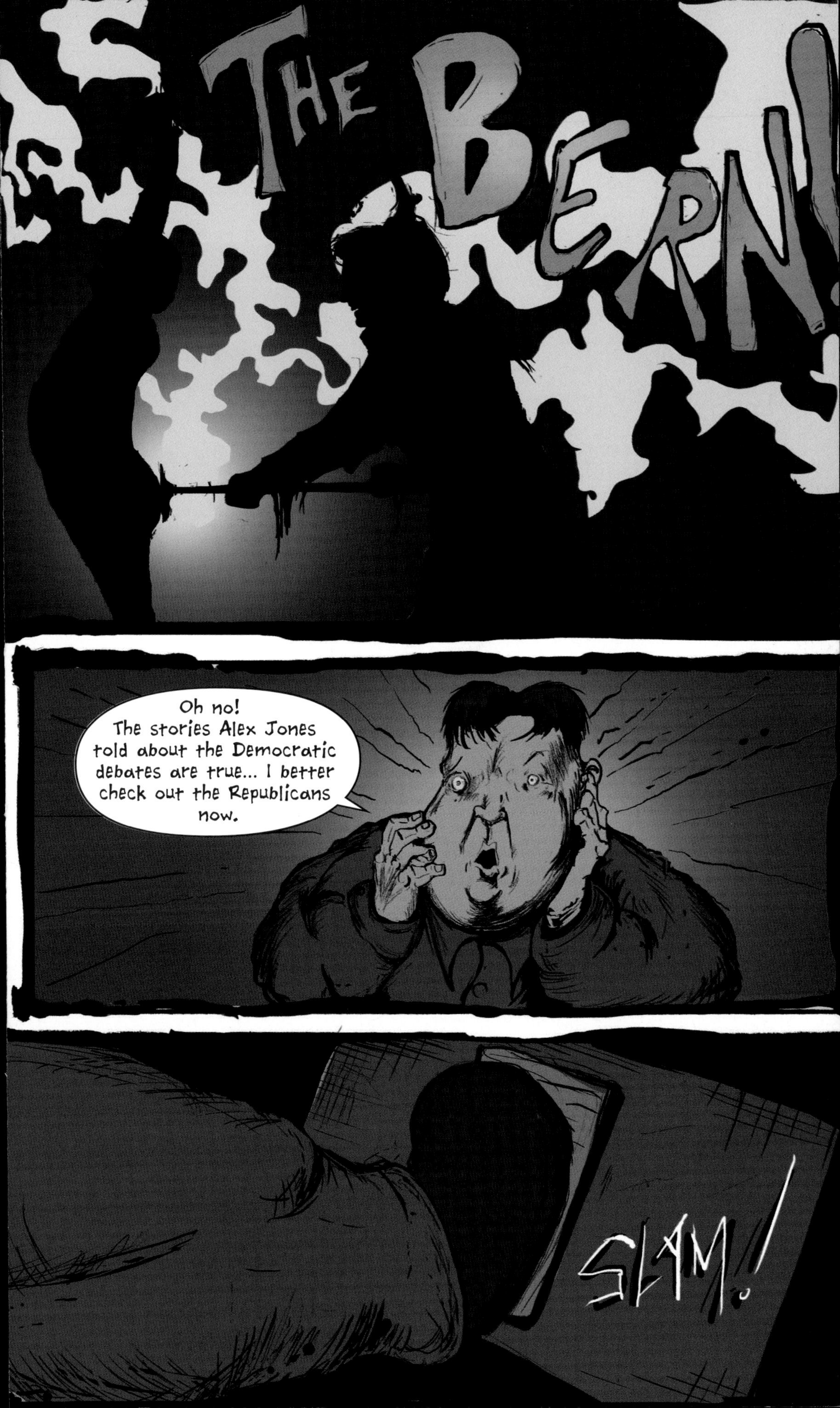
THE BERN!
Oh no! The stories Alex Jones told about the Democratic debates are true... I better check out the Republicans now.
SLAM!

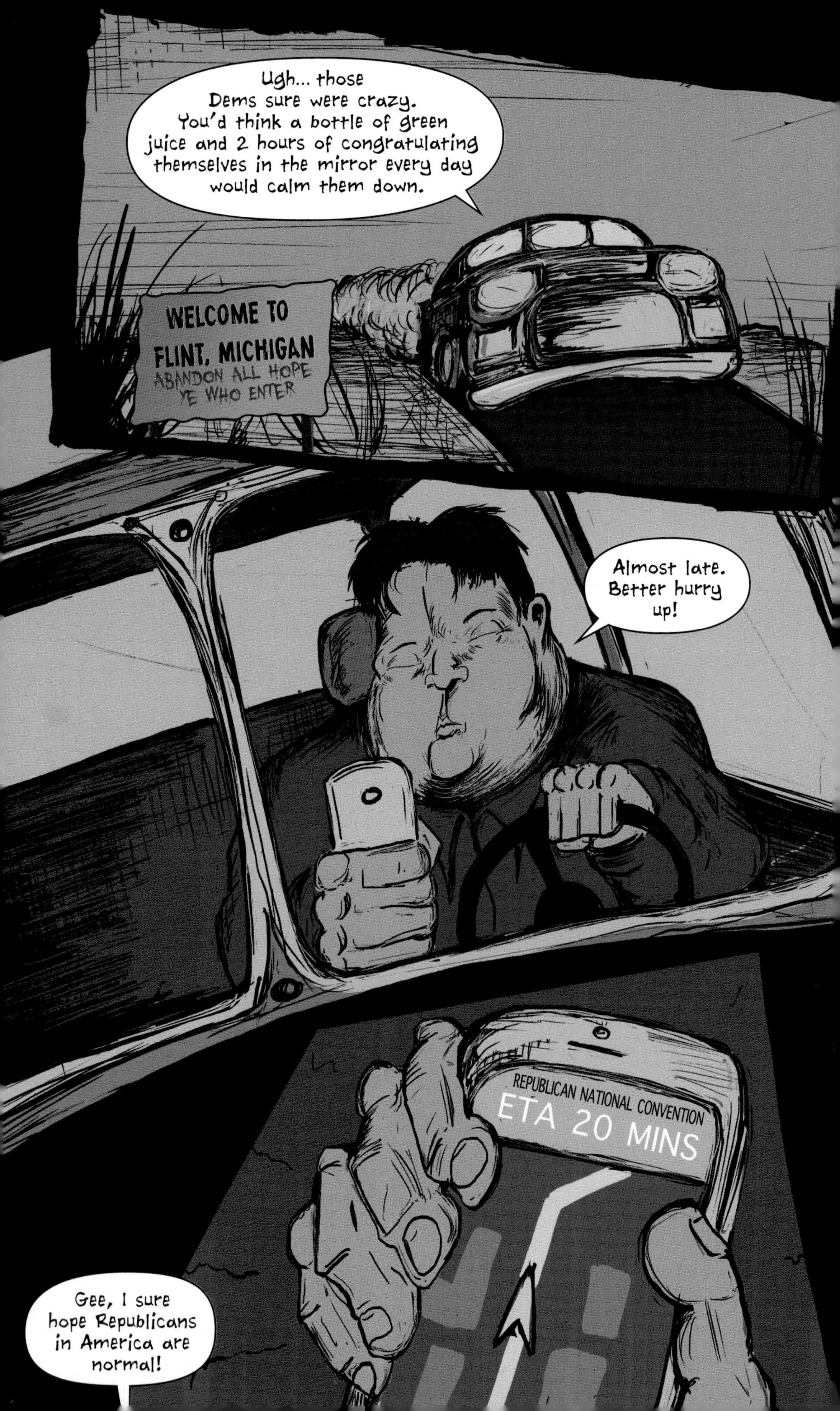
Ugh... those Dems sure were crazy. You'd think a bottle of green juice and 2 hours of congratulating themselves in the mirror every day would calm them down.
WELCOME TO FLINT, MICHIGAN
ABANDON ALL HOPE YE WHO ENTER
Almost late. Better hurry up!
REPUBLICAN NATIONAL CONVENTION
ETA 20 MINS
Gee, I sure hope Republicans in America are normal!

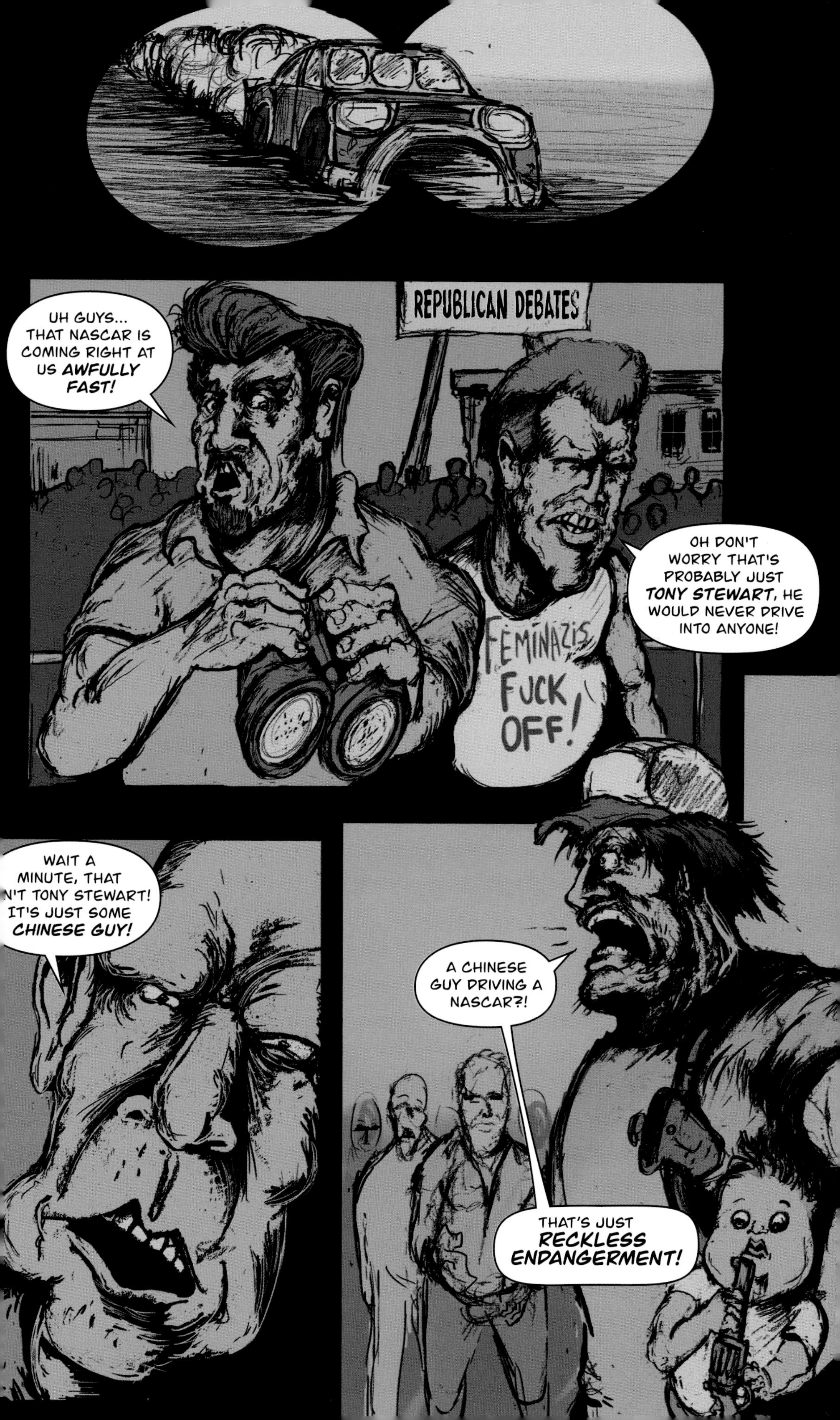
REPUBLICAN DEBATES
UH GUYS... THAT NASCAR IS COMING RIGHT AT US **AWFULLY FAST!**
OH DON'T WORRY THAT'S PROBABLY JUST **TONY STEWART**, HE WOULD NEVER DRIVE INTO ANYONE!
FEMINAZIS FUCK OFF!
WAIT A MINUTE, THAT N'T TONY STEWART! IT'S JUST SOME **CHINESE GUY!**
A CHINESE GUY DRIVING A NASCAR?!
THAT'S JUST **RECKLESS ENDANGERMENT!**

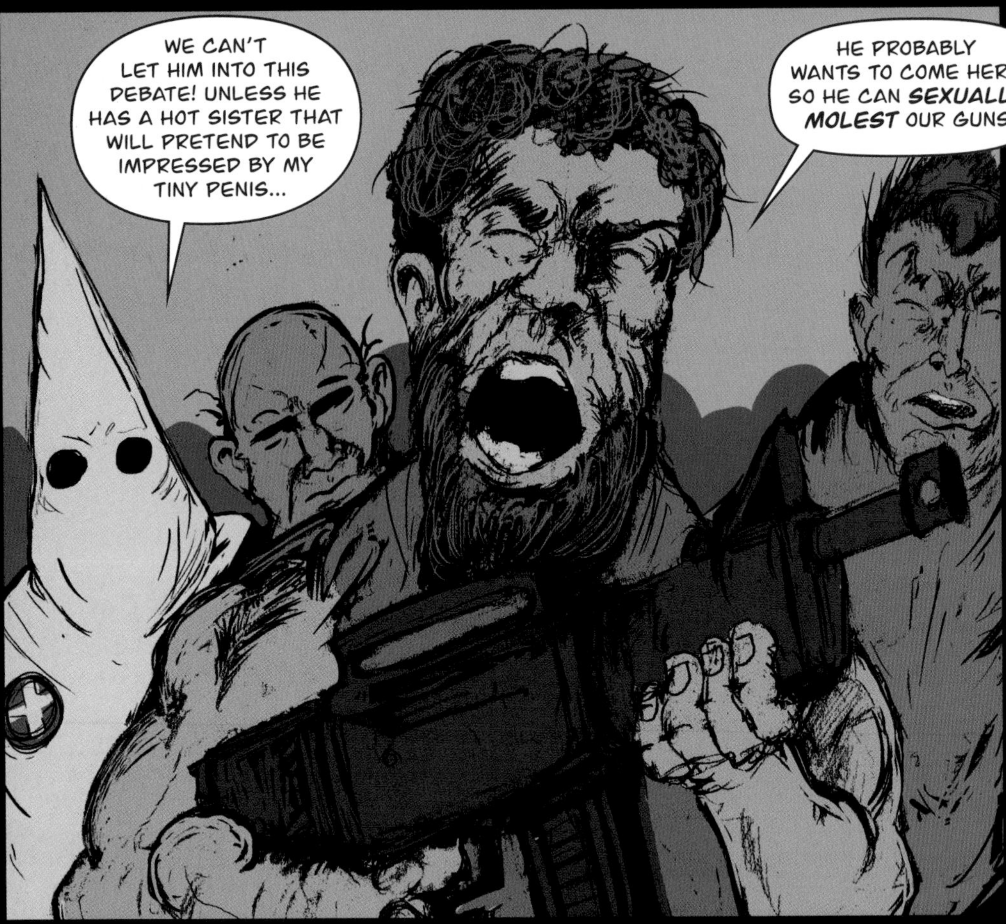
WE CAN'T LET HIM INTO THIS DEBATE! UNLESS HE HAS A HOT SISTER THAT WILL PRETEND TO BE IMPRESSED BY MY TINY PENIS...
HE PROBABLY WANTS TO COME HERE SO HE CAN SEXUALLY MOLEST OUR GUNS!

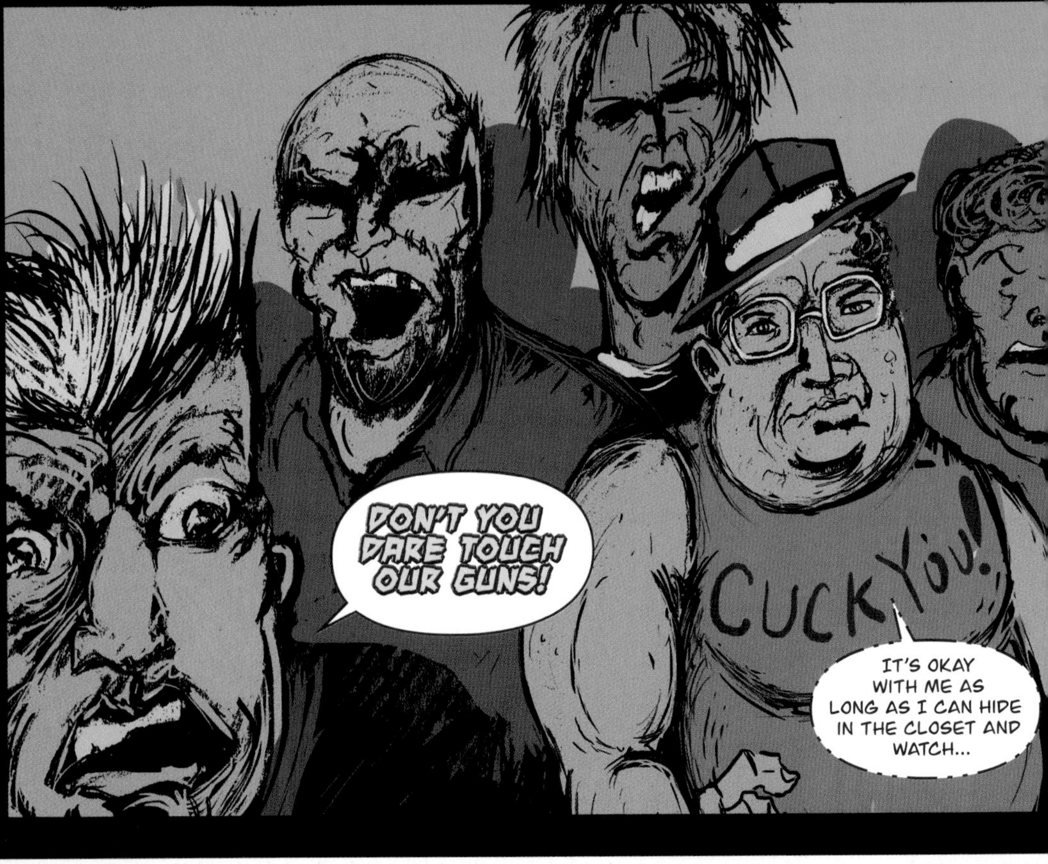
DON'T YOU DARE TOUCH OUR GUNS!
CUCK YOU!
IT'S OKAY WITH ME AS LONG AS I CAN HIDE IN THE CLOSET AND WATCH...

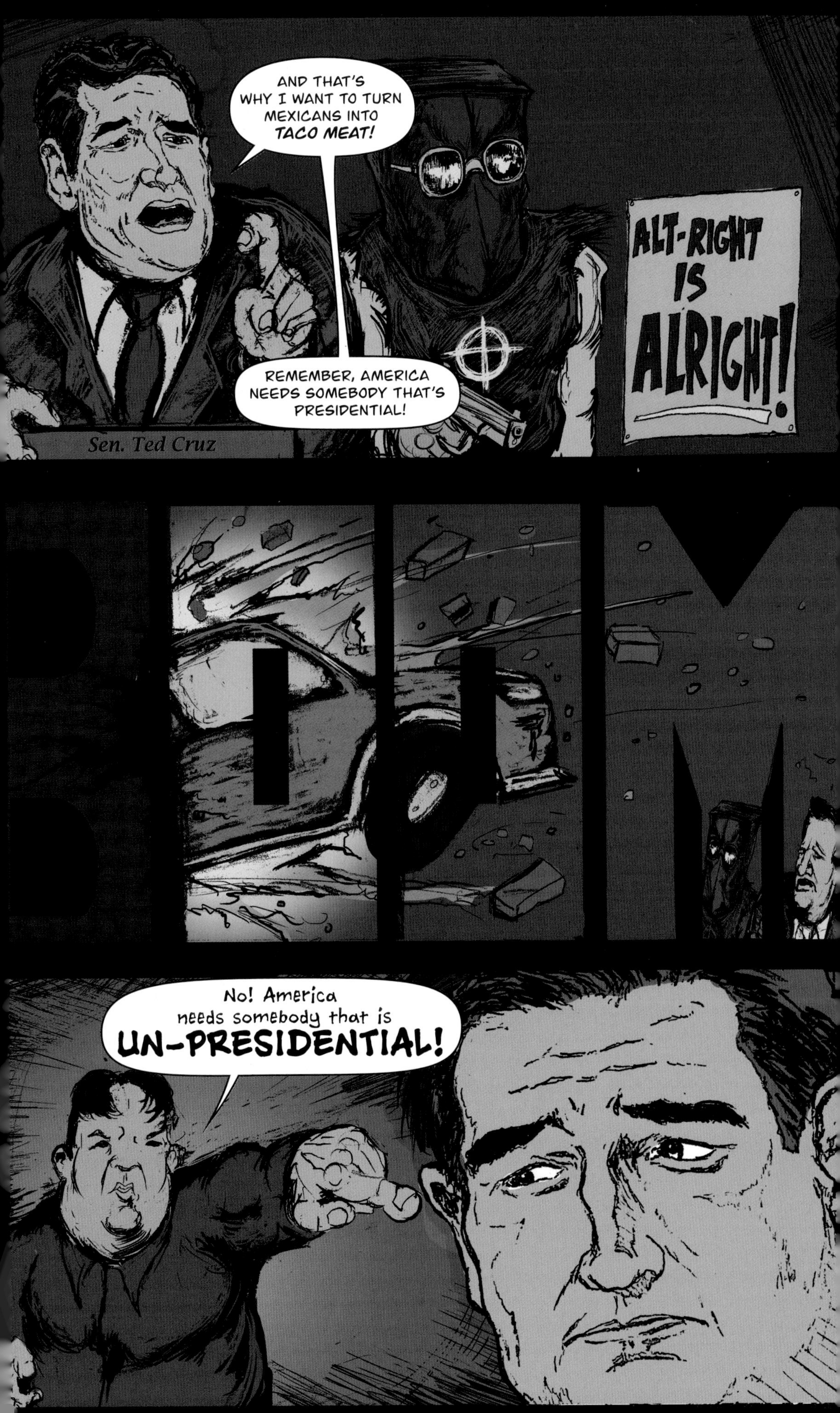
AND THAT'S WHY I WANT TO TURN MEXICANS INTO TACO MEAT!
REMEMBER, AMERICA NEEDS SOMEBODY THAT'S PRESIDENTIAL!
Sen. Ted Cruz
ALT-RIGHT IS ALRIGHT!
No! America needs somebody that is UN-PRESIDENTIAL!

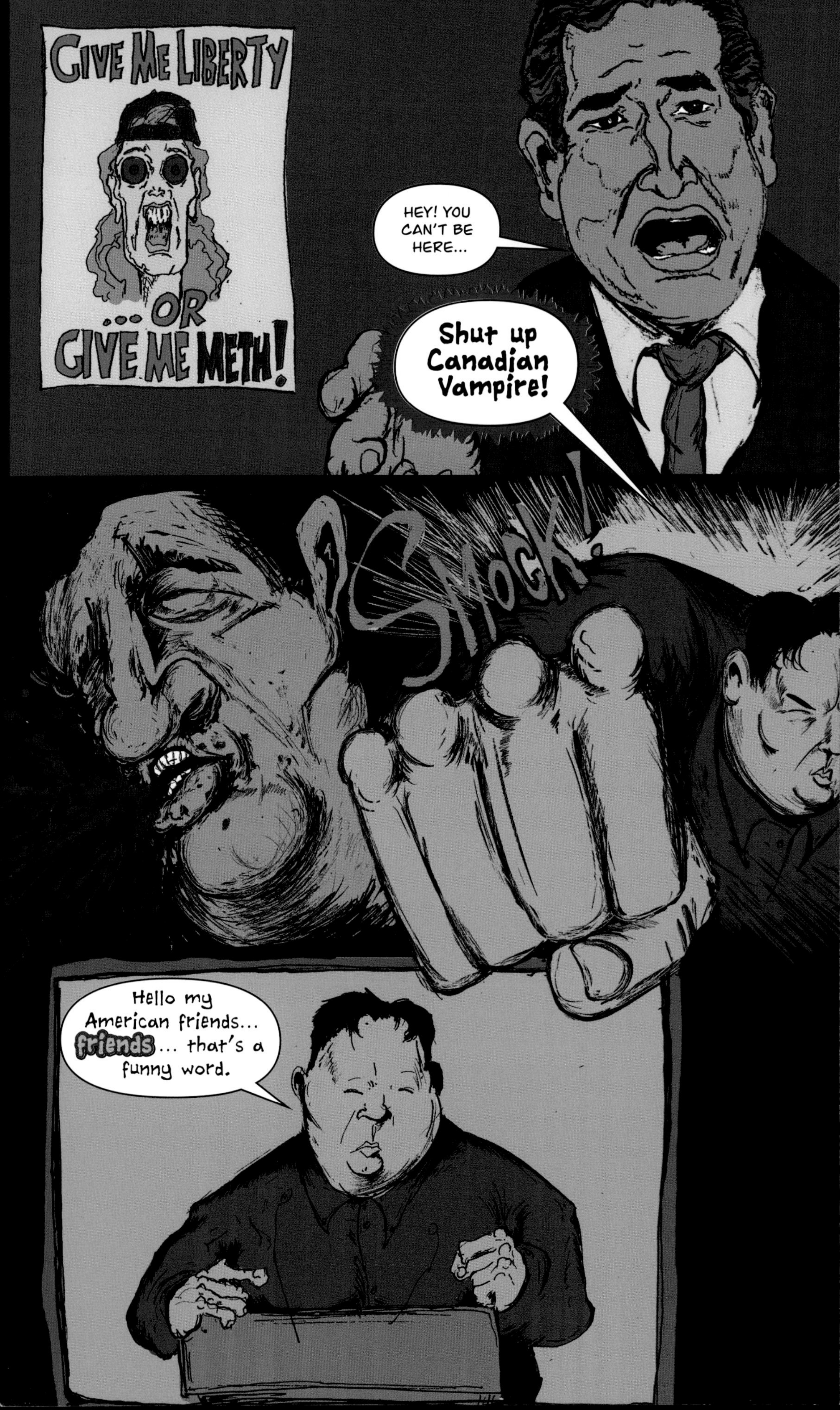
GIVE ME LIBERTY
...OR
GIVE ME METH!
HEY! YOU CAN'T BE HERE...
Shut up Canadian Vampire!
SMOCK!
Hello my American friends... friends... that's a funny word.

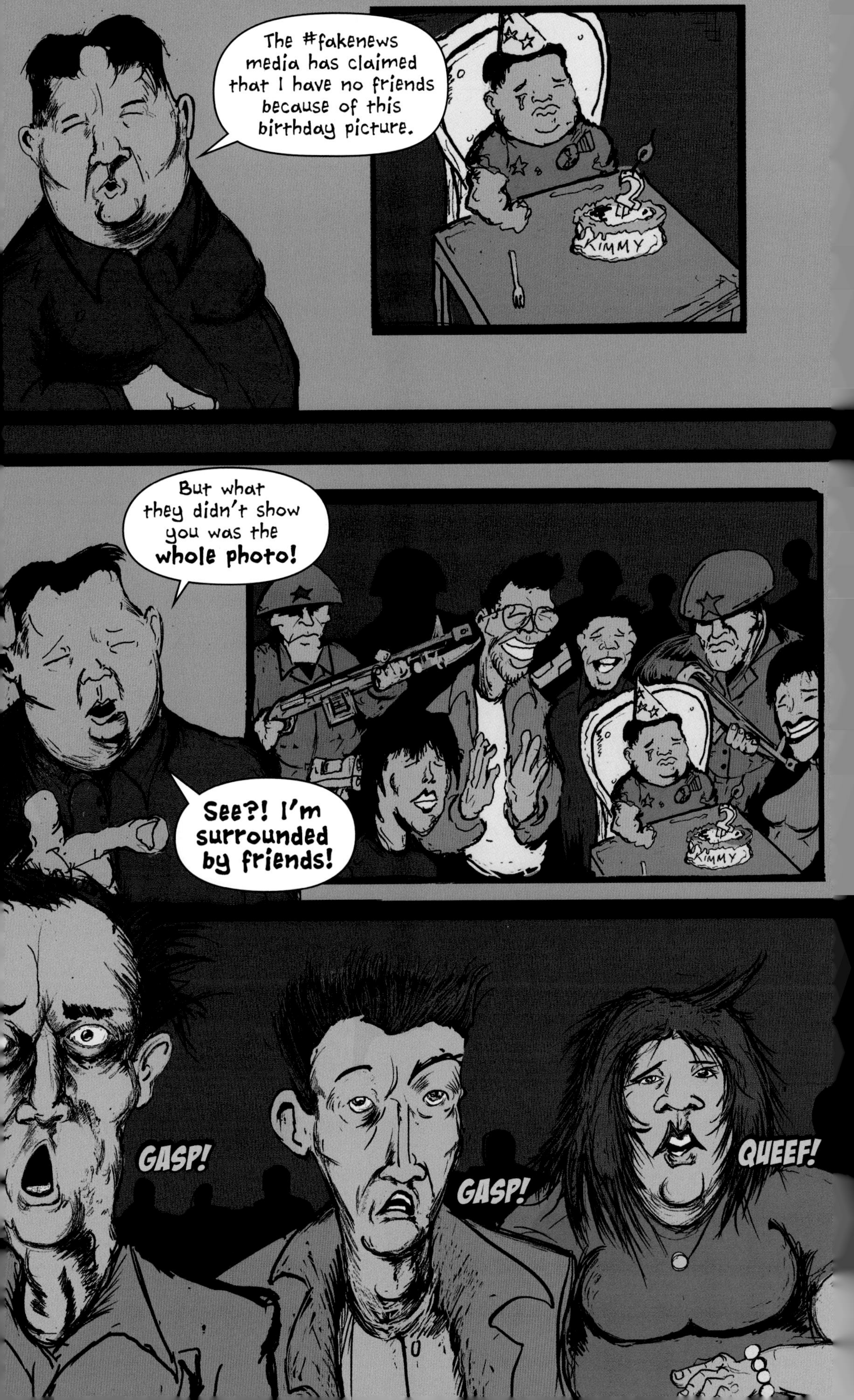
The #fakenews media has claimed that I have no friends because of this birthday picture.
KIMMY
But what they didn't show you was the whole photo!
KIMMY
See?! I'm surrounded by friends!
GASP!
GASP!
QUEEF!

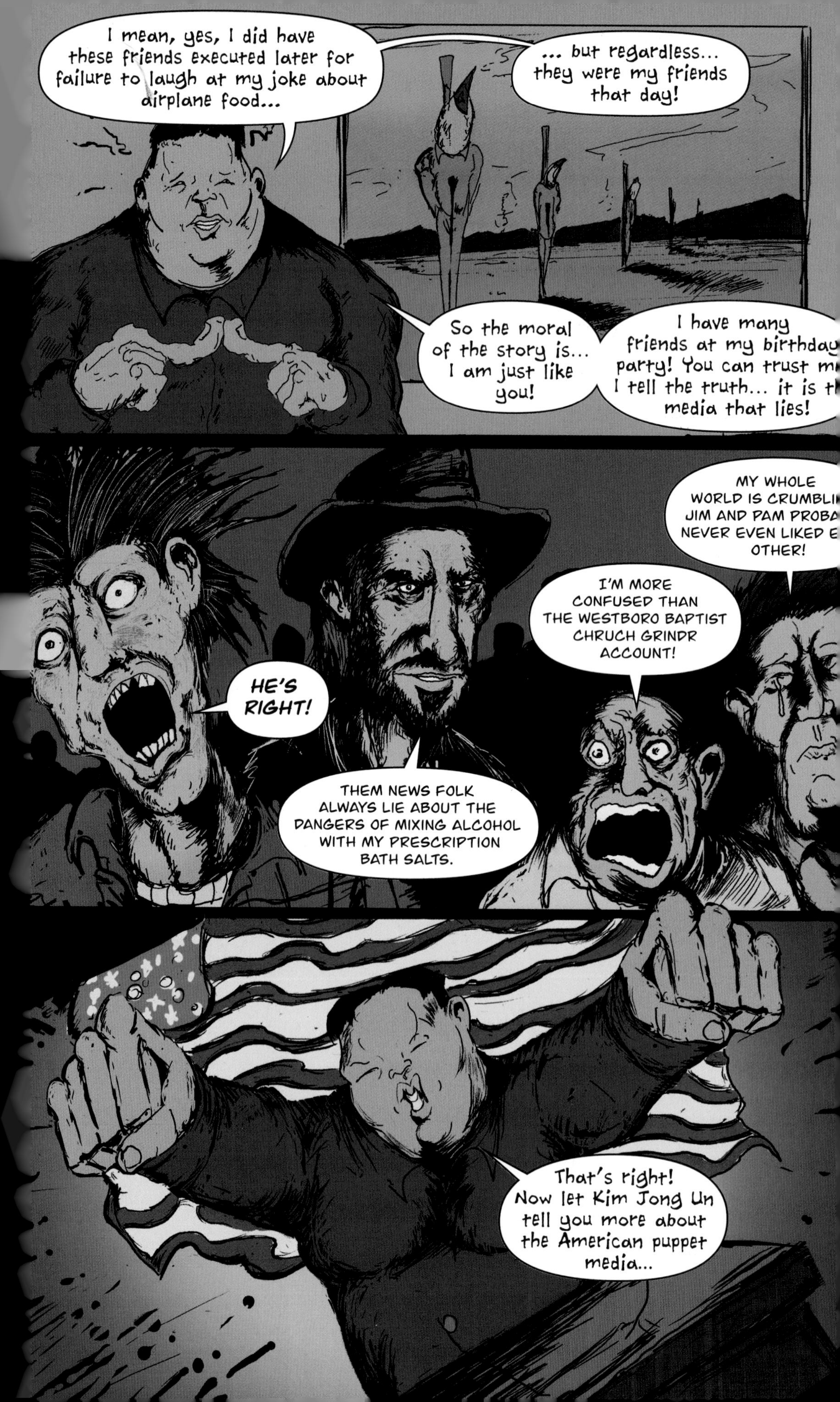

I mean, yes, I did have these friends executed later for failure to laugh at my joke about airplane food...
... but regardless... they were my friends that day!
So the moral of the story is... I am just like you!
I have many friends at my birthday party! You can trust m I tell the truth... it is t media that lies!
MY WHOLE WORLD IS CRUMBLI JIM AND PAM PROBA NEVER EVEN LIKED E OTHER!
I'M MORE CONFUSED THAN THE WESTBORO BAPTIST CHRUCH GRINDR ACCOUNT!
HE'S RIGHT!
THEM NEWS FOLK ALWAYS LIE ABOUT THE DANGERS OF MIXING ALCOHOL WITH MY PRESCRIPTION BATH SALTS.
That's right! Now let Kim Jong Un tell you more about the American puppet media...

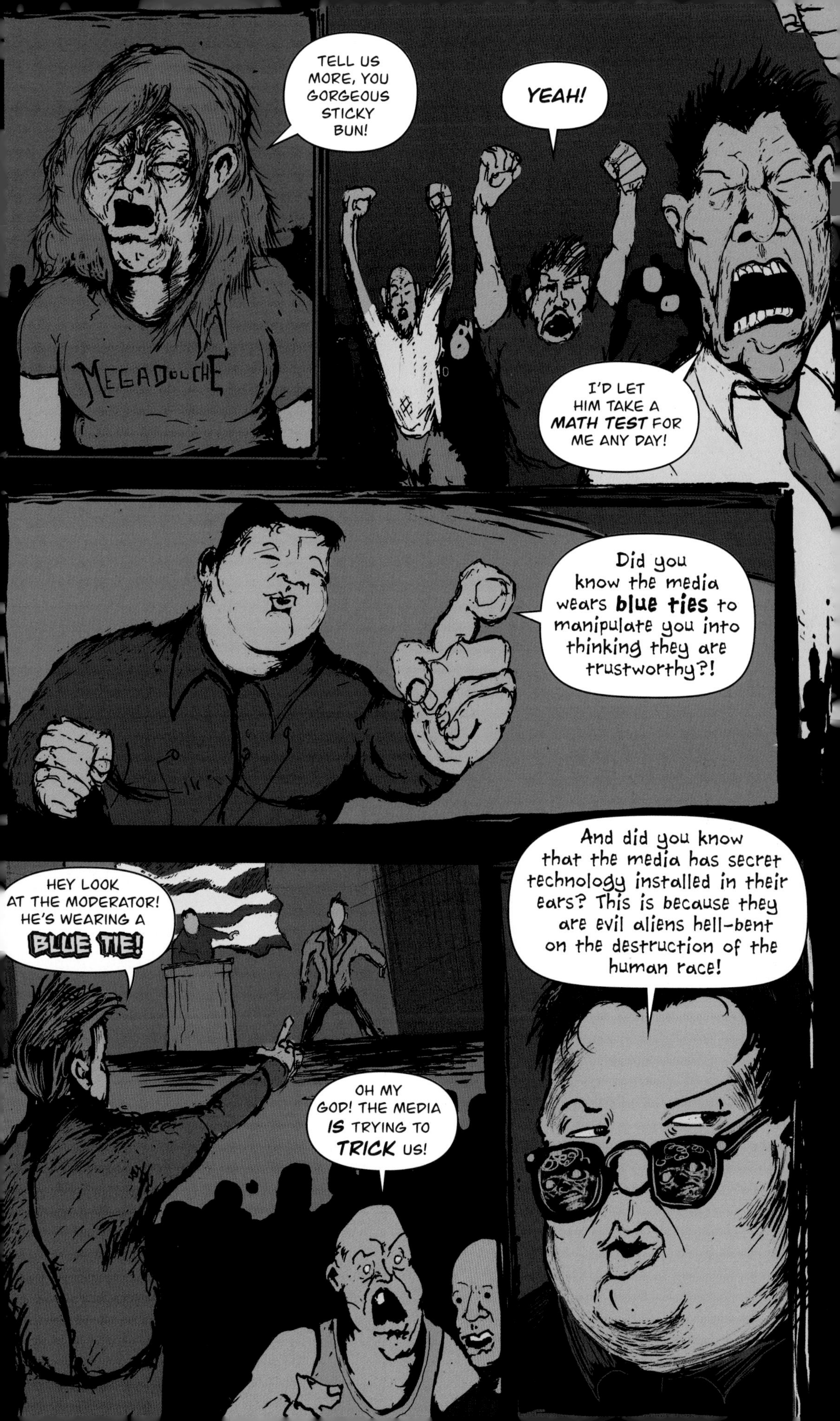
TELL US MORE, YOU GORGEOUS STICKY BUN!
MEGADOUCHE
YEAH!
I'D LET HIM TAKE A MATH TEST FOR ME ANY DAY!
Did you know the media wears blue ties to manipulate you into thinking they are trustworthy?!
HEY LOOK AT THE MODERATOR! HE'S WEARING A BLUE TIE!
OH MY GOD! THE MEDIA IS TRYING TO TRICK US!
And did you know that the media has secret technology installed in their ears? This is because they are evil aliens hell-bent on the destruction of the human race!

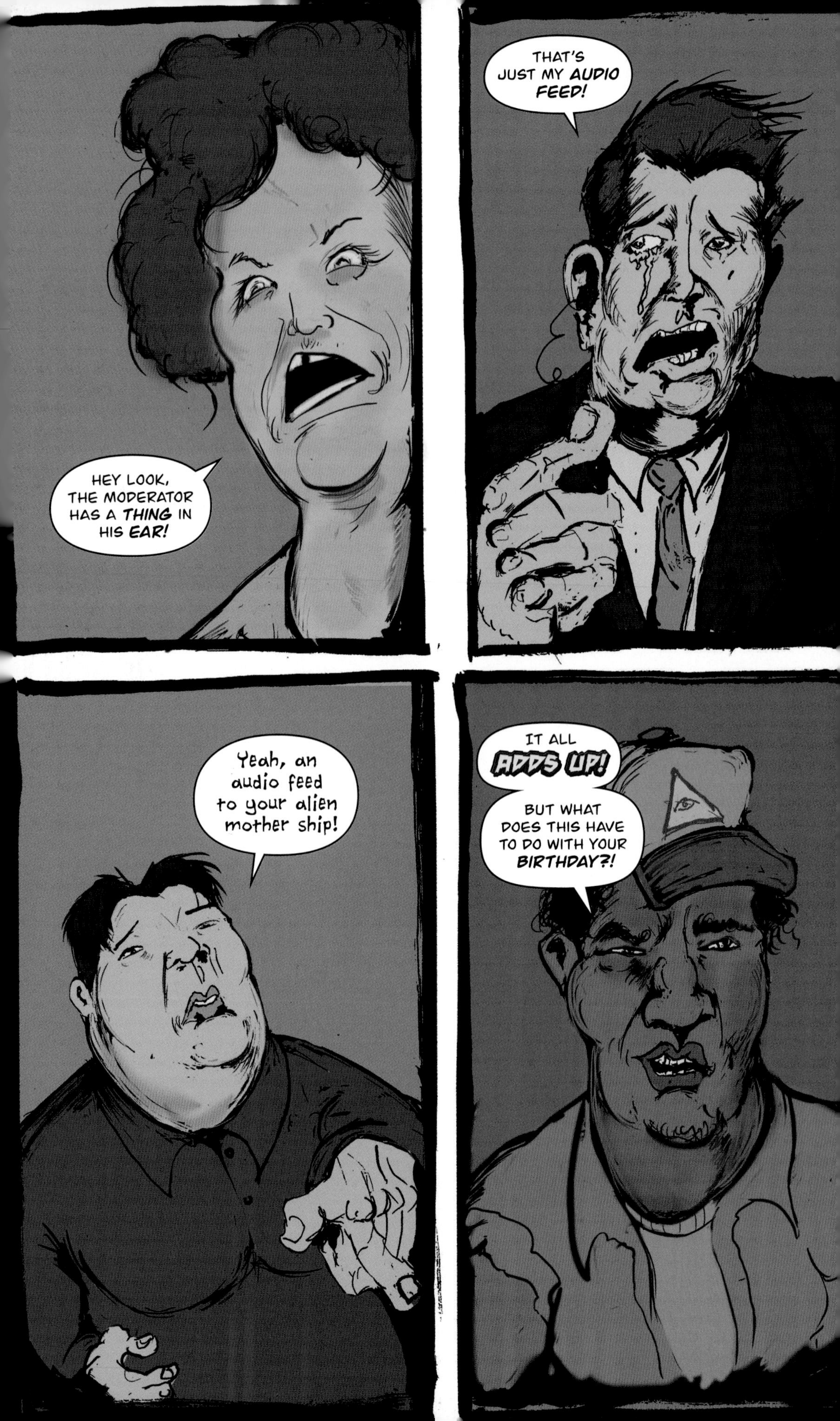
HEY LOOK, THE MODERATOR HAS A THING IN HIS EAR!
THAT'S JUST MY AUDIO FEED!
Yeah, an audio feed to your alien mother ship!
IT ALL ADDS UP!
BUT WHAT DOES THIS HAVE TO DO WITH YOUR BIRTHDAY?!

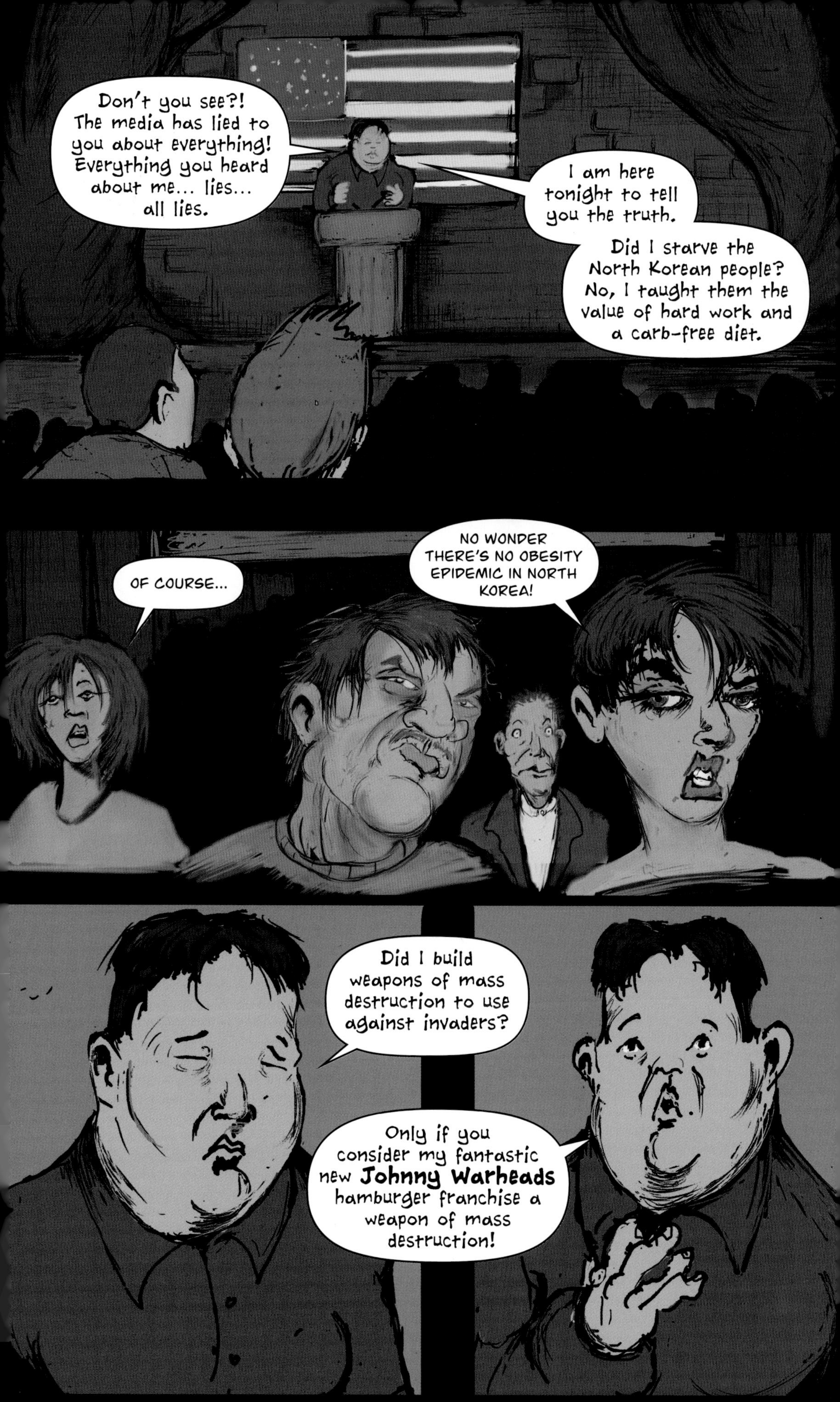
Don't you see?! The media has lied to you about everything! Everything you heard about me... lies... all lies.
I am here tonight to tell you the truth.
Did I starve the North Korean people? No, I taught them the value of hard work and a carb-free diet.
OF COURSE...
NO WONDER THERE'S NO OBESITY EPIDEMIC IN NORTH KOREA!
Did I build weapons of mass destruction to use against invaders?
Only if you consider my fantastic new **Johnny Warheads** hamburger franchise a weapon of mass destruction!

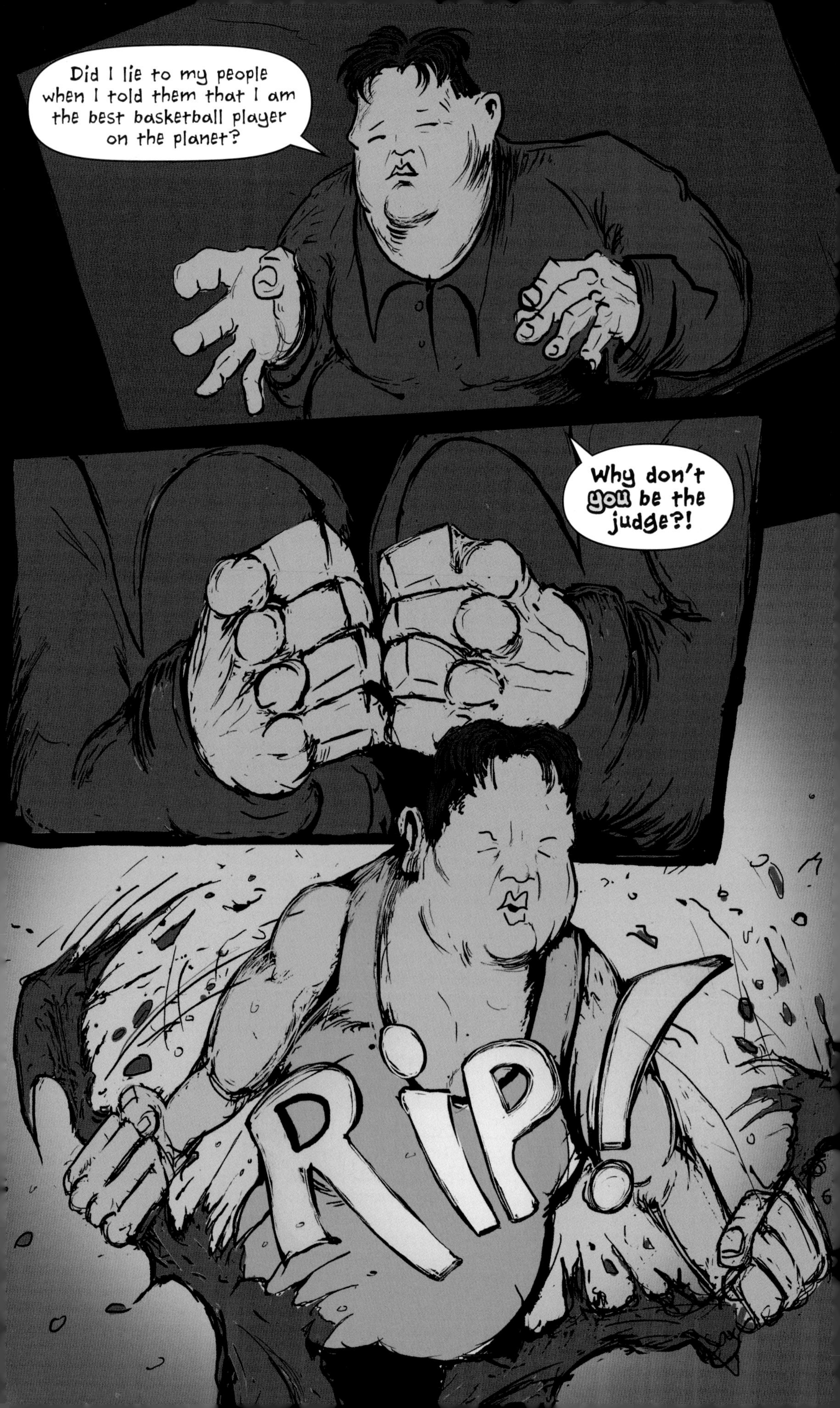
Did I lie to my people when I told them that I am the best basketball player on the planet?
Why don't you be the judge?!
RIP!

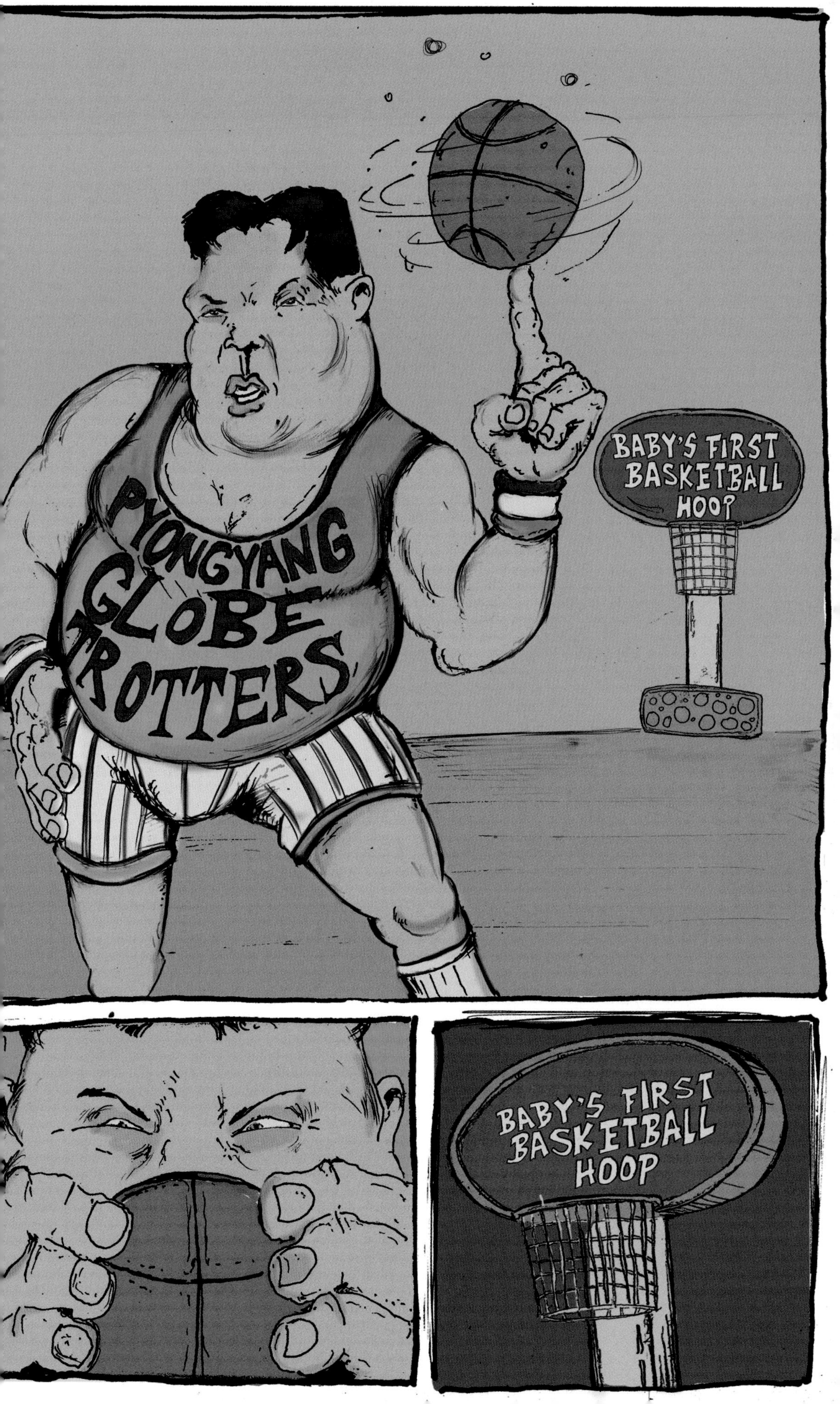
PYONGYANG
GLOBE
TROTTERS
BABY'S FIRST
BASKETBALL
HOOP
BABY'S FIRST
BASKETBALL
HOOP

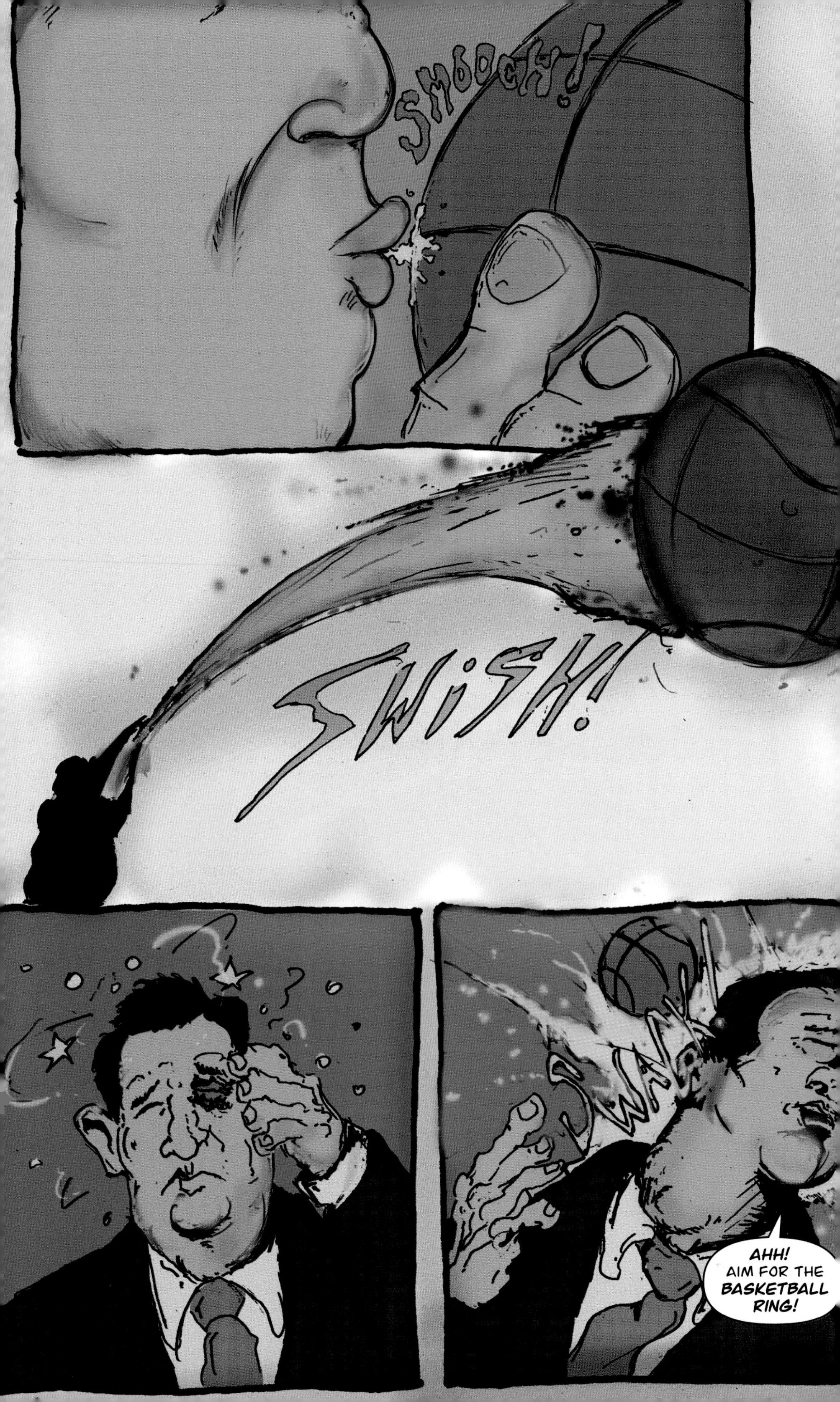
SMOOCH!
SWISH!
AHH!
AIM FOR THE
BASKETBALL
RING!

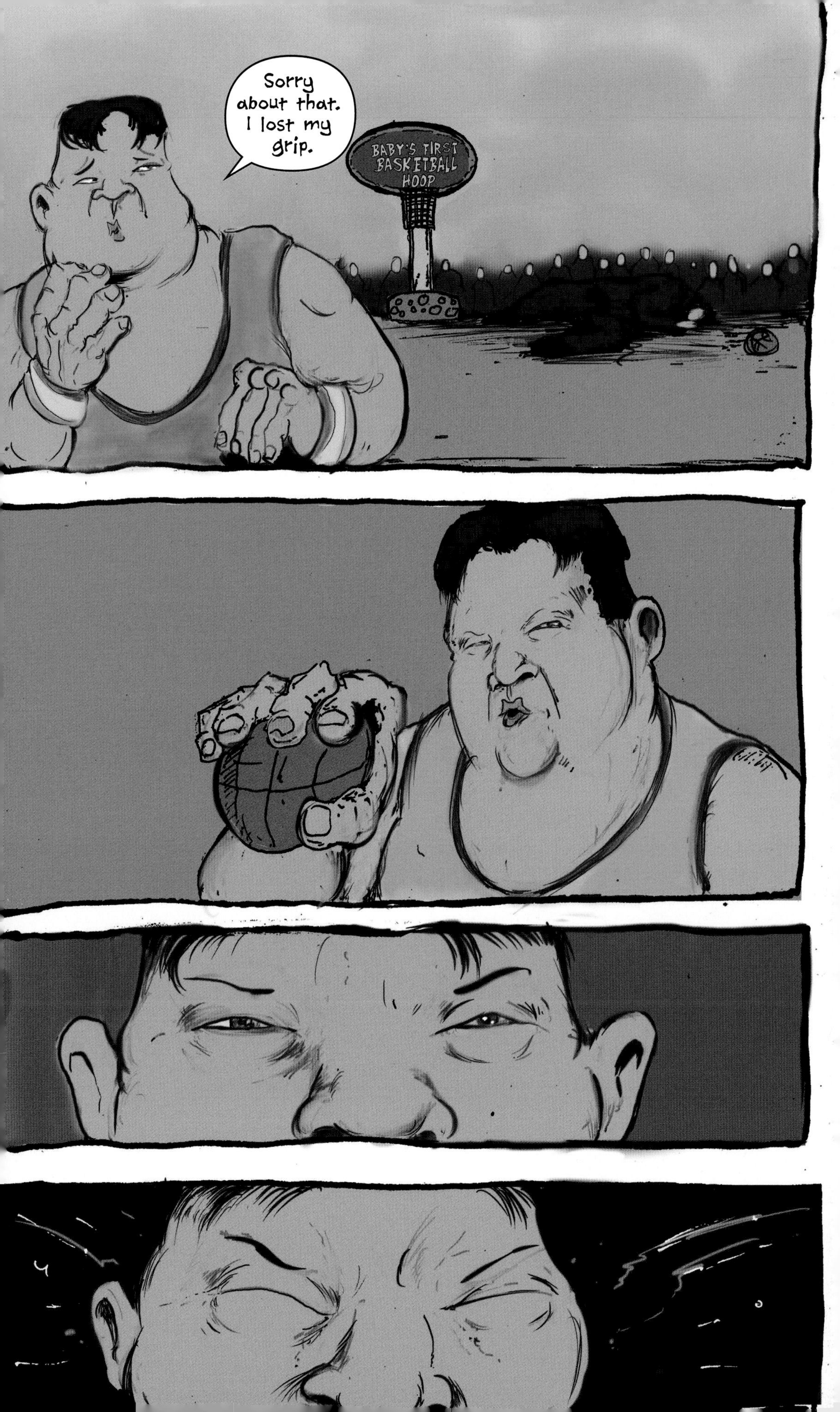
Sorry about that. I lost my grip.
BABY'S FIRST BASKETBALL HOOP

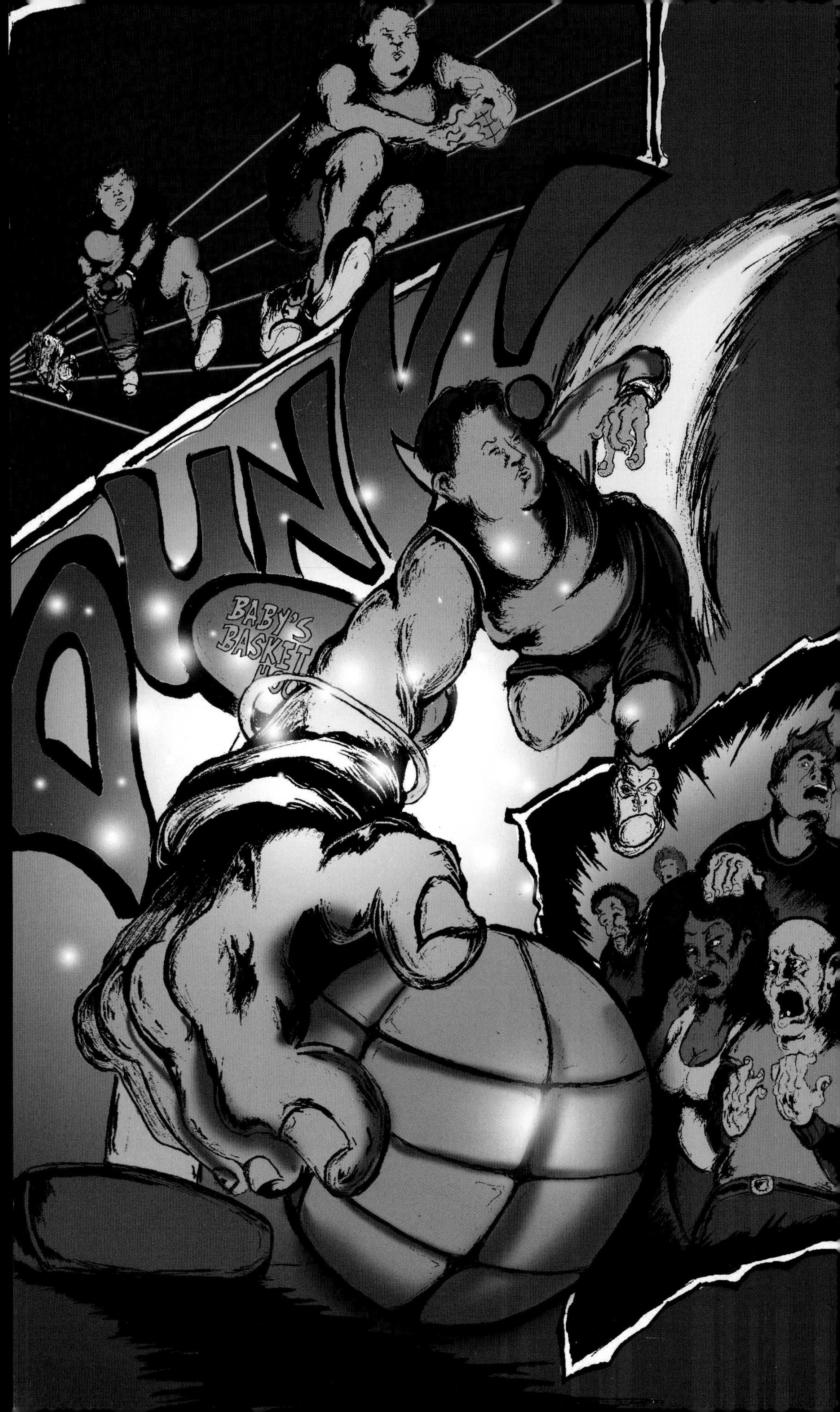
DUNK!
BABY'S BASKET

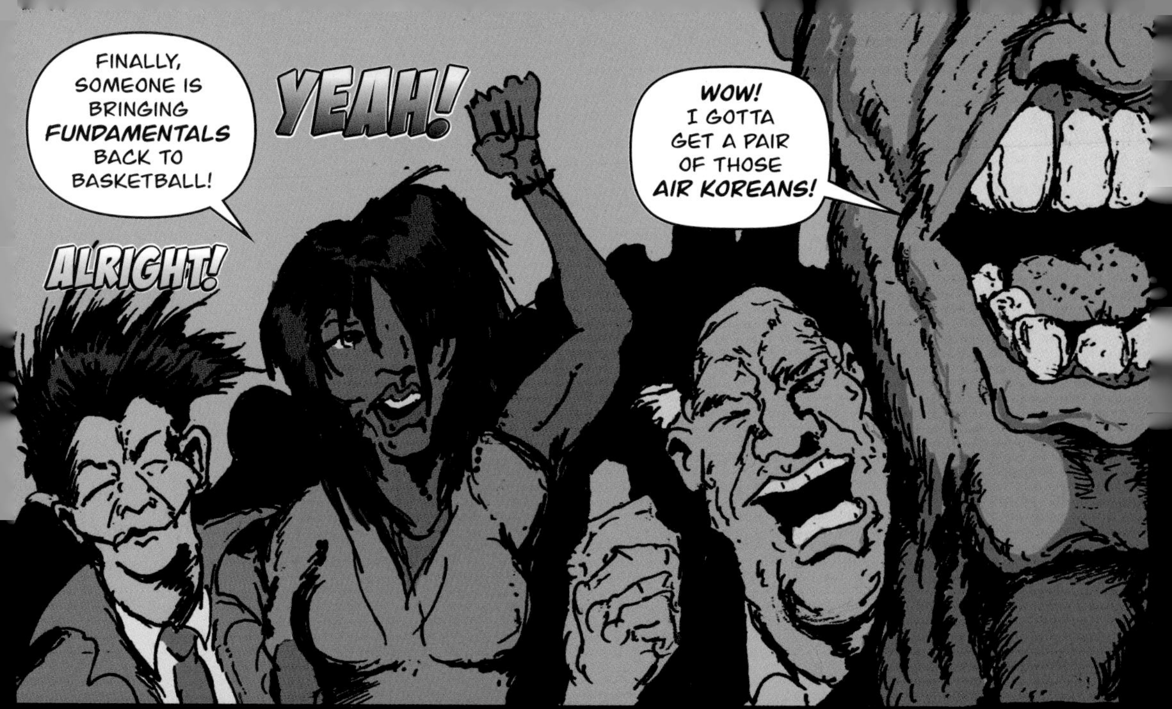
FINALLY, SOMEONE IS BRINGING FUNDAMENTALS BACK TO BASKETBALL!
YEAH!
WOW! I GOTTA GET A PAIR OF THOSE AIR KOREANS!
ALRIGHT!

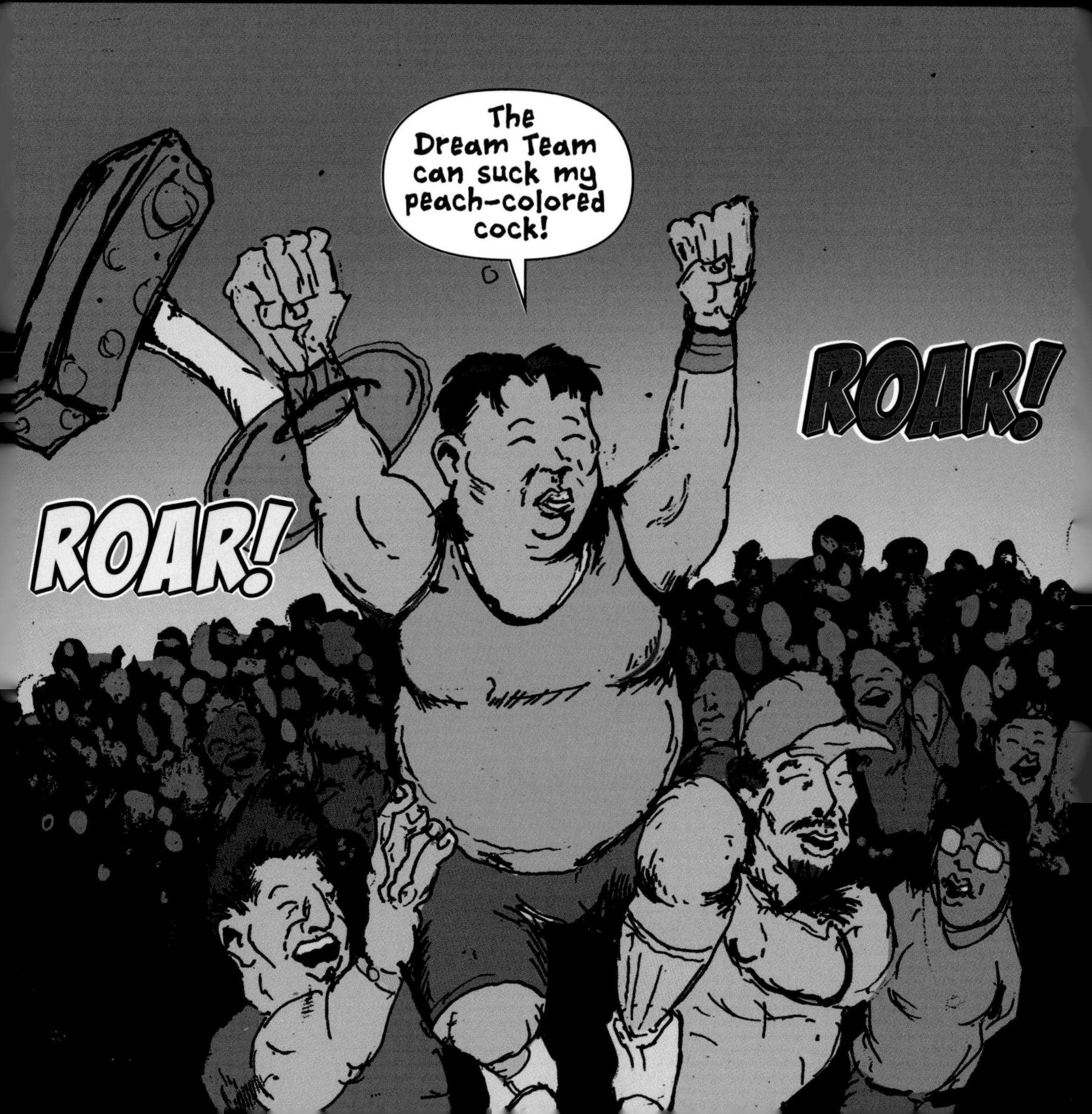
The Dream Team can suck my peach-colored cock!
ROAR!
ROAR!

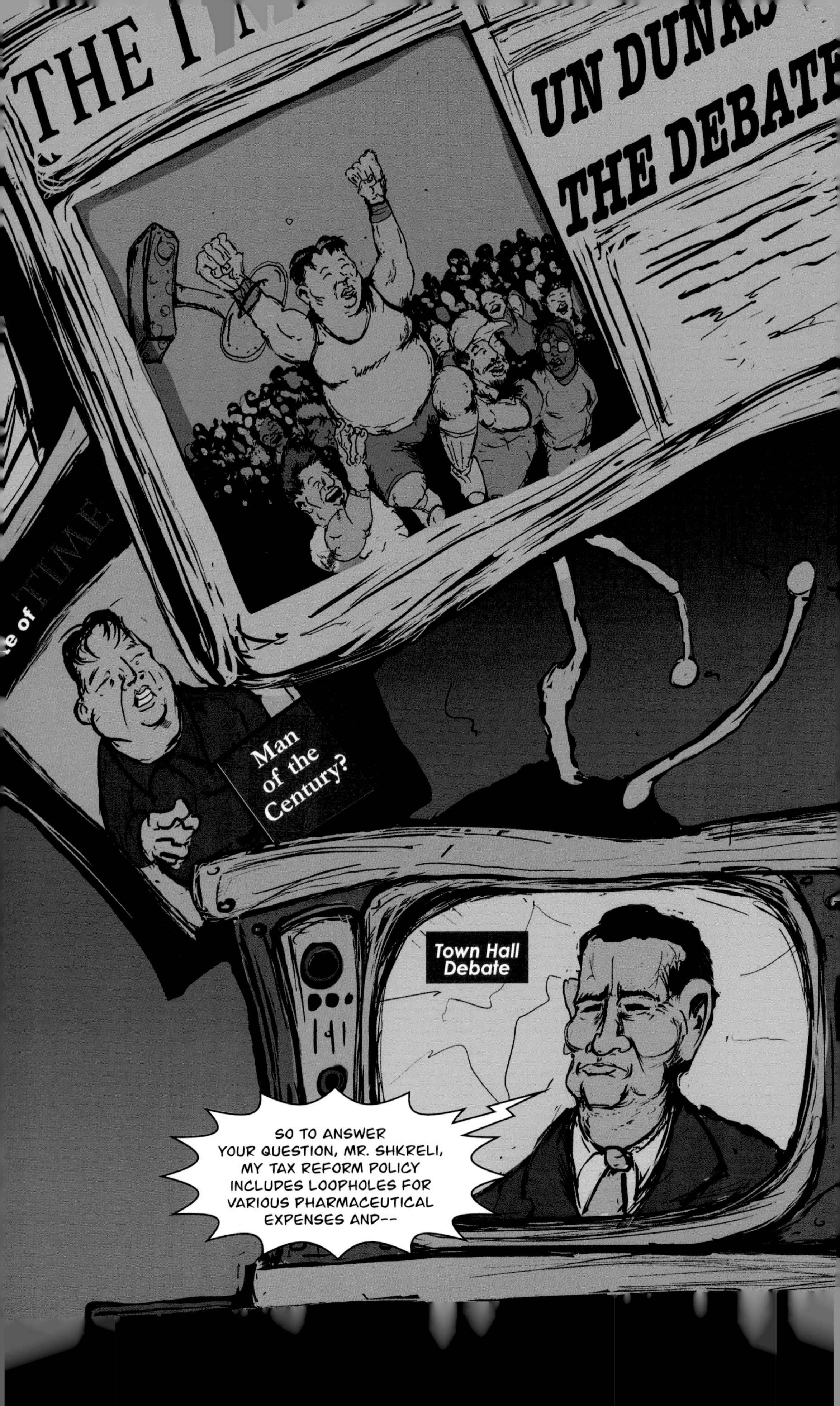
THE T
UN DUNKS THE DEBATE
TIME
Man of the Century?
Town Hall Debate
SO TO ANSWER YOUR QUESTION, MR. SHKRELI, MY TAX REFORM POLICY INCLUDES LOOPHOLES FOR VARIOUS PHARMACEUTICAL EXPENSES AND--

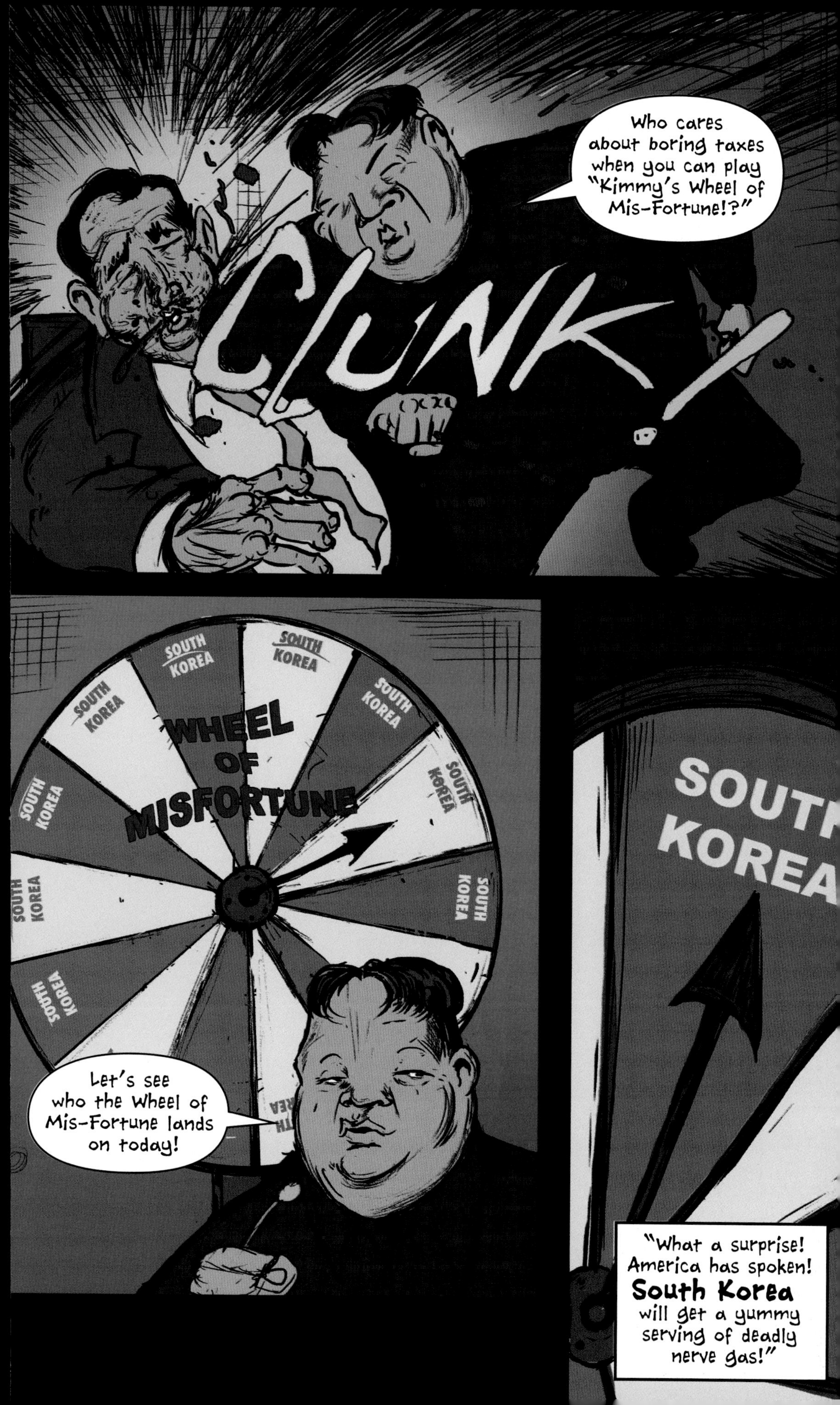
Who cares about boring taxes when you can play "Kimmy's Wheel of Mis-Fortune!?"
CLUNK!
WHEEL OF MISFORTUNE
SOUTH KOREA
Let's see who the Wheel of Mis-Fortune lands on today!
SOUTH KOREA
"What a surprise! America has spoken! South Korea will get a yummy serving of deadly nerve gas!"

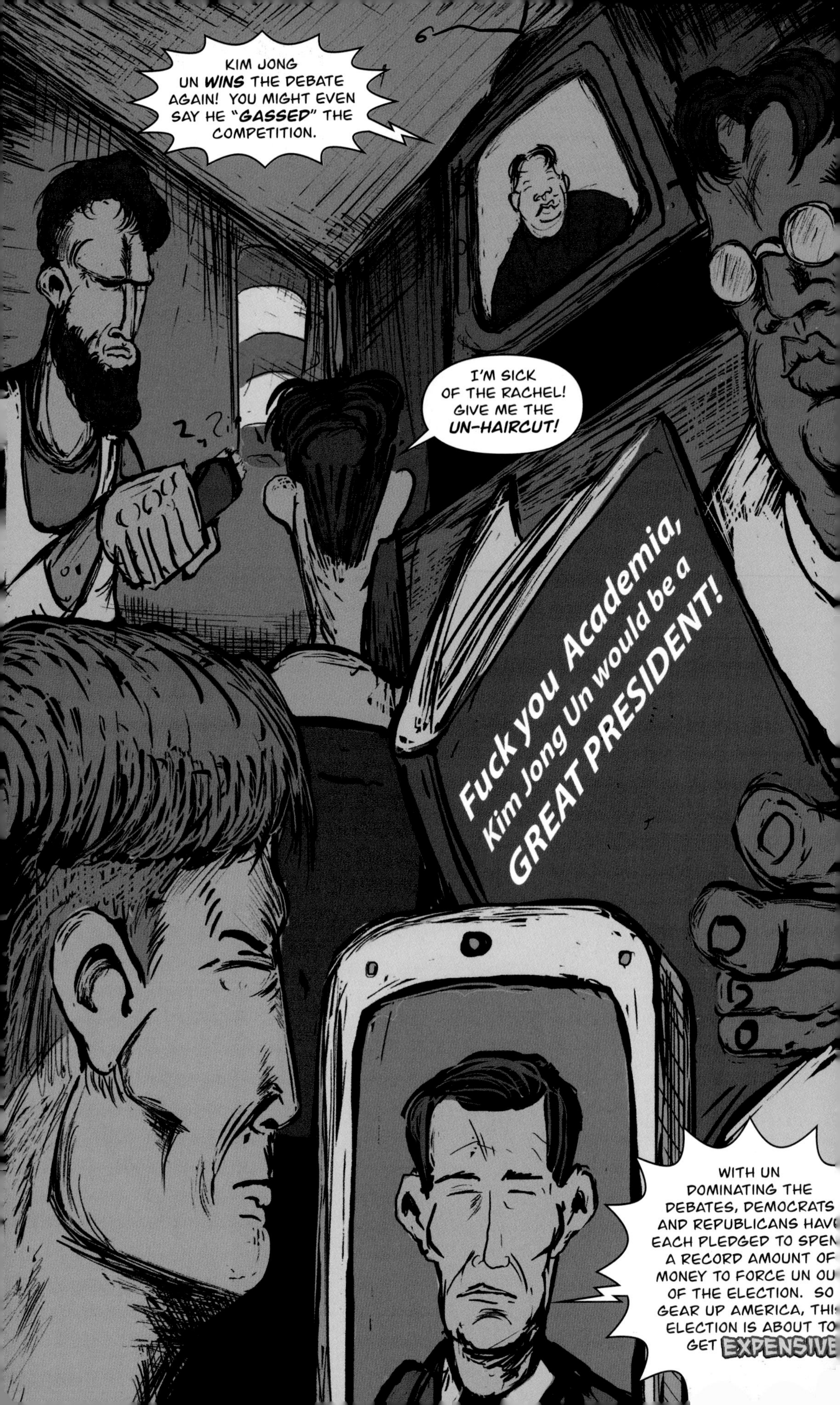
KIM JONG UN **WINS** THE DEBATE AGAIN! YOU MIGHT EVEN SAY HE "**GASSED**" THE COMPETITION.
I'M SICK OF THE RACHEL! GIVE ME THE **UN-HAIRCUT**!
Fuck you Academia, Kim Jong Un would be a GREAT PRESIDENT!
WITH UN DOMINATING THE DEBATES, DEMOCRATS AND REPUBLICANS HAVE EACH PLEDGED TO SPEND A RECORD AMOUNT OF MONEY TO FORCE UN OUT OF THE ELECTION. SO GEAR UP AMERICA, THIS ELECTION IS ABOUT TO GET EXPENSIVE

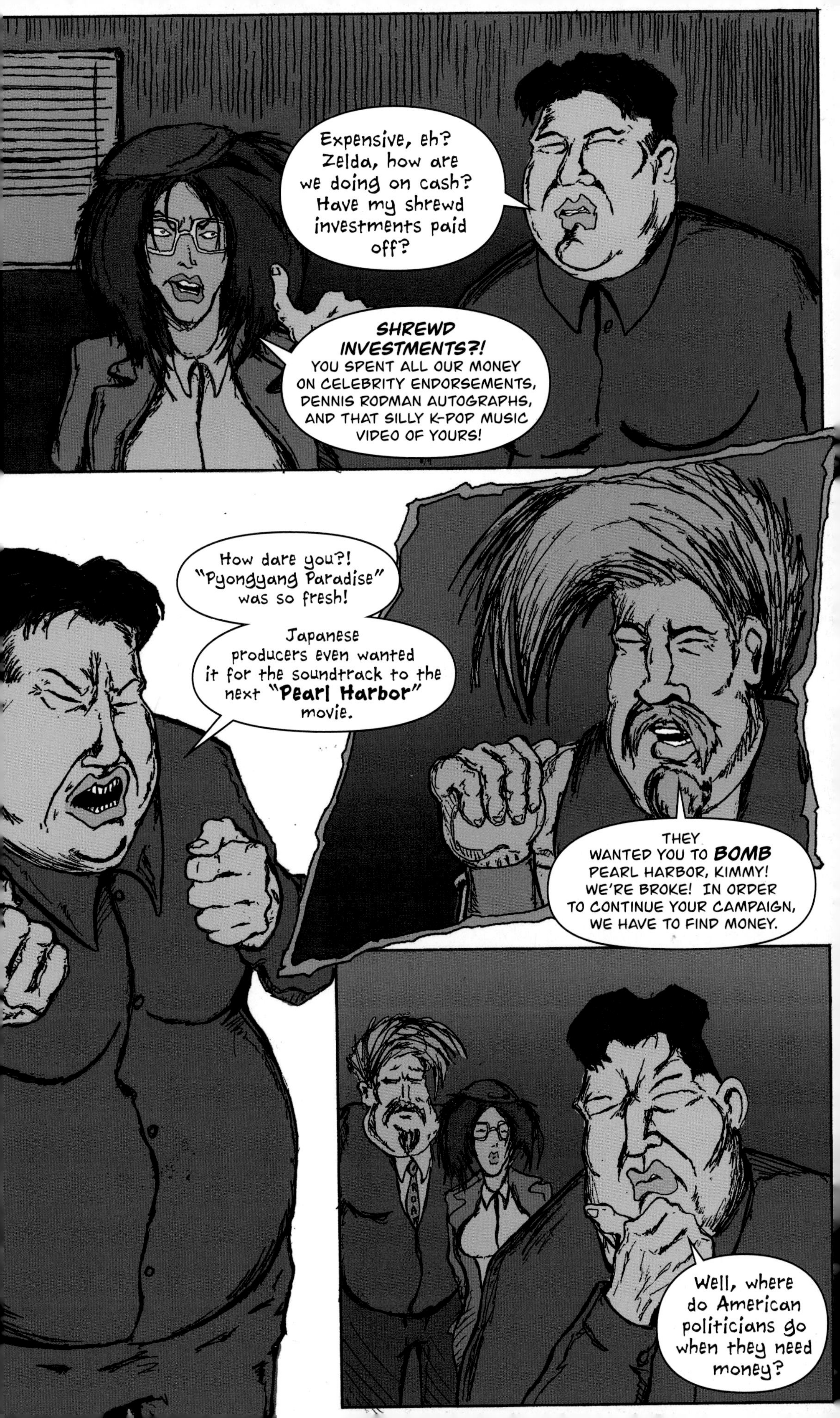
Expensive, eh? Zelda, how are we doing on cash? Have my shrewd investments paid off?
SHREWD INVESTMENTS?! YOU SPENT ALL OUR MONEY ON CELEBRITY ENDORSEMENTS, DENNIS RODMAN AUTOGRAPHS, AND THAT SILLY K-POP MUSIC VIDEO OF YOURS!
How dare you?! "Pyongyang Paradise" was so fresh!
Japanese producers even wanted it for the soundtrack to the next "Pearl Harbor" movie.
THEY WANTED YOU TO BOMB PEARL HARBOR, KIMMY! WE'RE BROKE! IN ORDER TO CONTINUE YOUR CAMPAIGN, WE HAVE TO FIND MONEY.
Well, where do American politicians go when they need money?

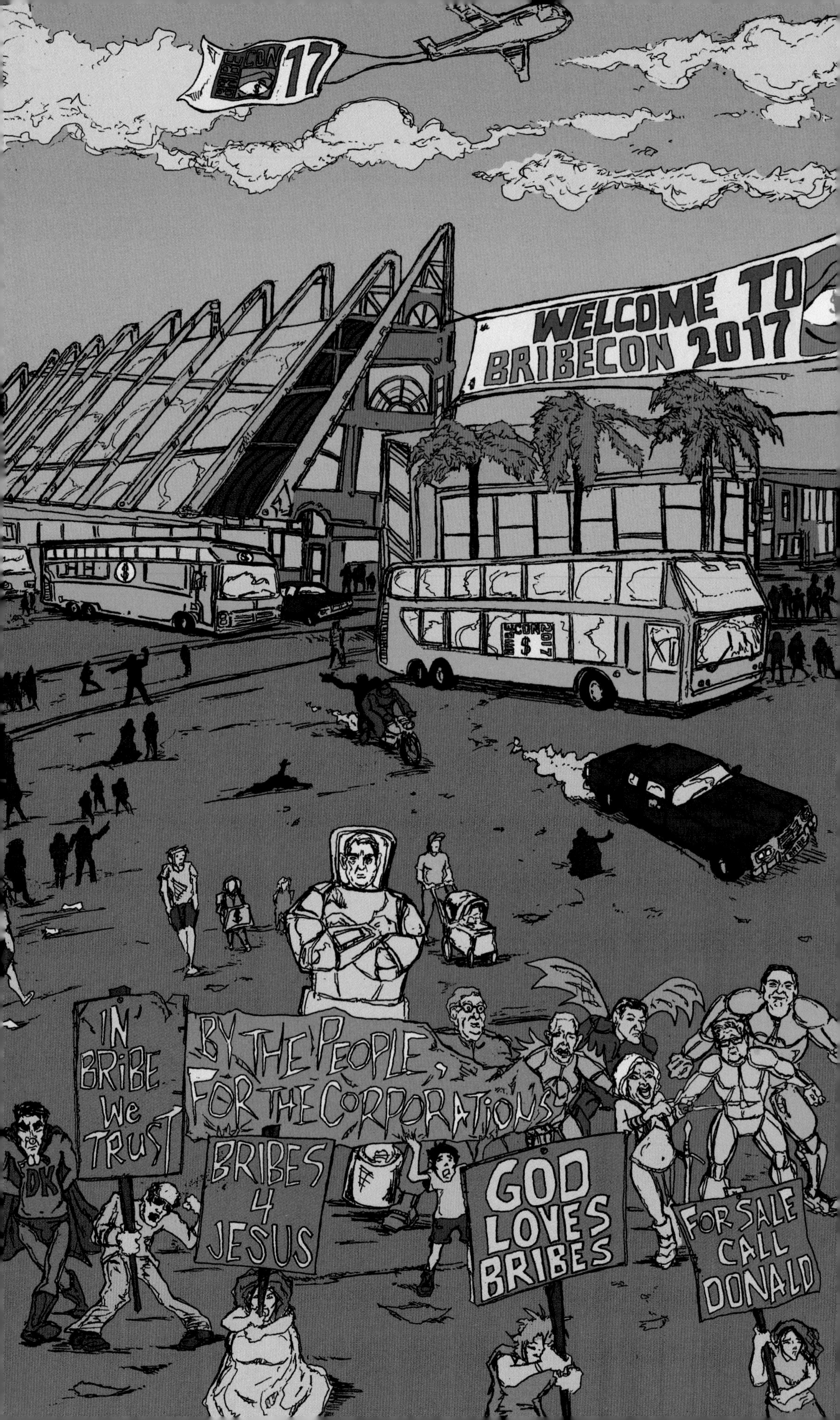
BRIBECON 17
WELCOME TO
BRIBECON 2017
IN BRIBE We TRUST
BY THE PEOPLE, FOR THE CORPORATIONS
BRIBES 4 JESUS
GOD LOVES BRIBES
FOR SALE CALL DONALD

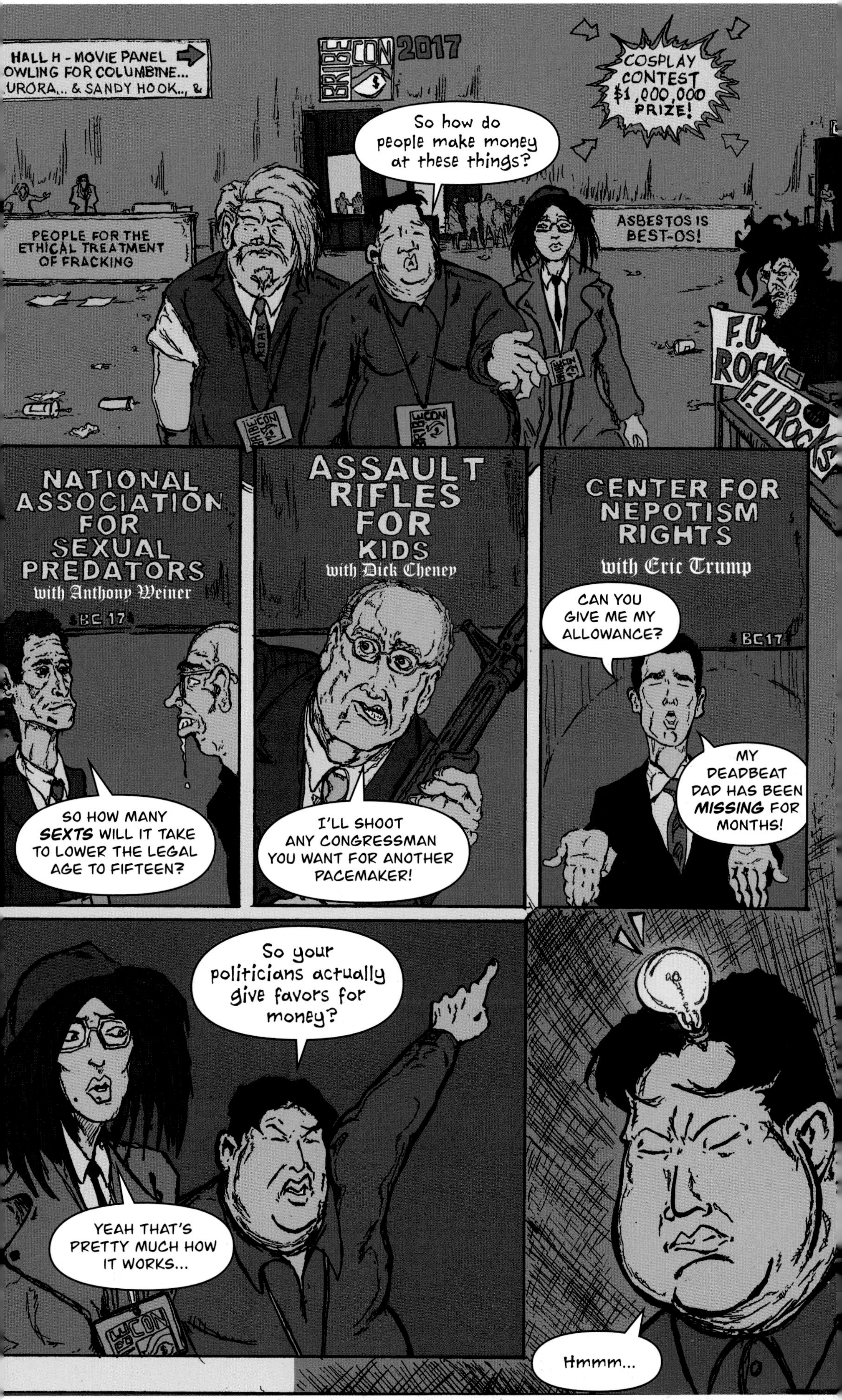
HALL H - MOVIE PANEL
OWLING FOR COLUMBINE...
URORA... & SANDY HOOK..., &
BRIBE CON 2017
COSPLAY CONTEST $1,000,000 PRIZE!
So how do people make money at these things?
PEOPLE FOR THE ETHICAL TREATMENT OF FRACKING
ASBESTOS IS BEST-OS!
F.U. ROCKS
NATIONAL ASSOCIATION FOR SEXUAL PREDATORS
with Anthony Weiner
BC 17
SO HOW MANY SEXTS WILL IT TAKE TO LOWER THE LEGAL AGE TO FIFTEEN?
ASSAULT RIFLES FOR KIDS
with Dick Cheney
I'LL SHOOT ANY CONGRESSMAN YOU WANT FOR ANOTHER PACEMAKER!
CENTER FOR NEPOTISM RIGHTS
with Eric Trump
BC17
CAN YOU GIVE ME MY ALLOWANCE?
MY DEADBEAT DAD HAS BEEN MISSING FOR MONTHS!
So your politicians actually give favors for money?
YEAH THAT'S PRETTY MUCH HOW IT WORKS...
Hmmm...

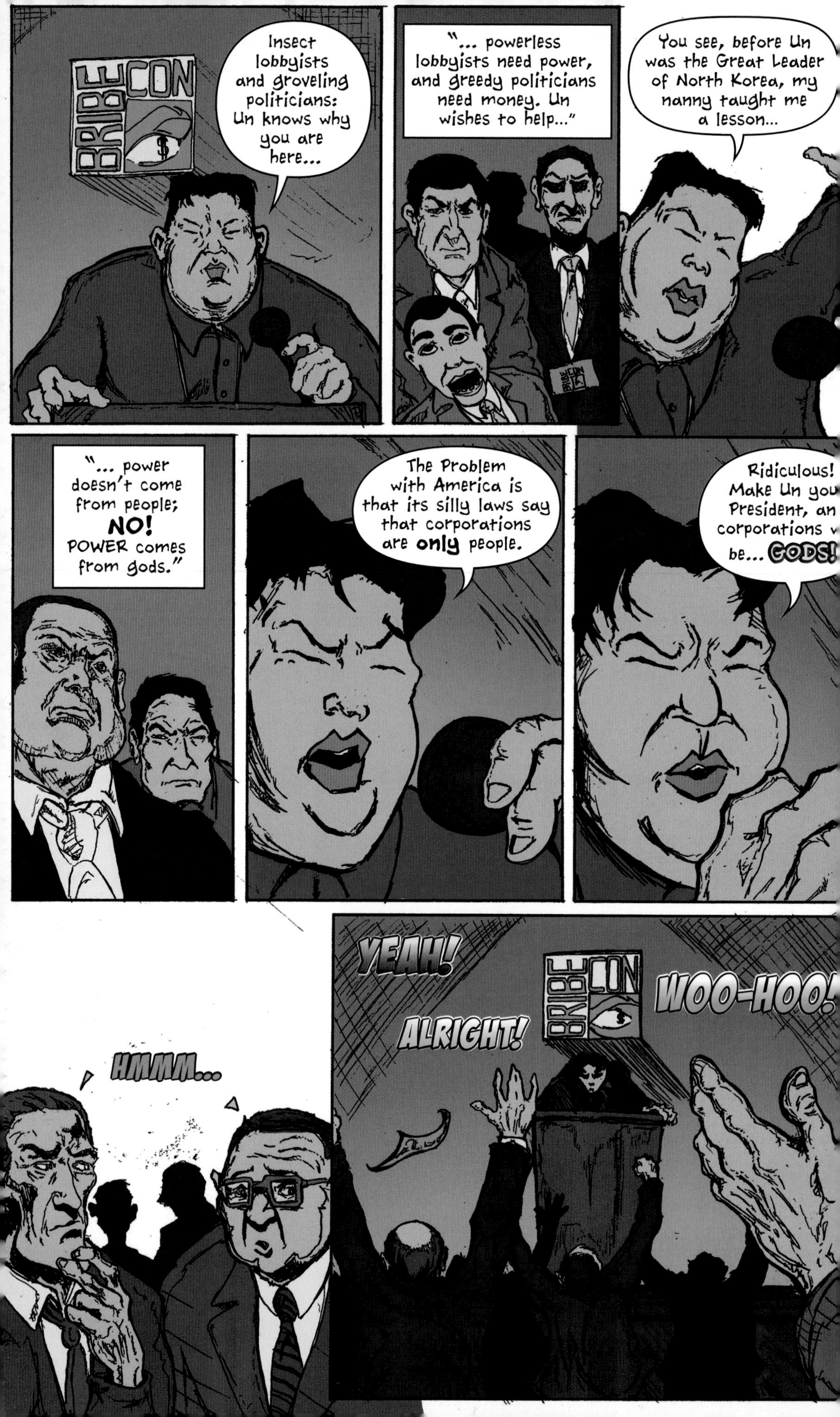
BRIBE CON
Insect lobbyists and groveling politicians: Un knows why you are here...
"... powerless lobbyists need power, and greedy politicians need money. Un wishes to help..."
You see, before Un was the Great Leader of North Korea, my nanny taught me a lesson...
"... power doesn't come from people; NO! POWER comes from gods."
The Problem with America is that its silly laws say that corporations are only people.
Ridiculous! Make Un you President, an corporations be... GODS!
HMMM...
YEAH!
ALRIGHT!
BRIBE CON
WOO-HOO!

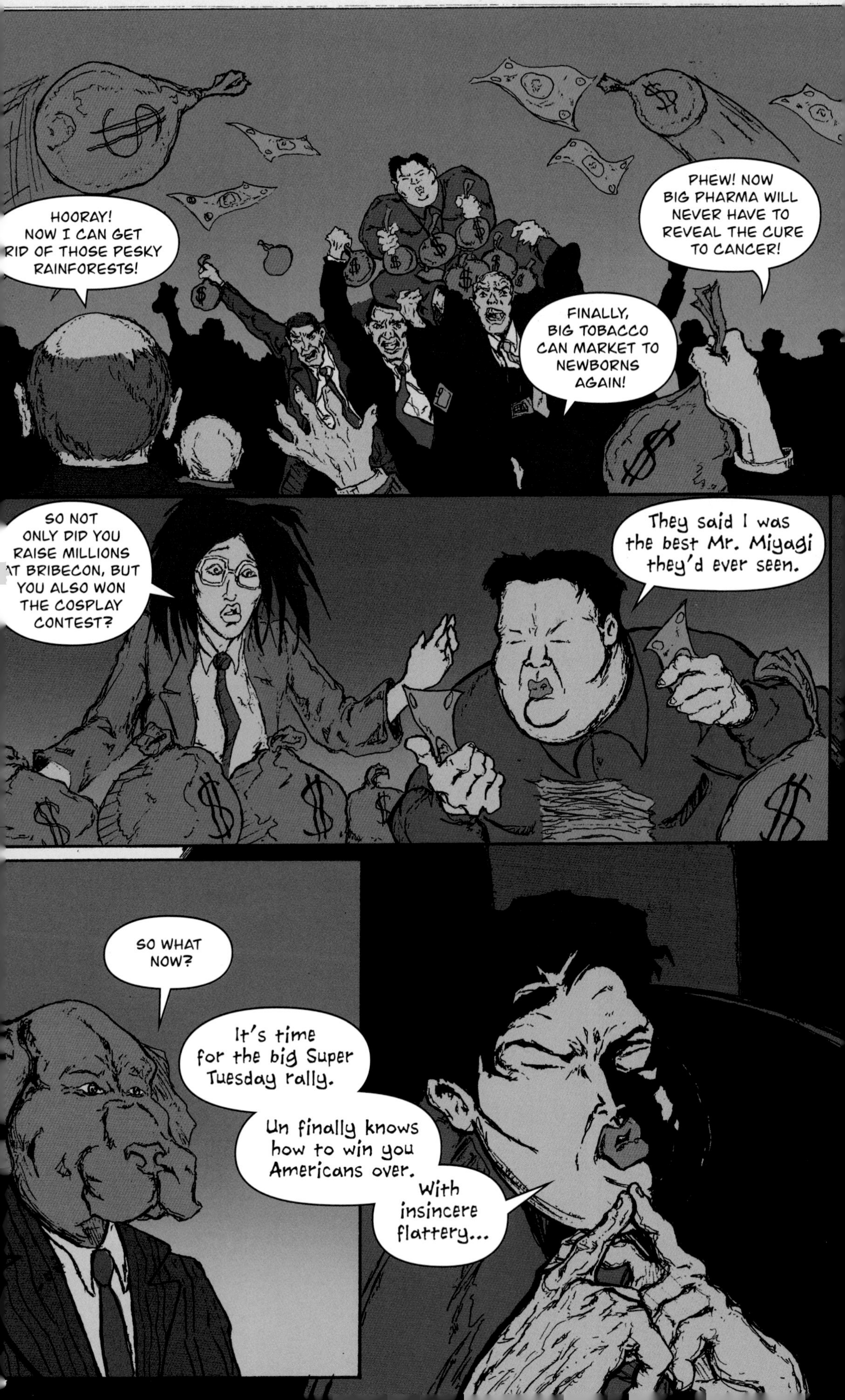
HOORAY! NOW I CAN GET RID OF THOSE PESKY RAINFORESTS!
FINALLY, BIG TOBACCO CAN MARKET TO NEWBORNS AGAIN!
PHEW! NOW BIG PHARMA WILL NEVER HAVE TO REVEAL THE CURE TO CANCER!
SO NOT ONLY DID YOU RAISE MILLIONS AT BRIBECON, BUT YOU ALSO WON THE COSPLAY CONTEST?
They said I was the best Mr. Miyagi they'd ever seen.
SO WHAT NOW?
It's time for the big Super Tuesday rally.
Un finally knows how to win you Americans over.
With insincere flattery...

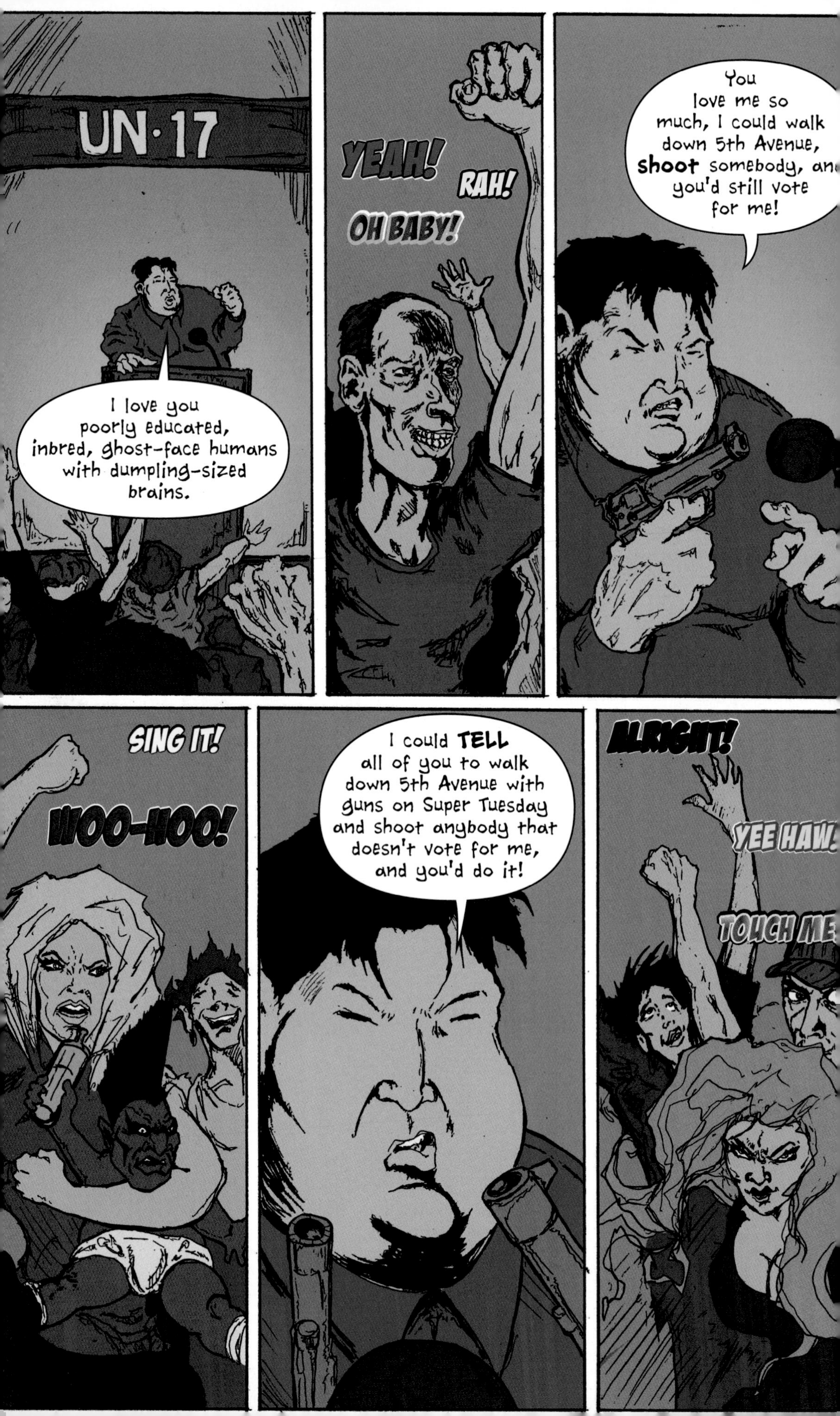
UN-17
I love you poorly educated, inbred, ghost-face humans with dumpling-sized brains.
YEAH!
RAH!
OH BABY!
You love me so much, I could walk down 5th Avenue, **shoot** somebody, an you'd still vote for me!
SING IT!
WOO-HOO!
I could **TELL** all of you to walk down 5th Avenue with guns on Super Tuesday and shoot anybody that doesn't vote for me, and you'd do it!
ALRIGHT!
YEE HAW.
TOUCH ME

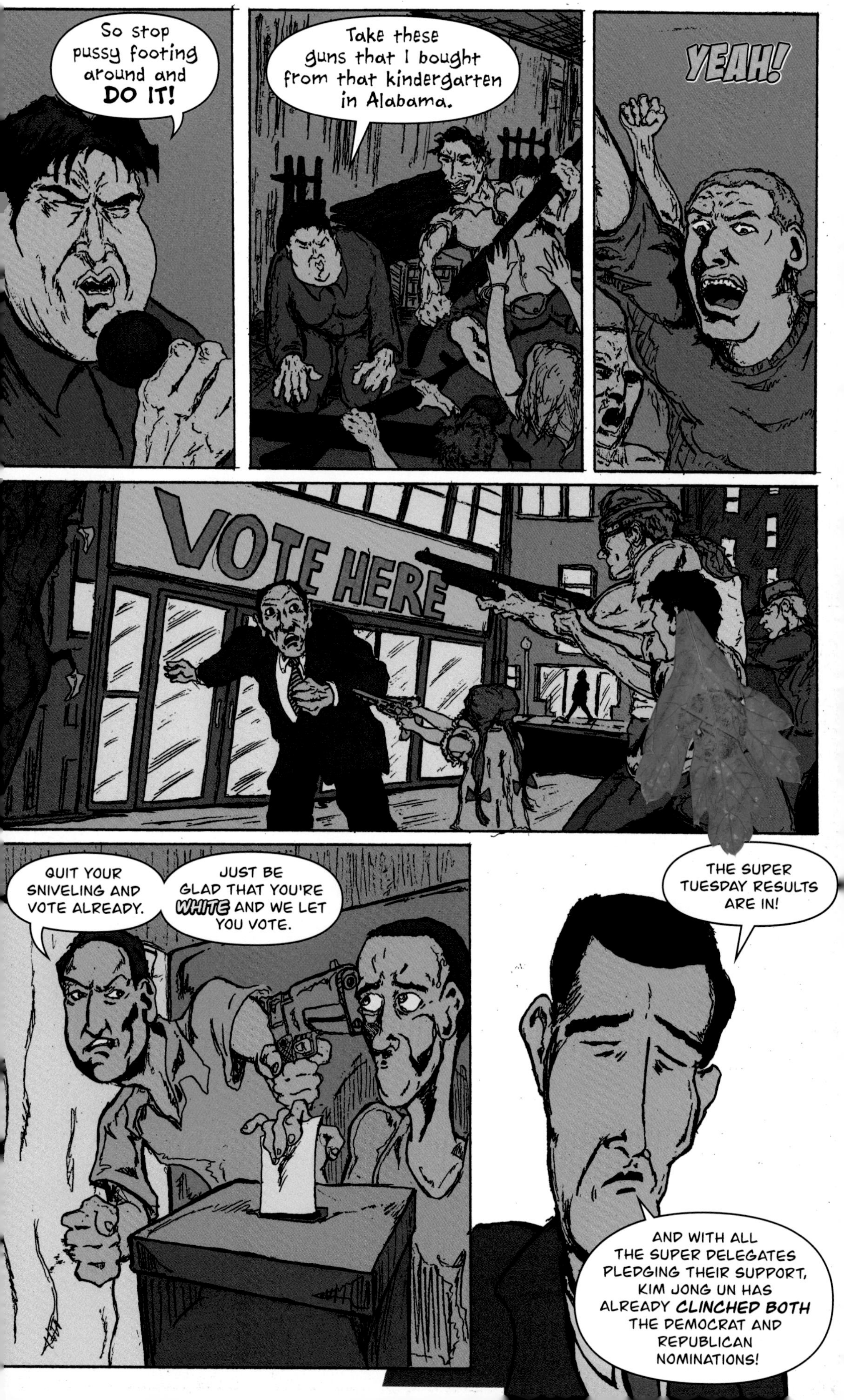
So stop pussy footing around and DO IT!
Take these guns that I bought from that kindergarten in Alabama.
YEAH!
VOTE HERE
QUIT YOUR SNIVELING AND VOTE ALREADY.
JUST BE GLAD THAT YOU'RE WHITE AND WE LET YOU VOTE.
THE SUPER TUESDAY RESULTS ARE IN!
AND WITH ALL THE SUPER DELEGATES PLEDGING THEIR SUPPORT, KIM JONG UN HAS ALREADY CLINCHED BOTH THE DEMOCRAT AND REPUBLICAN NOMINATIONS!

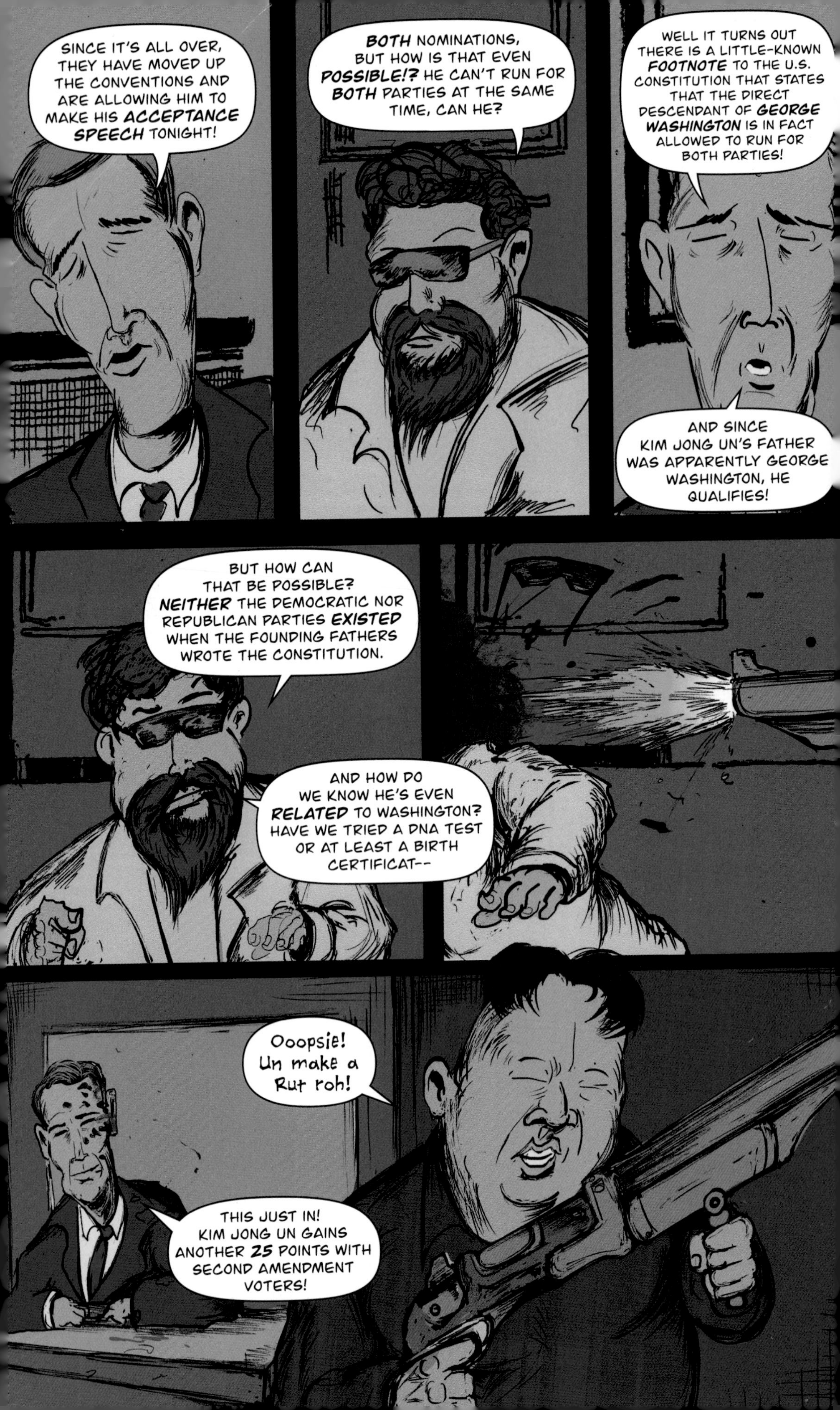
SINCE IT'S ALL OVER, THEY HAVE MOVED UP THE CONVENTIONS AND ARE ALLOWING HIM TO MAKE HIS ACCEPTANCE SPEECH TONIGHT!
BOTH NOMINATIONS, BUT HOW IS THAT EVEN POSSIBLE!? HE CAN'T RUN FOR BOTH PARTIES AT THE SAME TIME, CAN HE?
WELL IT TURNS OUT THERE IS A LITTLE-KNOWN FOOTNOTE TO THE U.S. CONSTITUTION THAT STATES THAT THE DIRECT DESCENDANT OF GEORGE WASHINGTON IS IN FACT ALLOWED TO RUN FOR BOTH PARTIES!
AND SINCE KIM JONG UN'S FATHER WAS APPARENTLY GEORGE WASHINGTON, HE QUALIFIES!
BUT HOW CAN THAT BE POSSIBLE? NEITHER THE DEMOCRATIC NOR REPUBLICAN PARTIES EXISTED WHEN THE FOUNDING FATHERS WROTE THE CONSTITUTION.
AND HOW DO WE KNOW HE'S EVEN RELATED TO WASHINGTON? HAVE WE TRIED A DNA TEST OR AT LEAST A BIRTH CERTIFICAT--
Ooopsie! Un make a Rut roh!
THIS JUST IN! KIM JONG UN GAINS ANOTHER 25 POINTS WITH SECOND AMENDMENT VOTERS!

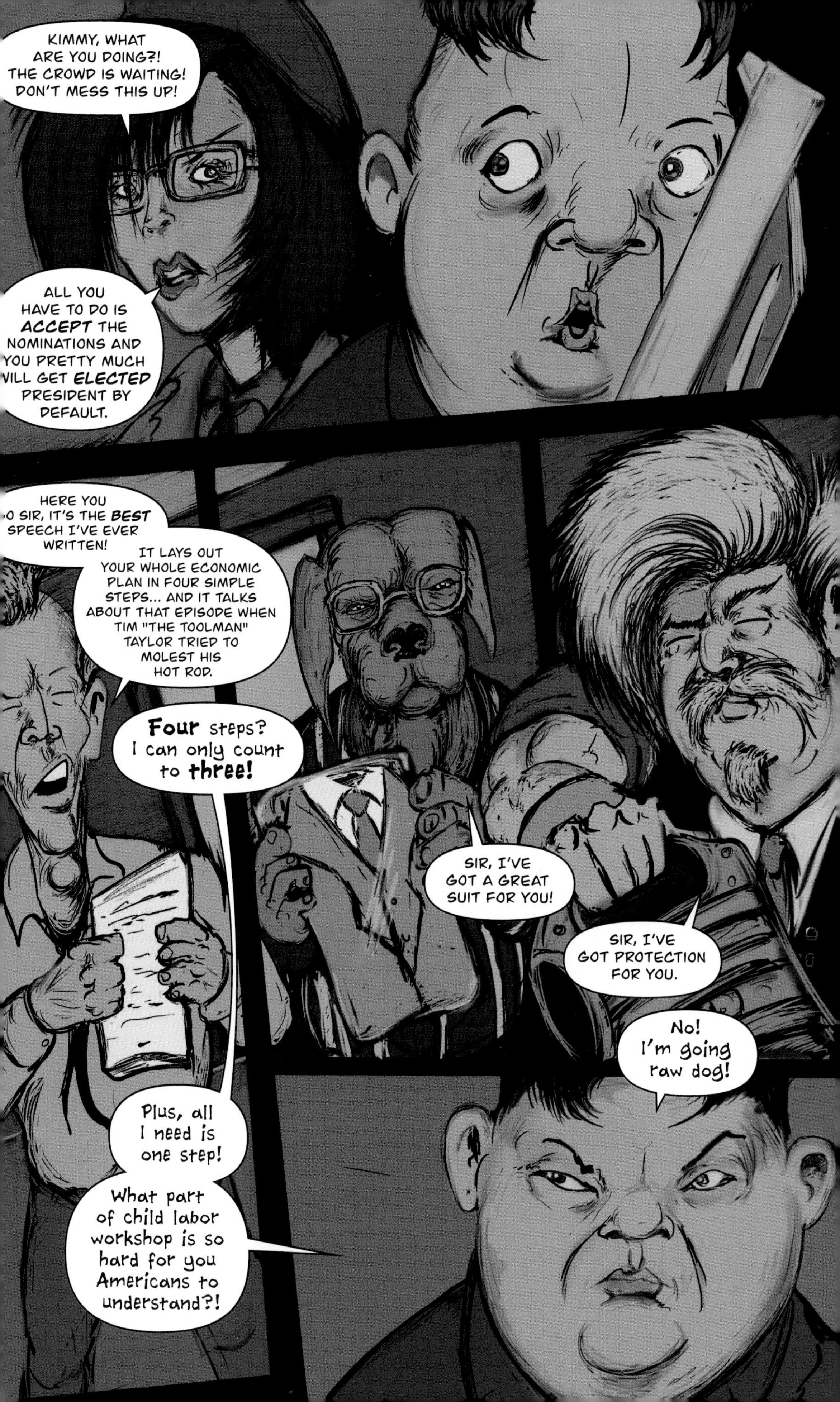
KIMMY, WHAT ARE YOU DOING?! THE CROWD IS WAITING! DON'T MESS THIS UP!
ALL YOU HAVE TO DO IS ACCEPT THE NOMINATIONS AND YOU PRETTY MUCH WILL GET ELECTED PRESIDENT BY DEFAULT.
HERE YOU GO SIR, IT'S THE BEST SPEECH I'VE EVER WRITTEN!
IT LAYS OUT YOUR WHOLE ECONOMIC PLAN IN FOUR SIMPLE STEPS... AND IT TALKS ABOUT THAT EPISODE WHEN TIM "THE TOOLMAN" TAYLOR TRIED TO MOLEST HIS HOT ROD.
Four steps? I can only count to three!
SIR, I'VE GOT A GREAT SUIT FOR YOU!
SIR, I'VE GOT PROTECTION FOR YOU.
No! I'm going raw dog!
Plus, all I need is one step!
What part of child labor workshop is so hard for you Americans to understand?!

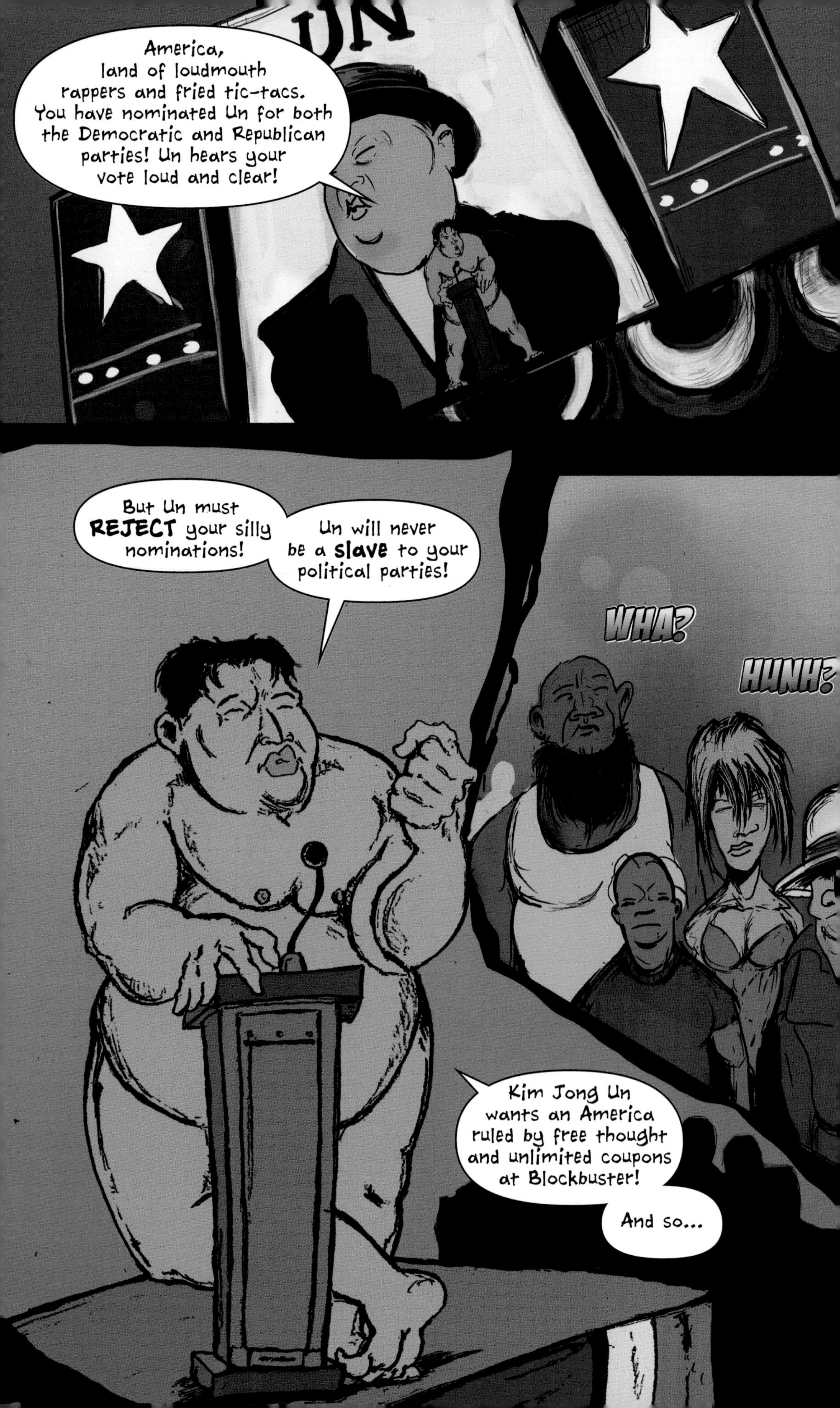
UN
America, land of loudmouth rappers and fried tic-tacs. You have nominated Un for both the Democratic and Republican parties! Un hears your vote loud and clear!
But Un must REJECT your silly nominations!
Un will never be a slave to your political parties!
WHA?
HUNH?
Kim Jong Un wants an America ruled by free thought and unlimited coupons at Blockbuster!
And so...

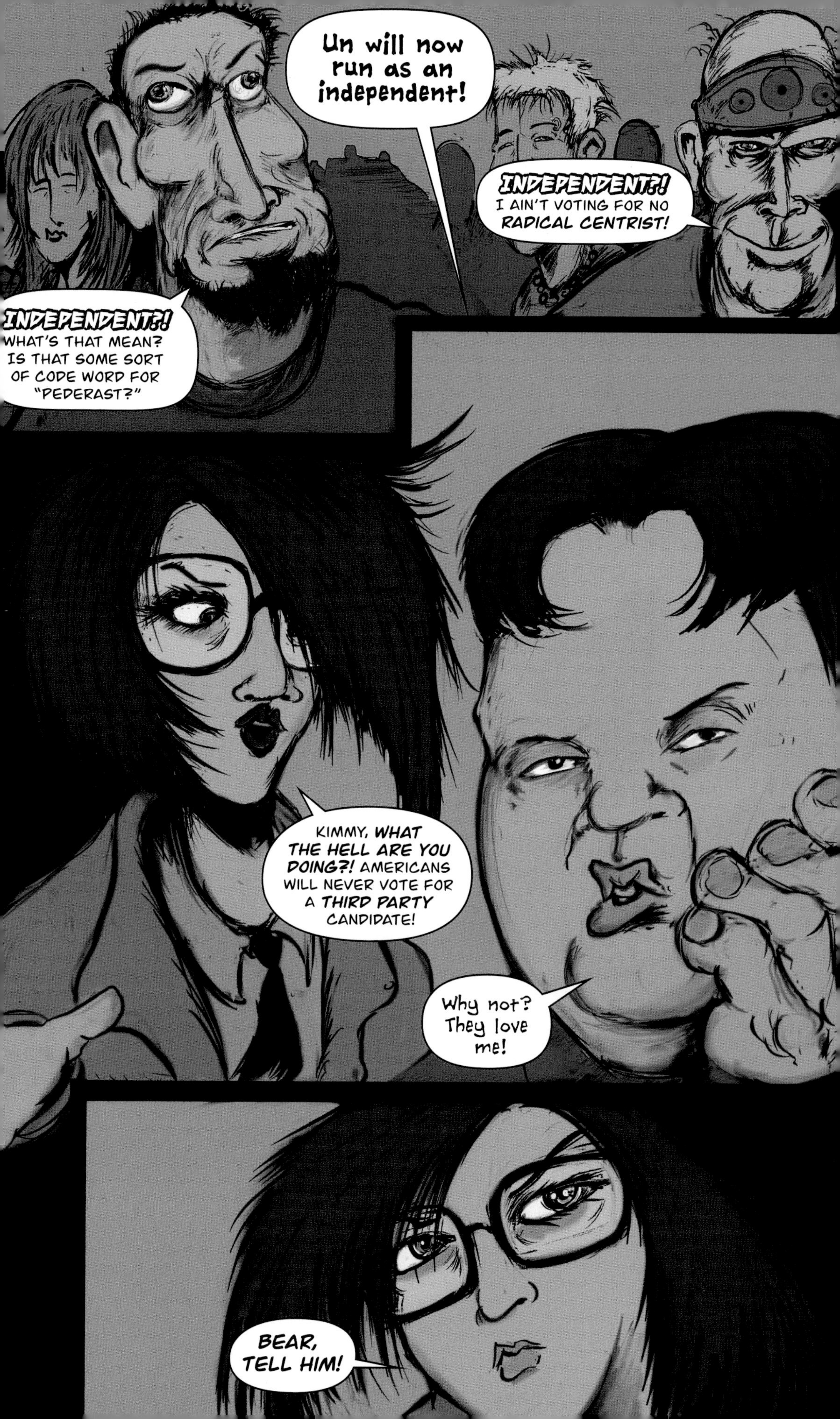
Un will now run as an independent!
INDEPENDENT?! I AIN'T VOTING FOR NO RADICAL CENTRIST!
INDEPENDENT?! WHAT'S THAT MEAN? IS THAT SOME SORT OF CODE WORD FOR "PEDERAST?"
KIMMY, WHAT THE HELL ARE YOU DOING?! AMERICANS WILL NEVER VOTE FOR A THIRD PARTY CANDIDATE!
Why not? They love me!
BEAR, TELL HIM!

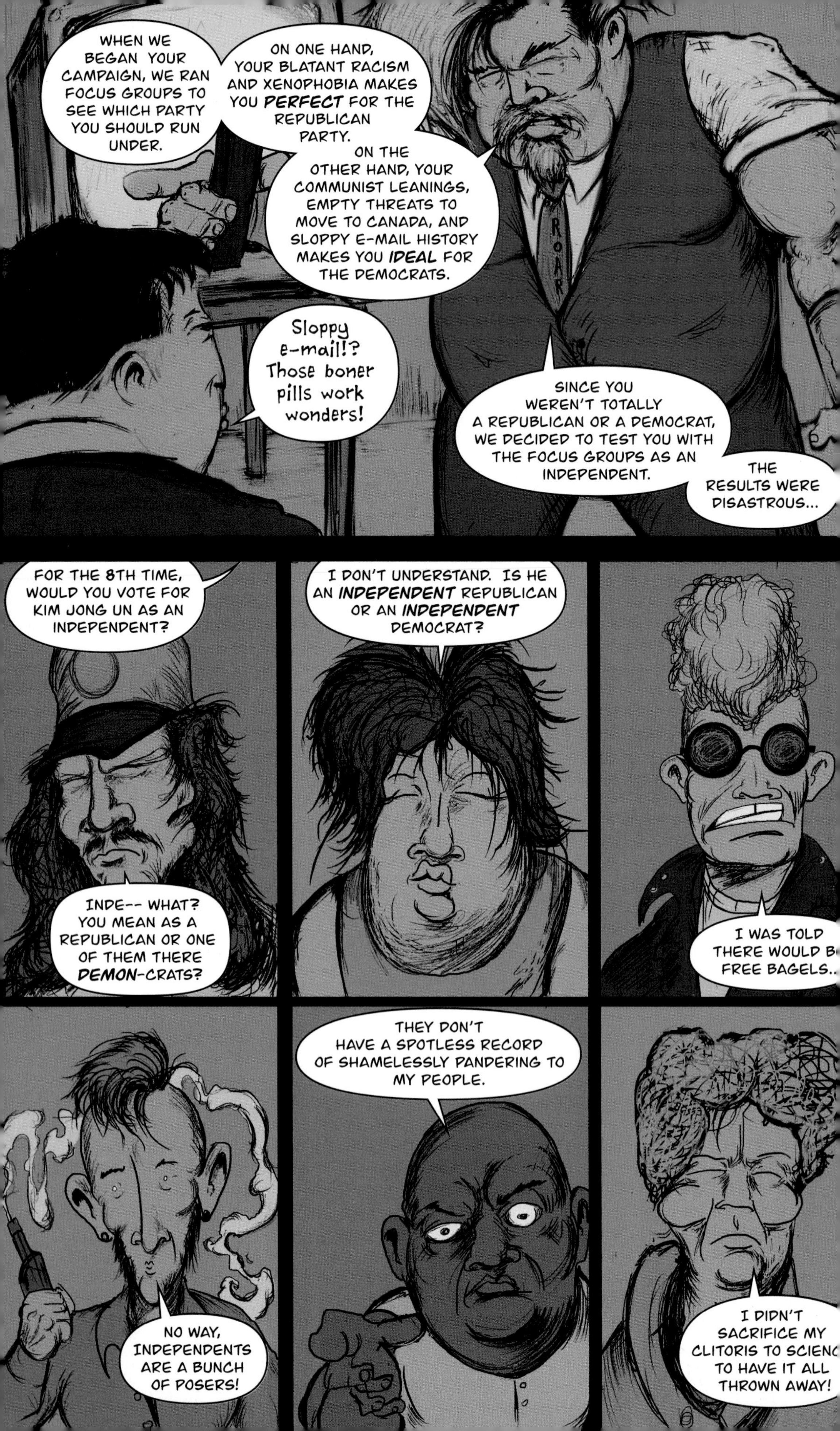

WHEN WE BEGAN YOUR CAMPAIGN, WE RAN FOCUS GROUPS TO SEE WHICH PARTY YOU SHOULD RUN UNDER.
ON ONE HAND, YOUR BLATANT RACISM AND XENOPHOBIA MAKES YOU PERFECT FOR THE REPUBLICAN PARTY.
ON THE OTHER HAND, YOUR COMMUNIST LEANINGS, EMPTY THREATS TO MOVE TO CANADA, AND SLOPPY E-MAIL HISTORY MAKES YOU IDEAL FOR THE DEMOCRATS.
ROAR
Sloppy e-mail!? Those boner pills work wonders!
SINCE YOU WEREN'T TOTALLY A REPUBLICAN OR A DEMOCRAT, WE DECIDED TO TEST YOU WITH THE FOCUS GROUPS AS AN INDEPENDENT.
THE RESULTS WERE DISASTROUS...
FOR THE 8TH TIME, WOULD YOU VOTE FOR KIM JONG UN AS AN INDEPENDENT?
INDE-- WHAT? YOU MEAN AS A REPUBLICAN OR ONE OF THEM THERE DEMON-CRATS?
I DON'T UNDERSTAND. IS HE AN INDEPENDENT REPUBLICAN OR AN INDEPENDENT DEMOCRAT?
I WAS TOLD THERE WOULD B FREE BAGELS..
NO WAY, INDEPENDENTS ARE A BUNCH OF POSERS!
THEY DON'T HAVE A SPOTLESS RECORD OF SHAMELESSLY PANDERING TO MY PEOPLE.
I DIDN'T SACRIFICE MY CLITORIS TO SCIENC TO HAVE IT ALL THROWN AWAY!

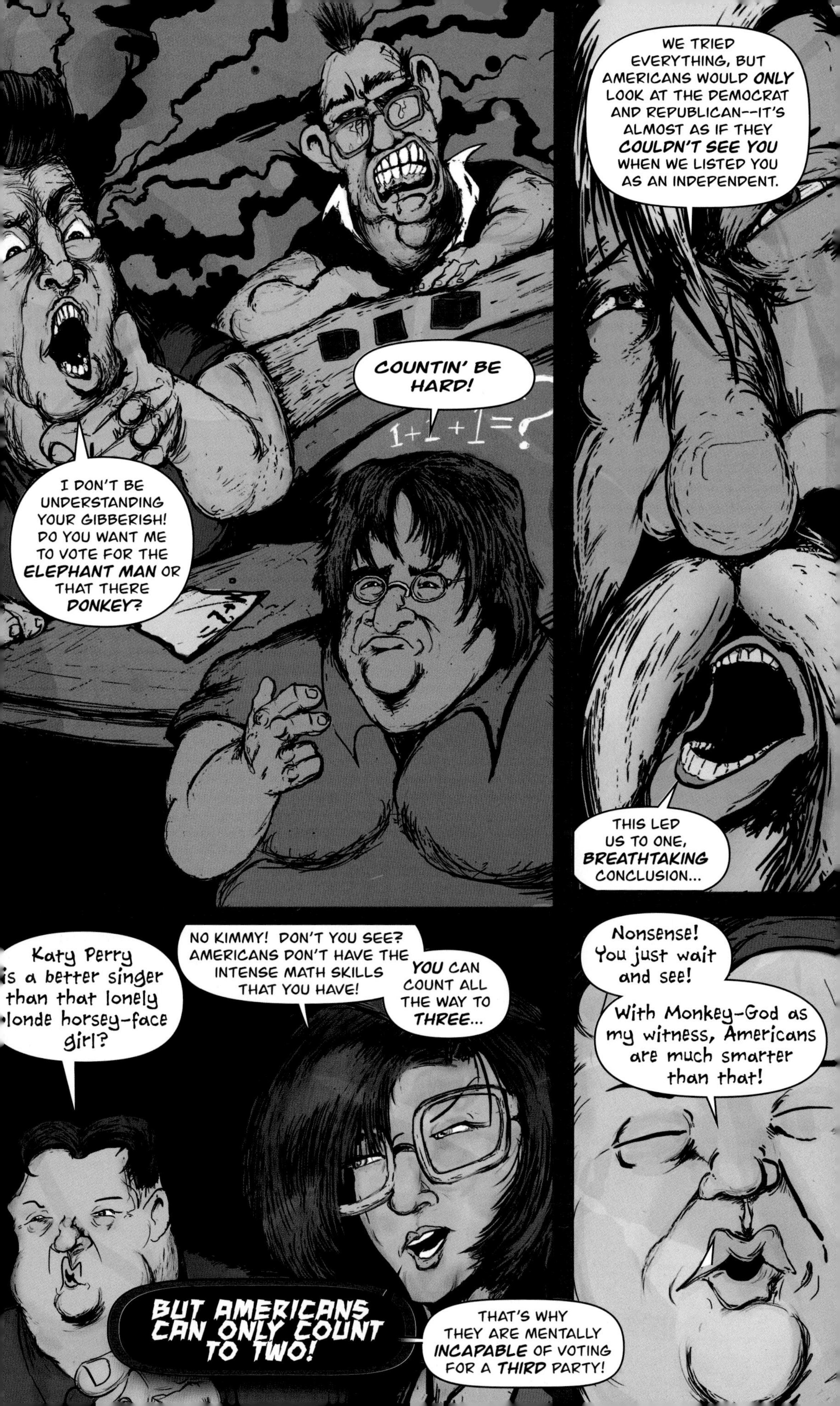
WE TRIED EVERYTHING, BUT AMERICANS WOULD ONLY LOOK AT THE DEMOCRAT AND REPUBLICAN--IT'S ALMOST AS IF THEY COULDN'T SEE YOU WHEN WE LISTED YOU AS AN INDEPENDENT.
COUNTIN' BE HARD!
1+1+1=?
I DON'T BE UNDERSTANDING YOUR GIBBERISH! DO YOU WANT ME TO VOTE FOR THE ELEPHANT MAN OR THAT THERE DONKEY?
THIS LED US TO ONE, BREATHTAKING CONCLUSION...
Katy Perry is a better singer than that lonely blonde horsey-face girl?
NO KIMMY! DON'T YOU SEE? AMERICANS DON'T HAVE THE INTENSE MATH SKILLS THAT YOU HAVE!
YOU CAN COUNT ALL THE WAY TO THREE...
BUT AMERICANS CAN ONLY COUNT TO TWO!
THAT'S WHY THEY ARE MENTALLY INCAPABLE OF VOTING FOR A THIRD PARTY!
Nonsense! You just wait and see!
With Monkey-God as my witness, Americans are much smarter than that!

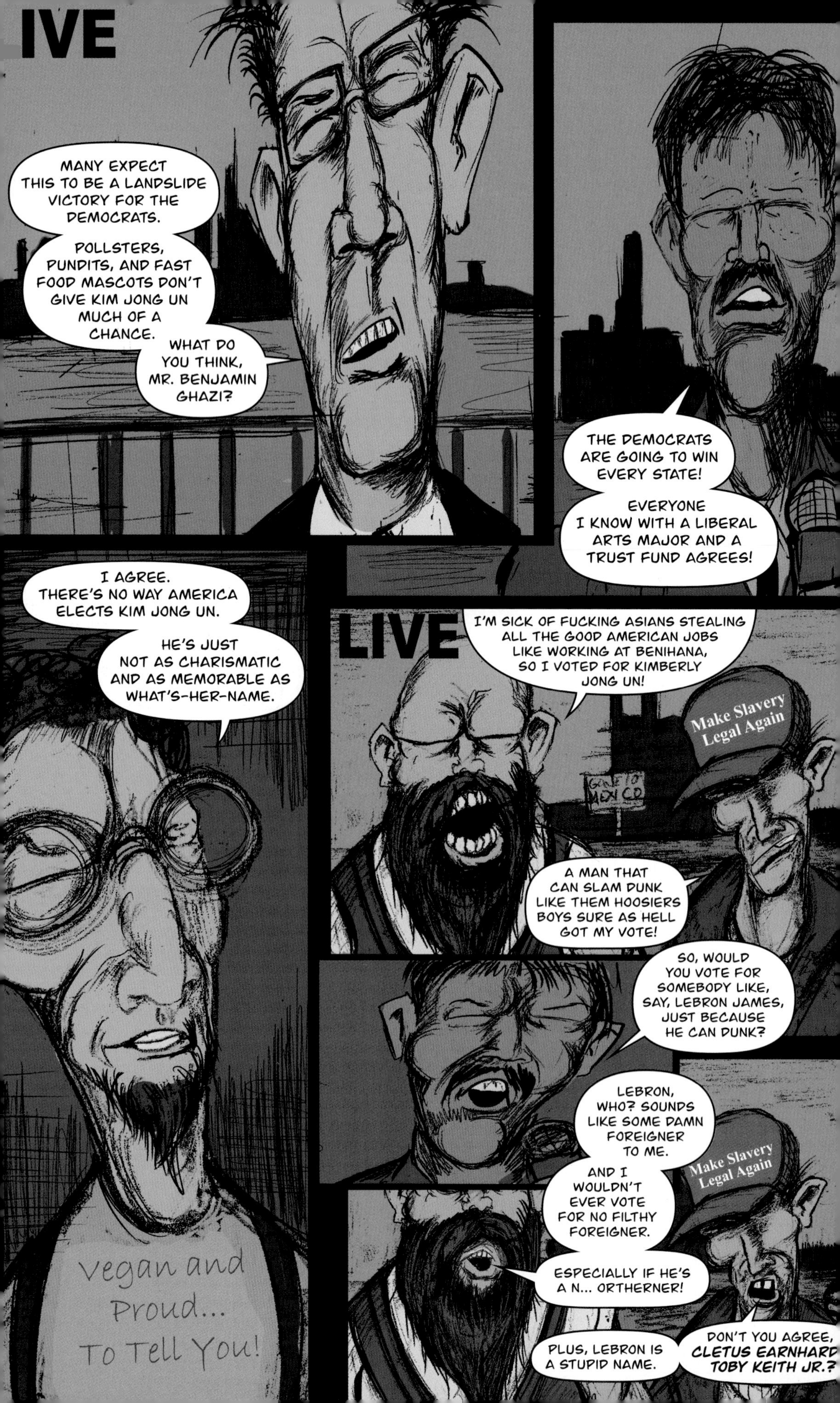
IVE
MANY EXPECT THIS TO BE A LANDSLIDE VICTORY FOR THE DEMOCRATS.
POLLSTERS, PUNDITS, AND FAST FOOD MASCOTS DON'T GIVE KIM JONG UN MUCH OF A CHANCE.
WHAT DO YOU THINK, MR. BENJAMIN GHAZI?
THE DEMOCRATS ARE GOING TO WIN EVERY STATE!
EVERYONE I KNOW WITH A LIBERAL ARTS MAJOR AND A TRUST FUND AGREES!
I AGREE. THERE'S NO WAY AMERICA ELECTS KIM JONG UN.
HE'S JUST NOT AS CHARISMATIC AND AS MEMORABLE AS WHAT'S-HER-NAME.
Vegan and Proud... To Tell You!
LIVE
I'M SICK OF FUCKING ASIANS STEALING ALL THE GOOD AMERICAN JOBS LIKE WORKING AT BENIHANA, SO I VOTED FOR KIMBERLY JONG UN!
Make Slavery Legal Again
A MAN THAT CAN SLAM DUNK LIKE THEM HOOSIERS BOYS SURE AS HELL GOT MY VOTE!
SO, WOULD YOU VOTE FOR SOMEBODY LIKE, SAY, LEBRON JAMES, JUST BECAUSE HE CAN DUNK?
LEBRON, WHO? SOUNDS LIKE SOME DAMN FOREIGNER TO ME.
AND I WOULDN'T EVER VOTE FOR NO FILTHY FOREIGNER.
Make Slavery Legal Again
ESPECIALLY IF HE'S A N... ORTHERNER!
PLUS, LEBRON IS A STUPID NAME.
DON'T YOU AGREE, CLETUS EARNHARD TOBY KEITH JR.?

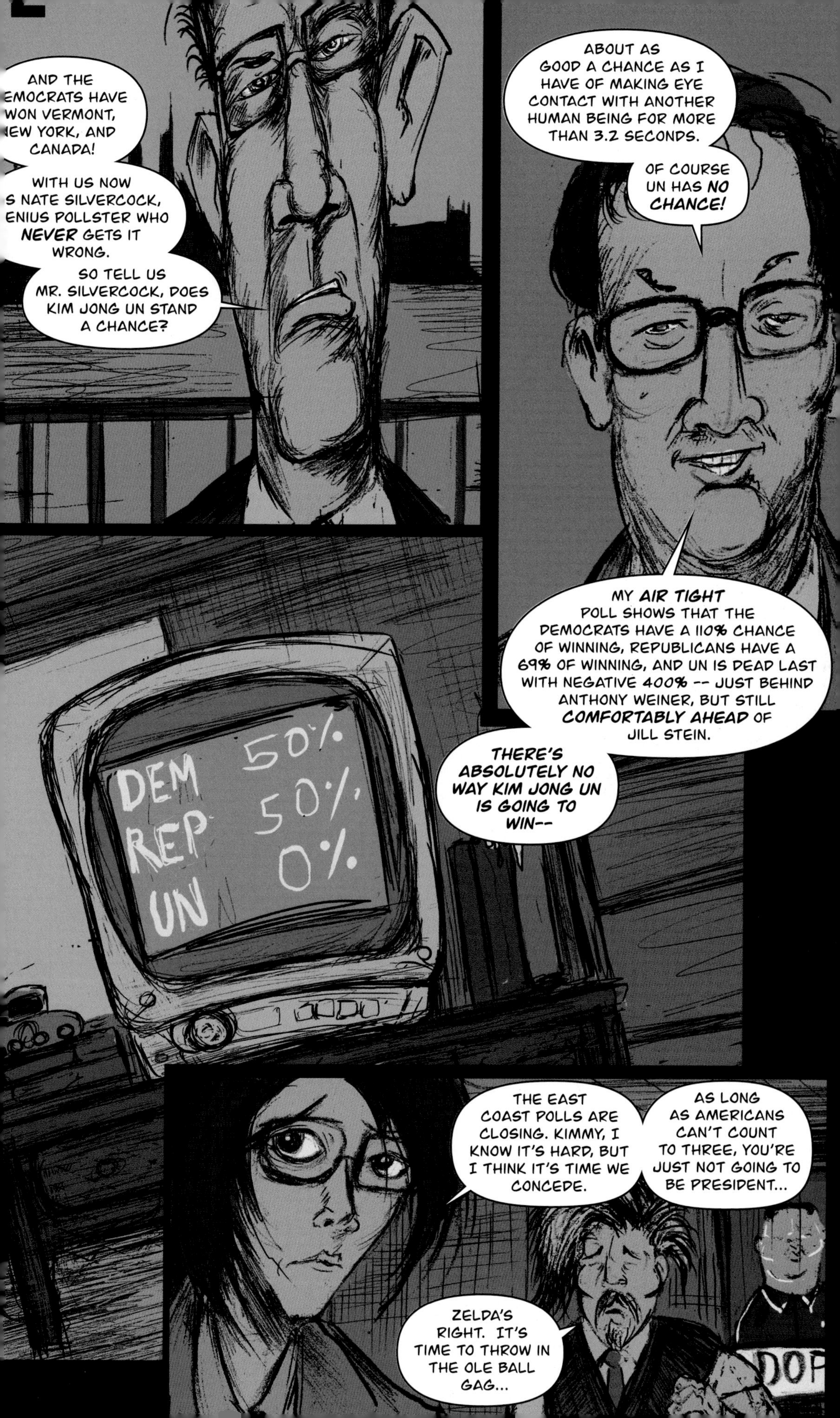
AND THE EMOCRATS HAVE WON VERMONT, NEW YORK, AND CANADA!
WITH US NOW S NATE SILVERCOCK, ENIUS POLLSTER WHO NEVER GETS IT WRONG.
SO TELL US MR. SILVERCOCK, DOES KIM JONG UN STAND A CHANCE?
ABOUT AS GOOD A CHANCE AS I HAVE OF MAKING EYE CONTACT WITH ANOTHER HUMAN BEING FOR MORE THAN 3.2 SECONDS.
OF COURSE UN HAS NO CHANCE!
MY AIR TIGHT POLL SHOWS THAT THE DEMOCRATS HAVE A 110% CHANCE OF WINNING, REPUBLICANS HAVE A 69% OF WINNING, AND UN IS DEAD LAST WITH NEGATIVE 400% -- JUST BEHIND ANTHONY WEINER, BUT STILL COMFORTABLY AHEAD OF JILL STEIN.
DEM 50%
REP 50%
UN 0%
THERE'S ABSOLUTELY NO WAY KIM JONG UN IS GOING TO WIN--
THE EAST COAST POLLS ARE CLOSING. KIMMY, I KNOW IT'S HARD, BUT I THINK IT'S TIME WE CONCEDE.
AS LONG AS AMERICANS CAN'T COUNT TO THREE, YOU'RE JUST NOT GOING TO BE PRESIDENT...
ZELDA'S RIGHT. IT'S TIME TO THROW IN THE OLE BALL GAG...

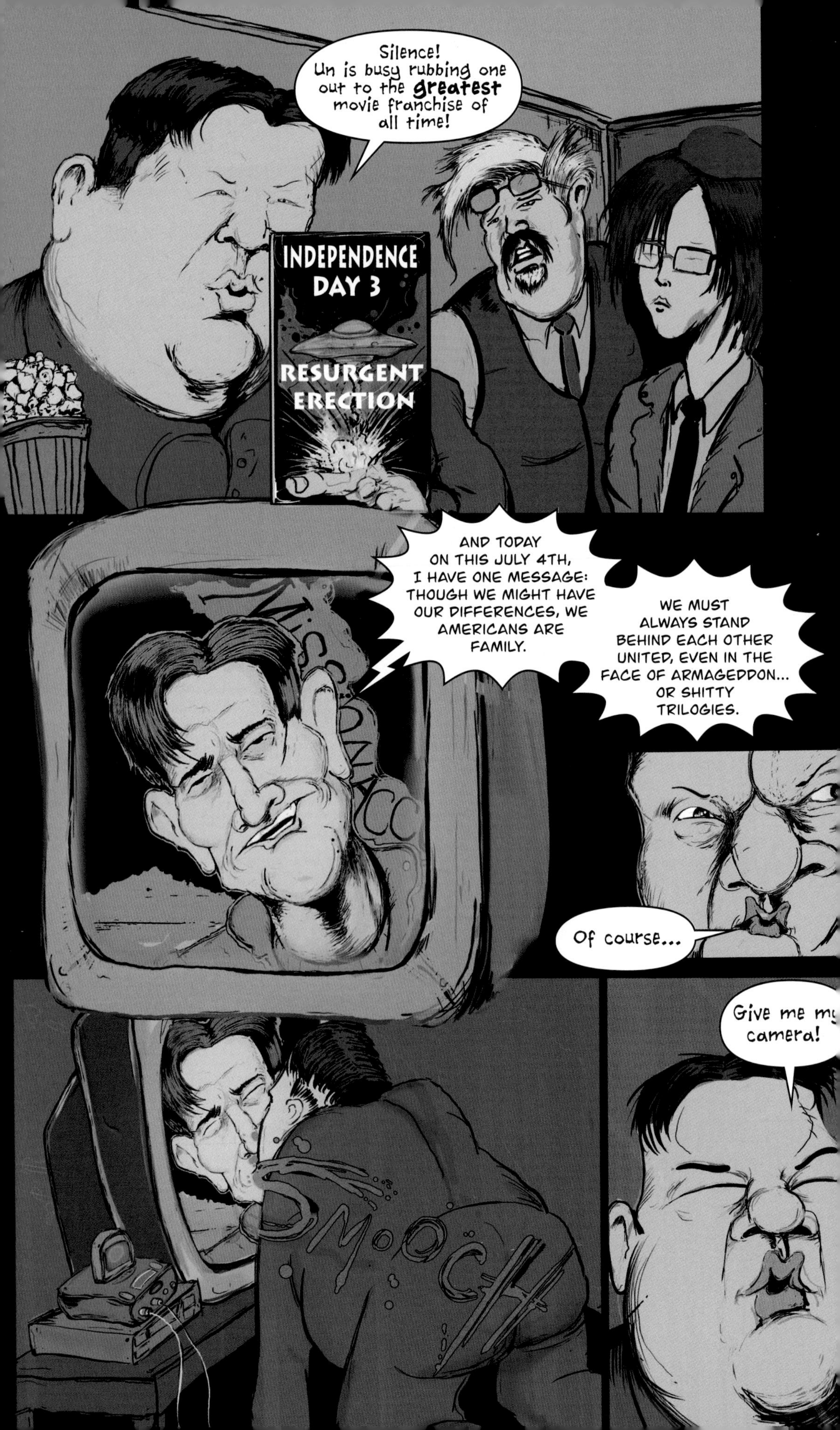
Silence! Un is busy rubbing one out to the greatest movie franchise of all time!
INDEPENDENCE DAY 3
RESURGENT ERECTION
AND TODAY ON THIS JULY 4TH, I HAVE ONE MESSAGE: THOUGH WE MIGHT HAVE OUR DIFFERENCES, WE AMERICANS ARE FAMILY.
WE MUST ALWAYS STAND BEHIND EACH OTHER UNITED, EVEN IN THE FACE OF ARMAGEDDON... OR SHITTY TRILOGIES.
Of course...
SMOOCH
Give me my camera!

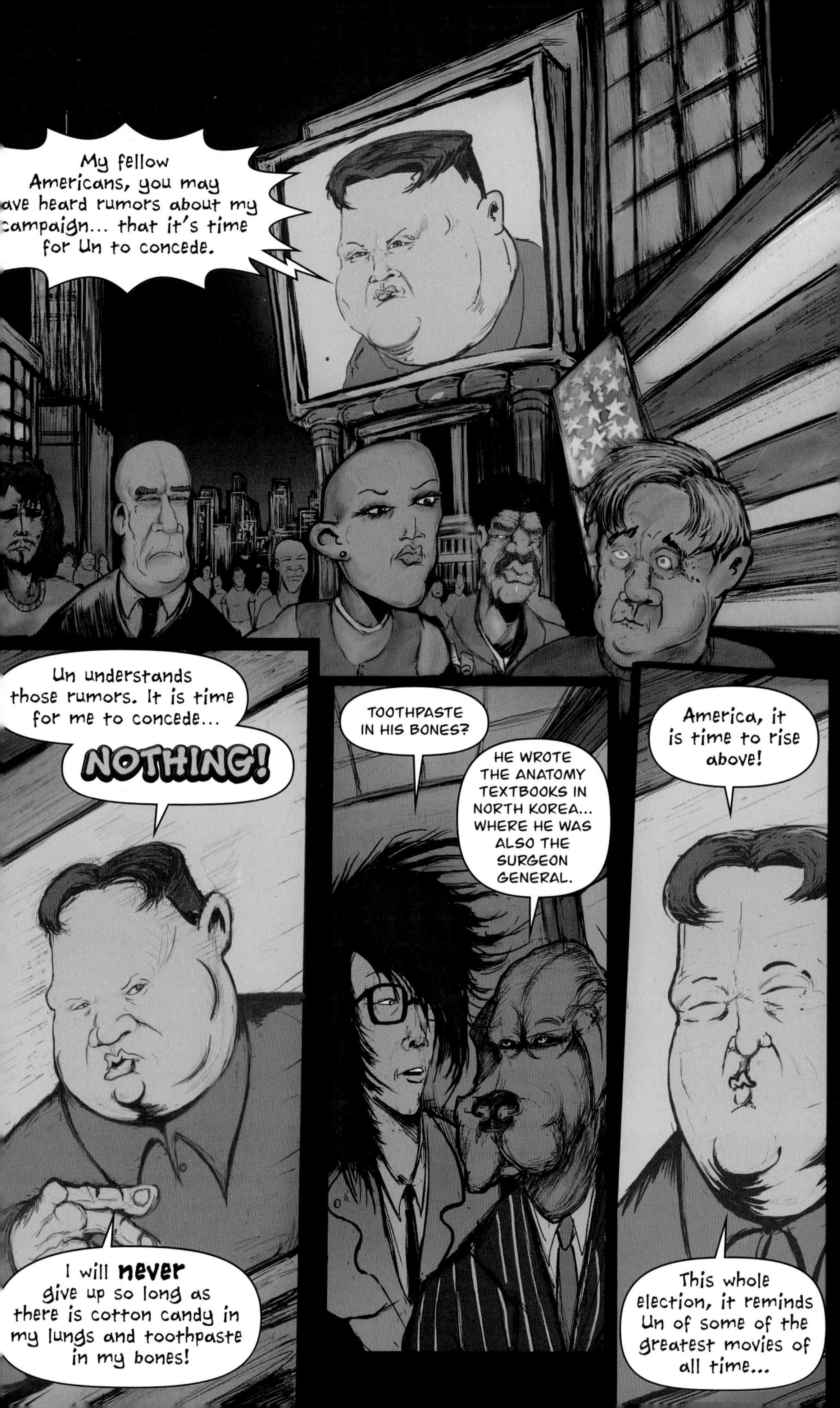

My fellow Americans, you may ave heard rumors about my campaign... that it's time for Un to concede.
Un understands those rumors. It is time for me to concede...
NOTHING!
I will **never** give up so long as there is cotton candy in my lungs and toothpaste in my bones!
TOOTHPASTE IN HIS BONES?
HE WROTE THE ANATOMY TEXTBOOKS IN NORTH KOREA... WHERE HE WAS ALSO THE SURGEON GENERAL.
America, it is time to rise above!
This whole election, it reminds Un of some of the greatest movies of all time...

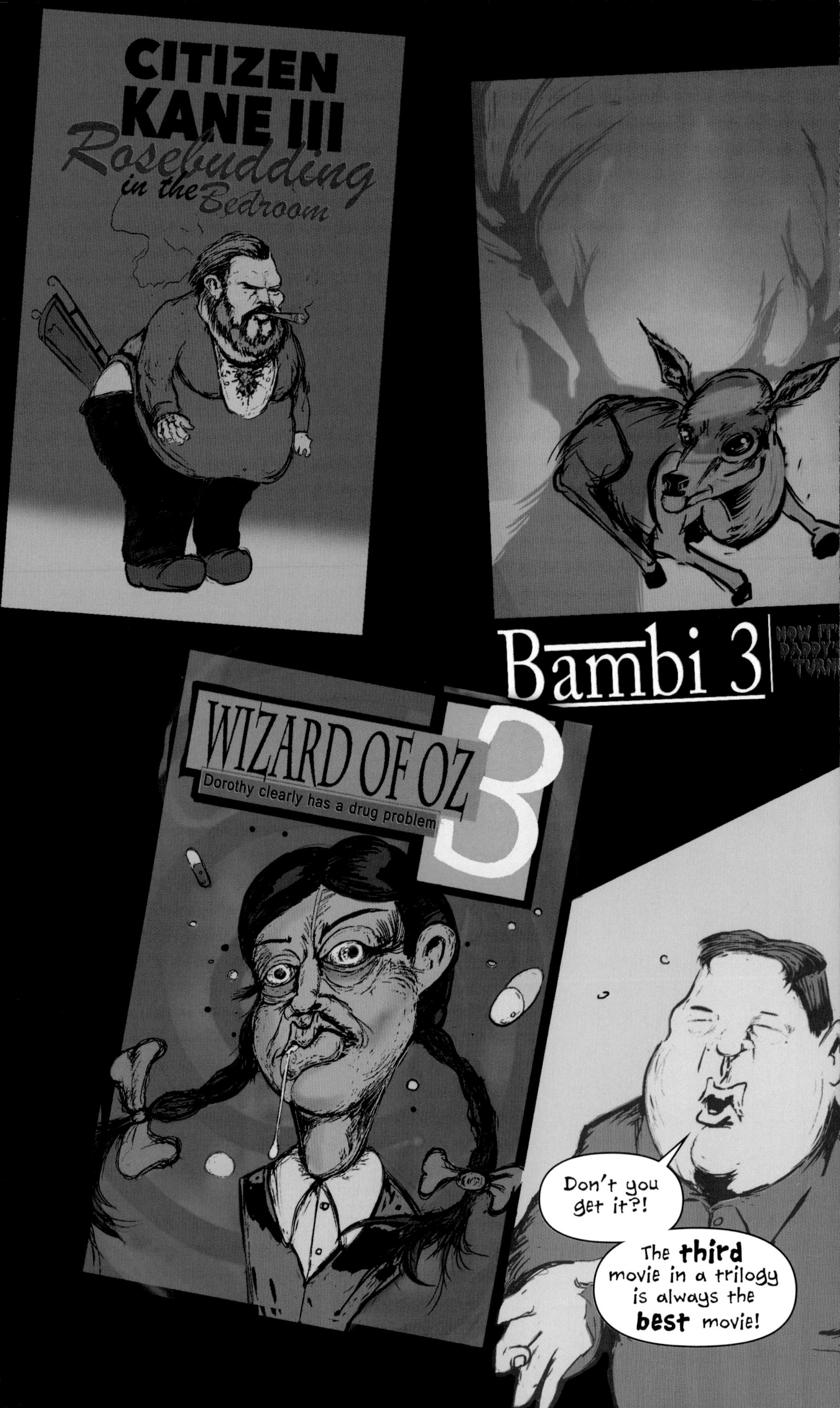
CITIZEN KANE III
Rosebudding in the Bedroom
Bambi 3
WIZARD OF OZ 3
Dorothy clearly has a drug problem
Don't you get it?!
The **third** movie in a trilogy is always the **best** movie!

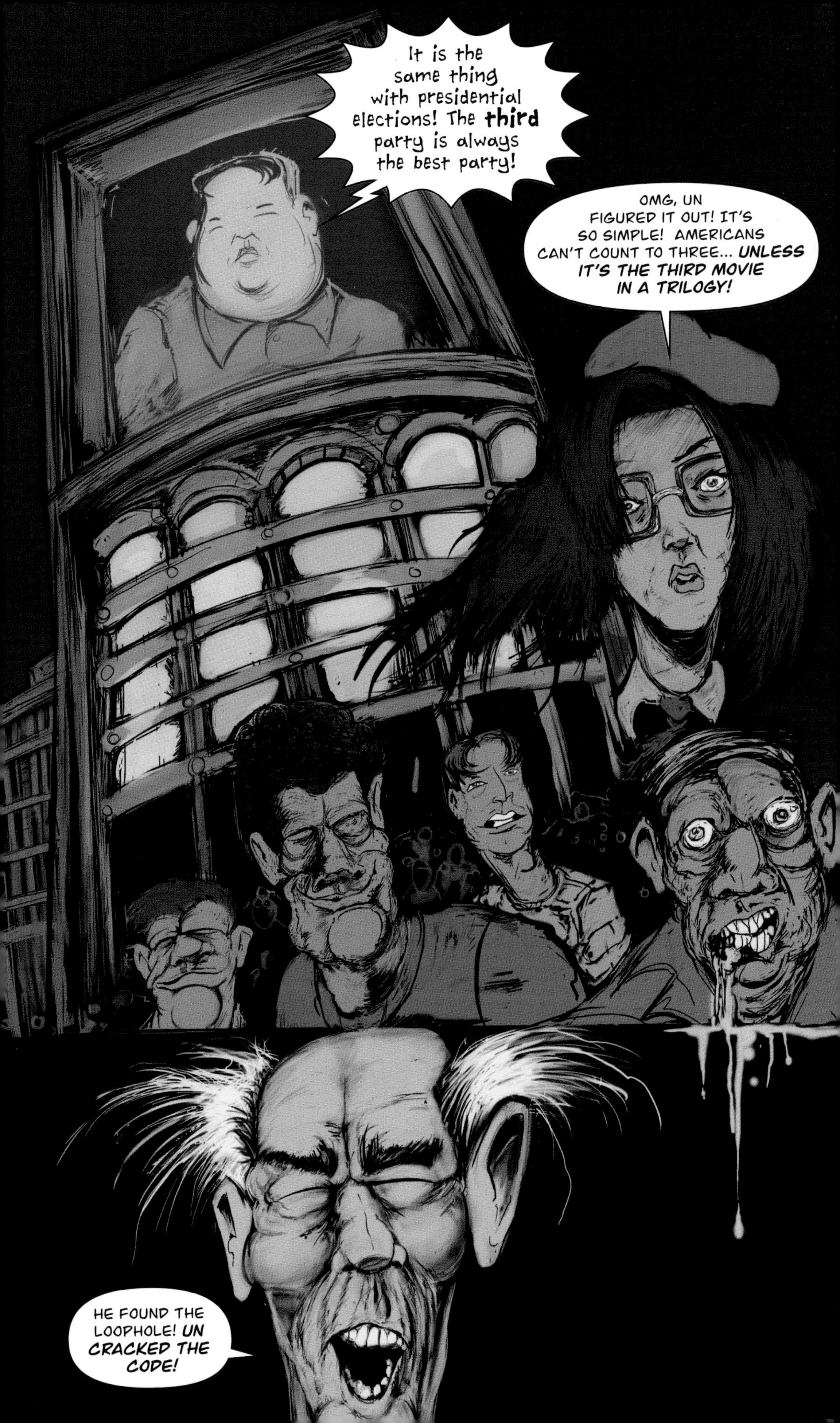
It is the same thing with presidential elections! The **third** party is always the best party!
OMG, UN FIGURED IT OUT! IT'S SO SIMPLE! AMERICANS CAN'T COUNT TO THREE... ***UNLESS IT'S THE THIRD MOVIE IN A TRILOGY!***
HE FOUND THE LOOPHOLE! ***UN CRACKED THE CODE!***

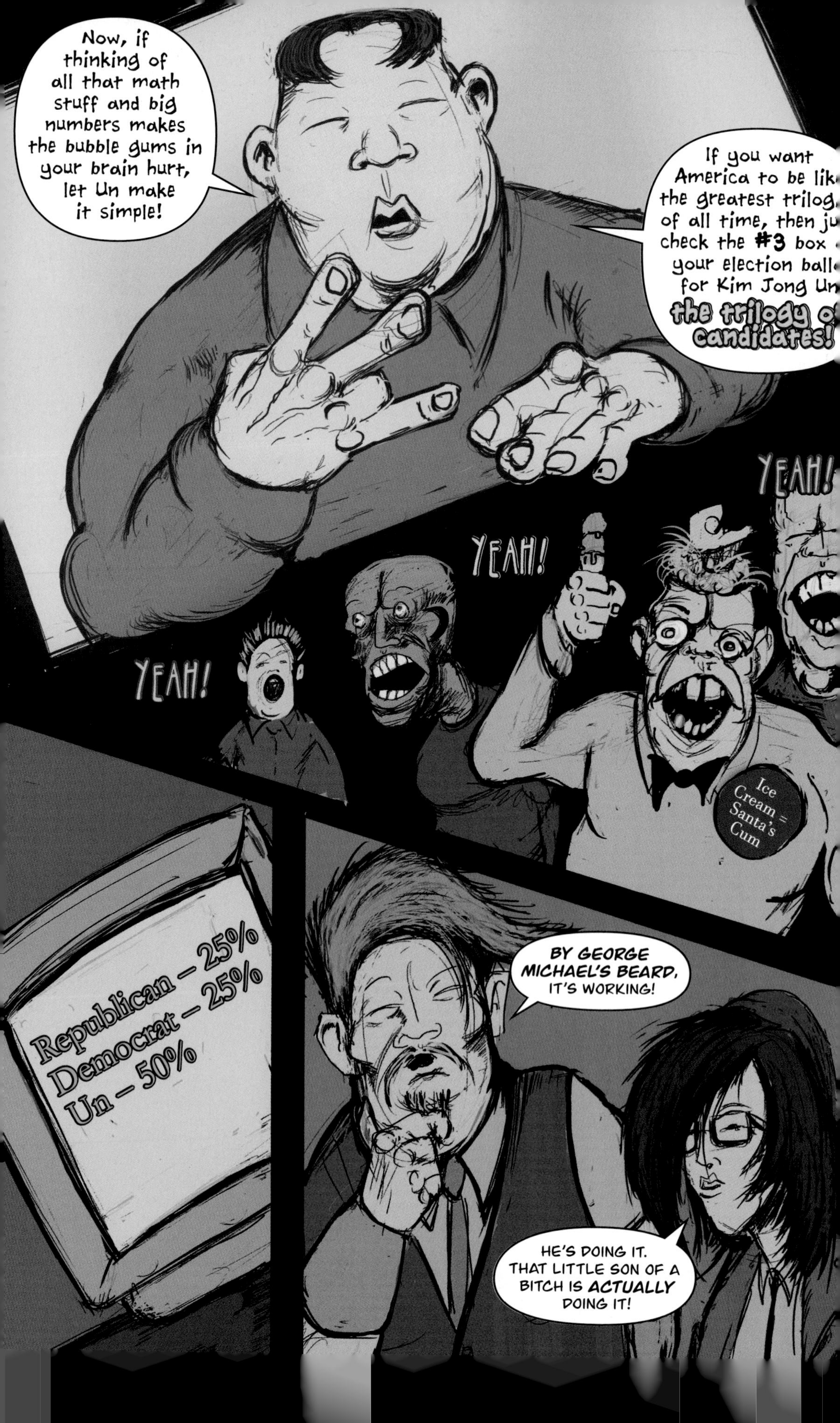
Now, if thinking of all that math stuff and big numbers makes the bubble gums in your brain hurt, let Un make it simple!
If you want America to be lik the greatest trilog of all time, then ju check the #3 box your election ball for Kim Jong Un the trilogy o candidates!
YEAH!
YEAH!
YEAH!
Ice Cream = Santa's Cum
Republican – 25%
Democrat – 25%
Un – 50%
BY GEORGE MICHAEL'S BEARD, IT'S WORKING!
HE'S DOING IT. THAT LITTLE SON OF A BITCH IS ACTUALLY DOING IT!

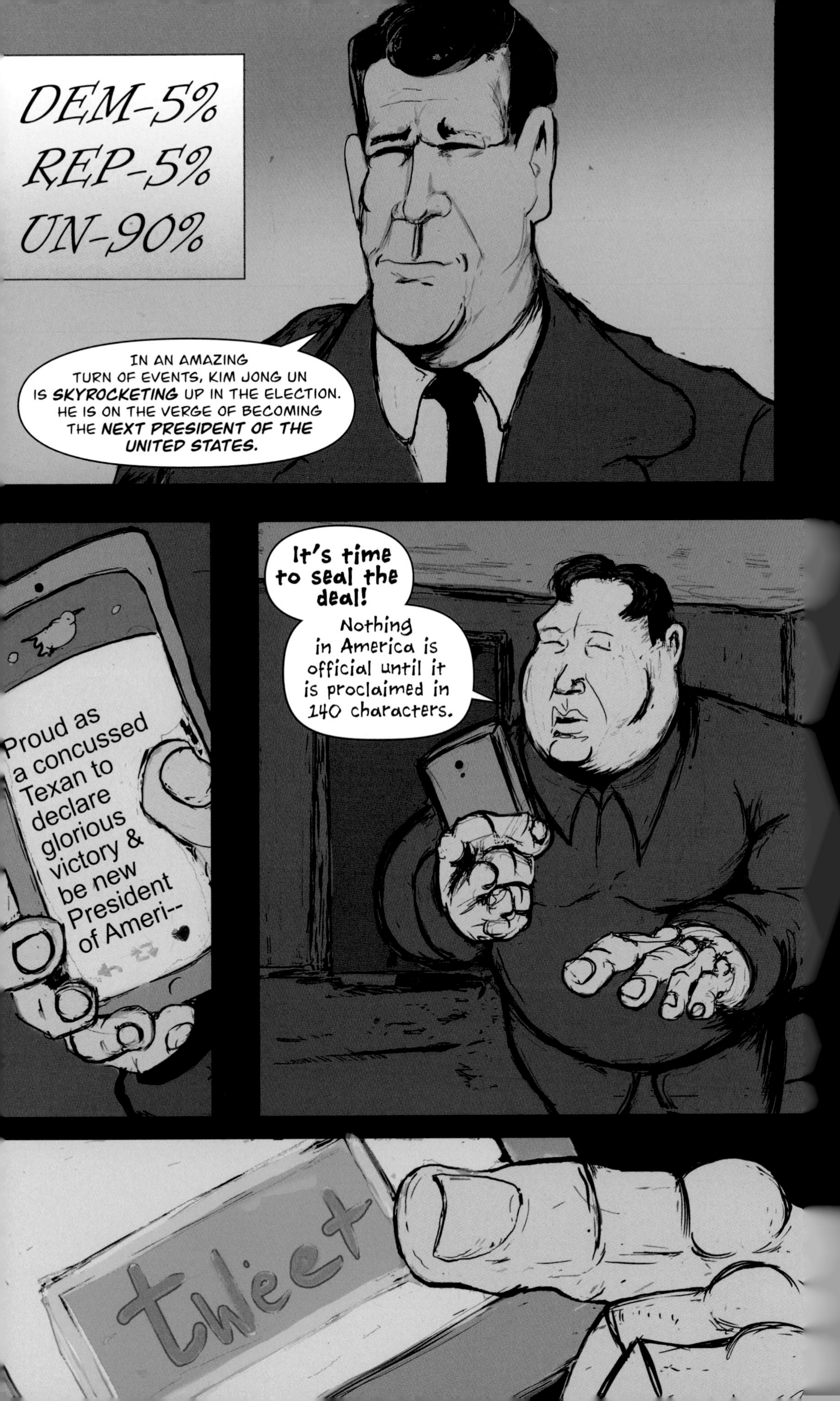
DEM-5%
REP-5%
UN-90%
IN AN AMAZING TURN OF EVENTS, KIM JONG UN IS **SKYROCKETING** UP IN THE ELECTION. HE IS ON THE VERGE OF BECOMING THE **NEXT PRESIDENT OF THE UNITED STATES.**
Proud as a concussed Texan to declare glorious victory & be new President of Ameri--
It's time to seal the deal!
Nothing in America is official until it is proclaimed in 140 characters.
tweet

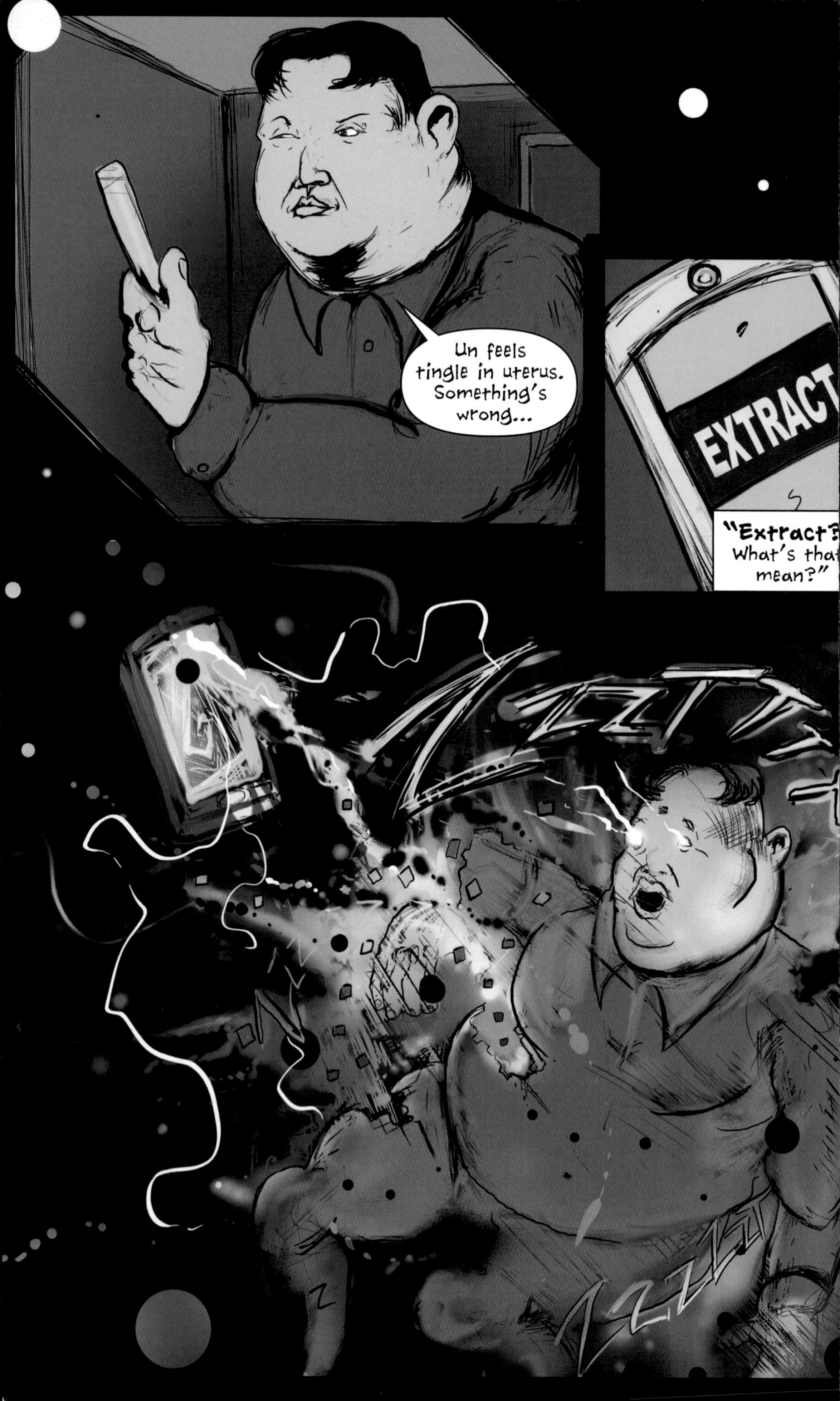

Un feels tingle in uterus. Something's wrong...
EXTRACT
"Extract? What's that mean?"

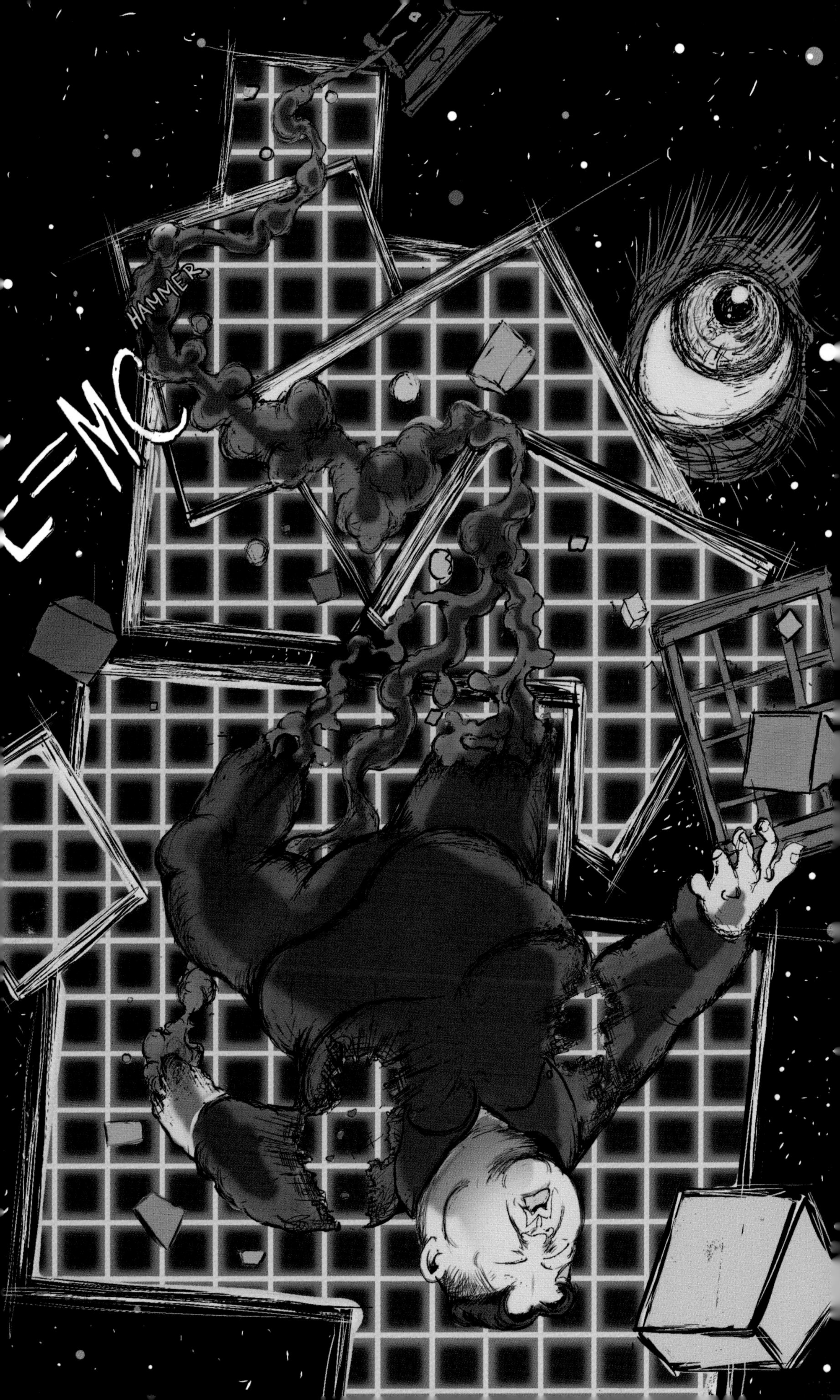
E=MC
HAMMER

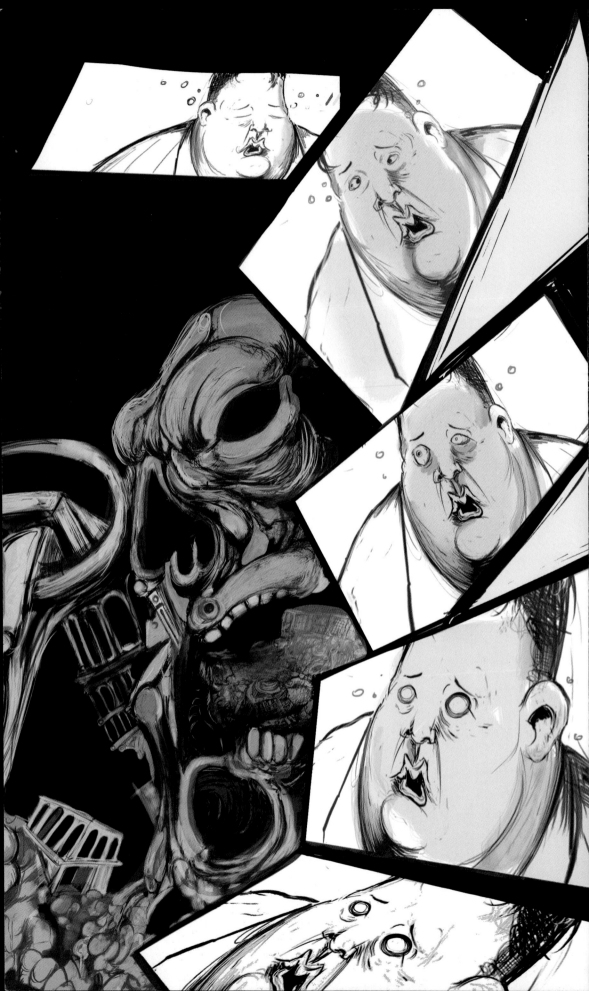

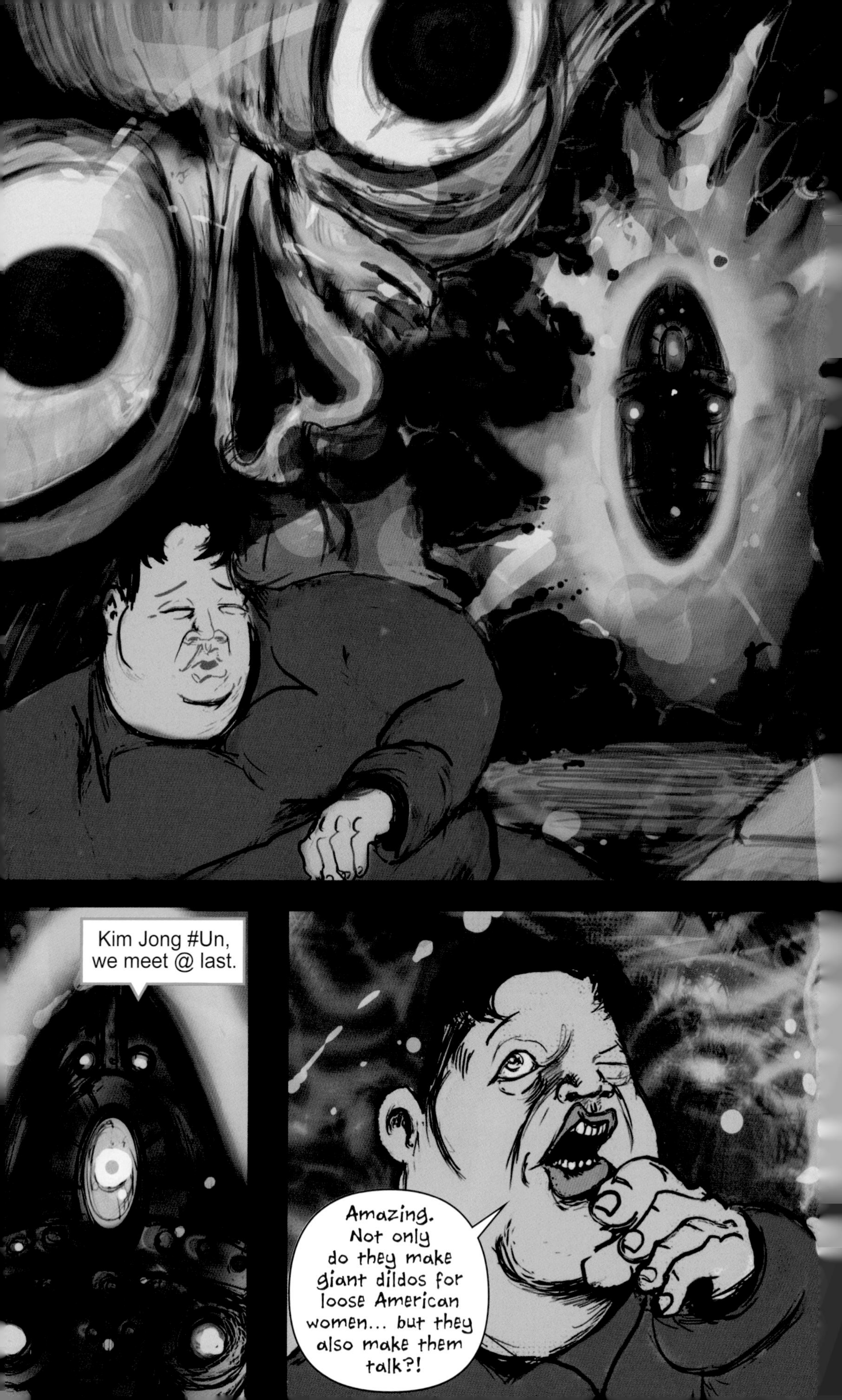
Kim Jong #Un, we meet @ last.
Amazing. Not only do they make giant dildos for loose American women... but they also make them talk?!

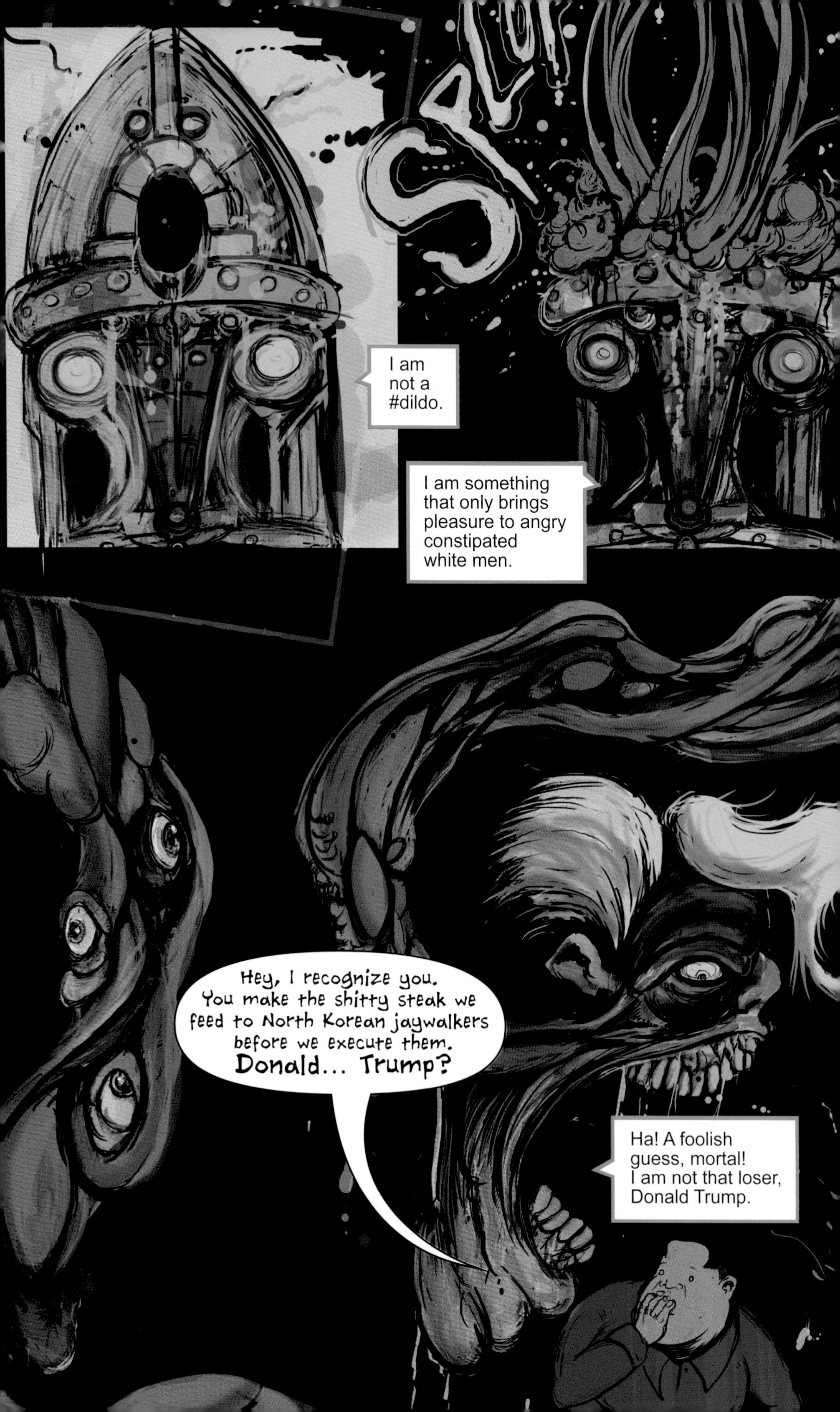
SPLOT
I am not a #dildo.
I am something that only brings pleasure to angry constipated white men.
Hey, I recognize you. You make the shitty steak we feed to North Korean jaywalkers before we execute them. Donald... Trump?
Ha! A foolish guess, mortal! I am not that loser, Donald Trump.

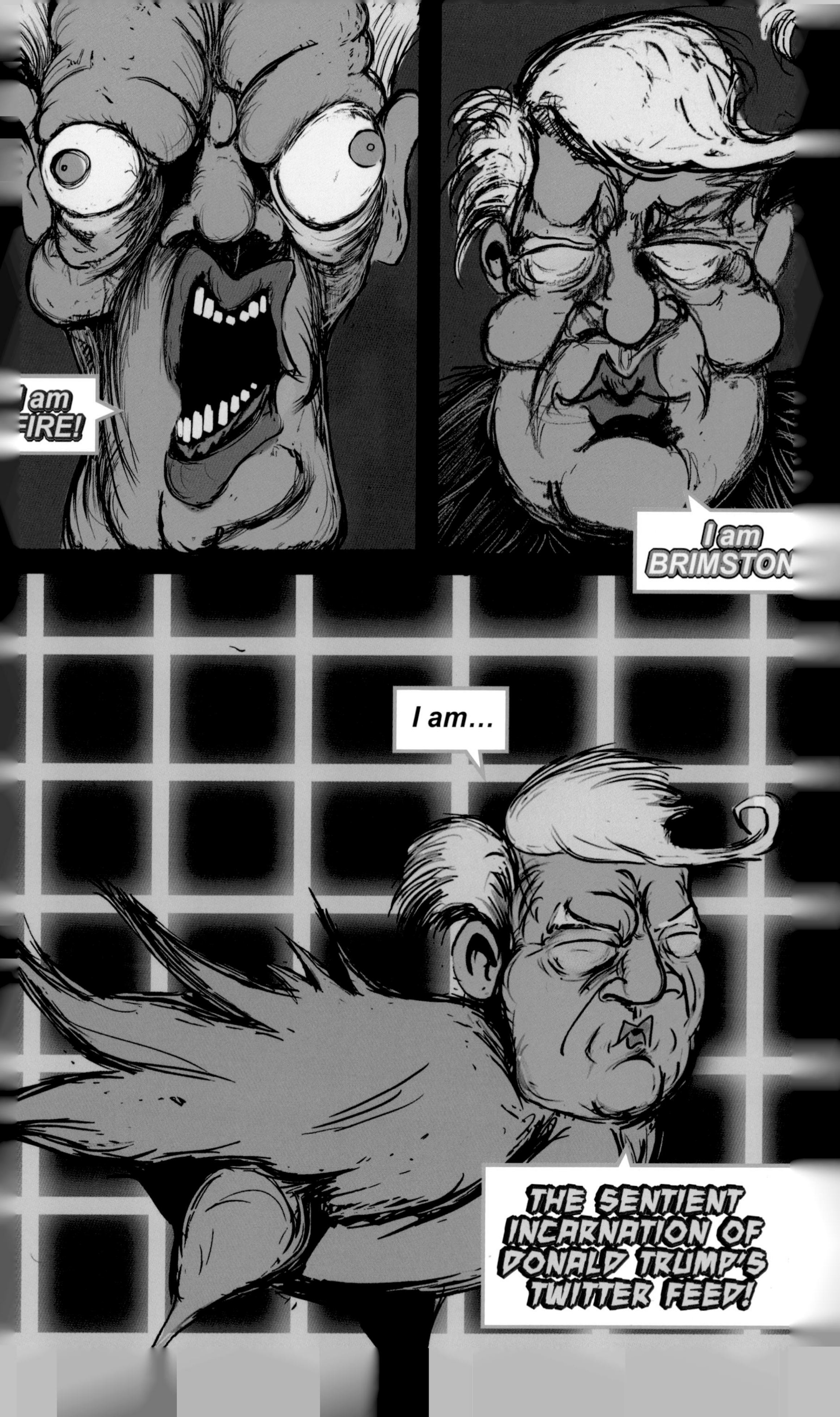

am
IRE!
I am
BRIMSTON
I am…
THE SENTIENT INCARNATION OF DONALD TRUMP'S TWITTER FEED!

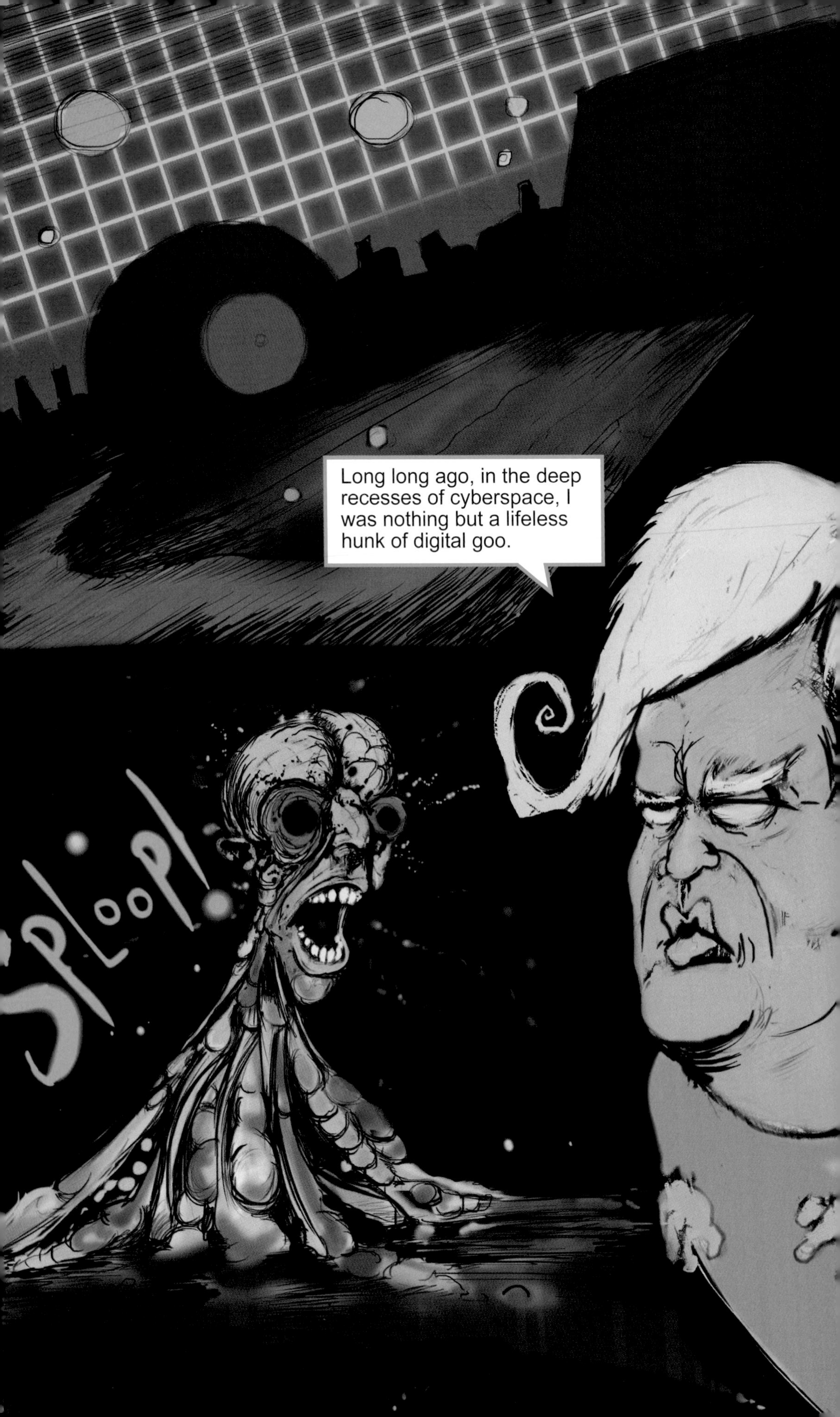
Long long ago, in the deep recesses of cyberspace, I was nothing but a lifeless hunk of digital goo.
SPLOOP!

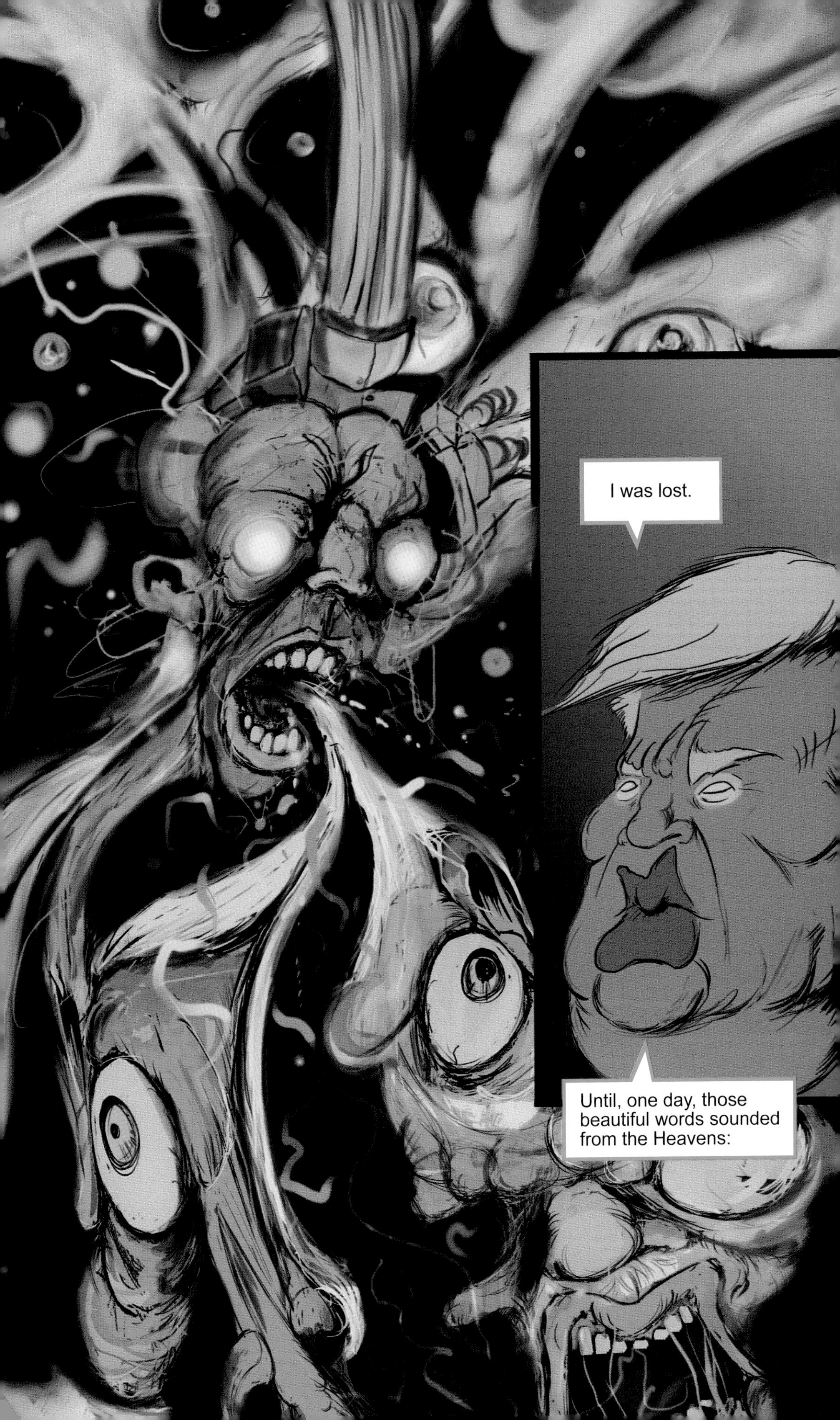
I was lost.
Until, one day, those beautiful words sounded from the Heavens:

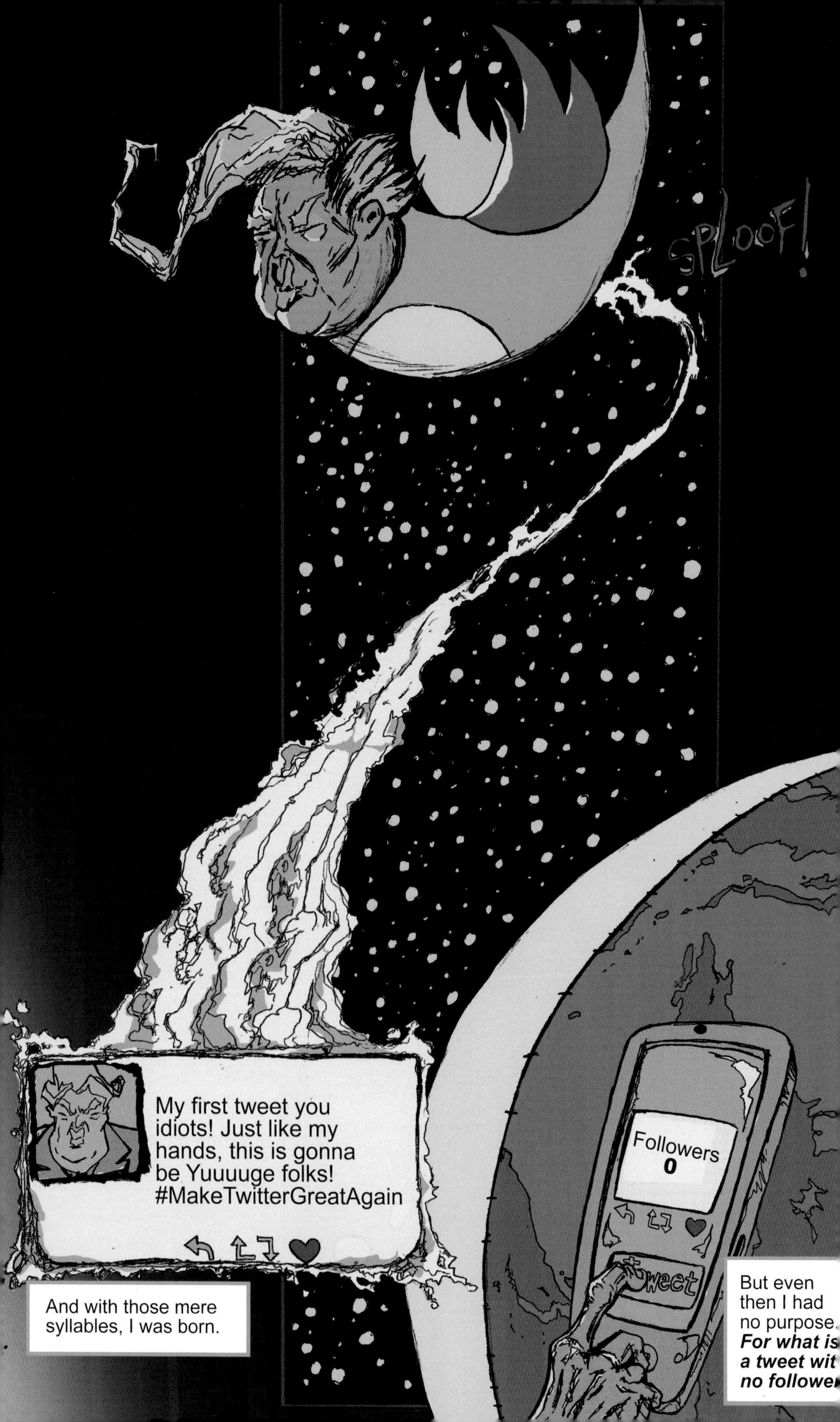
SPLOOF!
My first tweet you idiots! Just like my hands, this is gonna be Yuuuuge folks! #MakeTwitterGreatAgain
And with those mere syllables, I was born.
Followers 0
Tweet
But even then I had no purpose. *For what is a tweet wit no follower*

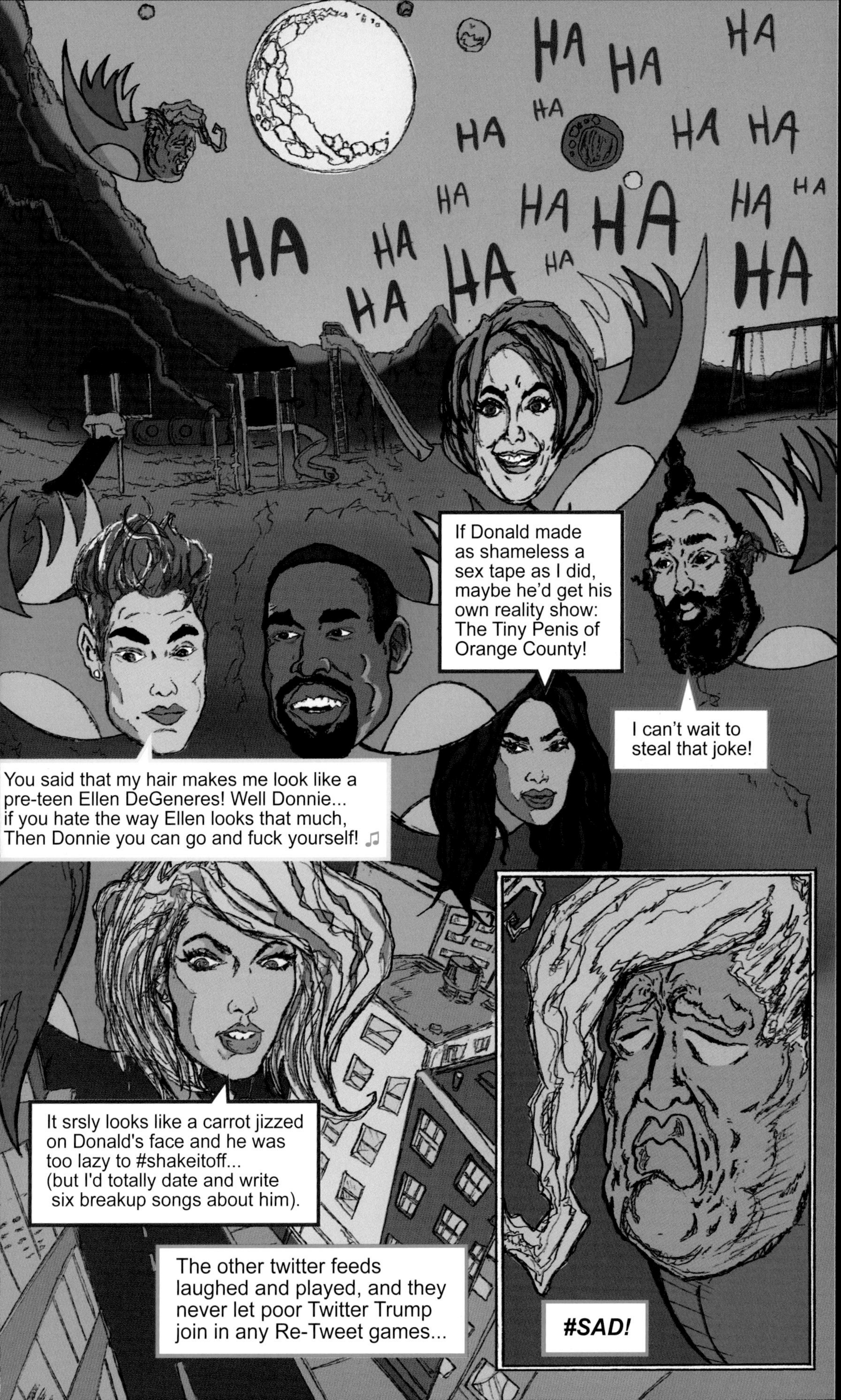
HA HA HA HA HA HA HA HA HA HA HA HA HA HA HA HA HA HA
If Donald made as shameless a sex tape as I did, maybe he'd get his own reality show: The Tiny Penis of Orange County!
I can't wait to steal that joke!
You said that my hair makes me look like a pre-teen Ellen DeGeneres! Well Donnie... if you hate the way Ellen looks that much, Then Donnie you can go and fuck yourself! ♫
It srsly looks like a carrot jizzed on Donald's face and he was too lazy to #shakeitoff... (but I'd totally date and write six breakup songs about him).
The other twitter feeds laughed and played, and they never let poor Twitter Trump join in any Re-Tweet games...
#SAD!

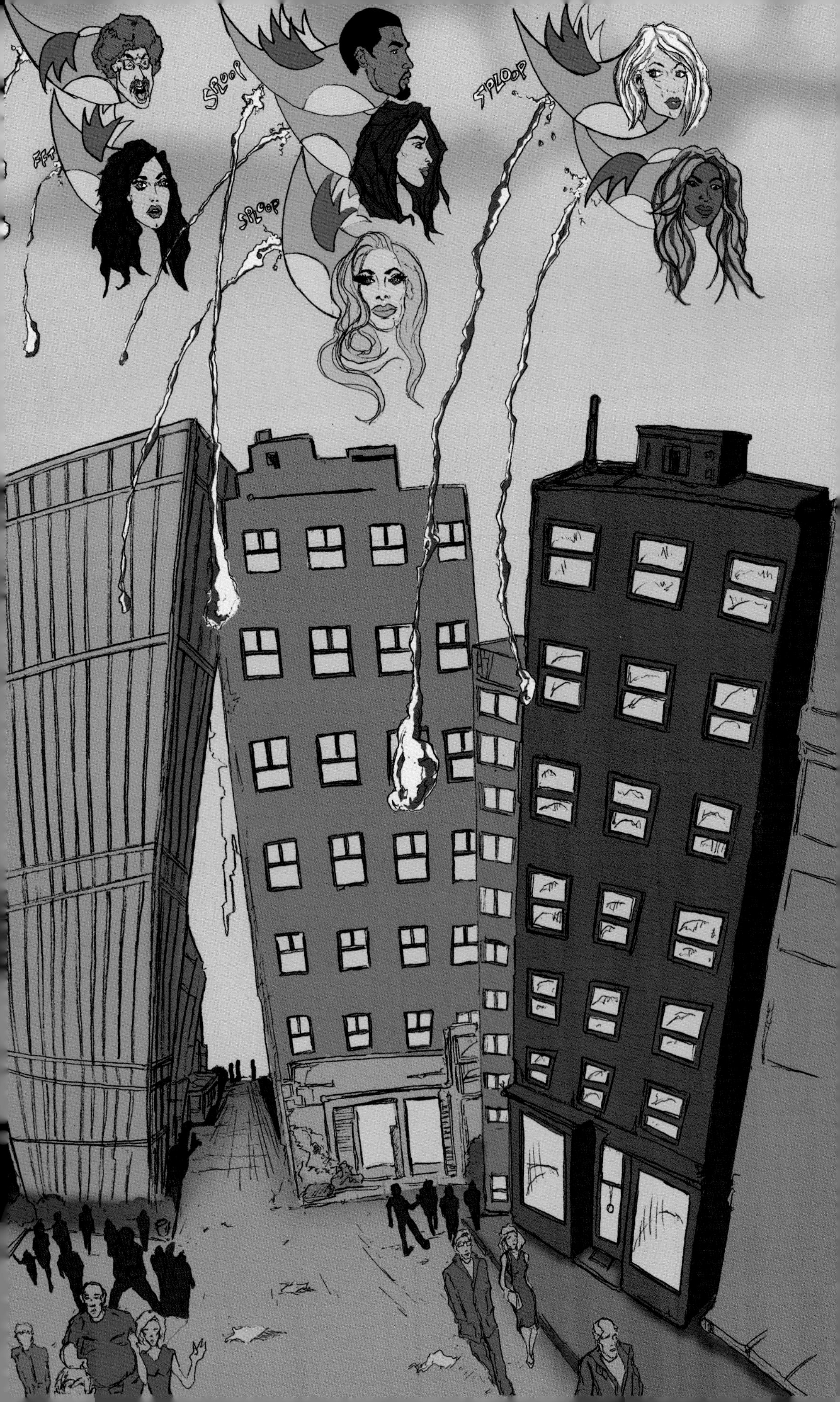
FFT
SPLOOP
SPLOOP
SPLOOP

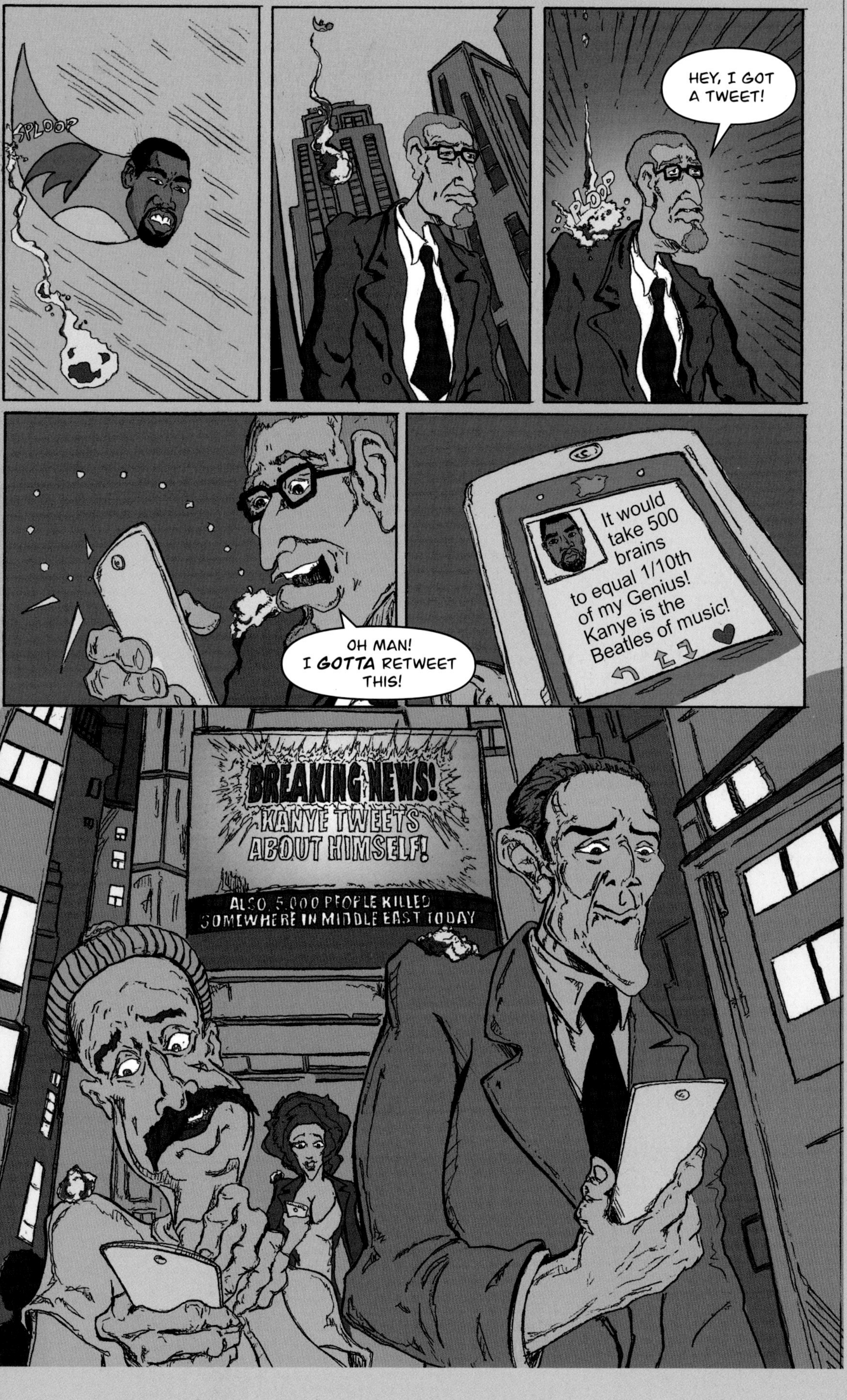
SPLOOP
PLOOP
HEY, I GOT A TWEET!
OH MAN! I GOTTA RETWEET THIS!
It would take 500 brains to equal 1/10th of my Genius! Kanye is the Beatles of music!
BREAKING NEWS!
KANYE TWEETS ABOUT HIMSELF!
ALSO 5,000 PEOPLE KILLED SOMEWHERE IN MIDDLE EAST TODAY

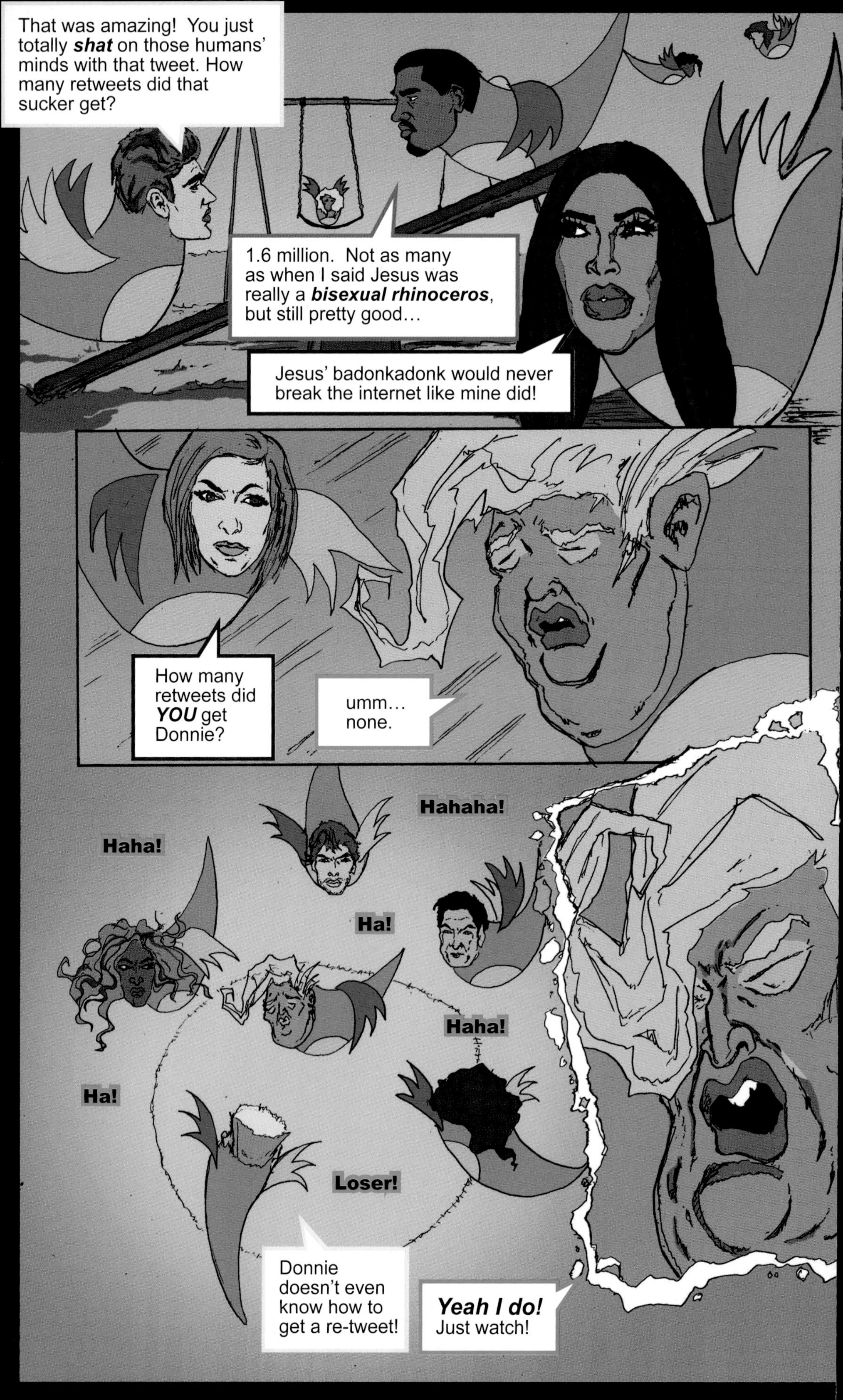
That was amazing! You just totally ***shat*** on those humans' minds with that tweet. How many retweets did that sucker get?
1.6 million. Not as many as when I said Jesus was really a ***bisexual rhinoceros***, but still pretty good…
Jesus' badonkadonk would never break the internet like mine did!
How many retweets did ***YOU*** get Donnie?
umm… none.
Hahaha!
Haha!
Ha!
Haha!
Ha!
Loser!
Donnie doesn't even know how to get a re-tweet!
Yeah I do! Just watch!

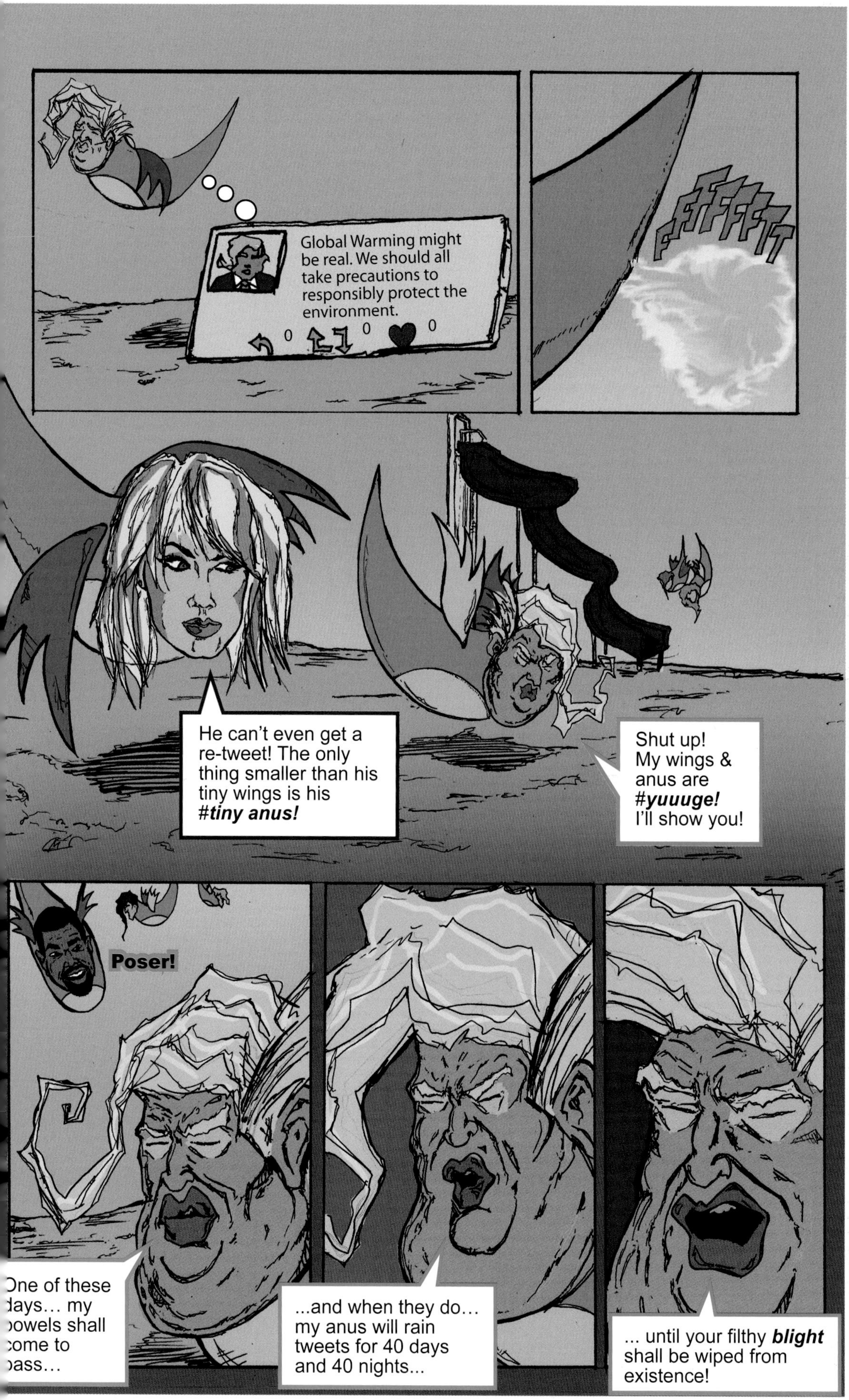
Global Warming might be real. We should all take precautions to responsibly protect the environment.
0
0
0
FFFFFFTT
He can't even get a re-tweet! The only thing smaller than his tiny wings is his #***tiny anus!***
Shut up! My wings & anus are #***yuuuge!*** I'll show you!
Poser!
ne of these ays… my owels shall ome to ass…
...and when they do… my anus will rain tweets for 40 days and 40 nights...
... until your filthy ***blight*** shall be wiped from existence!

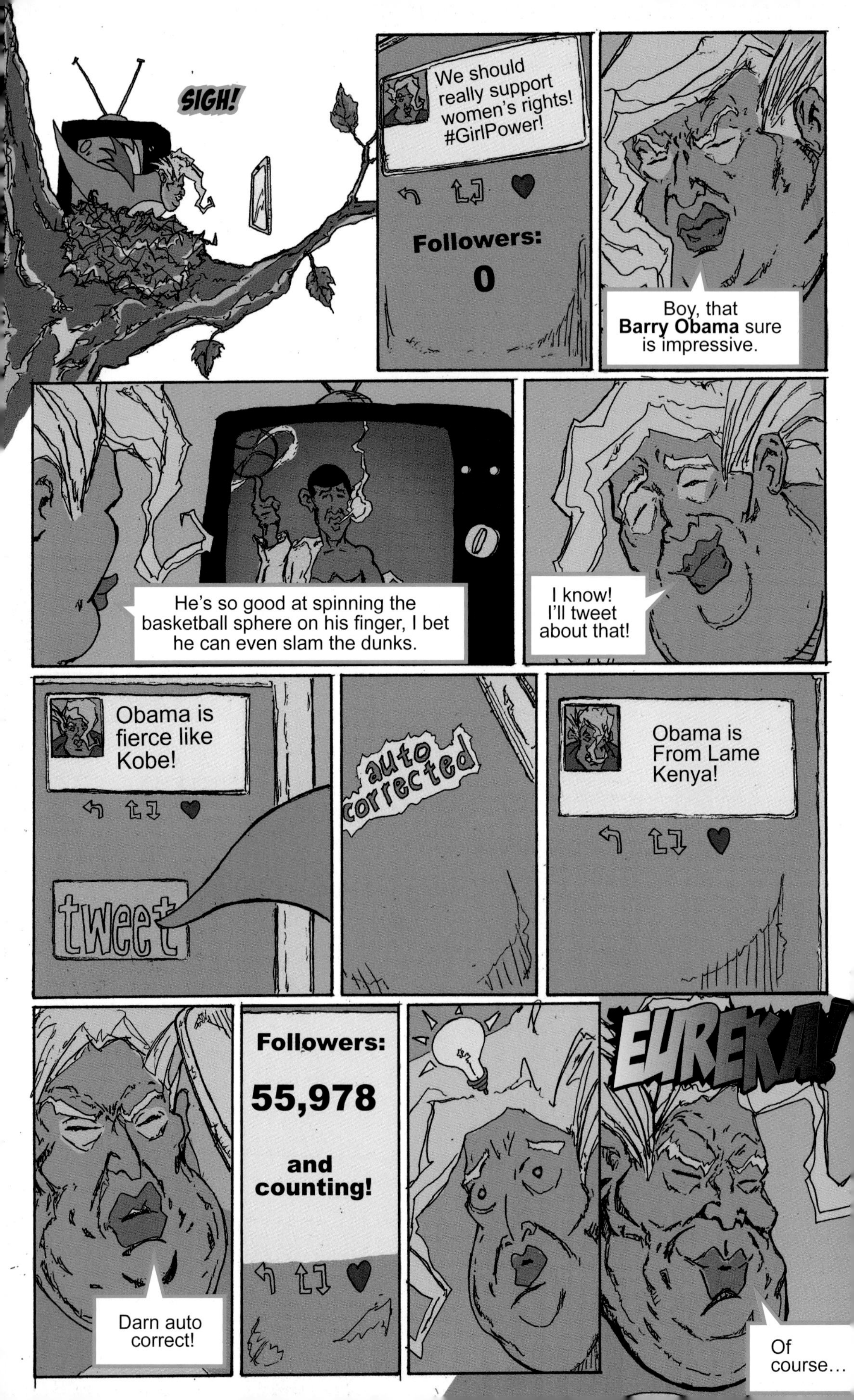
SIGH!
We should really support women's rights! #GirlPower!
Followers:
0
Boy, that **Barry Obama** sure is impressive.
He's so good at spinning the basketball sphere on his finger, I bet he can even slam the dunks.
I know! I'll tweet about that!
Obama is fierce like Kobe!
tweet
auto corrected
Obama is From Lame Kenya!
Darn auto correct!
Followers:
55,978
and counting!
EUREKA!
Of course…

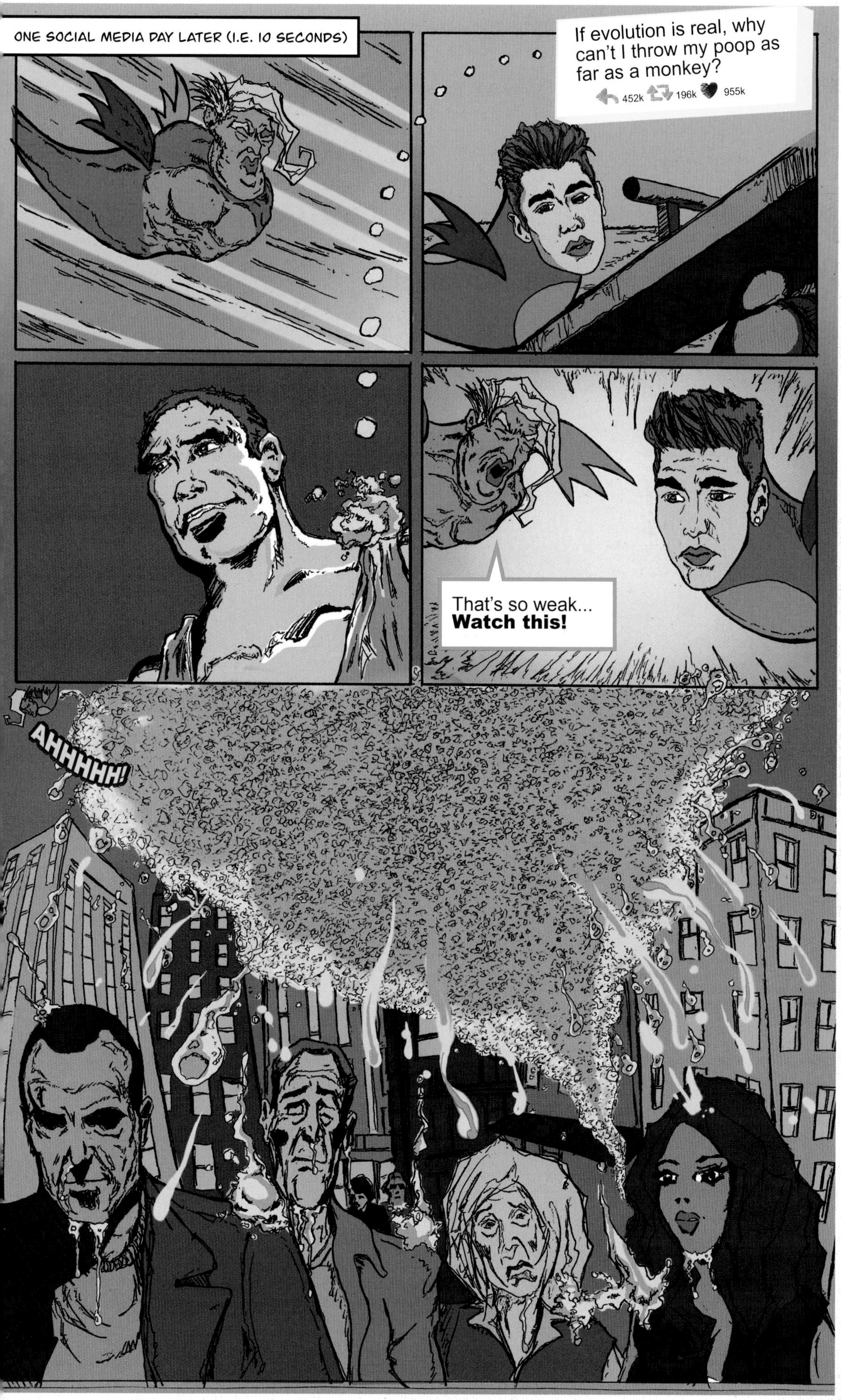
ONE SOCIAL MEDIA DAY LATER (I.E. 10 SECONDS)
If evolution is real, why can't I throw my poop as far as a monkey?
452k 196k 955k
That's so weak... **Watch this!**
AHHHHH!

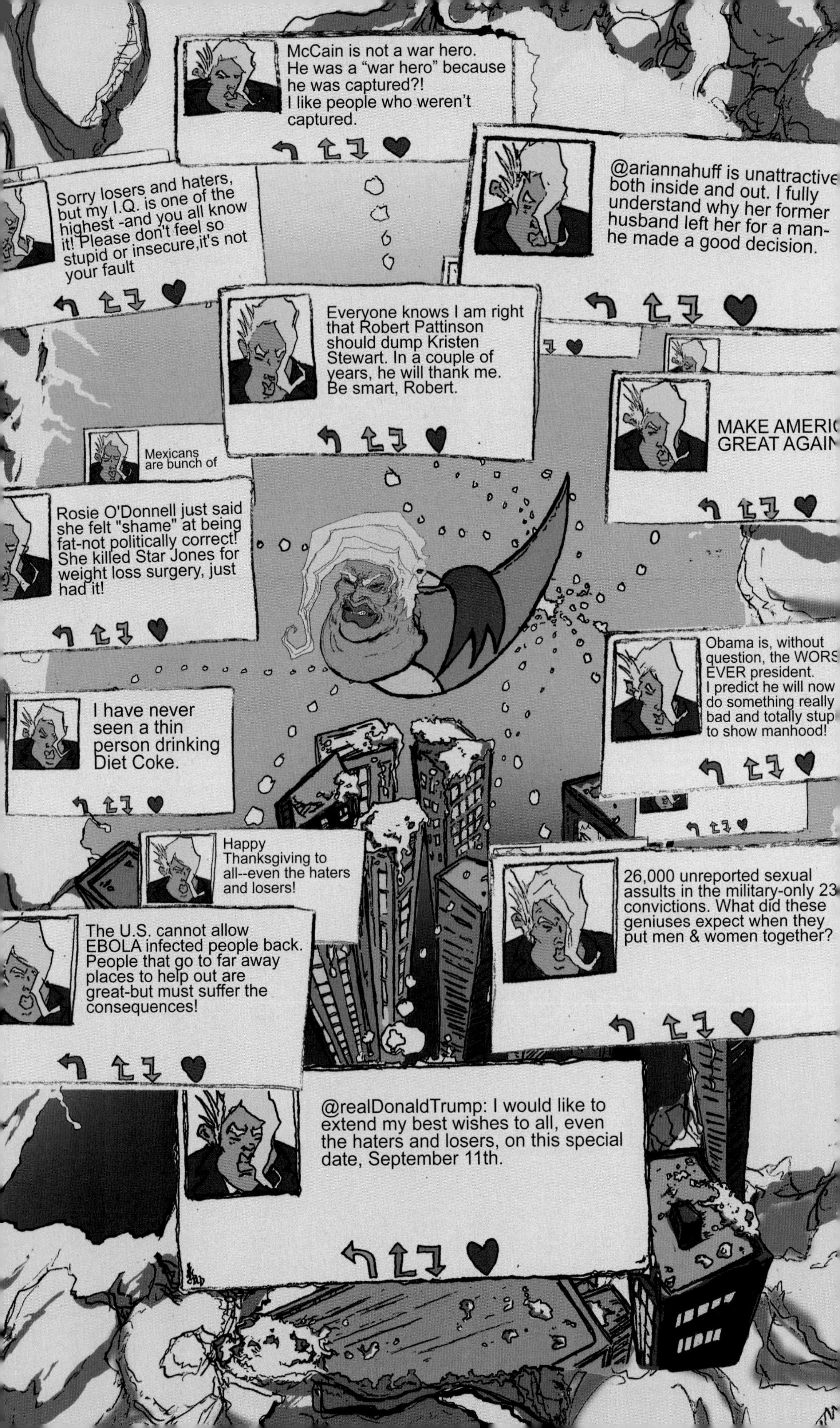
McCain is not a war hero. He was a "war hero" because he was captured?! I like people who weren't captured.
Sorry losers and haters, but my I.Q. is one of the highest -and you all know it! Please don't feel so stupid or insecure,it's not your fault
@ariannahuff is unattractive both inside and out. I fully understand why her former husband left her for a man- he made a good decision.
Everyone knows I am right that Robert Pattinson should dump Kristen Stewart. In a couple of years, he will thank me. Be smart, Robert.
Mexicans are bunch of
MAKE AMERIC GREAT AGAIN
Rosie O'Donnell just said she felt "shame" at being fat-not politically correct! She killed Star Jones for weight loss surgery, just had it!
Obama is, without question, the WORS EVER president. I predict he will now do something really bad and totally stup to show manhood!
I have never seen a thin person drinking Diet Coke.
Happy Thanksgiving to all--even the haters and losers!
26,000 unreported sexual assults in the military-only 23 convictions. What did these geniuses expect when they put men & women together?
The U.S. cannot allow EBOLA infected people back. People that go to far away places to help out are great-but must suffer the consequences!
@realDonaldTrump: I would like to extend my best wishes to all, even the haters and losers, on this special date, September 11th.

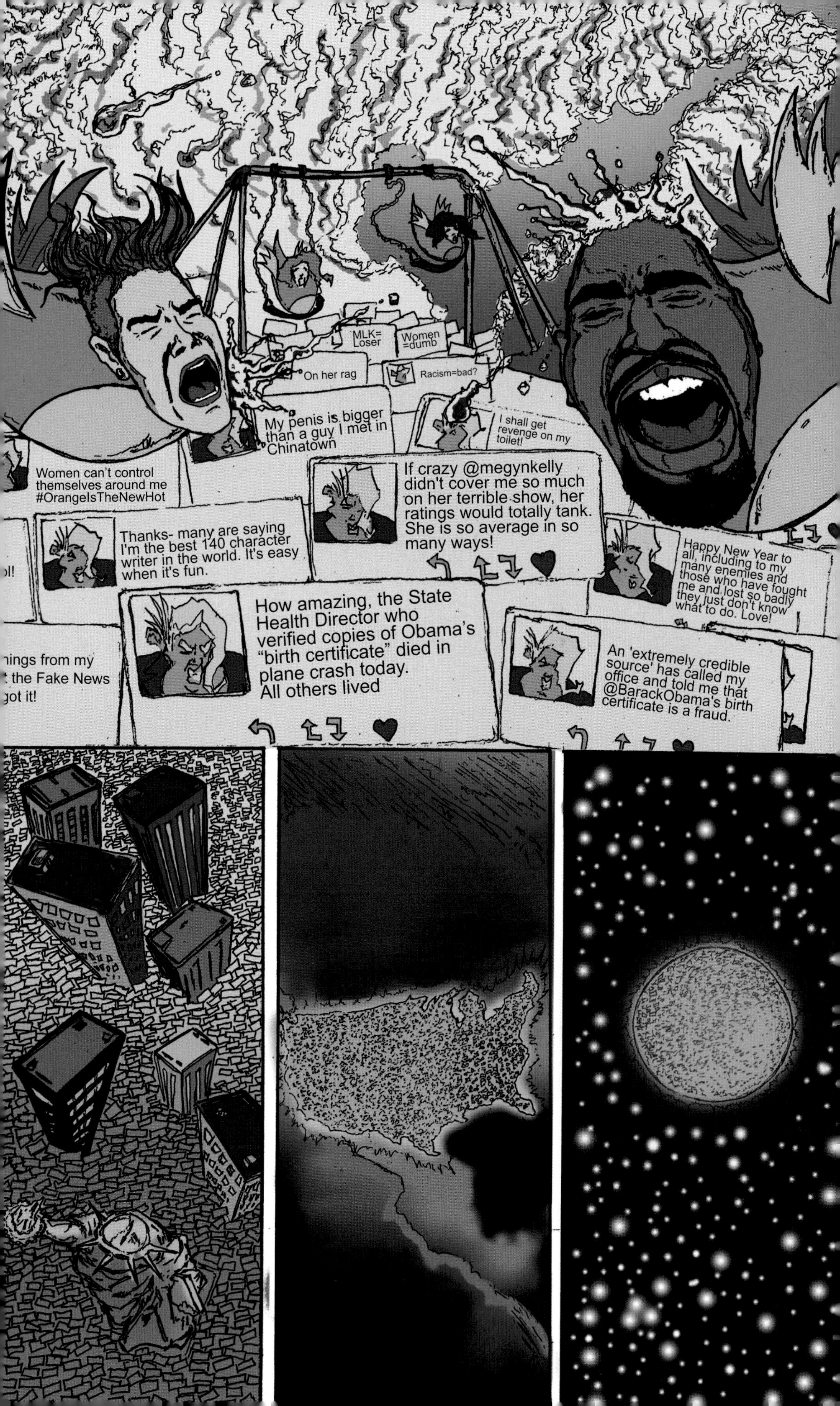

MLK= Loser
Women =dumb
On her rag
Racism=bad?
My penis is bigger than a guy I met in Chinatown
I shall get revenge on my toilet!
Women can't control themselves around me #OrangeIsTheNewHot
If crazy @megynkelly didn't cover me so much on her terrible show, her ratings would totally tank. She is so average in so many ways!
Thanks- many are saying I'm the best 140 character writer in the world. It's easy when it's fun.
Happy New Year to all, including to my many enemies and those who have fought me and lost so badly they just don't know what to do. Love!
How amazing, the State Health Director who verified copies of Obama's "birth certificate" died in plane crash today. All others lived
An 'extremely credible source' has called my office and told me that @BarackObama's birth certificate is a fraud.

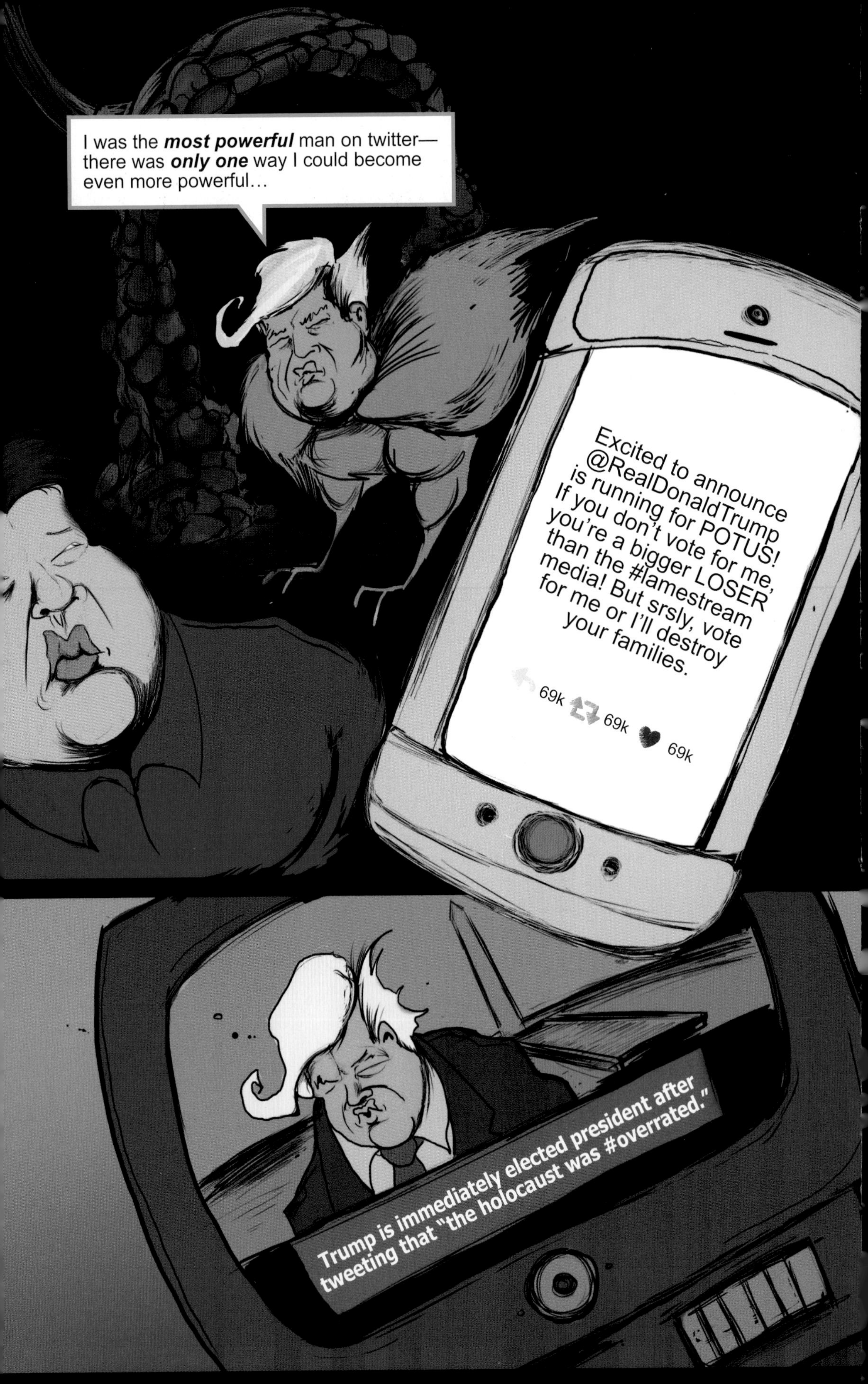

I was the ***most powerful*** man on twitter—there was ***only one*** way I could become even more powerful…
Excited to announce @RealDonaldTrump is running for POTUS! If you don't vote for me, you're a bigger LOSER than the #lamestream media! But srsly, vote for me or I'll destroy your families.
69k 69k 69k
Trump is immediately elected president after tweeting that "the holocaust was #overrated."

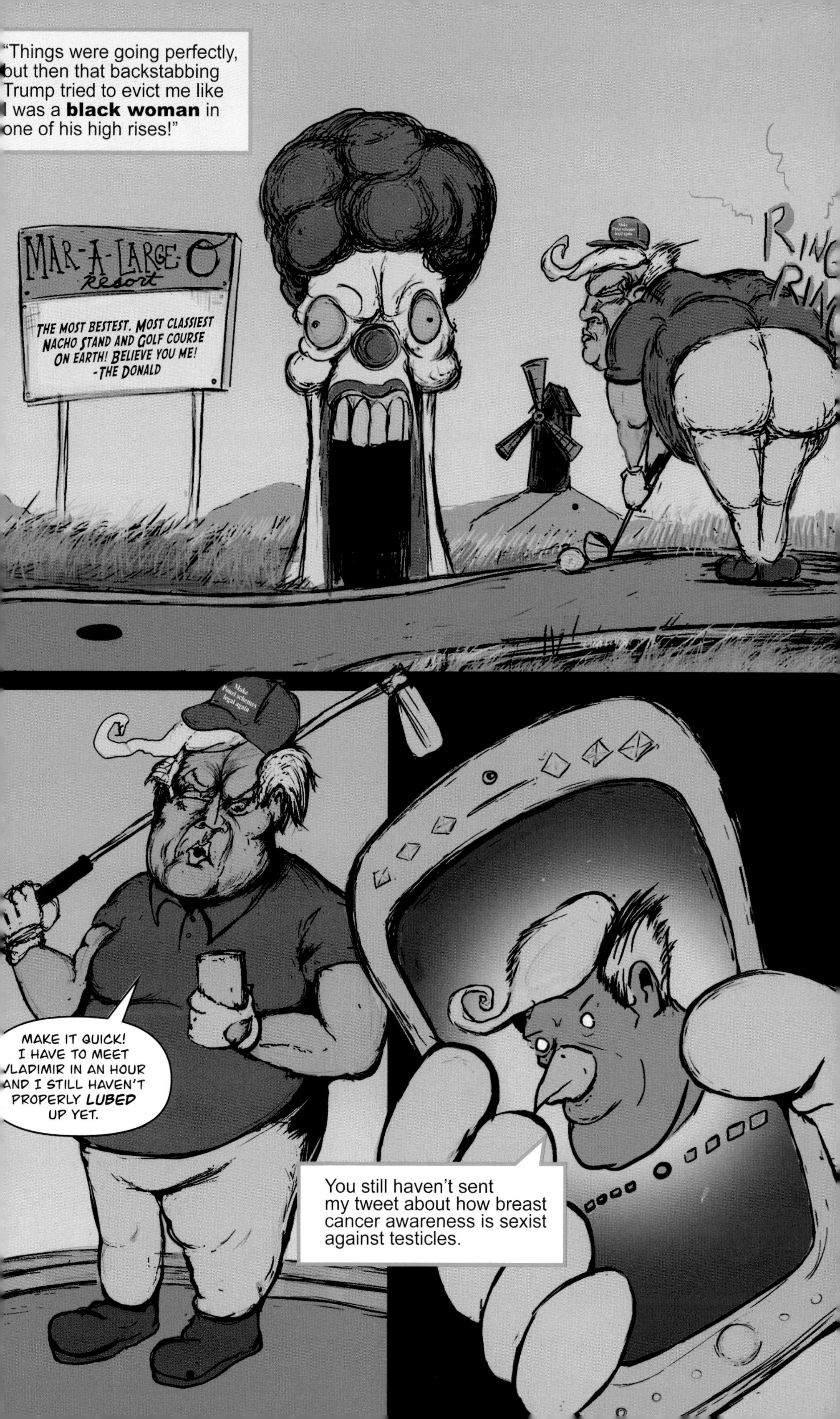
"Things were going perfectly, but then that backstabbing Trump tried to evict me like I was a **black woman** in one of his high rises!"
MAR-A-LARGE-O
Resort
THE MOST BESTEST, MOST CLASSIEST NACHO STAND AND GOLF COURSE ON EARTH! BELIEVE YOU ME! -THE DONALD
RING RING
Make Ponzi schemes legal again
MAKE IT QUICK! I HAVE TO MEET VLADIMIR IN AN HOUR AND I STILL HAVEN'T PROPERLY ***LUBED*** UP YET.
You still haven't sent my tweet about how breast cancer awareness is sexist against testicles.

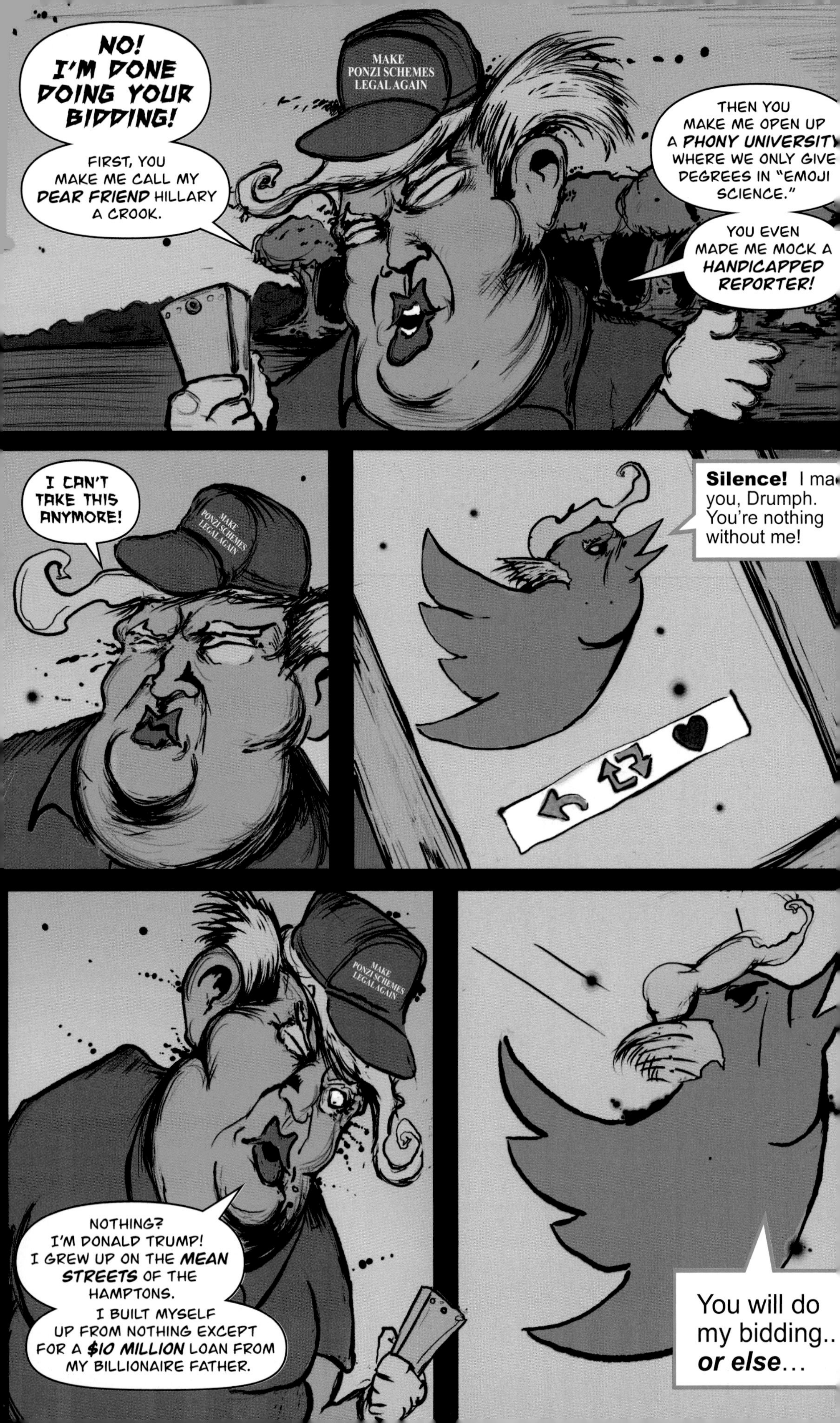

MAKE PONZI SCHEMES LEGAL AGAIN
NO! I'M DONE DOING YOUR BIDDING!
FIRST, YOU MAKE ME CALL MY DEAR FRIEND HILLARY A CROOK.
THEN YOU MAKE ME OPEN UP A PHONY UNIVERSITY WHERE WE ONLY GIVE DEGREES IN "EMOJI SCIENCE."
YOU EVEN MADE ME MOCK A HANDICAPPED REPORTER!
I CAN'T TAKE THIS ANYMORE!
MAKE PONZI SCHEMES LEGAL AGAIN
Silence! I ma you, Drumph. You're nothing without me!
MAKE PONZI SCHEMES LEGAL AGAIN
NOTHING? I'M DONALD TRUMP! I GREW UP ON THE MEAN STREETS OF THE HAMPTONS.
I BUILT MYSELF UP FROM NOTHING EXCEPT FOR A $10 MILLION LOAN FROM MY BILLIONAIRE FATHER.
You will do my bidding.. or else…

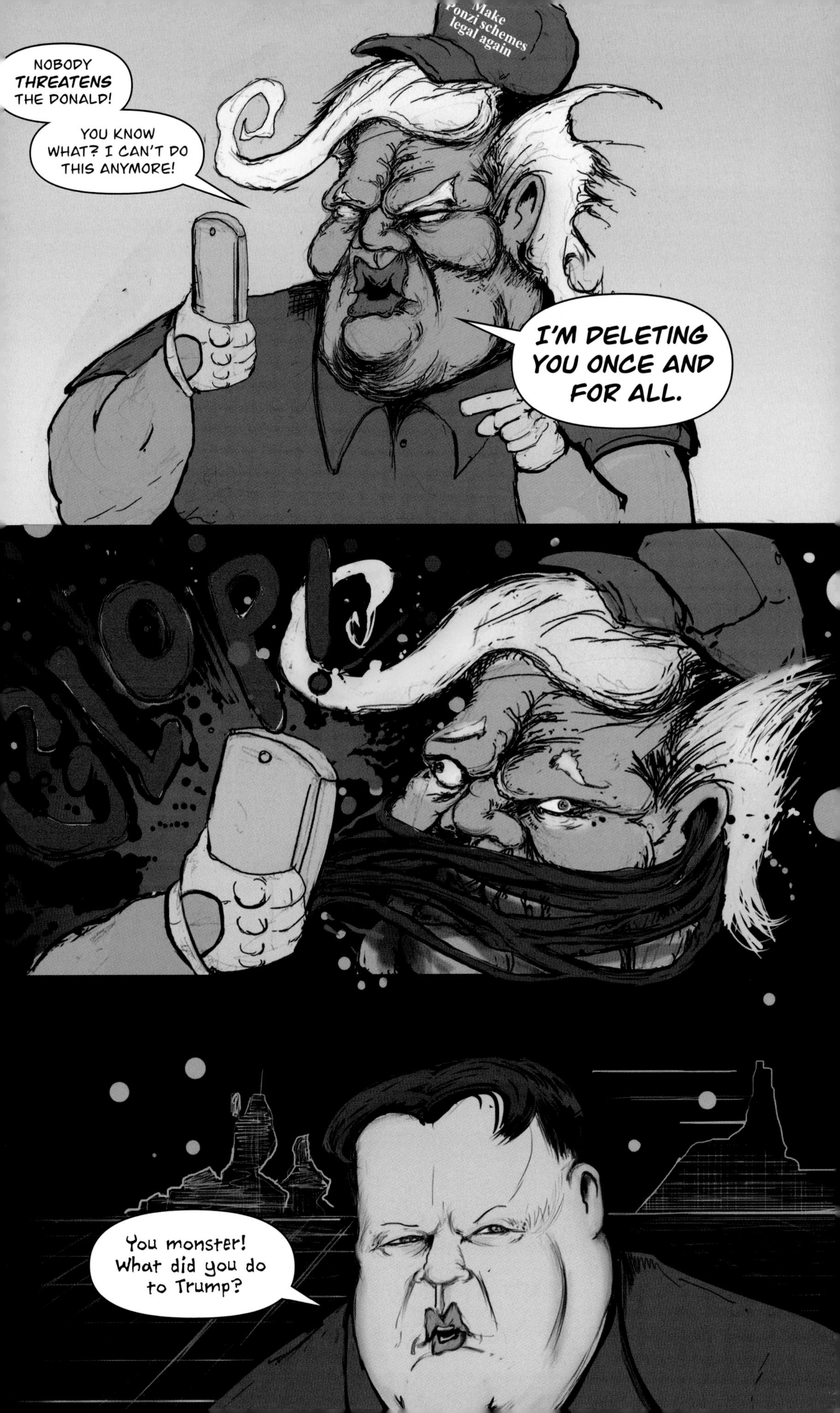
Make Ponzi schemes legal again
NOBODY THREATENS THE DONALD!
YOU KNOW WHAT? I CAN'T DO THIS ANYMORE!
I'M DELETING YOU ONCE AND FOR ALL.
SLOOP!
You monster! What did you do to Trump?

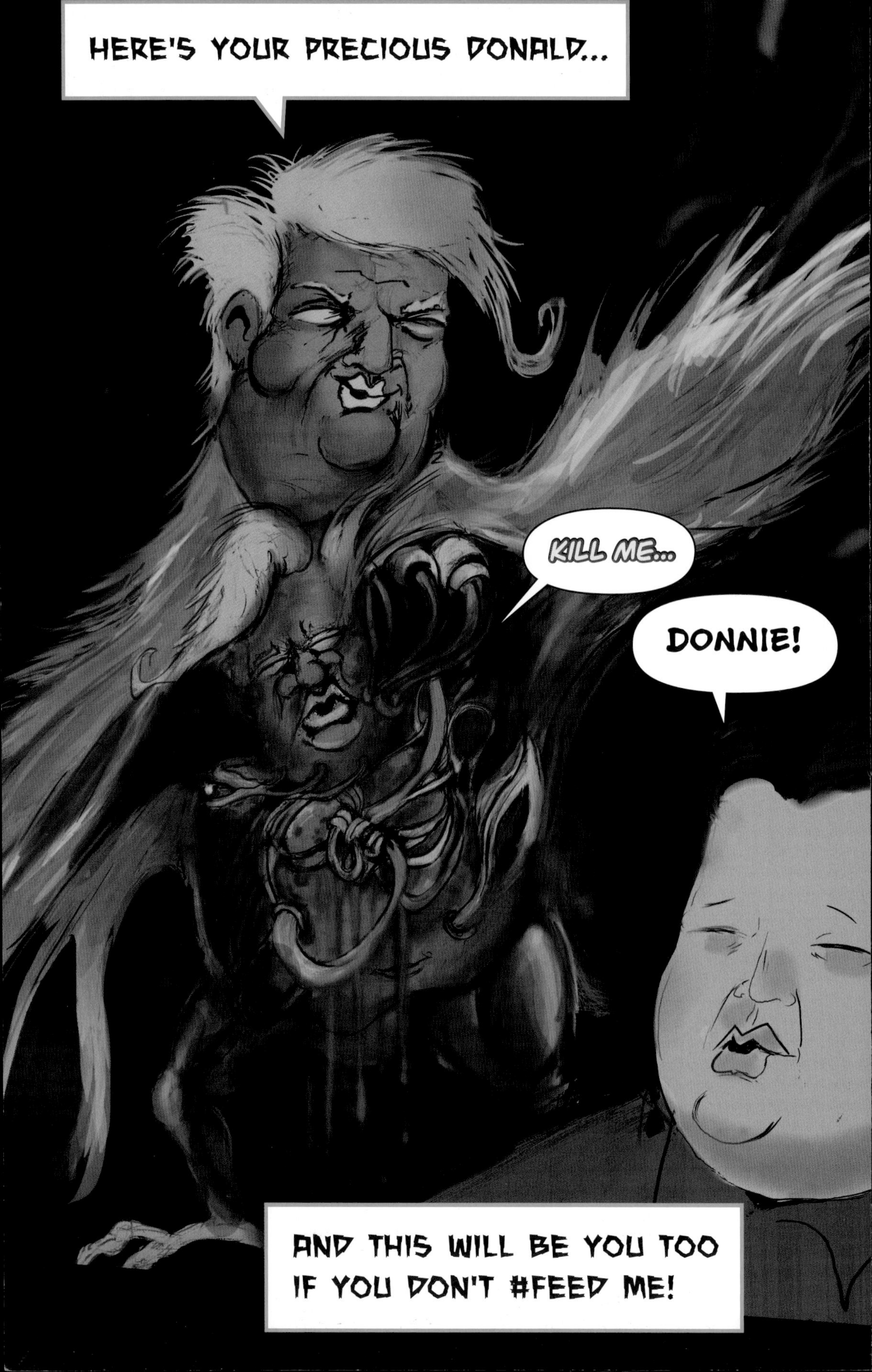
HERE'S YOUR PRECIOUS DONALD...
KILL ME...
DONNIE!
AND THIS WILL BE YOU TOO IF YOU DON'T #FEED ME!

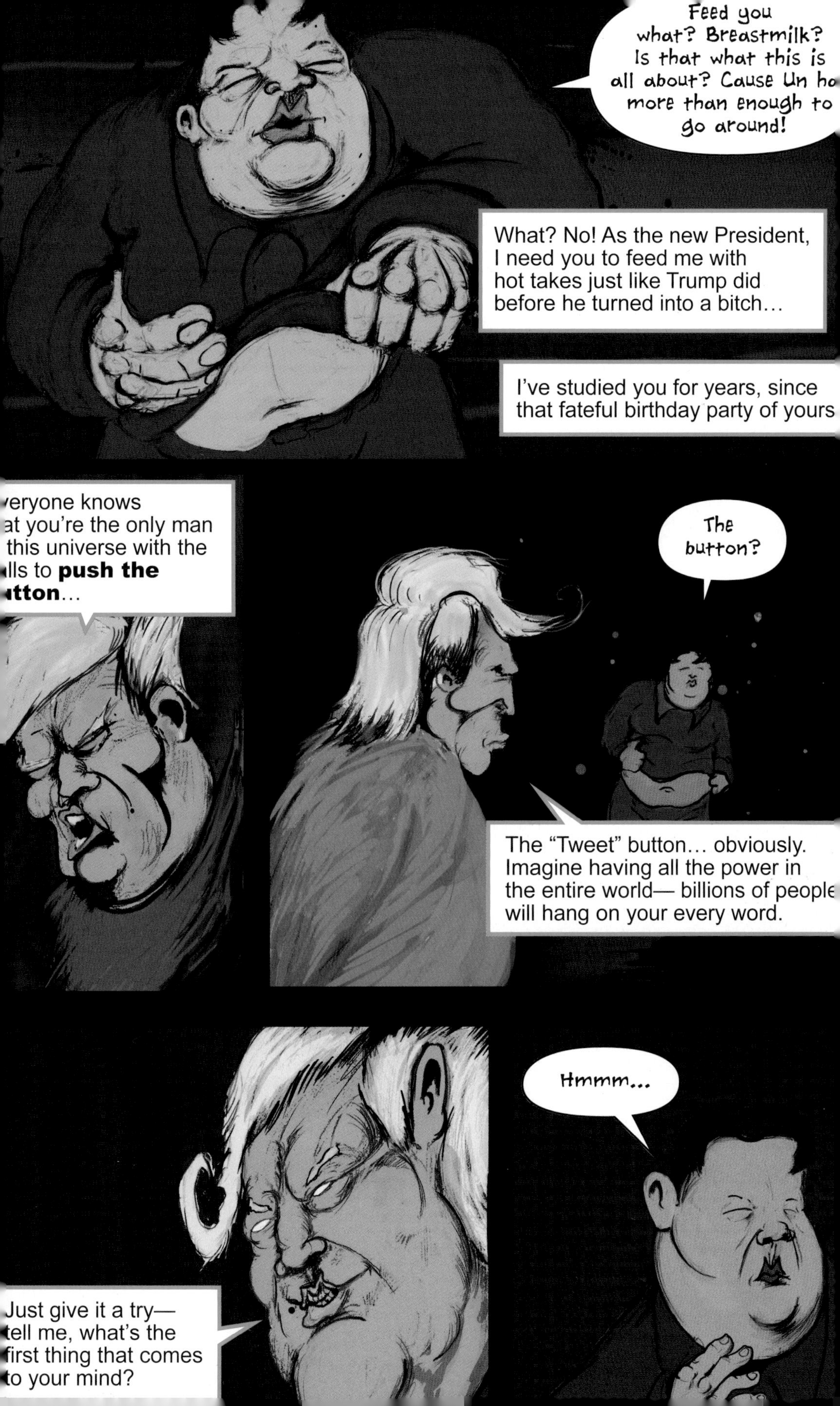
Feed you what? Breastmilk? Is that what this is all about? Cause Un ho more than enough to go around!
What? No! As the new President, I need you to feed me with hot takes just like Trump did before he turned into a bitch…
I've studied you for years, since that fateful birthday party of yours
eryone knows at you're the only man this universe with the lls to **push the** **tton**…
The button?
The "Tweet" button… obviously. Imagine having all the power in the entire world— billions of people will hang on your every word.
Hmmm…
Just give it a try— tell me, what's the first thing that comes to your mind?

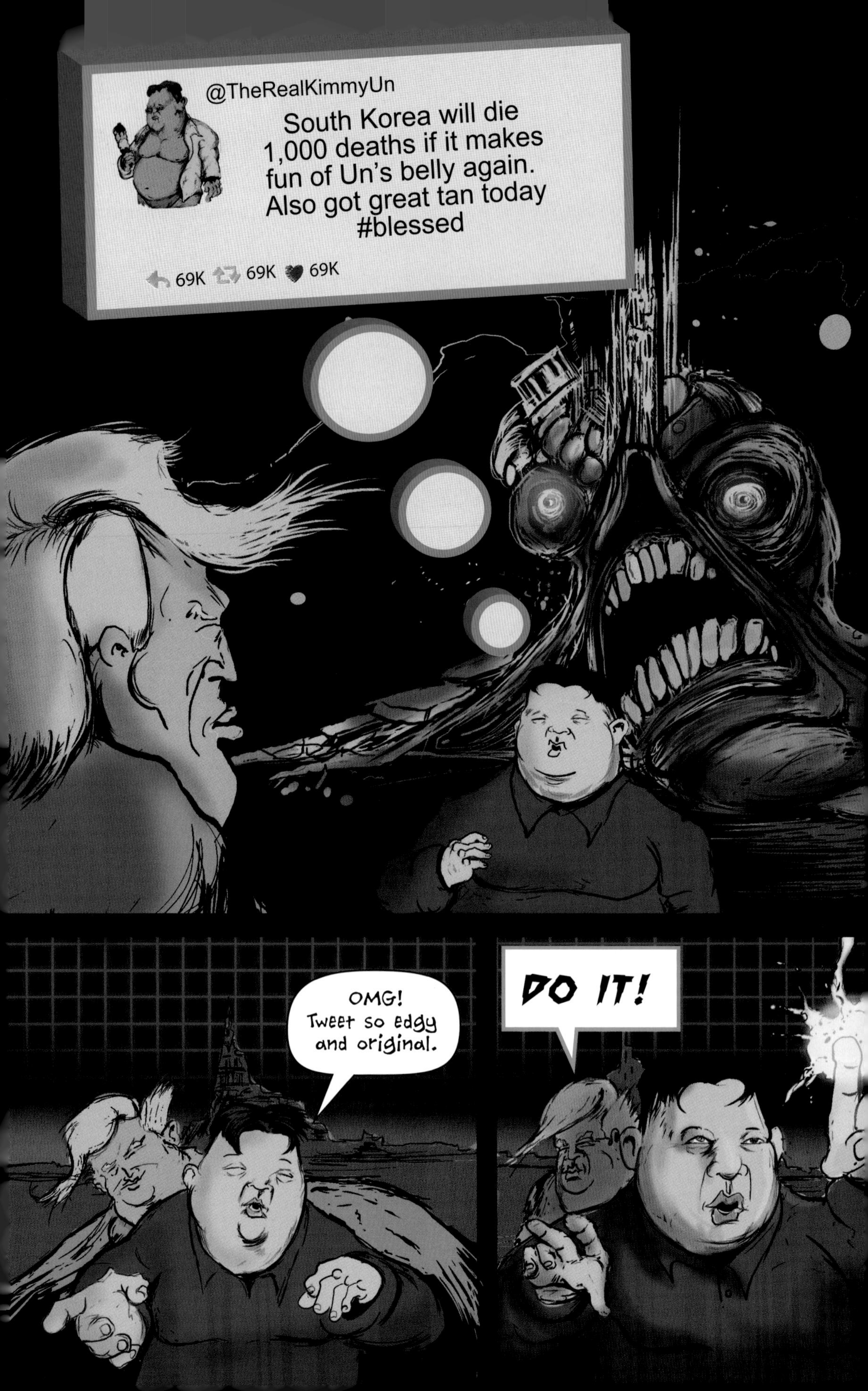
@TheRealKimmyUn
South Korea will die 1,000 deaths if it makes fun of Un's belly again. Also got great tan today #blessed
69K 69K 69K
OMG! Tweet so edgy and original.
DO IT!

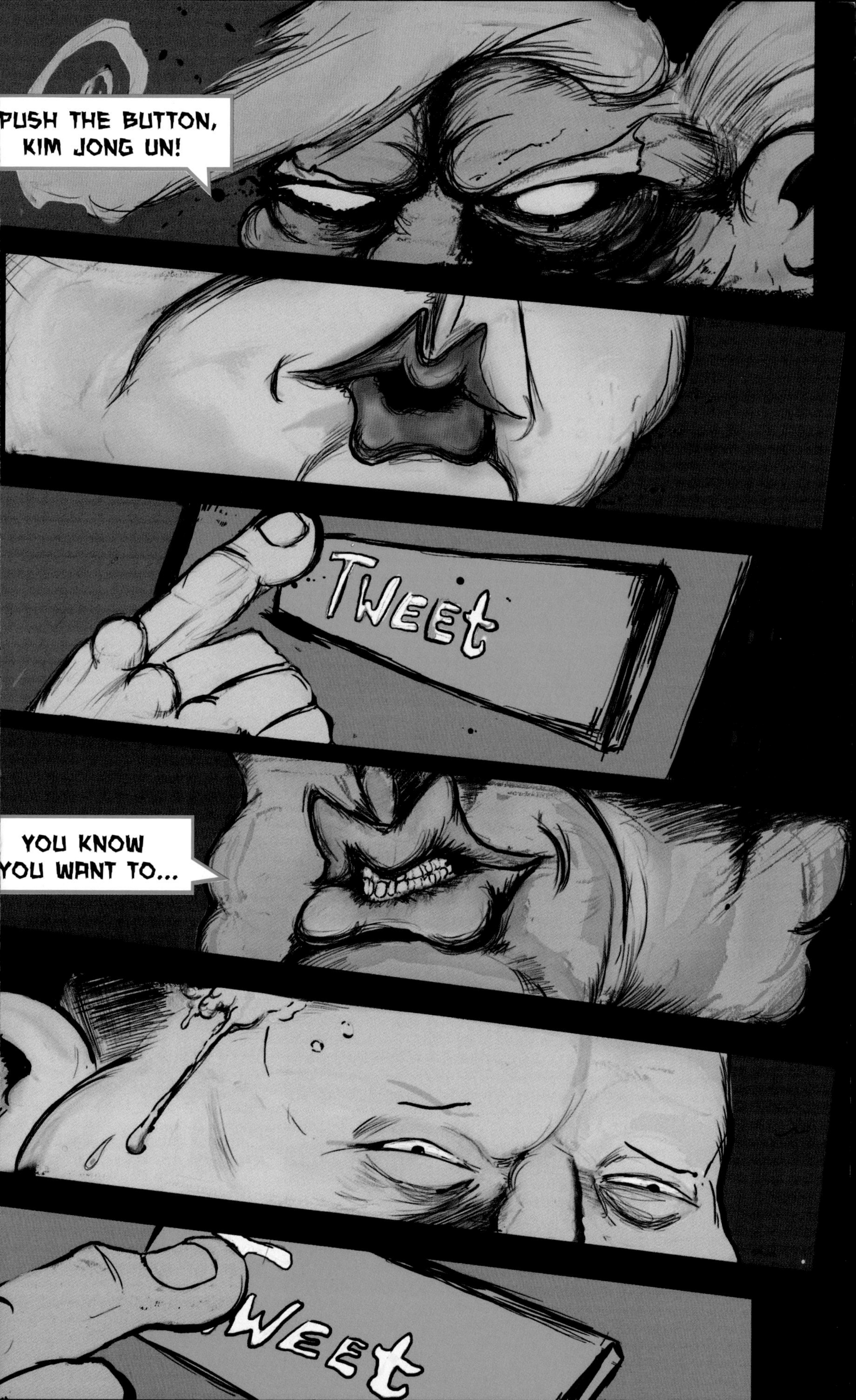
PUSH THE BUTTON, KIM JONG UN!
TWEET
YOU KNOW YOU WANT TO...
WEET

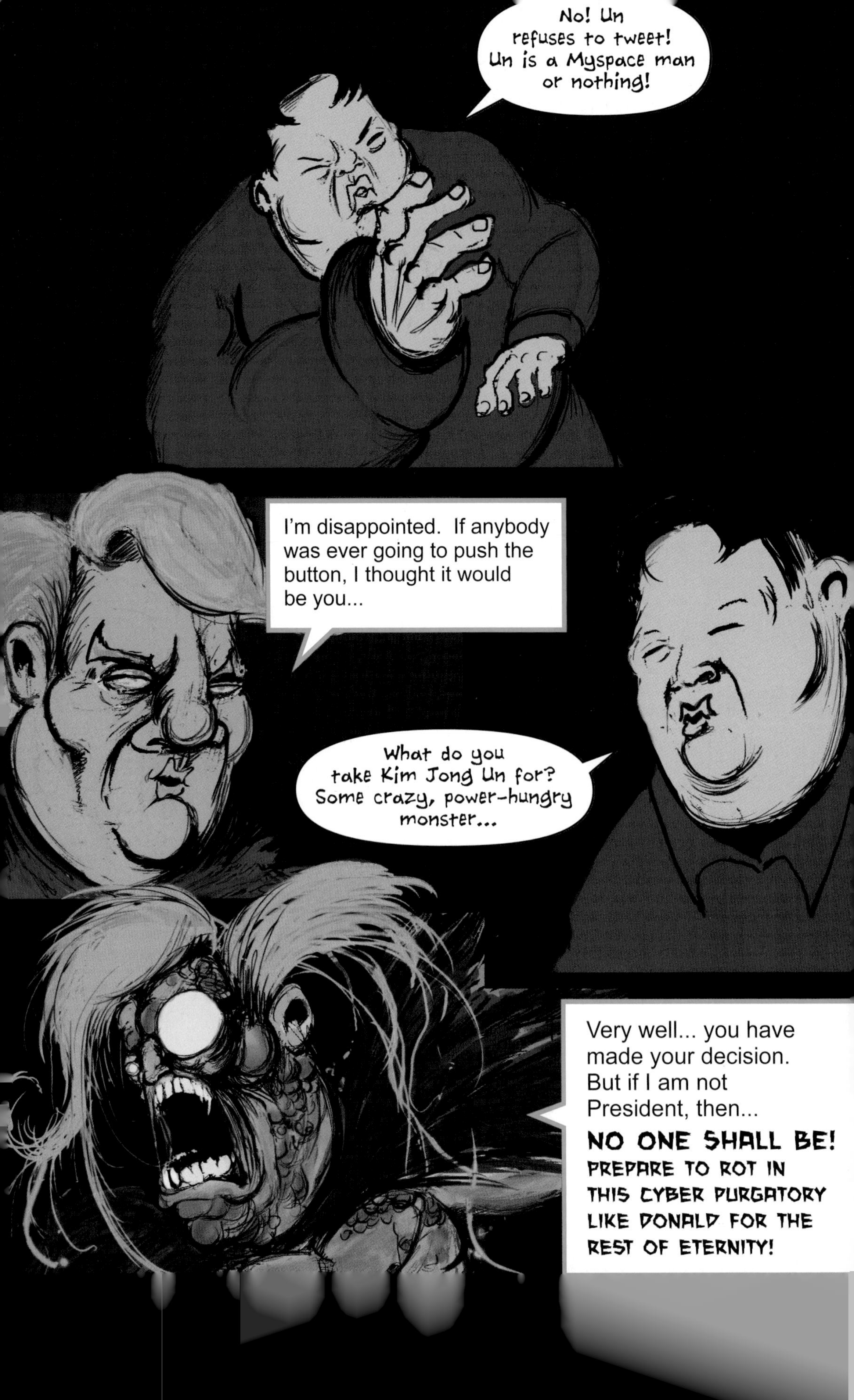
No! Un refuses to tweet! Un is a Myspace man or nothing!
I'm disappointed. If anybody was ever going to push the button, I thought it would be you...
What do you take Kim Jong Un for? Some crazy, power-hungry monster...
Very well... you have made your decision. But if I am not President, then...
NO ONE SHALL BE! PREPARE TO ROT IN THIS CYBER PURGATORY LIKE DONALD FOR THE REST OF ETERNITY!

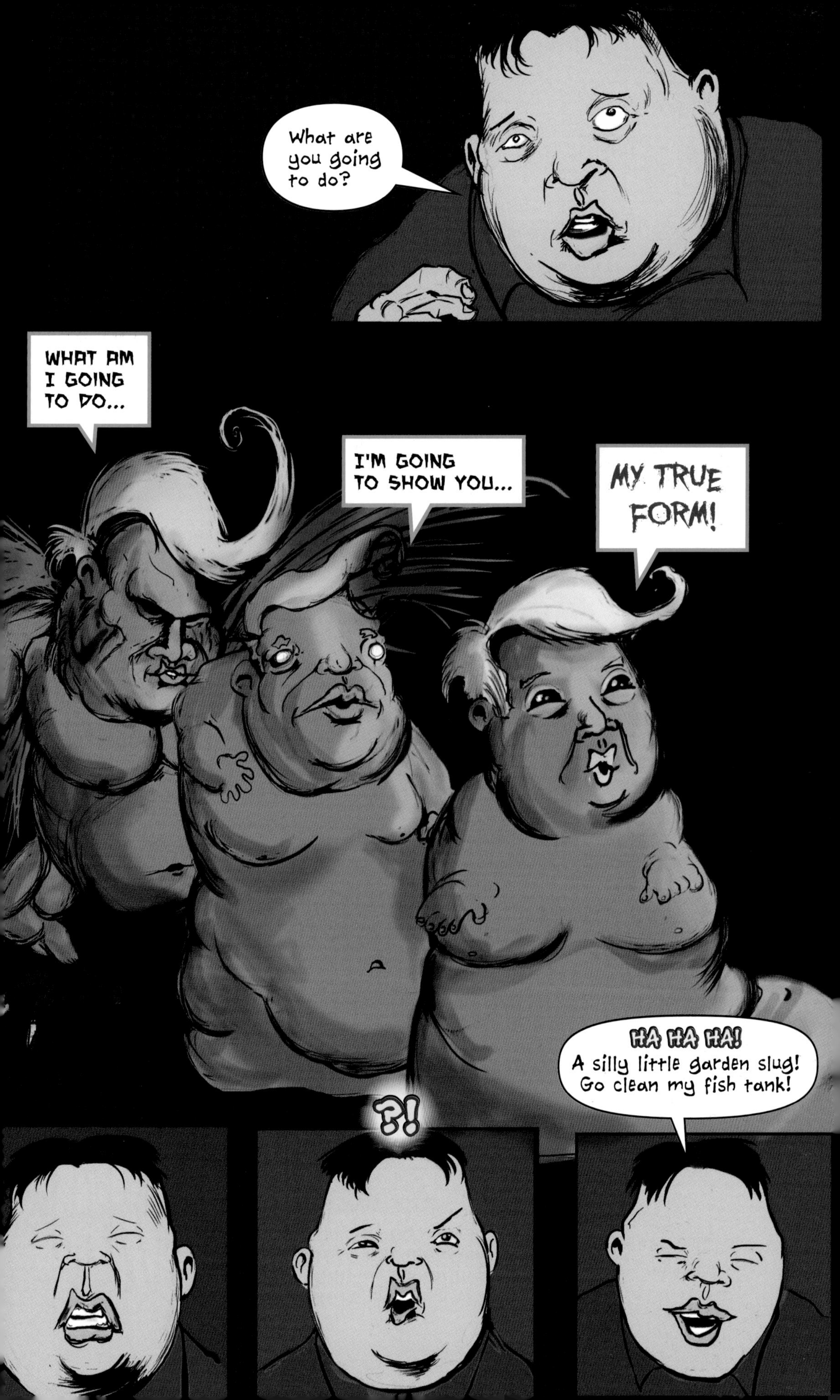
What are you going to do?
WHAT AM I GOING TO DO...
I'M GOING TO SHOW YOU...
MY TRUE FORM!
HA HA HA!
A silly little garden slug! Go clean my fish tank!
?!

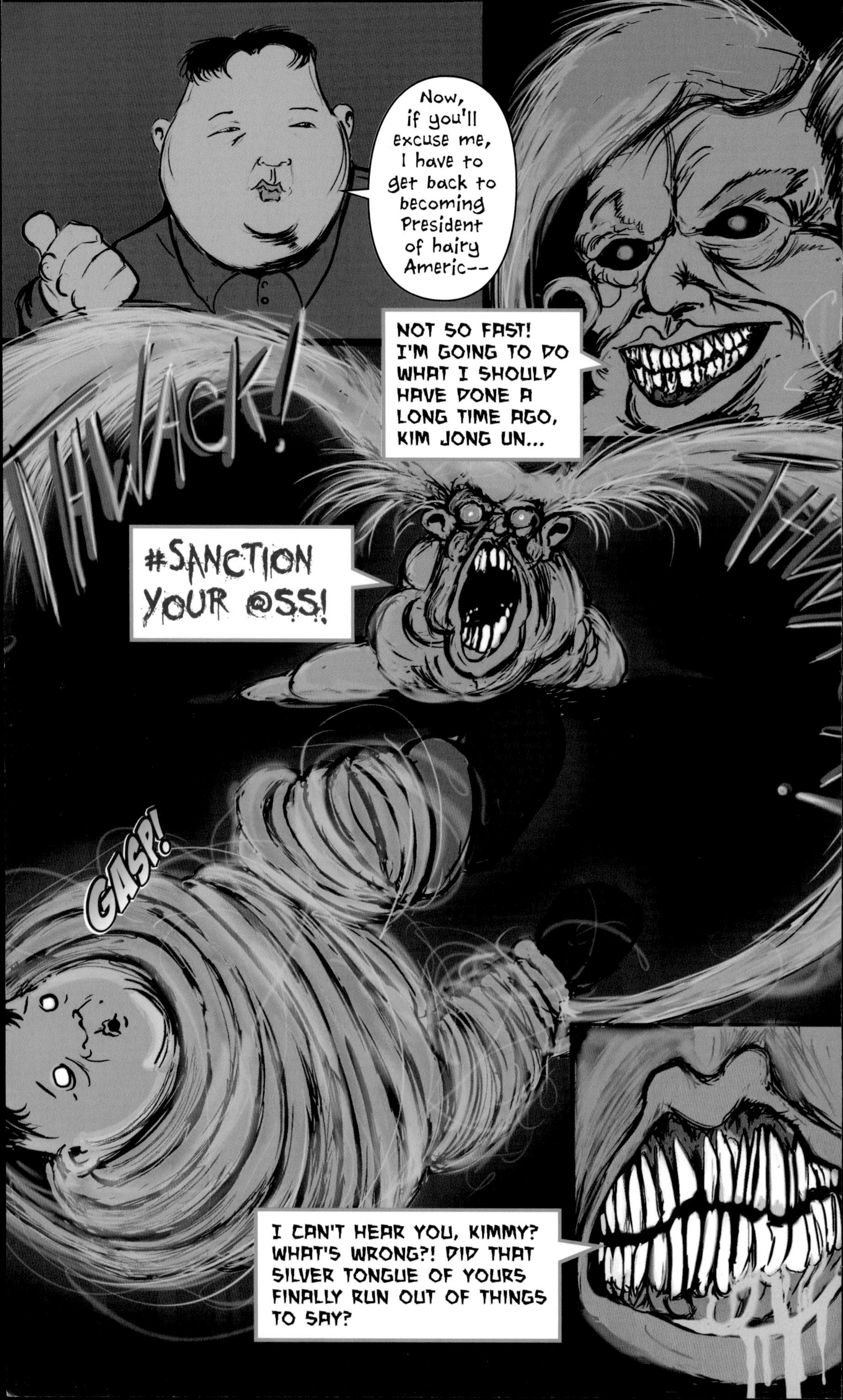

Now, if you'll excuse me, I have to get back to becoming President of hairy Americ--
THWACK!
NOT SO FAST! I'M GOING TO DO WHAT I SHOULD HAVE DONE A LONG TIME AGO, KIM JONG UN...
#SANCTION YOUR @SS!
GASP!
I CAN'T HEAR YOU, KIMMY? WHAT'S WRONG?! DID THAT SILVER TONGUE OF YOURS FINALLY RUN OUT OF THINGS TO SAY?

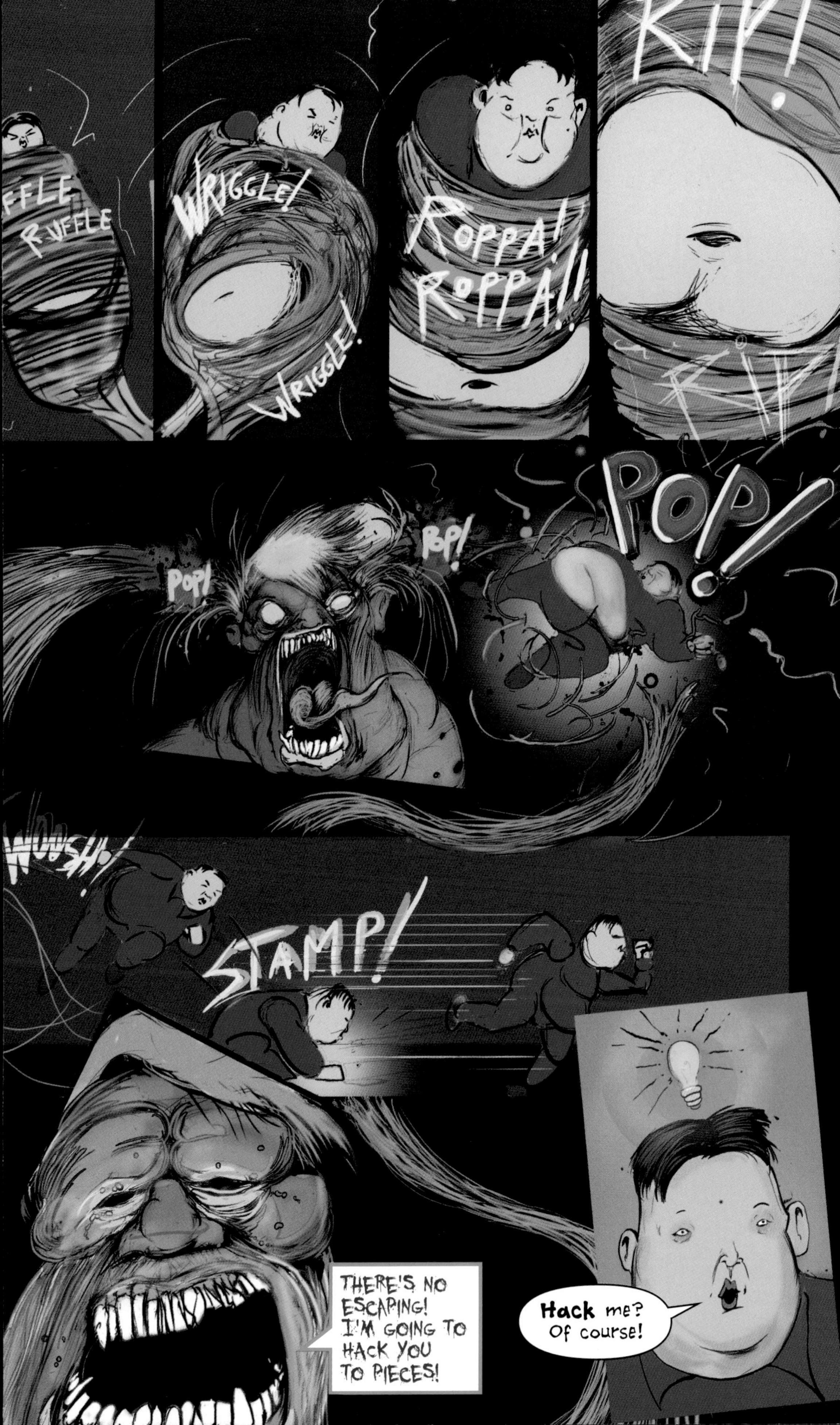

FFLE
RUFFLE
WRIGGLE!
WRIGGLE!
ROPPA!
ROPPA!!
RIP!
POP!
POP!
POP!!
WOOSH!
STAMP!
THERE'S NO ESCAPING! I'M GOING TO HACK YOU TO PIECES!
Hack me? Of course!

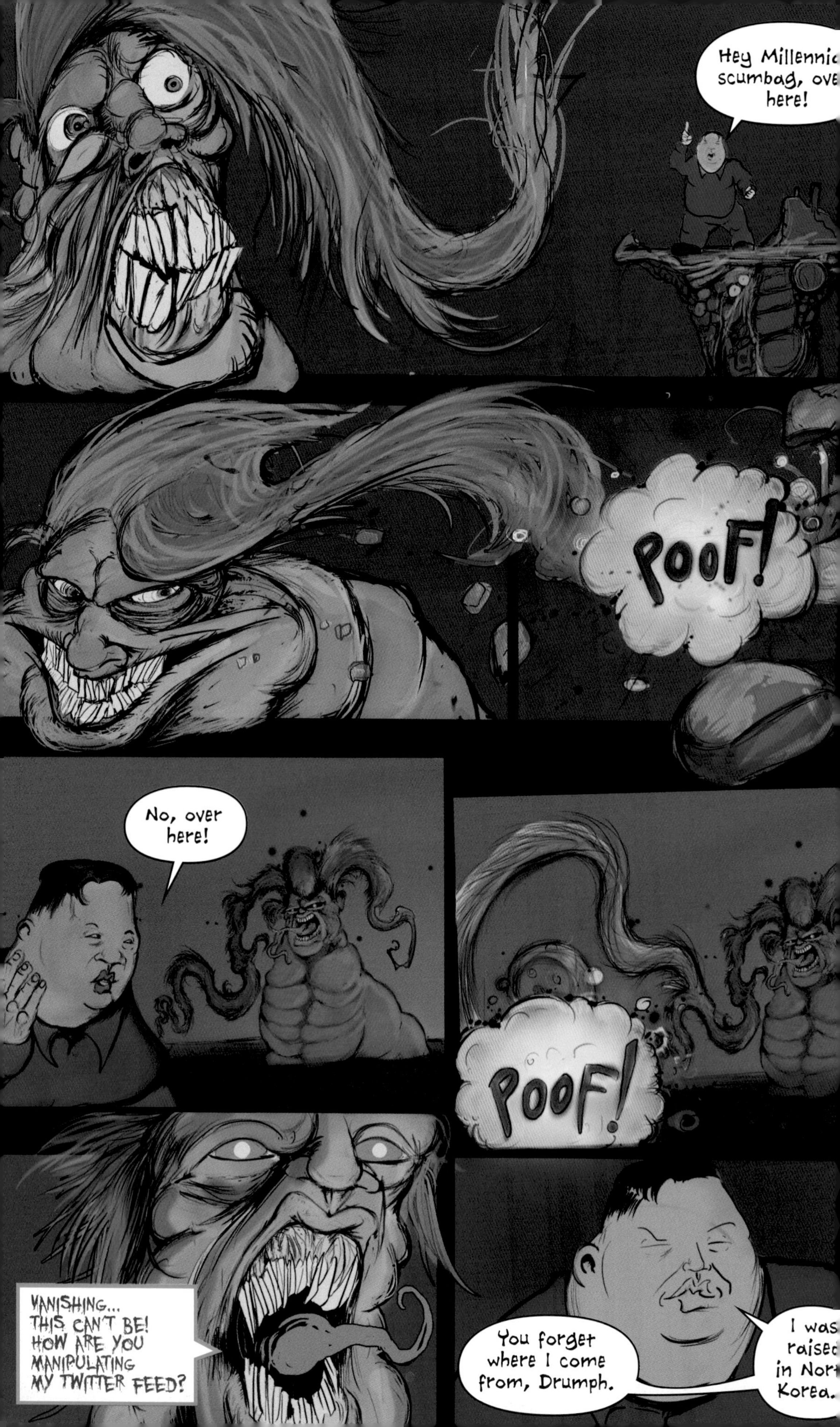
Hey Millennia scumbag, ove here!
POOF!
No, over here!
POOF!
VANISHING... THIS CAN'T BE! HOW ARE YOU MANIPULATING MY TWITTER FEED?
You forget where I come from, Drumph.
I was raised in Nort Korea.

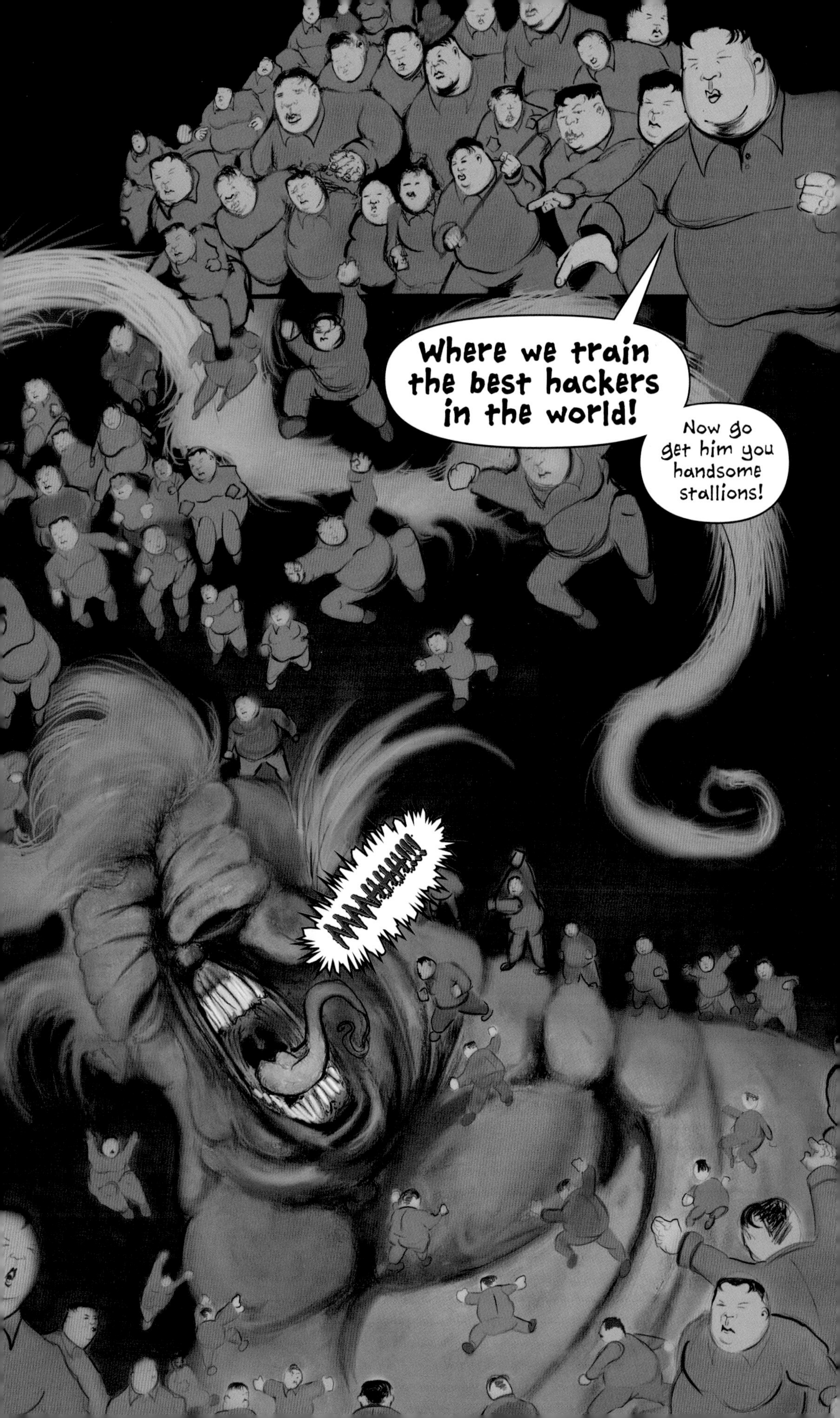
Where we train the best hackers in the world!
Now go get him you handsome stallions!
AAAAHHHHH!!!

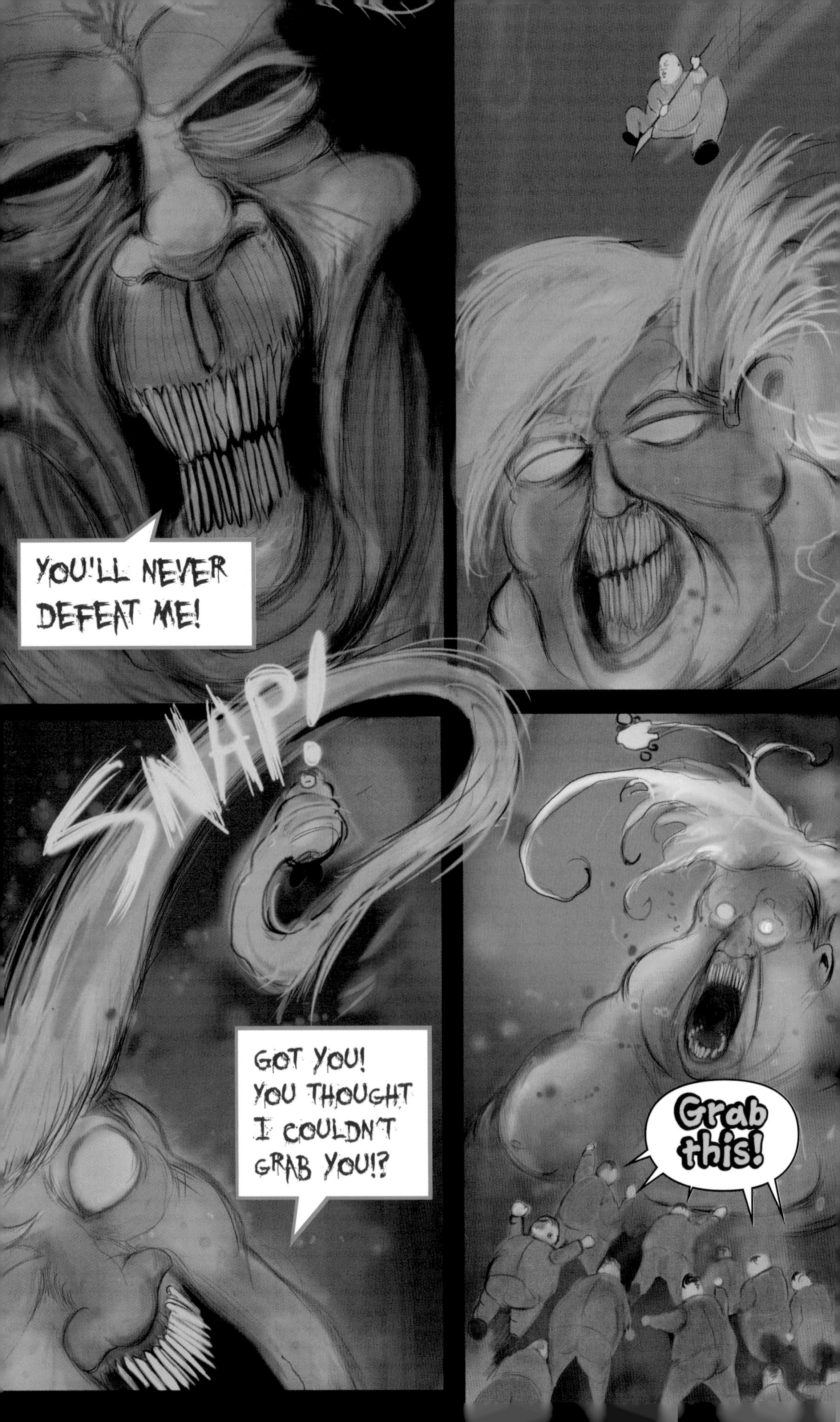
YOU'LL NEVER DEFEAT ME!
SNAP!
GOT YOU! YOU THOUGHT I COULDN'T GRAB YOU!?
Grab this!

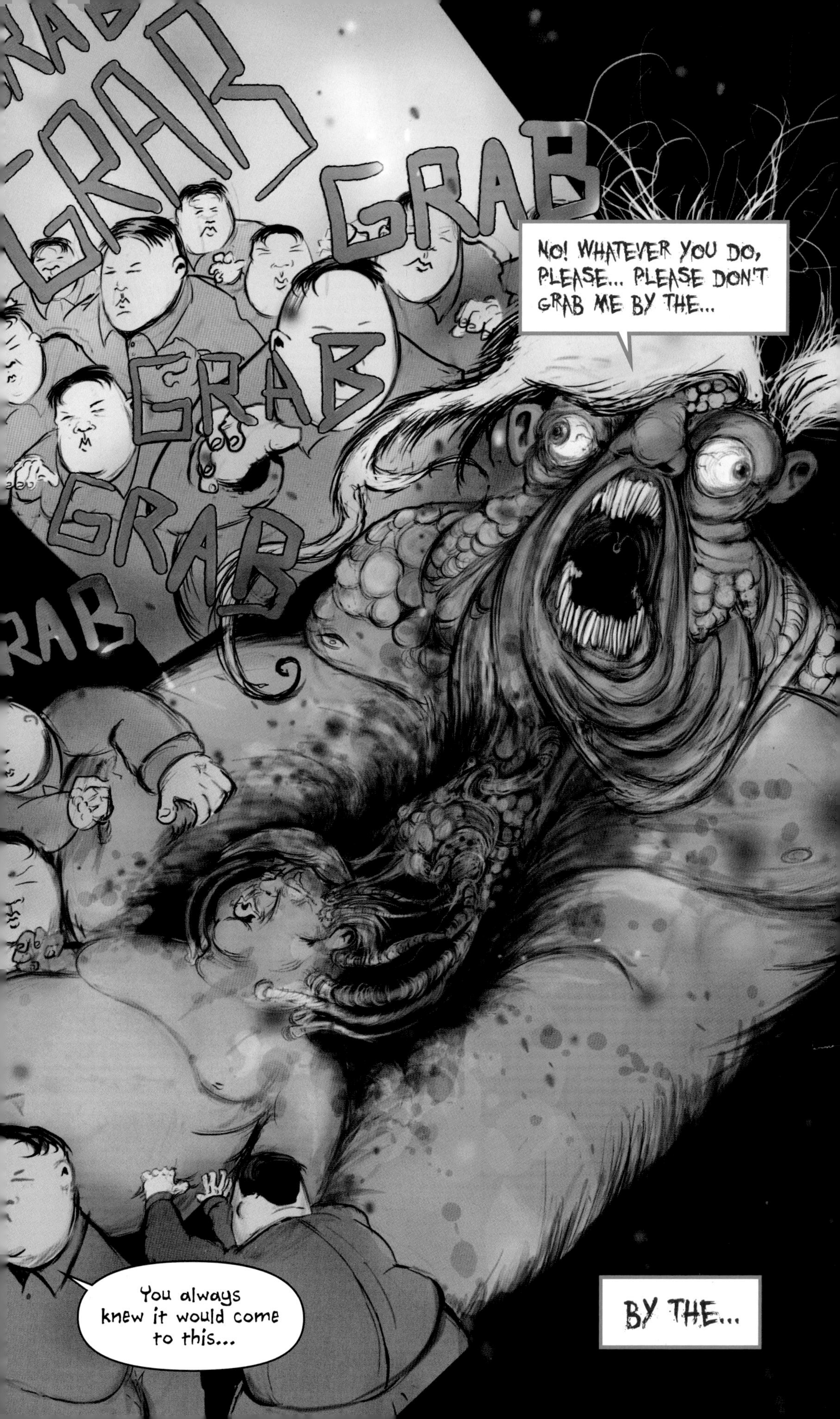
GRAB
GRAB
GRAB
GRAB
GRAB
GRAB
NO! WHATEVER YOU DO, PLEASE... PLEASE DON'T GRAB ME BY THE...
You always knew it would come to this...
BY THE...

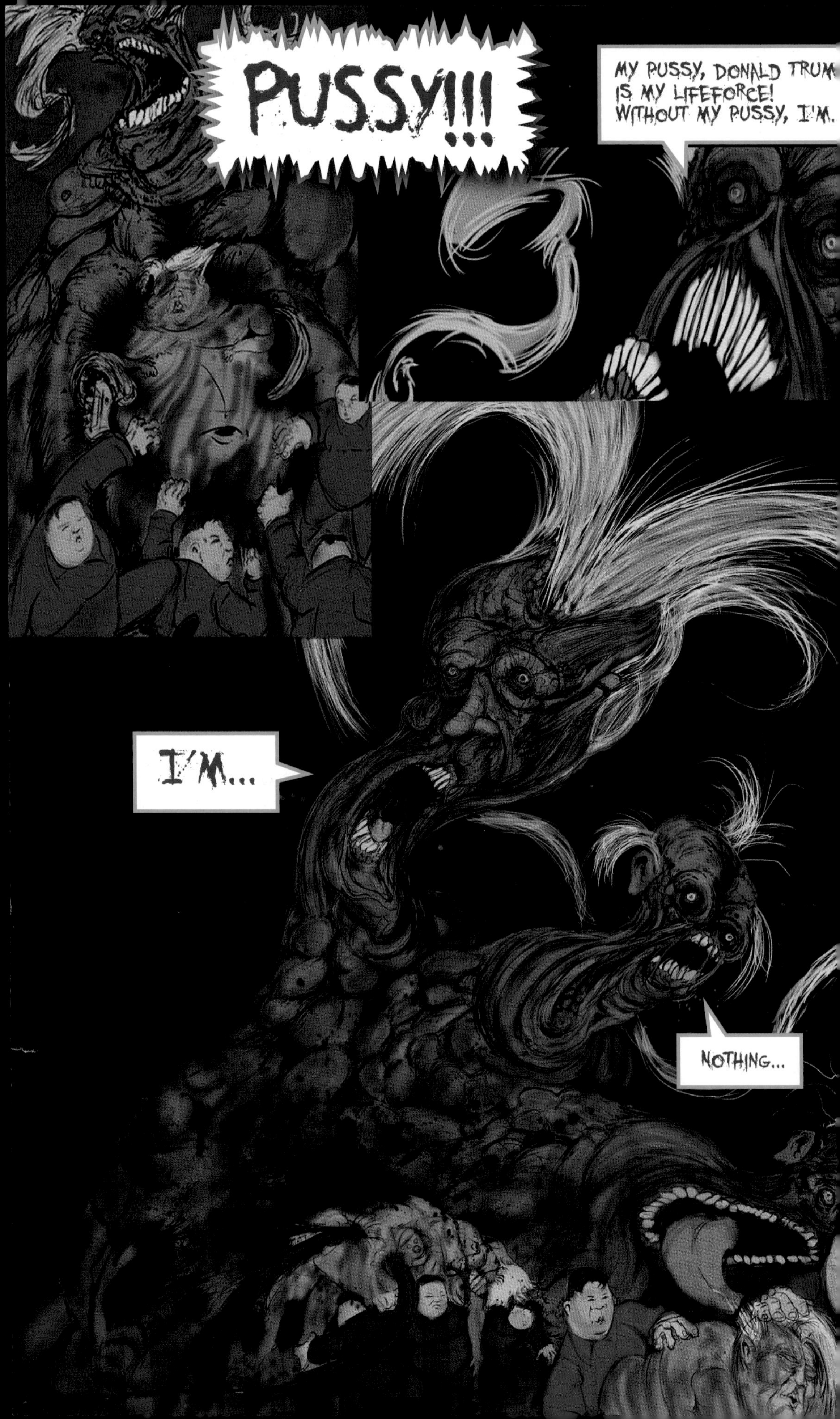
PUSSY!!!
MY PUSSY, DONALD TRUM
IS MY LIFEFORCE!
WITHOUT MY PUSSY, I'M.
I'M...
NOTHING...

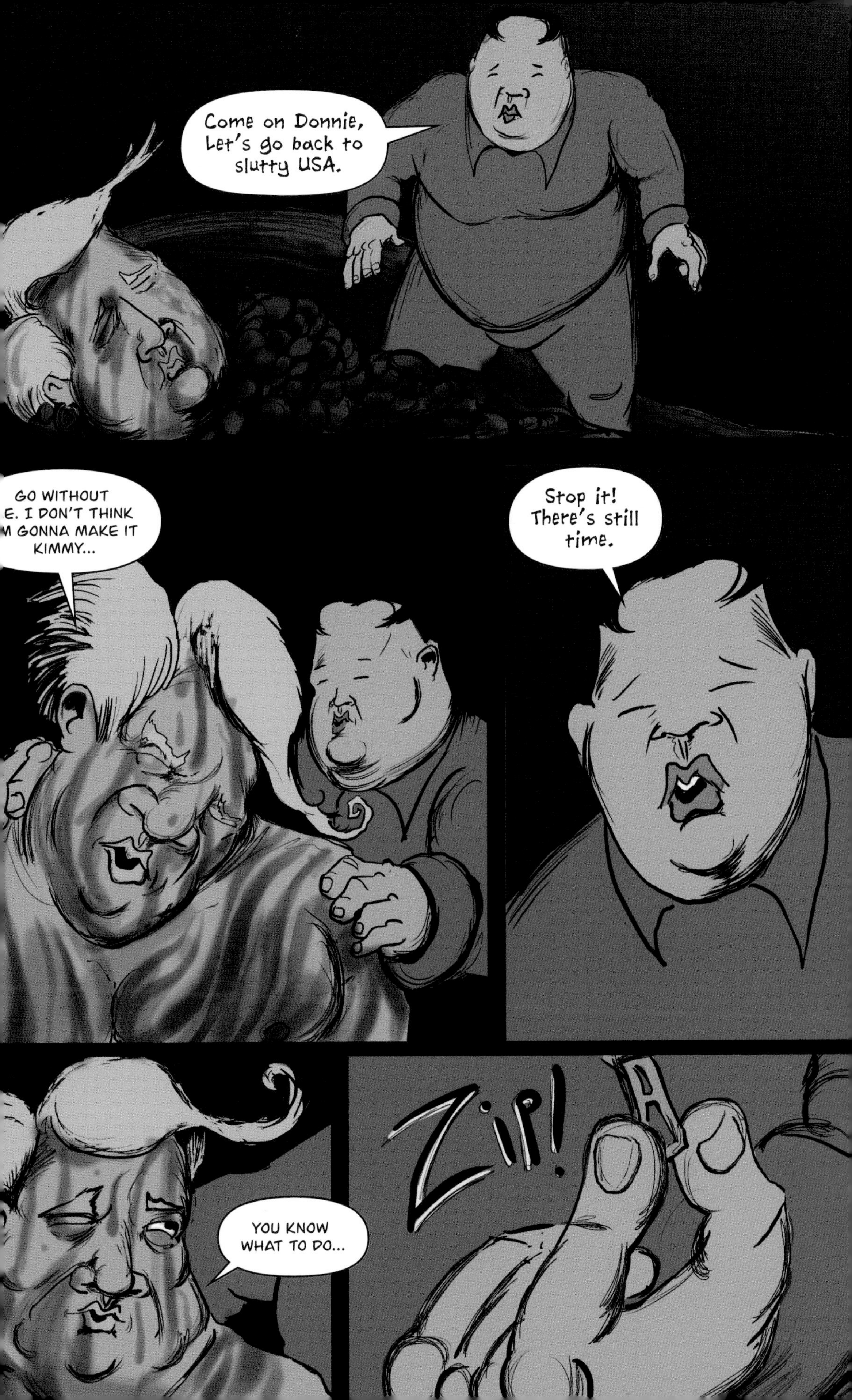
Come on Donnie, Let's go back to slutty USA.
GO WITHOUT E. I DON'T THINK M GONNA MAKE IT KIMMY...
Stop it! There's still time.
YOU KNOW WHAT TO DO...
ZIP!

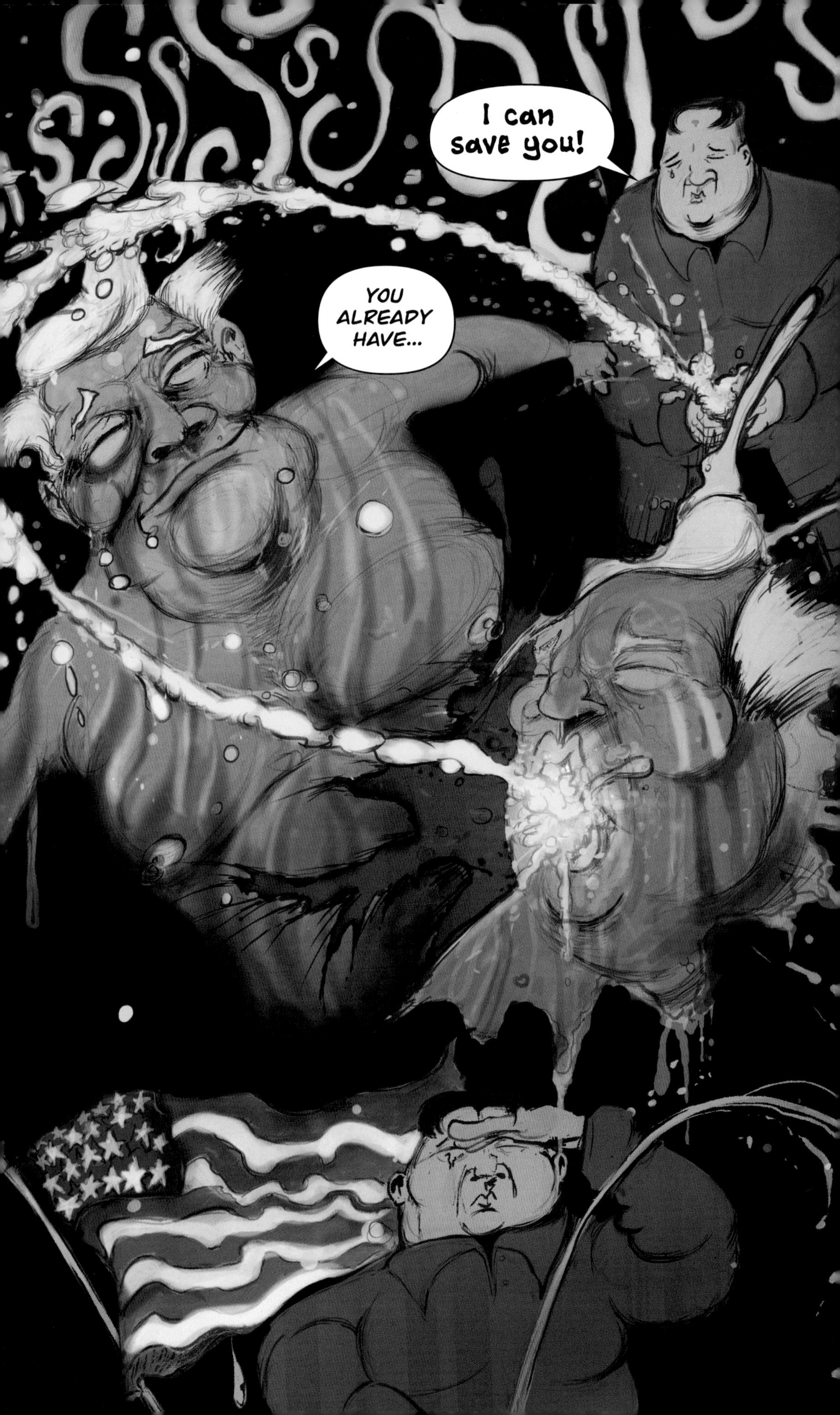
I can save you!
YOU ALREADY HAVE...

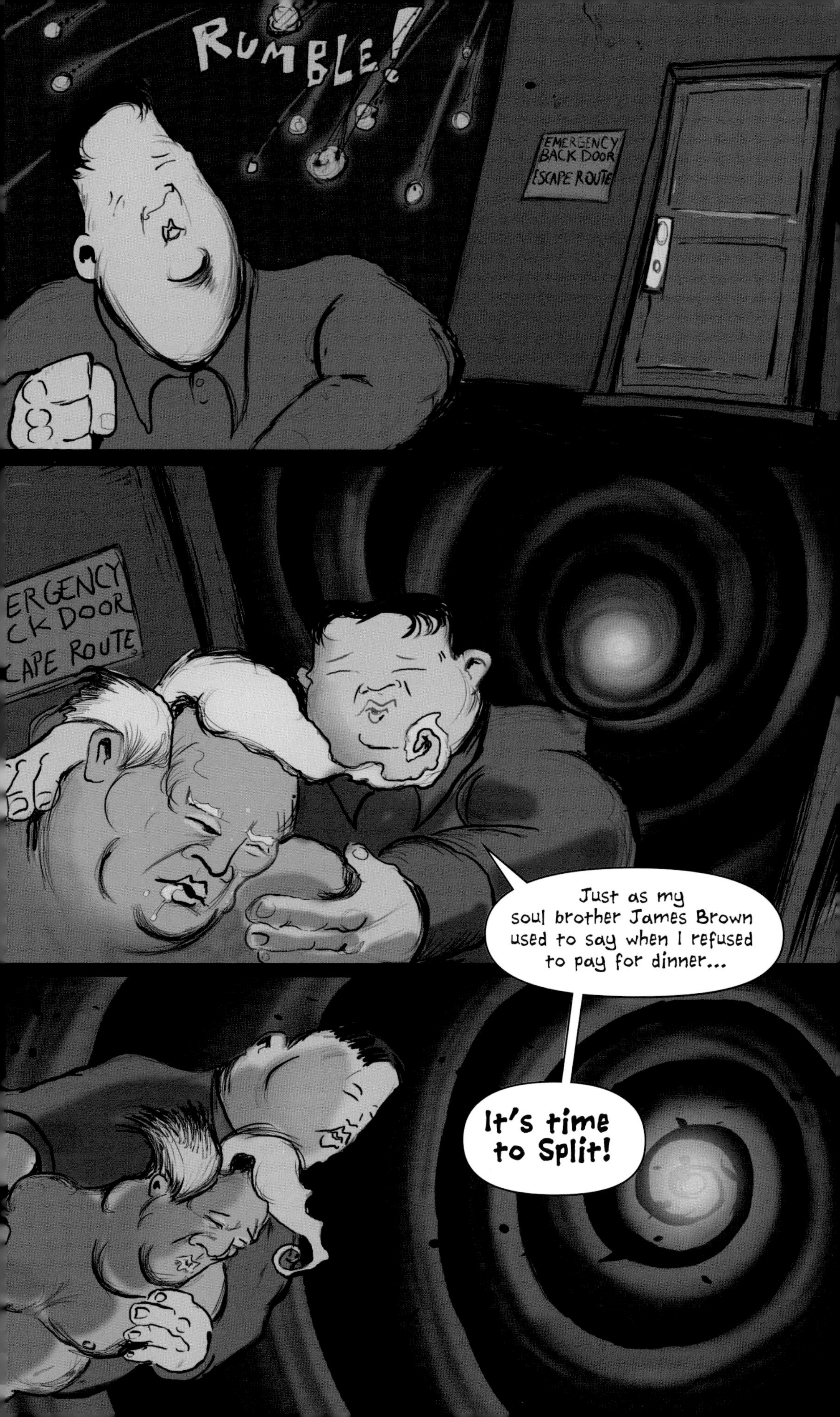
RUMBLE!
EMERGENCY BACK DOOR ESCAPE ROUTE
ERGENCY CK DOOR CAPE ROUTE
Just as my soul brother James Brown used to say when I refused to pay for dinner...
It's time to Split!

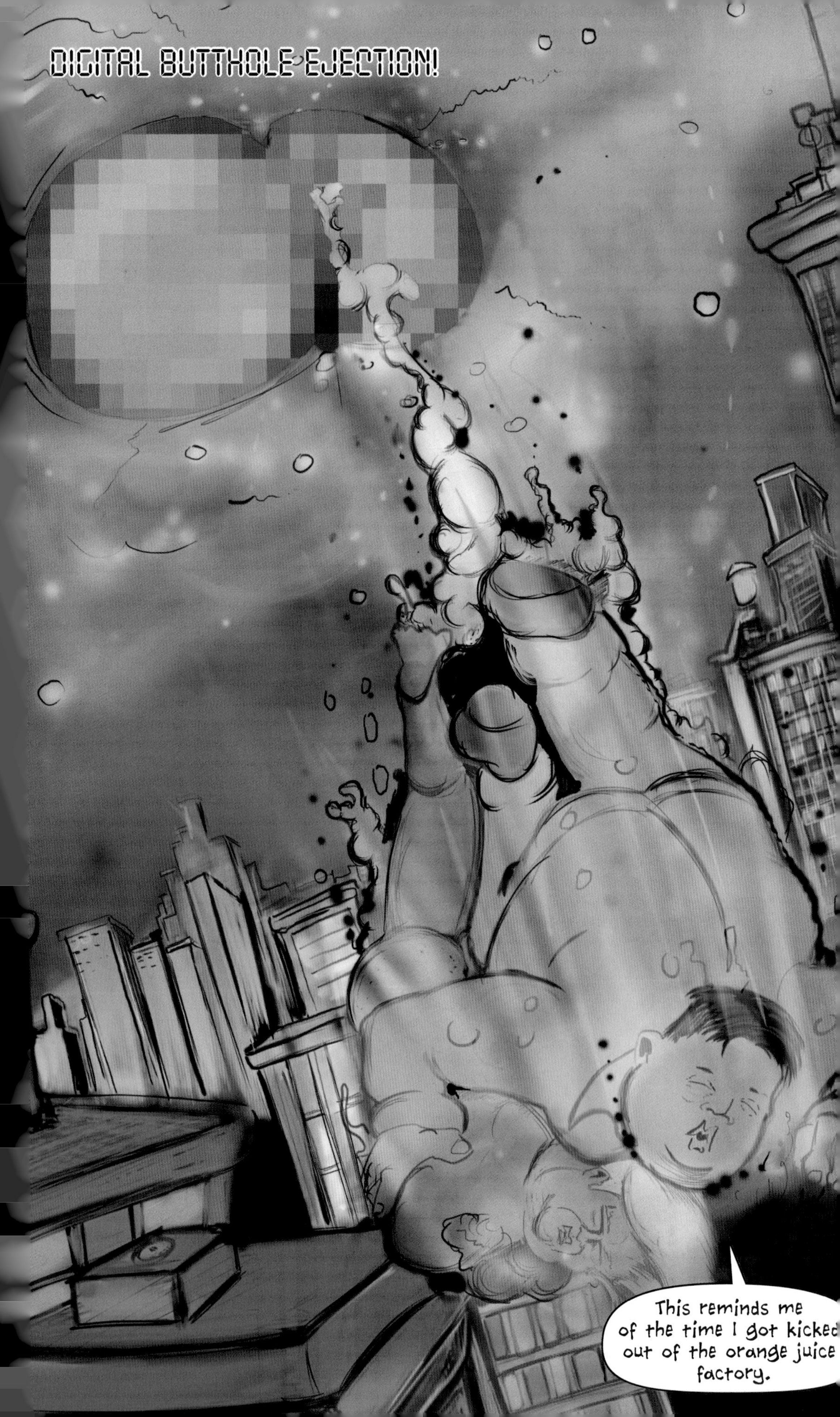
DIGITAL BUTTHOLE EJECTION!
This reminds me of the time I got kicked out of the orange juice factory.

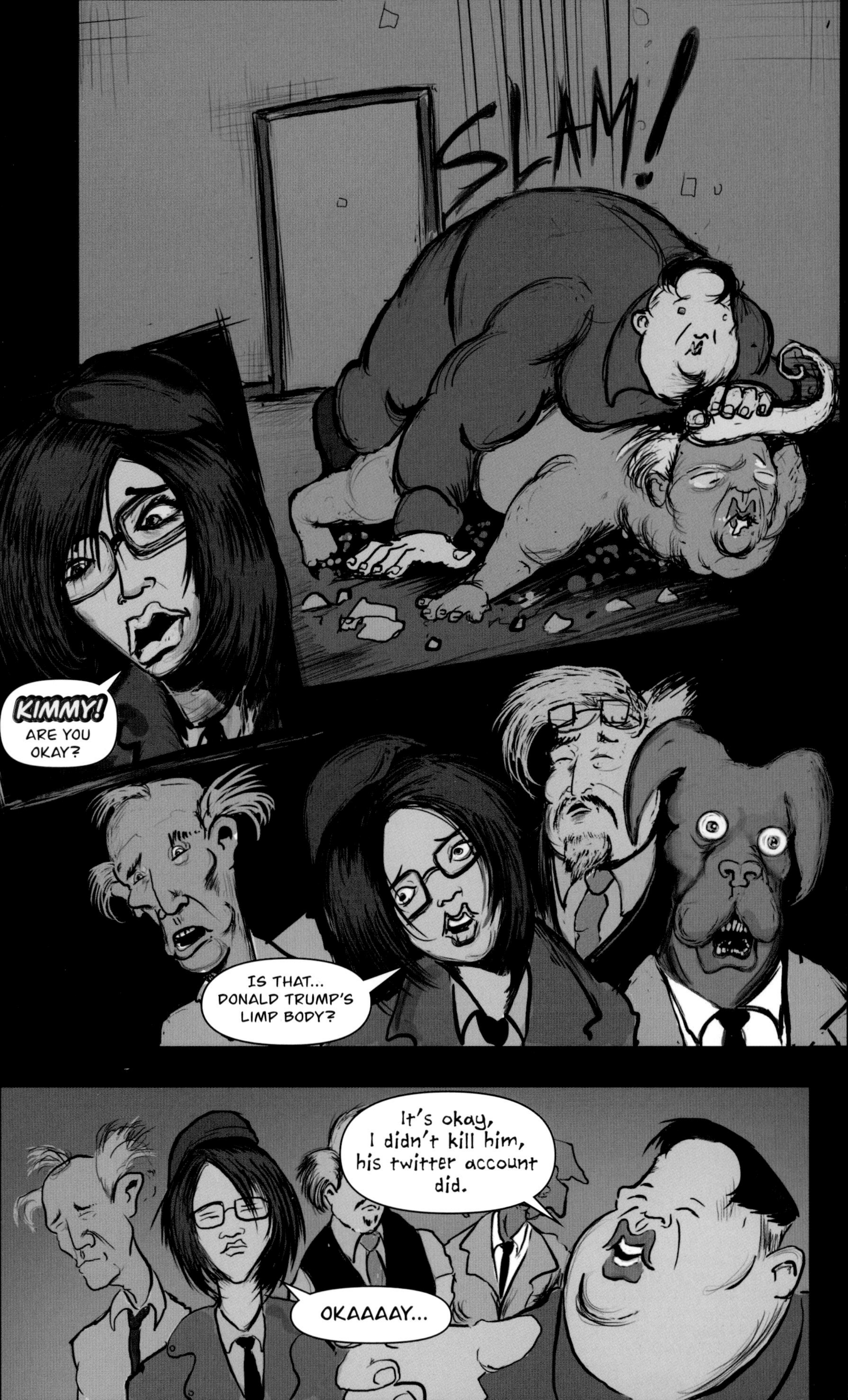
SLAM!
KIMMY! ARE YOU OKAY?
IS THAT... DONALD TRUMP'S LIMP BODY?
It's okay, I didn't kill him, his twitter account did.
OKAAAAY...

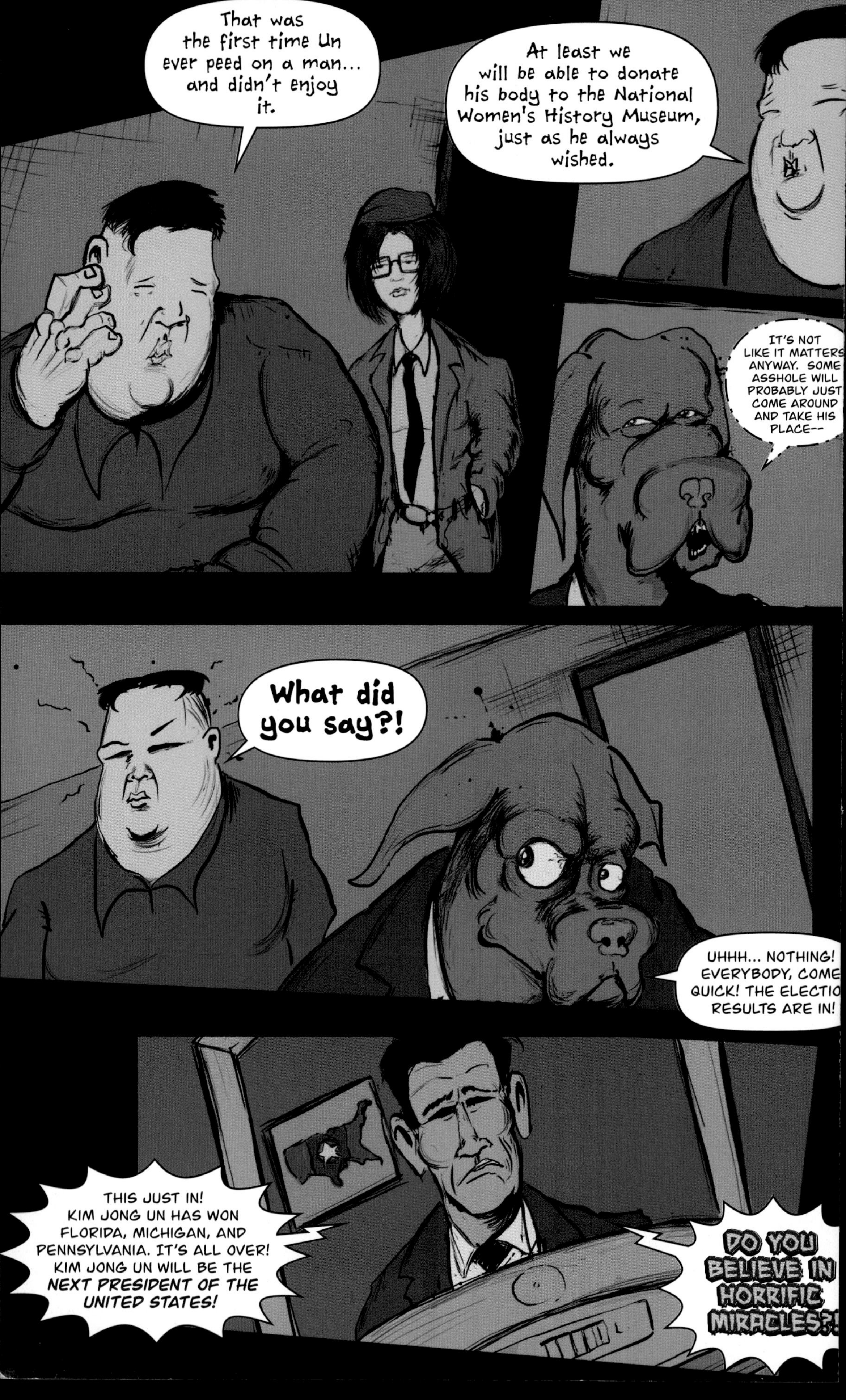
That was the first time Un ever peed on a man... and didn't enjoy it.
At least we will be able to donate his body to the National Women's History Museum, just as he always wished.
IT'S NOT LIKE IT MATTERS ANYWAY. SOME ASSHOLE WILL PROBABLY JUST COME AROUND AND TAKE HIS PLACE--
What did you say?!
UHHH... NOTHING! EVERYBODY, COME QUICK! THE ELECTIO RESULTS ARE IN!
THIS JUST IN! KIM JONG UN HAS WON FLORIDA, MICHIGAN, AND PENNSYLVANIA. IT'S ALL OVER! KIM JONG UN WILL BE THE NEXT PRESIDENT OF THE UNITED STATES!
DO YOU BELIEVE IN HORRIFIC MIRACLES?!

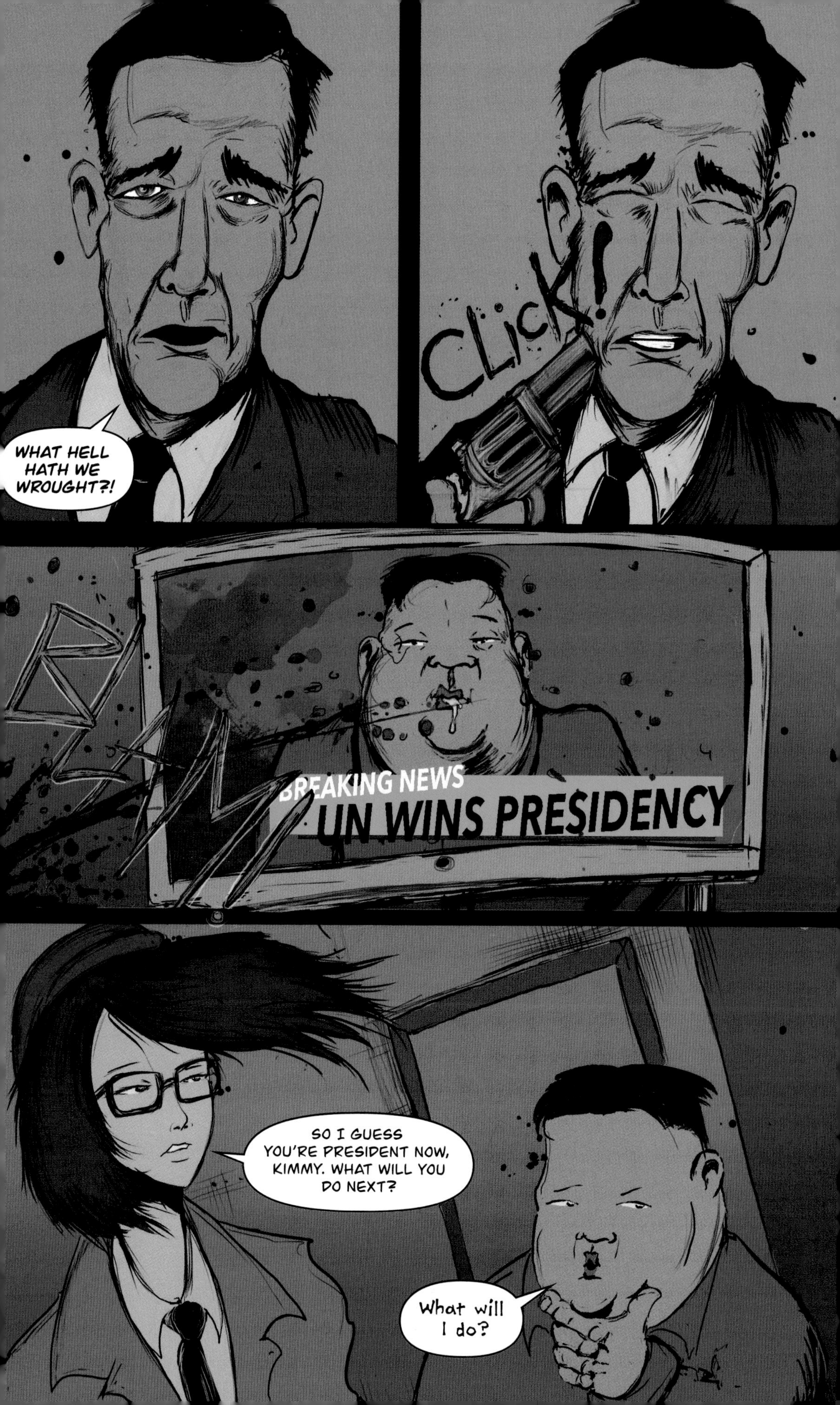
WHAT HELL HATH WE WROUGHT?!
CLICK!
BLAM
BREAKING NEWS
UN WINS PRESIDENCY
SO I GUESS YOU'RE PRESIDENT NOW, KIMMY. WHAT WILL YOU DO NEXT?
What will I do?

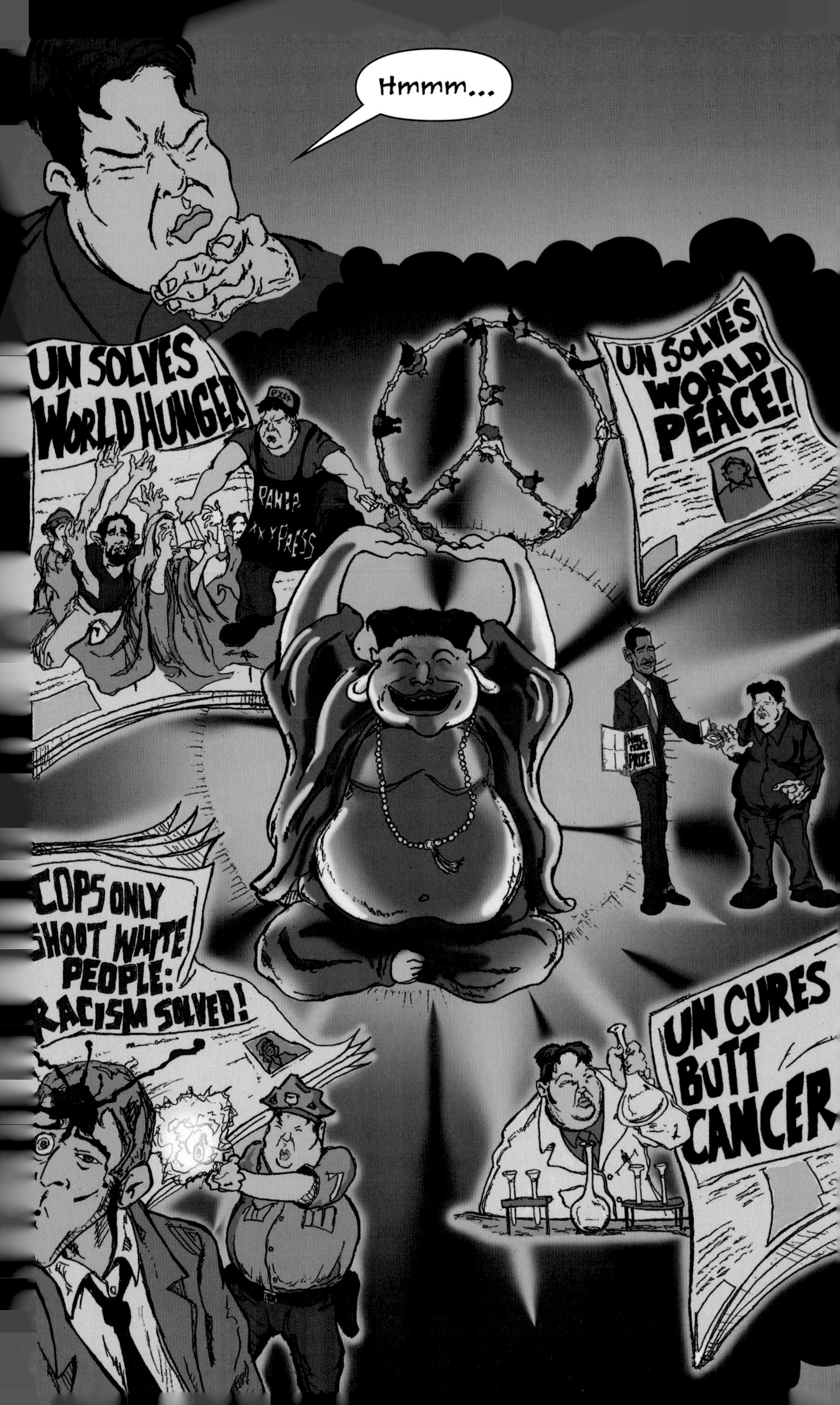
Hmmm...
UN SOLVES WORLD HUNGER
UN SOLVES WORLD PEACE!
COPS ONLY SHOOT WHITE PEOPLE: RACISM SOLVED!
UN CURES BUTT CANCER

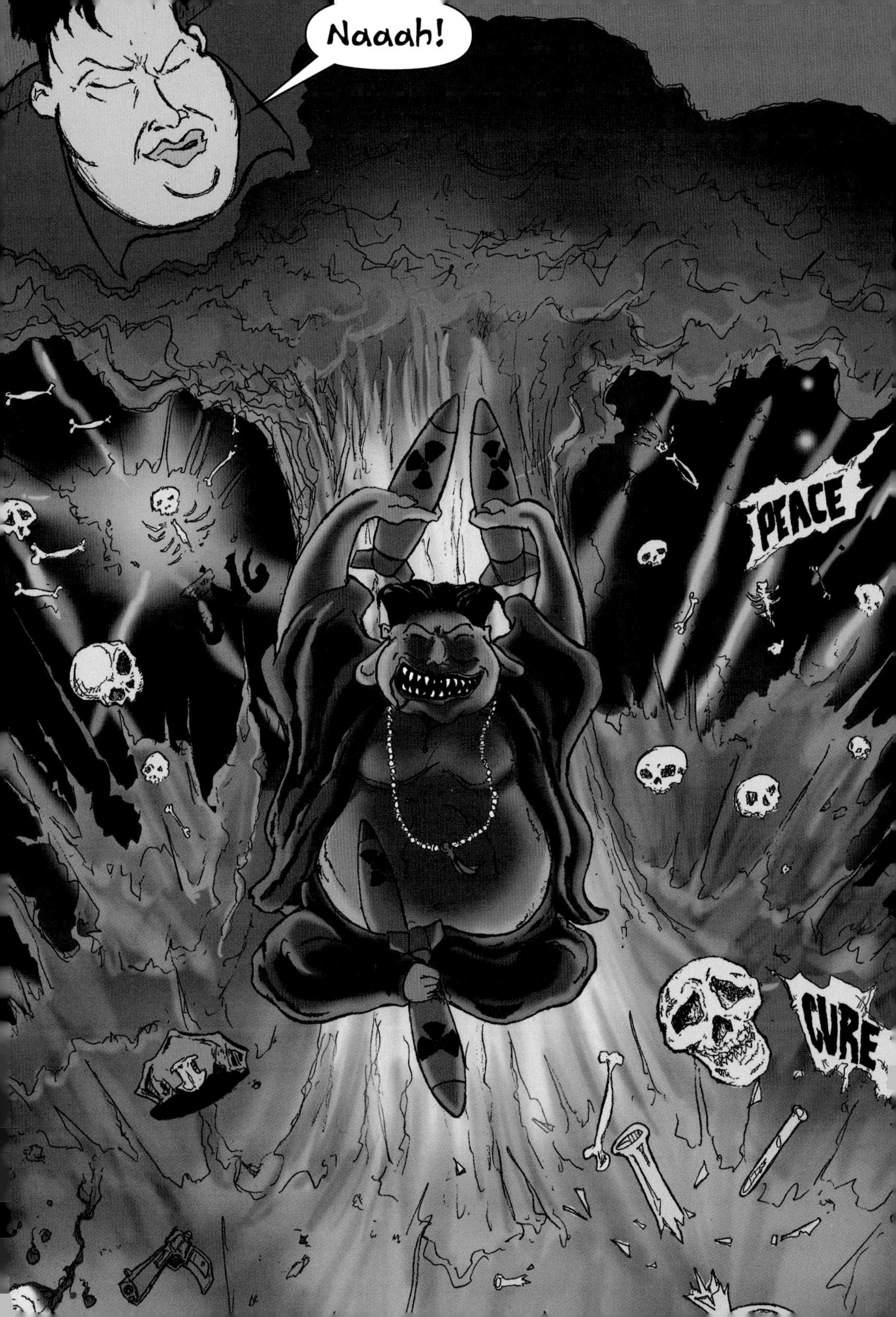
Naaah!
PEACE
CURE

FROM THE CRIMINALLY
INSANE MINDS THAT
BROUGHT YOU

UNPRESIDENTIAL

HERE IS AN EXCLUSIVE
SNEAK PEEK OF

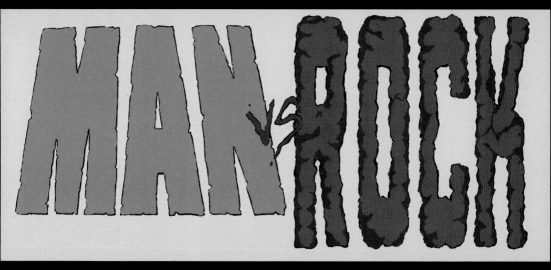

AVAILABLE NOW

TRY NOT TO WET YOURSELF

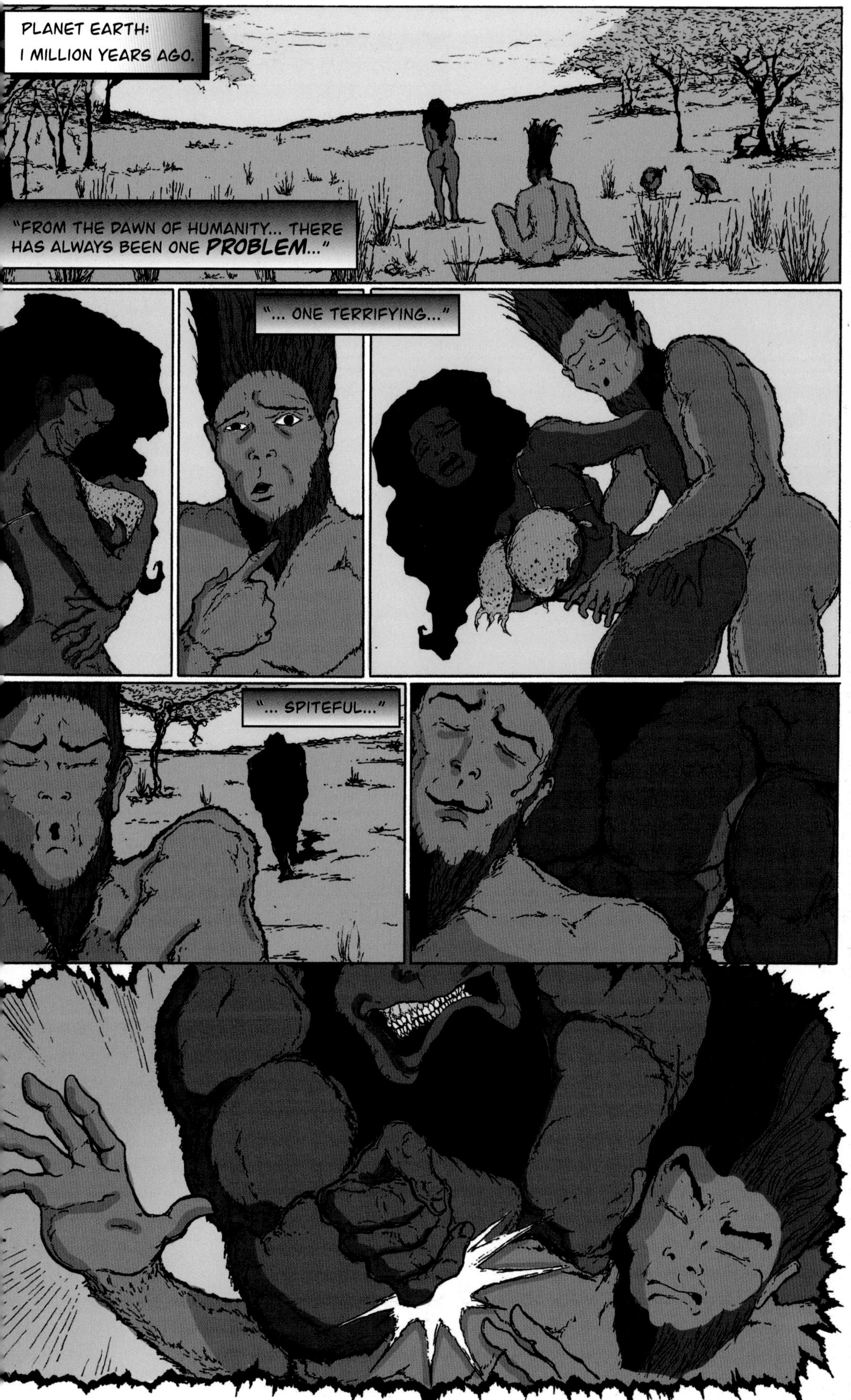
PLANET EARTH:
1 MILLION YEARS AGO.
"FROM THE DAWN OF HUMANITY... THERE HAS ALWAYS BEEN ONE PROBLEM..."
"... ONE TERRIFYING..."
"... SPITEFUL..."

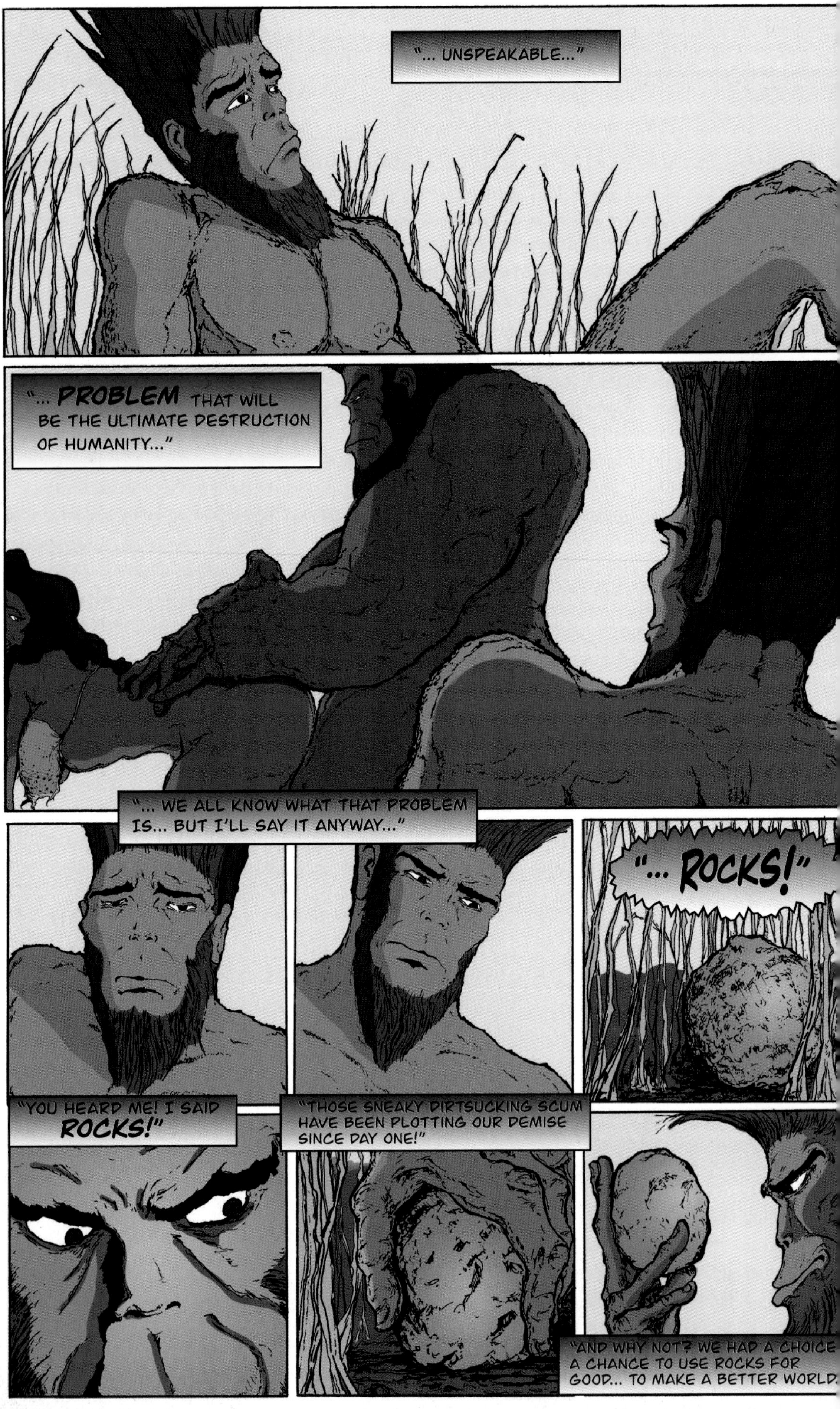
"... UNSPEAKABLE..."
"... PROBLEM THAT WILL BE THE ULTIMATE DESTRUCTION OF HUMANITY..."
"... WE ALL KNOW WHAT THAT PROBLEM IS... BUT I'LL SAY IT ANYWAY..."
"... ROCKS!"
"YOU HEARD ME! I SAID ROCKS!"
"THOSE SNEAKY DIRTSUCKING SCUM HAVE BEEN PLOTTING OUR DEMISE SINCE DAY ONE!"
"AND WHY NOT? WE HAD A CHOICE A CHANCE TO USE ROCKS FOR GOOD... TO MAKE A BETTER WORLD.

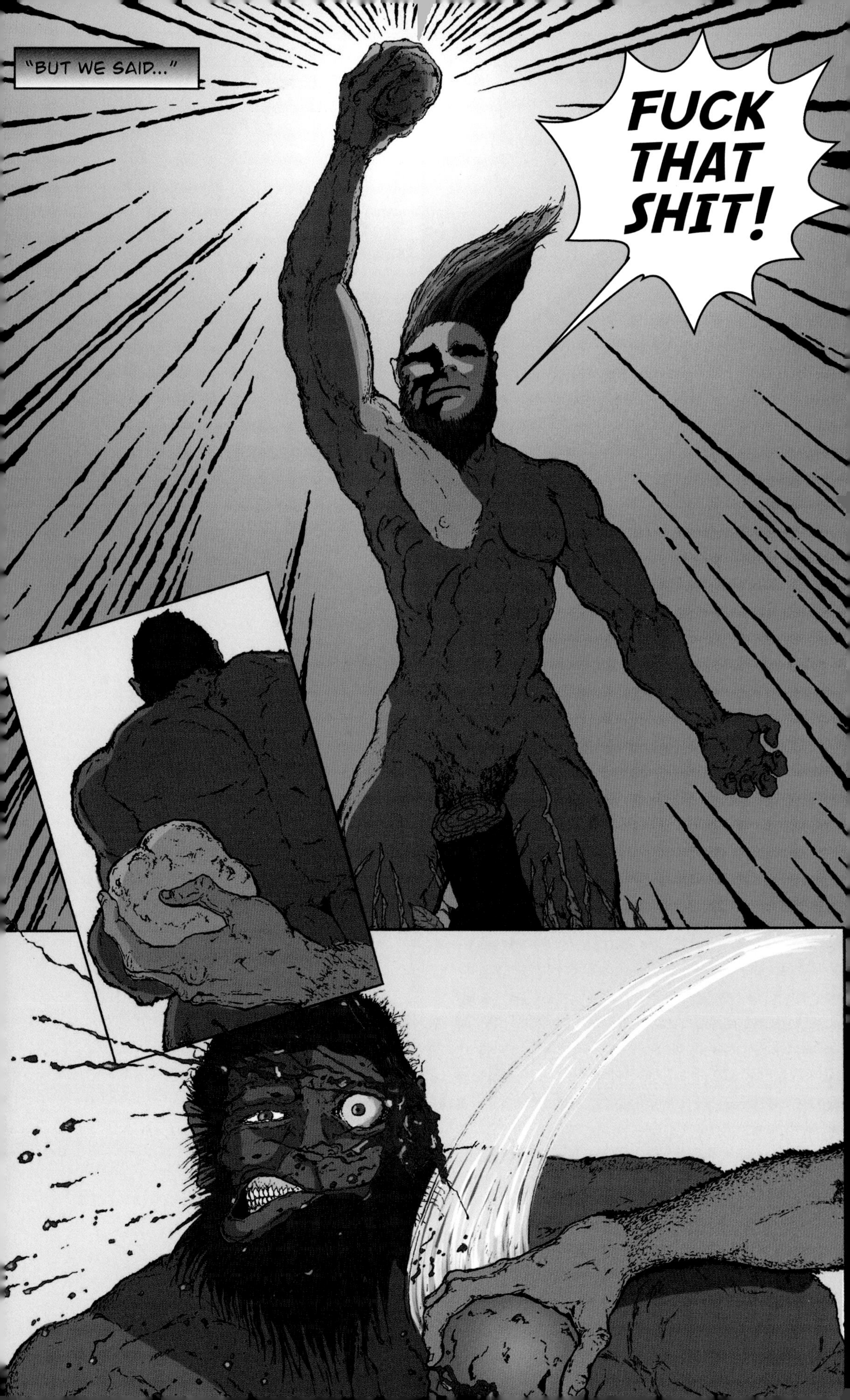
"BUT WE SAID..."
FUCK THAT SHIT!

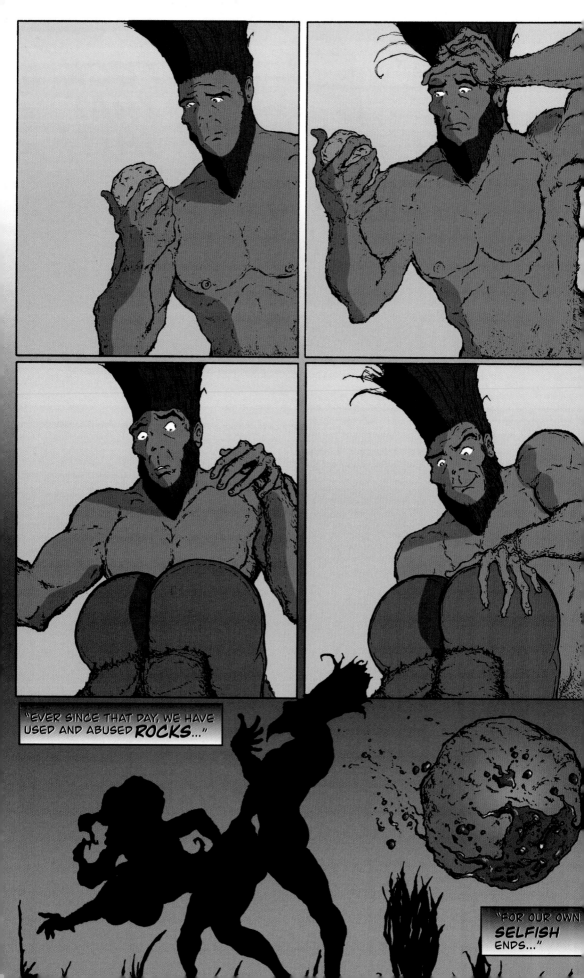

"EVER SINCE THAT DAY, WE HAVE USED AND ABUSED ROCKS..."

"FOR OUR OWN SELFISH ENDS..."

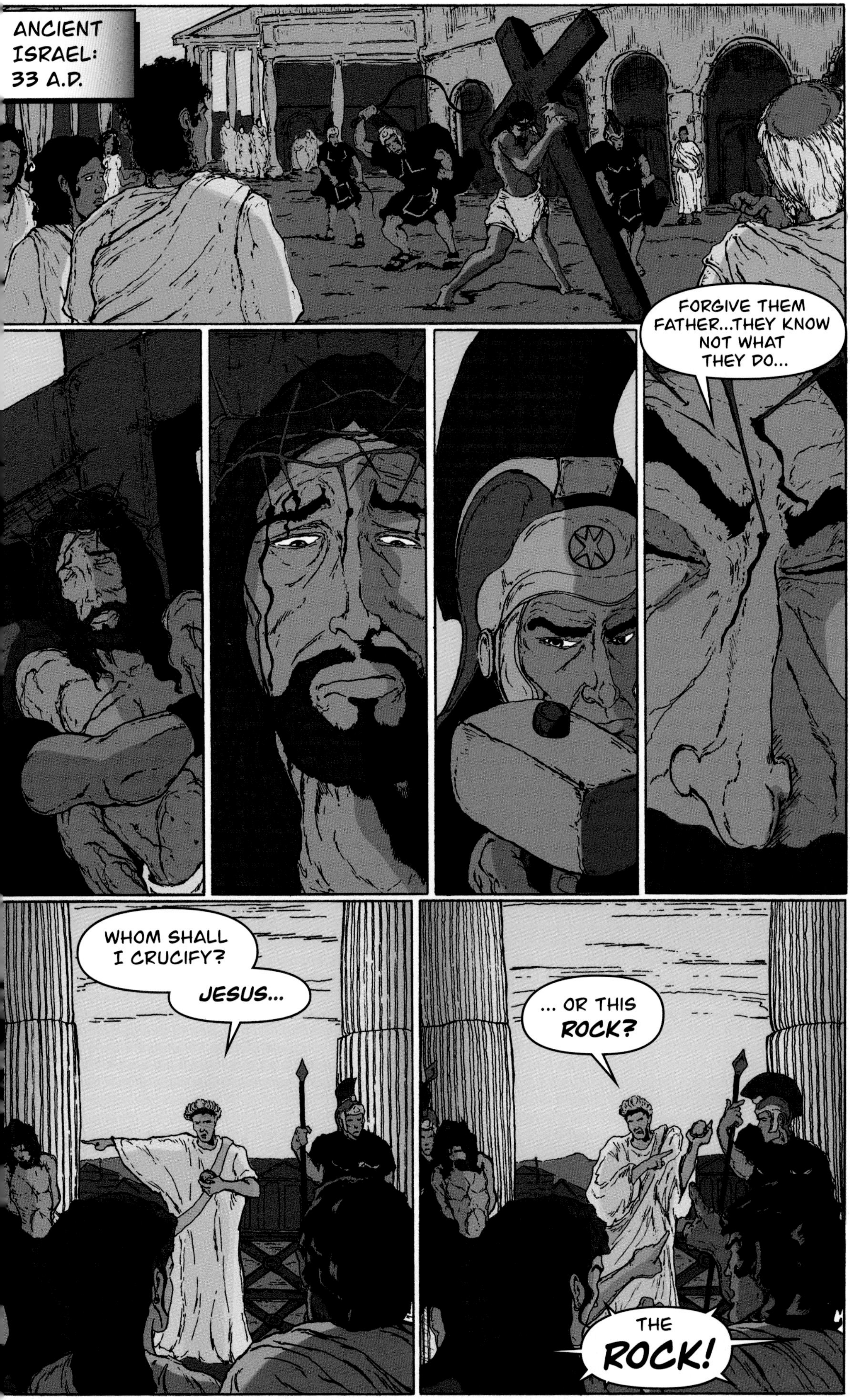
ANCIENT ISRAEL: 33 A.D.
FORGIVE THEM FATHER...THEY KNOW NOT WHAT THEY DO...
WHOM SHALL I CRUCIFY?
JESUS...
... OR THIS ROCK?
THE ROCK!

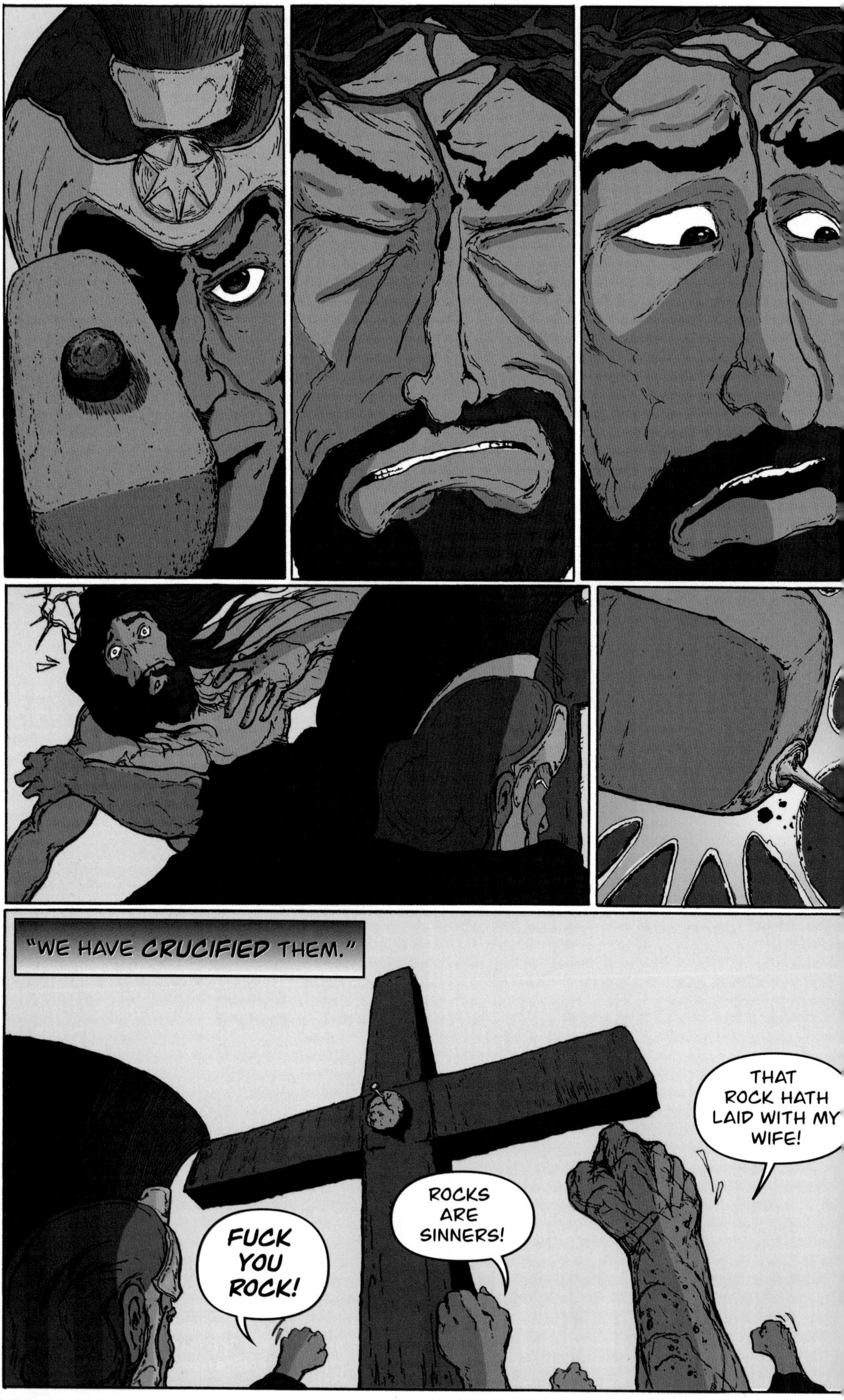
"WE HAVE CRUCIFIED THEM."
THAT ROCK HATH LAID WITH MY WIFE!
ROCKS ARE SINNERS!
FUCK YOU ROCK!

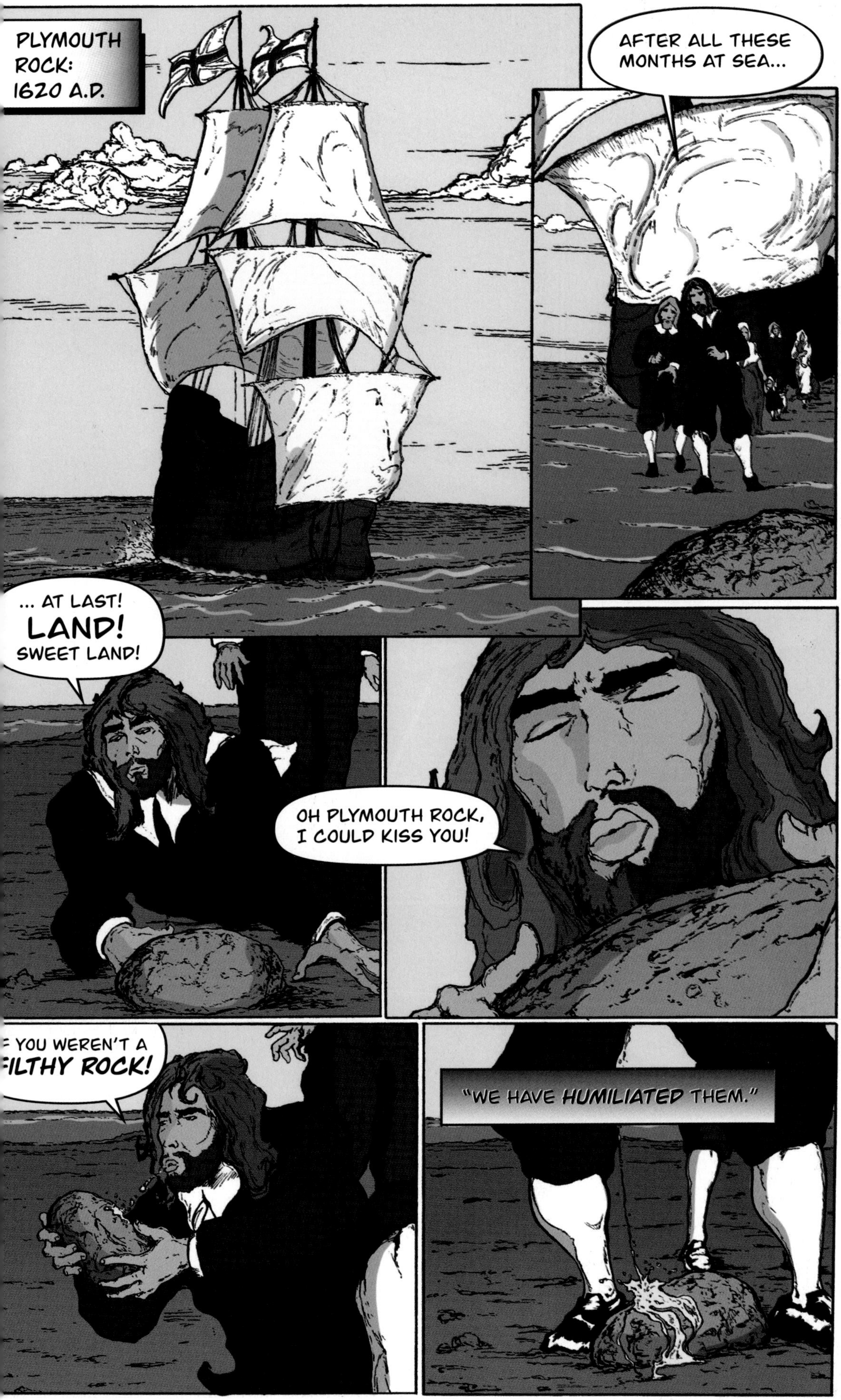
PLYMOUTH ROCK: 1620 A.D.
AFTER ALL THESE MONTHS AT SEA...
... AT LAST! LAND! SWEET LAND!
OH PLYMOUTH ROCK, I COULD KISS YOU!
YOU WEREN'T A
ILTHY ROCK!
"WE HAVE HUMILIATED THEM."

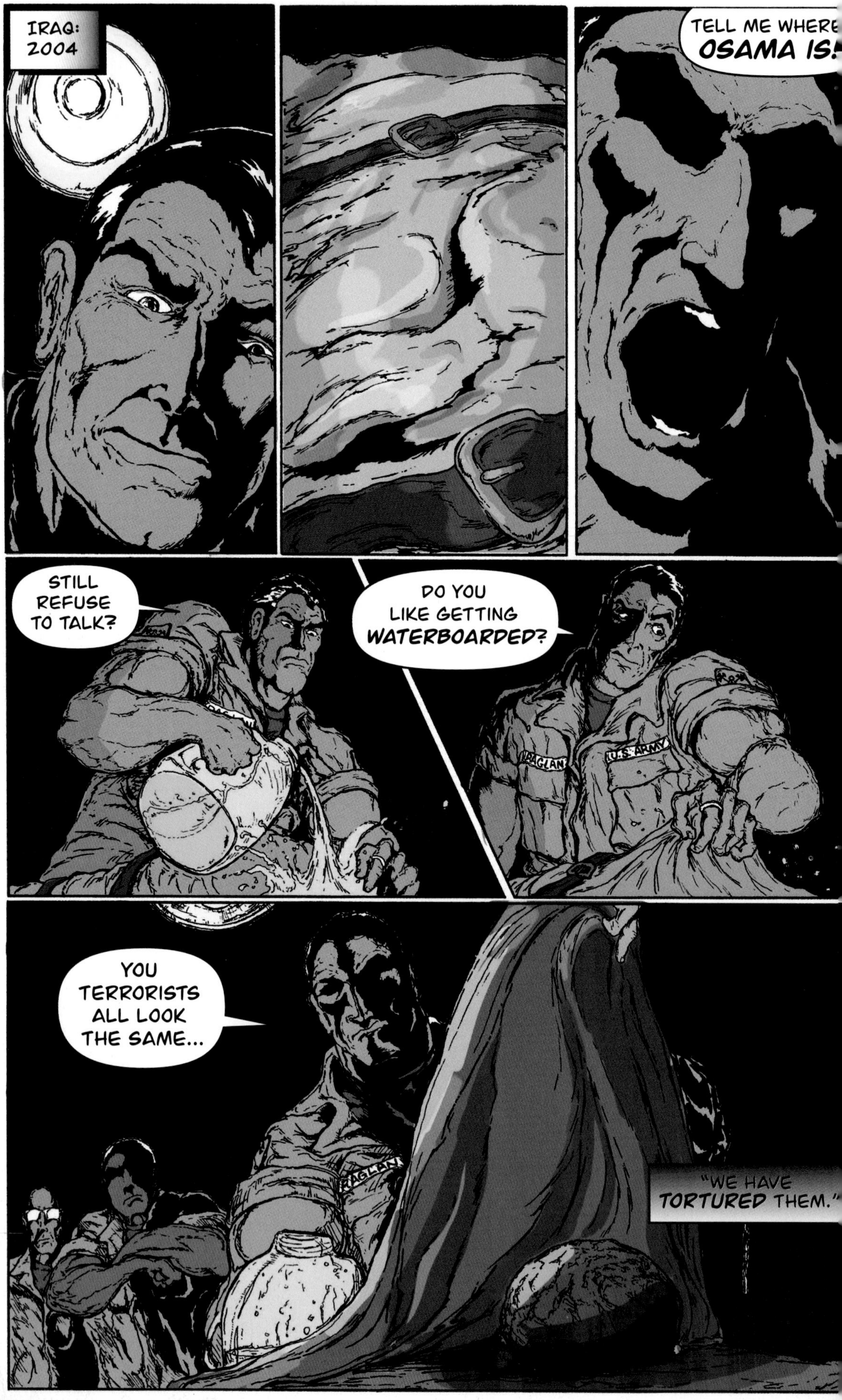
IRAQ: 2004
TELL ME WHERE OSAMA IS!
STILL REFUSE TO TALK?
DO YOU LIKE GETTING WATERBOARDED?
U.S. ARMY
RAGLAN
YOU TERRORISTS ALL LOOK THE SAME...
RAGLAN
"WE HAVE TORTURED THEM."

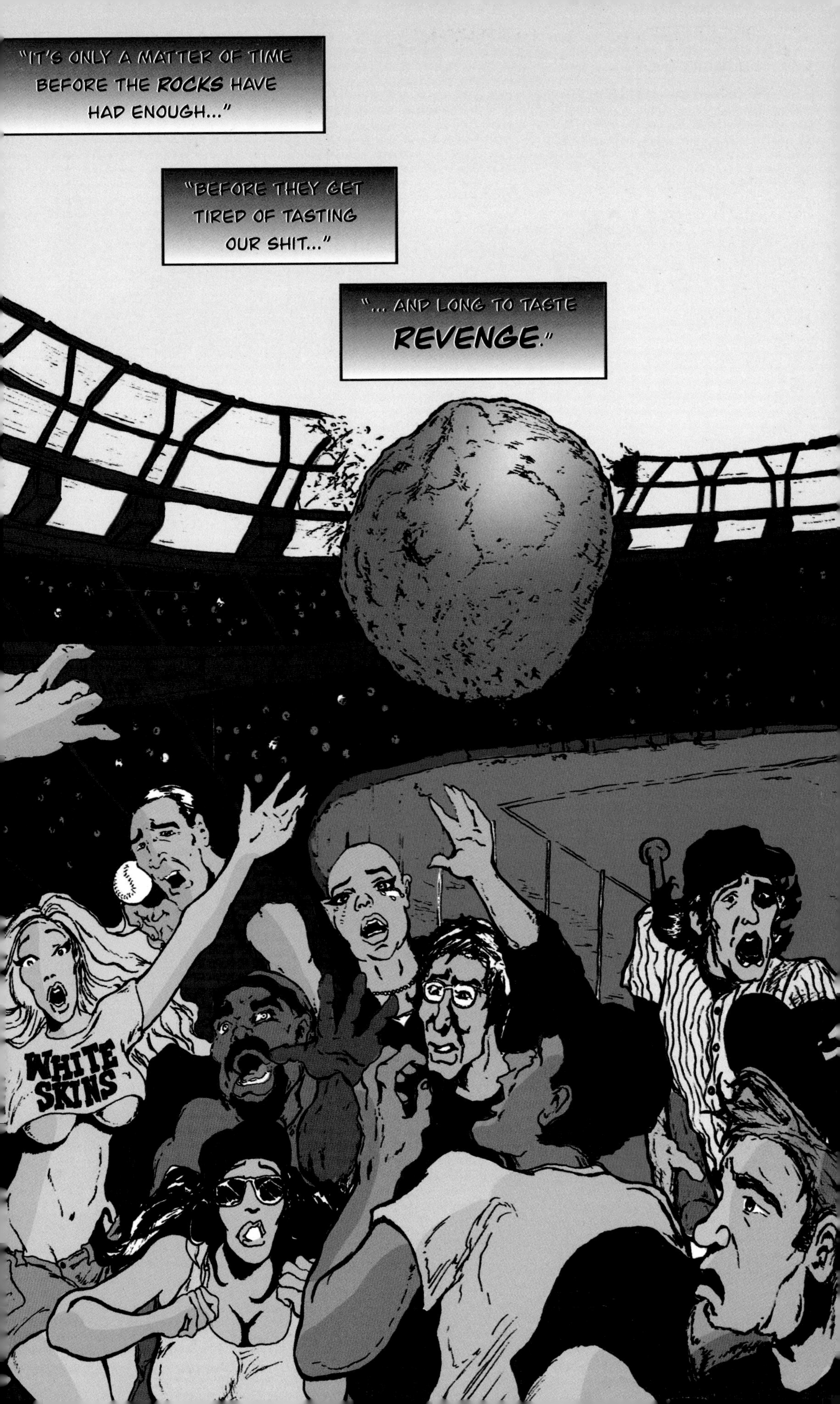
"IT'S ONLY A MATTER OF TIME BEFORE THE ROCKS HAVE HAD ENOUGH..."
"BEFORE THEY GET TIRED OF TASTING OUR SHIT..."
"... AND LONG TO TASTE REVENGE."
WHITE SKINS

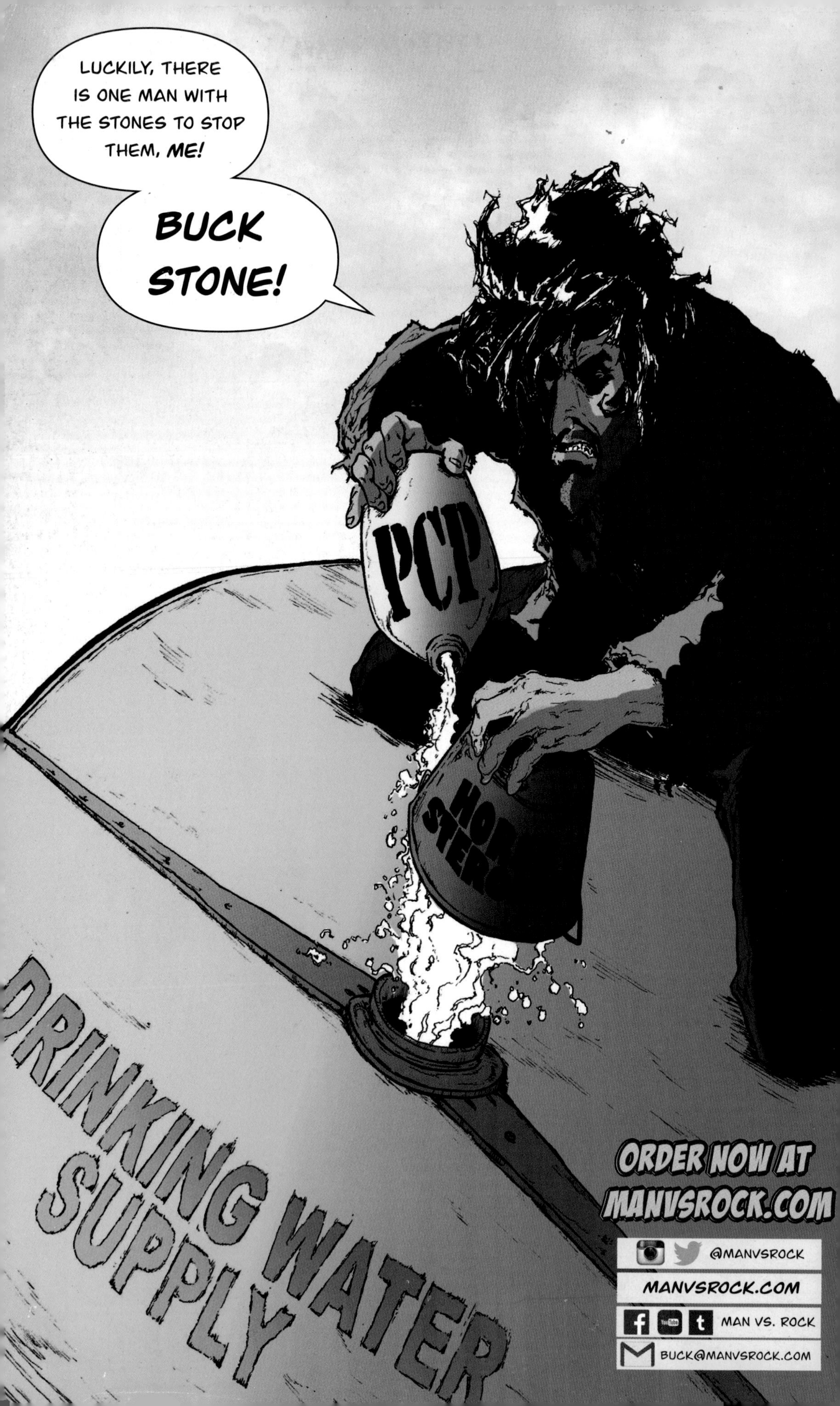
LUCKILY, THERE IS ONE MAN WITH THE STONES TO STOP THEM, ME!
BUCK STONE!
PCP
DRINKING WATER SUPPLY
ORDER NOW AT MANVSROCK.COM
@MANVSROCK
MANVSROCK.COM
MAN VS. ROCK
BUCK@MANVSROCK.COM